GENERAL SHOP

WOODWORKING

GENERAL SHOP
WOODWORKING

VERNE C. FRYKLUND
President Emeritus
Stout State University
Menomonie, Wisconsin

ARMAND J. LA BERGE
Formerly Instructor of
Industrial Arts
University of Minnesota
Minneapolis, Minnesota

McKNIGHT & McKNIGHT Publishing Company Bloomington, Illinois

SEVENTH EDITION

1972

Lithographed in U.S.A.

SBN: 87345-031-0

Library of Congress
Card Catalog Number: 70-183260

McKNIGHT & McKNIGHT PUBLISHING COMPANY

This publication was prepared by the McKnight & McKnight Editorial Staff under the direction of:

Ronald E. Dale
Managing Editor

Donna Faull
Production Editor

Bettye King
Copy Editor

Elizabeth Purcell
Art Editor

Mick Netherton
Printing Production
Illinois Graphics, Inc.
Bloomington, Illinois

Peoria Typographers
Peoria, Illinois
Compositor

Foreword

This text was written to provide instruction in the fundamentals of hand and machine woodworking. *General Shop Woodworking* is an appropriate text for any of the several types of shop organization and is easily used with any teaching method. It is also a practical book for the home workshop.

Subject aims used in the preparation of this text were conceived from well-known general education and industrial education aims. These aims are:

1. Provide experiences in processing wood and give information concerning industries and occupations relating to wood and its many uses.
2. Teach certain general and usable skills in safely modifying wood for personal needs.
3. Inspire appreciation of good workmanship and good design in wood products.
4. Develop habits of careful planning and methodical procedure in construction of wood products.
5. Foster development of intelligent discrimination in the selection of wood products, such as wood furniture and woodwork in the home.
6. Develop appreciation of one's dependence upon wood and wood products, and the importance of conservation.
7. Give training and experience in the reading of working drawings, especially those used in woodworking.
8. Inspire avocational interests in woodcrafts.

Any aim that suggests development of initiative and planning ability is very important. A dynamic society requires problem-solving abilities of those who would create as well as keep pace with change. In any creative field or subject, problems exist and they are solved by elements put together in combinations as is done in mathematics. Knowledge of and command of these elements are gained from training and experiences in the particular activity. The solutions for problems, therefore, do not "come out of the air." The individual must be trained in the fundamentals and in their applications; and this training should be so thorough that the fundamentals can be used readily in the solution of problems that are common to the activity.

Related academic instruction is desirable in conjunction with manipulative instruction. Technical information is needed in combination with hand and machine skills in the solution of shop problems. This kind of knowledge enables the learner to better form judgments in making his projects. There is need also for general knowledge relating to woodworking. And, if there is to be the best possible contribution to the realization of the aims, guidance topics should be added to the foregoing. Because of their growing importance, certain of these units have been brought forward from their former location in the related academic section of earlier editions. Flexibility in methods of using any of the units in this book, which was the original intent in preparing the very first edition, is still possible, but this rearrangement will make these units more likely to be noted early in planning for their study.

General Shop Woodworking provides the basic instruction on operations and related academic information, all of which have broadening cultural as well as technical values.

Method is relative and its success in instruction depends in large measure upon a rather fundamental idea; that is, that the teacher must distinguish clearly his responsibilities and the learner's responsibilities in connection with instruction. The teacher must teach the operations, demonstrate them, and teach how to plan procedures, and the learner must solve the problems of the shop. The learner therefore must plan his procedures and do the manipulative work properly in order to create and produce. This much is basic in all good shop teaching. Many proved teaching techniques and much ingenuity should be employed to make instruction effective in coping with individual differences in learning.

Experience has proved the effectiveness of the sketches used to portray clearly the important operational steps. In addition to the preface on working safely in the woodshop, instructions on safe work procedures are integrated in all units so as to make sure that safe work practices are fully presented.

The vocabulary has been carefully checked with recognized word lists, and even junior high school pupils experience little difficulty in achieving complete understanding of the study units. There are a few words, especially technical ones, that may tax the average pupil but this is to be expected as learning progresses.

There must be a program of testing to determine the success of the teaching and learning. Test questions also serve as study aids for the learners. For these reasons, questions are included at the end of each unit. These can be reconstructed and used in various ways, as well as repeated in the formal tests which should be administered from time to time. The questions are narrow in scope so as to leave opportunity for selection of other types of questions for formal tests. Formal tests are also available for use with the text.

This book has been written in clear and understandable language. The vocabulary has been carefully checked with recognized word lists, and even junior high school pupils experience little difficulty in achieving complete understanding of the study units. There are a few words, especially technical ones, that may tax the average pupil but this is to be expected as learning progresses.

Acknowledgments

Authors cannot succeed alone. There must be assisting agencies in every publication; and the following acknowledgments are gladly made. The authors were granted permission to use certain drawings, which have appeared previously under their separate names, by the *Industrial Education Magazine, Industrial Arts and Vocational Education,* and *Popular Homecraft Magazine*. The Saalfield Publishing Company, the Whitman Publishing Company, the Brodhead-Garrett Company, Stanley Tools, File Filosophy, Nicholson File Company, Sterling Furniture, Inc., Acme Hardware Company of Los Angeles, Traction Division of Allis Chalmers, American Forest Products, and United States Forest Service furnished photographs and information. Mr. Roy L. Sayre and Mr. Francis Zwickey rendered assistance in the preparation of sketches and drawings.

The following persons have given technical assistance and professional suggestions in preparing the seventh edition:

Dr. David P. Barnard and Dr. Robert Swanson of Stout State University, Menomonie, Wisconsin; Dr. Gordon Funk, Supervisor of Industrial Education, Los Angeles City Schools; and Dr. David O. Taxis, Consultant in Industrial Arts Education, Los Angeles County Schools. The authors are grateful for their assistance.

Verne C. Fryklund
Armand J. LaBerge

Contents

SECTION FOUR — Surfacing and Squaring Stock

SECTION FIVE — Shaping Irregular and Round Pieces

SECTION SIX — Cutting Holes

SECTION SEVEN — Joinery and Table Construction

SECTION EIGHT — Common Assembly Operations and Materials

Working Safely in the Woodshop

Your shop is a safe place in which to work. You will enjoy the work and you will learn many things that you can use later, outside of school, if your attitudes and habits of work are productive and safe. Proper shop procedures usually are safe procedures.

In the instructions in this book, each operation is explained so that it may be performed in the safest and quickest way and also the most economical way in the use of material. Safety instructions are included in each unit so you should follow the instructions carefully.

There are some general safety precautions you should follow in all the work that you do. They are presented here separately.

1. Know all safety rules and obey them.
2. Develop the habit of working safely at all times. If in doubt about the correct use of a tool, ask your teacher for assistance.
3. Hand tools and machines cannot and will not reach out to hurt you. They are dangerous only if you put your fingers in the wrong place while using them.
4. If you should have an accident, even a minor one, report it to your instructor so you can receive first aid.
5. All hand tools and machines must be kept in perfect operating condition.
6. Arrange tools on your work bench so they will not fall off and so the cutting edges will not catch on your hands or clothes.
7. Carry tools with cutting edges pointed down. If you wish to hand a tool to another person, pass it so he can grasp the handle.
8. If a tool handle becomes loose or cracked, call your instructor's attention to it so the handle can be replaced or repaired promptly.
9. Keep the tools sharp and it will be easier for you to work safely.
10. Wear an apron to protect your clothes. Special protective garments are worn in some shops.
11. Enjoy your work, but do not play or interfere with others while in the shop. Running is prohibited in all shops in school or in industry.
12. Remove outer garments, such as jackets, coats, vests, and loose sweaters, and place them in a designated place while you work.
13. Long neckties and sleeves may get caught in your work. Remove your tie and roll up your sleeves.
14. If your hair is not trimmed short, wear a shop cap, a hair band, or a visor. Long hair may get caught in the work or get in your way so you cannot see properly.
15. Keep your hands clean and do not put them in your mouth or rub your eyes. Infections usually start through such carelessness.
16. Jewelry is attractive, but it is dangerous when worn in the shop, and should be removed. Rings are especially dangerous because they are easily caught in moving parts.
17. Do not put tools, nails, screws, brads and the like in your mouth. You may pick up an infection or swallow the object.

18. Keep the floor clear of pieces of wood and blocks so no one will stumble on them.
19. Remove protruding nails and screws from wooden pieces that are not to be immediately used in construction.
20. Lumber must always be piled orderly. Two persons should carry long pieces. Take care to see that the way is clear as you walk.
21. Place dirty and oily rags and waste in special metal containers to prevent fire.
22. You must learn the fire drill signals. The instructor will explain the procedure for leaving the room and for returning. Stop work immediately when you hear the signal and follow orders quietly and calmly.

SECTION

One

Design, Problem Solving, Guidance

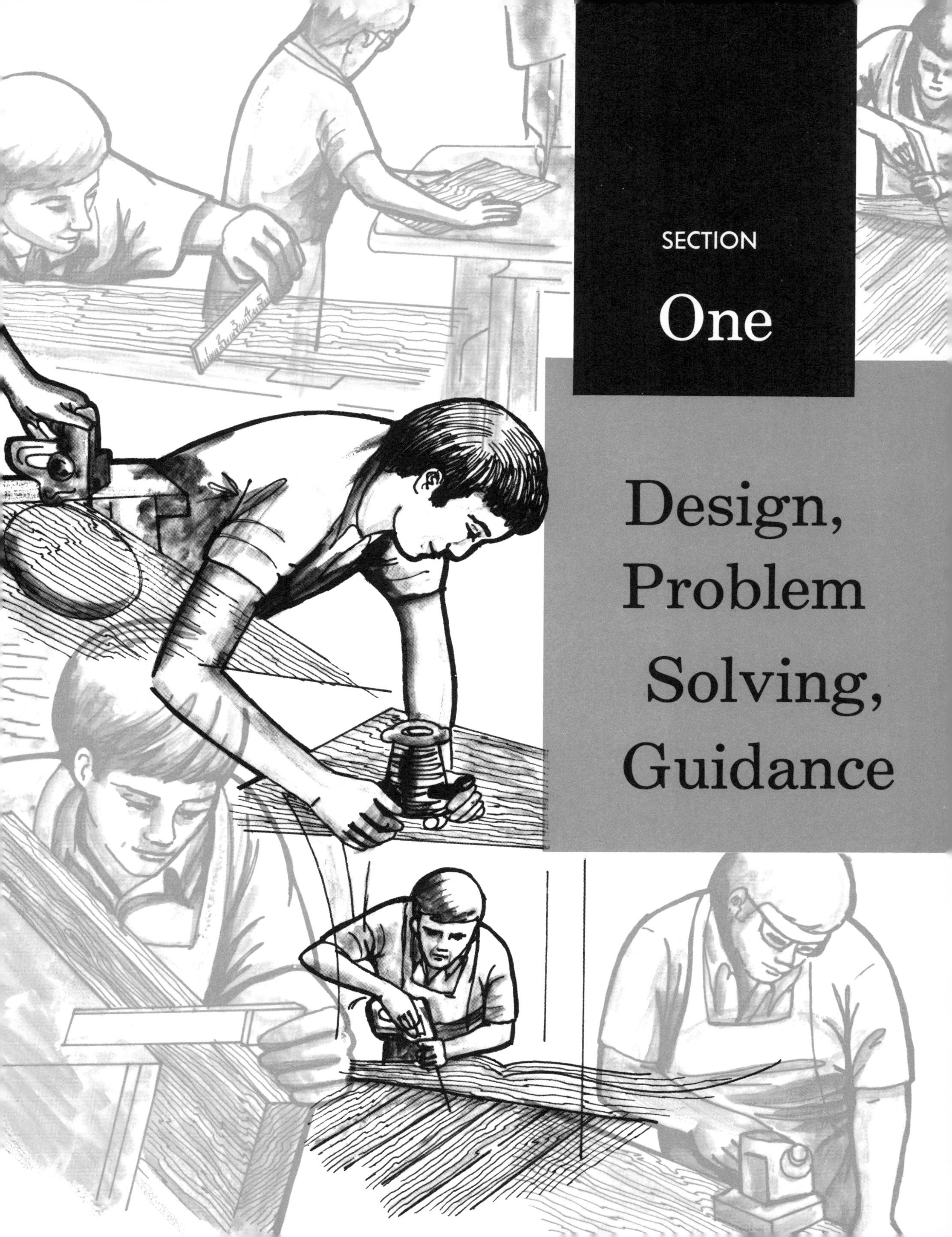

UNIT 1

Design in Woodworking

You should learn the principles of good design so you can plan and design your own projects in woodworking, or give a personal touch to a design you have selected. You will learn that careful planning and good design and workmanship all combine to produce a useful object of beauty. The following will be helpful in your study of contemporary design in today's living.

Contemporary Design

We live in an age of speed, jet planes, beautiful streamlined motor cars, majestic buildings with much glass, and low rambling, well-lighted ranch type homes. Our environment suggests a type of furniture which is simple, beautiful and useful. Simplicity, good proportion, utility, lightness in appearance and sturdiness combine in contemporary design of household furnishings to make them lasting in their beauty. Some people like to call contemporary design tomorrow's design as well as today's design.

There are many manufactured wood materials of beauty and strength that can be combined with traditional solid woods to produce easy and attractive variations in furniture designs of the present. Plywoods are examples of manufactured wood materials that tend to simplify the design and enhance the beauty of modern furniture. See Unit 82. The developments of the past are used in new variations to make the attractive designs of the present.

The designer of today utilizes the principles of balance, simple straight and curved lines, improved construction and finishing materials to create new and attractive designs in modern furniture.

Contemporary or Modern Pieces

The dining table and chairs shown in Fig. 1 are attractive and beautifully designed contemporary pieces of furniture. They are simple in design, durably constructed, and well finished.

Current furniture shows a definite trend in today's design. The sofa and coffee or oc-

Fig. 1. Beautiful, Efficient, and Pleasing Pieces (Douglas)

casional table shown in Fig. 2 make excellent use of the natural beauty and charm of wood surfaces. These simple pieces make economical use of materials and they are practical and pleasing. The long sofa is especially light in weight in relation to its overall dimensions.

The occasional chair, Fig. 3, is a functional chair which may be used in a reception room, a living room, or a recreation room.

The group of occasional chairs shown in Fig. 4 illustrate the possibilities of variety within the framework of a single basic design. Note the differences in upholstering among the pieces and the variety of materials. They reflect the trend of contemporary design in furniture.

Some Points in Good Design

In good design, at least three things should be kept in mind. The project should be useful for its purpose, it should be lasting or durable, and it should be beautiful.

An object is useful when it is designed and constructed with consideration as to where it is to be placed and how it is to be used when completed. It should be of proper size; for example, many furniture pieces have standard heights and widths. Chairs are usually 18 inches, dining tables 30 inches, and coffee tables 17 inches in height. Many new tables of the occasional and stacking type vary in heights and widths, however. Durability of a project is obtained through good construction and the use of suitable materials. A project cannot be called durable unless it has a lasting and beautiful finish.

Good proportions, well-divided spaces, simplicity, appropriate materials, and a finish in keeping with its surroundings combine to make a beautiful piece.

Fig. 2. Simple Design, Durable Construction and Lasting Finish (Mersman)

Fig. 3. Inviting Contemporary Chair (Douglas)

Fig. 4. Variety and Beauty with Single Basic Design (Broyhill Furniture Co.)

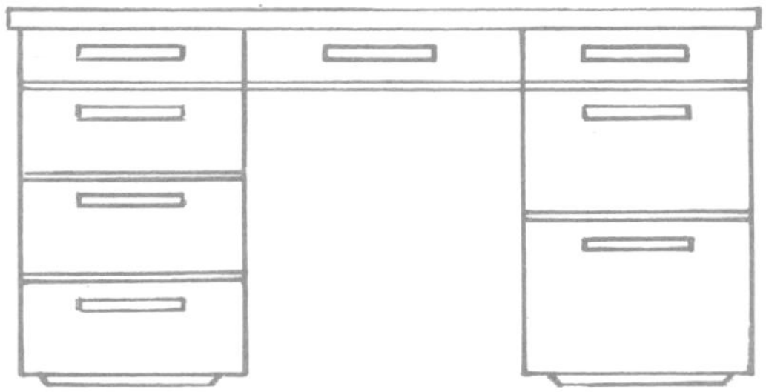

Fig. 5. Division of Space

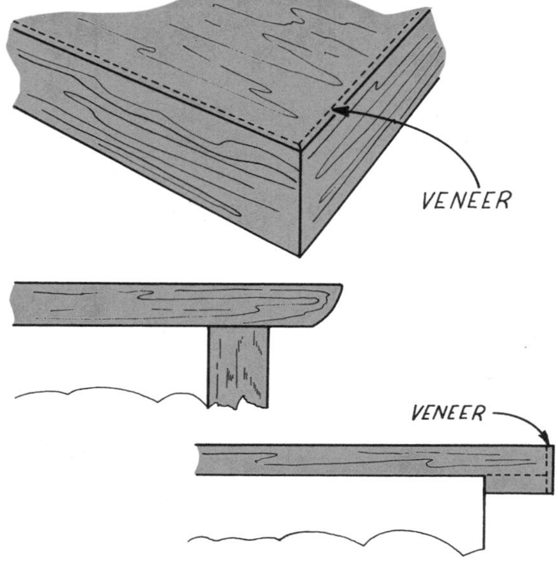

Fig. 6. Treatments for Edges[1]

Proportions

Proportion is the relationship of the length to the width of an entire project and also of each part. An article must have good proportions in order to be attractive. In other words, each part must have harmonious dimensions and the complete unit must be in harmony with the proportions of the parts.

A designer must have the ability to think of the articles as a whole. This ability may be developed by studying the whole project, its design and construction in small freehand sketches. Many of these small sketches help to develop possible designs to solve a design problem.

The practical use of proportions and dimensions in designing is necessary in project planning. Proportions are first studied and determined in sketches without reference to exact dimensions. The dimensions are then considered and added after the basic proportions have been determined. The golden proportion theory holds that the best proportions, in order to obtain beauty, are those of two to three. That is, the widths and lengths should be approximately two units and three units. Many good proportions vary from this relationship. Judgment should be developed regarding these relationships and the variation possible in the solution of a particular design problem. When the overall size and individual proportions of a piece have something in common but are not readily seen as something similar, they are pleasing. Proportions that are similar in the various parts of an article are sure to be pleasing.

Division of Space

Some suggestions for the division of space may be helpful.

1. If a vertical line divides the whole space into two divisions, these divisions should be equal or in the relationship of two to three.
2. If vertical lines divide the whole space in three divisions, the center portion is usually larger than the others, but the latter are usually equal, Fig. 5. The subdivision or smaller portions can also be treated in a similar manner, as the top desk compartments in Fig. 5. Observe the divisions of doors and grouping of windows according to this suggested principle.
3. If the primary mass is divided into three parts by horizontal lines, the middle part is usually larger than the upper and lower parts. The upper and lower parts are usually unlike. The middle part or the main structure of a building is larger than its base or top piece. This suggested rule could be applied to almost any industrial arts project.

Simplicity

Simplicity in good design is really more than the word itself suggests. It is apparent in the

[1] See also Unit 47.

finished article because the piece as a whole appears simple, but often the construction is not as simple as appearances indicate. Well designed pieces often involve hidden joints such as the miter, rabbet, and dado; and these joints must be well made. Poorly made joints have no place in any kind of furniture or project. Pieces with slightly rounded corners, soft edges, spindle bases, beveled edges, and mitered joints are characteristic of the simplicity of contemporary design, Figs. 1 and 6. Note the simplicity of the smooth table top and bevelled edges shown in Fig. 2 and the light sofa in Fig. 1.

A popular and simple way of treating edges and corners is shown in Fig. 6.

Materials and Finish

There is no finish more beautiful than that of natural wood, particularly on such woods as walnut, oak, mahogany, cherry, maple, and red gum. Their beauty is accentuated when two shades of the natural wood are used. Enamels and lacquers in tints and shades may also be used in finishing, but they are most appropriately used to cover the cheaper woods.

For several reasons there is little ornamentation in contemporary design. For economy in mass production and simple maintenance, decoration by carving, inlay, and striping are not used. Every effort is made to secure beauty of line without decoration. The finished piece should be simple, decorative, and useful.

Questions

1. Is a knowledge of the principles of design essential in planning?
2. What is contemporary design?
3. What are some characteristics of contemporary design?
4. What three main points should be kept in mind to obtain good design?
5. Name some furniture pieces that have standard heights.
6. What are some requirements to make projects beautiful?
7. What is the basis of durability in a project?
8. What is meant by the following: Proportion? Golden rectangle? Division of space?
9. What kind of wood is used in contemporary furniture?
10. Is surface decoration much used today?

UNIT 2 Planning the Procedure for Your Work

Before starting work on a project, you should plan carefully a step-by-step procedure. Such thoughtful planning will help you make a wise choice of materials, use the proper tools, and proceed in an orderly way.

Your project may be considered a problem that requires solution, just as a problem in mathematics. It must be studied thoroughly in order to decide what steps are necessary to make it. Careful planning saves you time and energy and makes possible the best use of materials. If you plan your work well, you should have a successful project.

Planning in Business

In the business world, procedures are carefully thought out in advance. The men who design and construct buildings, bridges, dams, power plants, railroads and airplanes must prepare plans and step-by-step procedures in their undertakings. The surgeon must visualize beforehand every detail of an operation in its proper order. A mistake or a wrong move might prove fatal. Anyone who really does things in the world, anyone who creates, must plan an orderly procedure for everything he undertakes to do.

Planning in Your Work

Whether your project is large or small, your first or fifteenth, you must plan your procedure and write it out. You should do things in the right way to be capable and self-reliant. The individual who can analyze a task, determine what needs to be done, how and in what order to do it has the necessary qualities to do the bigger things in the world outside of school.

In order that you will have an opportunity to learn how to plan carefully and systematically, your teacher may give you a special form on which to do your planning. On this form, you will list the general steps in proper order, determine the costs, and list the tools you will need. Hand it to your teacher so he can determine whether you are planning an orderly procedure for your project.

When your teacher has approved your plan, begin work according to your plan and follow it step by step. When you complete step one, mark it with a check. Mark each step as you proceed. Then you will know where you left off and your teacher will know the progress being made. Do not lose your plan sheet.

An Example

A sample form is shown here to give assistance and guidance in project planning. If a similar form is not available, this one can be copied for use in setting down a definite procedure for each project.

PLAN OF PROCEDURE

Name..

Project..

Date started.......................... Date finished.......................... Time..........................

Materials required:

Tools required:

Procedure:

Before performing the operations with which you are not thoroughly familiar, study your textbook carefully. List the steps in the order in which they should be performed, using as many of the spaces as needed.

1. ....
2. ....
3. ....
4. ....
5. ....
6. ....
7. ....
8. ....
9. ....
10. ....

Are you sure that you know how to perform each step in your plan?..........................

In order to help you in making your first plan, the plan of procedure in column two is included as an example. This plan was made by an eighth grade boy and approved by the teacher before the coat and hat rack was started.

Problem:

Select three projects which you know you can make and plan a procedure for each of them.

A SIMPLE PLAN OF PROCEDURE
For Making Coat and Hat Rack

Materials required: One piece of pine 1″ x 4″ x 60″ surfaced on two sides. Sandpaper, 12 clothes hooks, and 8—1¾″ No. 10 F. H. B. screws.

Tools required: Try square, pencil, rule, saw, jack plane, sandpaper block, awl, brace, bits, screwdriver.

Procedure:

1. Square up the stock to the size given in the drawing.
2. Pencil gage for the chamfer.
3. Clamp in the vise and plane the chamfer.
4. Sand the best surface and the edges — be sure to sand one way on the ends.
5. Finish.
6. Attach the hooks.
7. Fasten the rail in place with the screws.

UNIT 3 Reading a Working Drawing

A working drawing gives all the information required to make a project. If you attempted to describe in writing the appearance and dimensions of a project to be built, it would take pages and pages of description. Pictures are not satisfactory because they do not show accurately all parts of an object. A working drawing gives in condensed form the information needed to do a job.

The working drawing really is a *universal language*. It can be understood by technicians in all parts of the world. There could be little progress without drawings because it is through them that most information regarding construction must be given. Books, magazines and newspapers include drawings, diagrams, and graphs of various kinds because writing alone is inadequate to convey certain kinds of information.

Drawings in Life

The home owner, builder, engineer, lawyer, doctor, dentist, and the skilled workman must be able to read working drawings. While the drawings which these persons must understand are not exactly alike, they are similar and the same principles are used in making them. The working drawings used in the shops follow the same principles as those used in the world outside of school. What you learn now about reading a working drawing will be useful to you in reading other working drawings.

Working Drawings

A working drawing is a representation of an object by means of "views" on a flat surface, or "plane." The exact shape and size of the

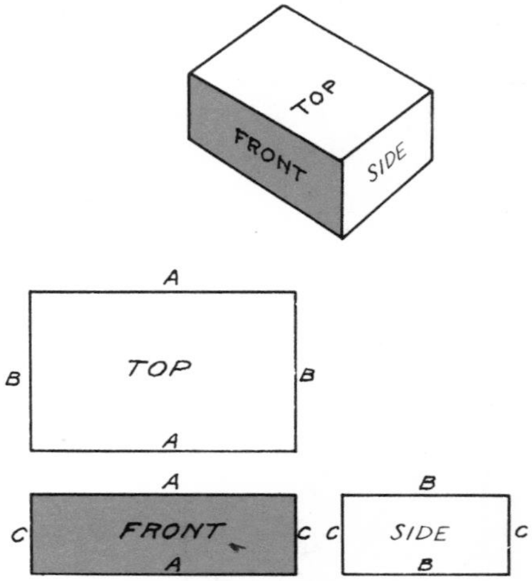

Fig. 7. Arrangement of Views in a Three-View Drawing

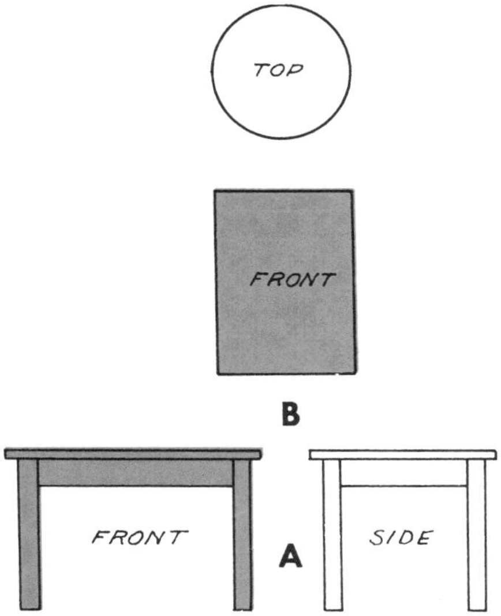

Fig. 8. Two-View Drawing May Show Top and Front Views or Side and Front Views

object and every part of it is shown accurately. A definite system is used in arranging the views.

Views of a Drawing

In a working drawing, an object may be represented by one, two or three views. Two- and three-view drawings are common. Fig. 7 shows the views of a block without dimensions. In the top part of the figure is a perspective view and below is a working drawing. Observe that the top view is placed directly above the front view and the side view is placed directly to one side of the front view. This is usually the arrangement of views in a three-view drawing. In a two-view drawing, either the top or side view may appear with the front view. In Fig. 8 examples of objects requiring only two views are shown.

Examine Fig. 7 and notice that the lines marked with letters in the views represent identical distances. Line A represents length; line *B* stands for width; and the height (or thickness) is shown by line *C*.

These drawings give information about the shapes of the objects but they do not give the sizes. To make a project, it is necessary to know the thickness, width and length of each piece.

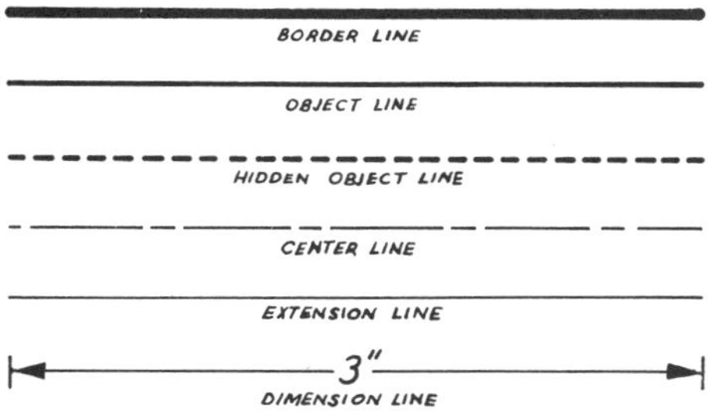

Fig. 9. Lines for Working Drawings, Often Called the Alphabet of Lines

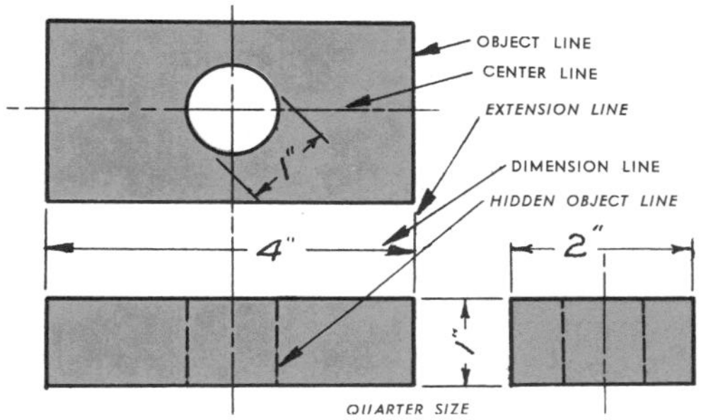

Fig. 10. Lines in a Drawing

Lines of a Drawing

In a complete working drawing, it is necessary to use certain kinds of lines. These lines have definite meanings just as words have meanings. An incorrect use of a line is as wrong as the incorrect use of a word. Study the lines in Fig. 9. This set of lines is known as the alphabet of lines because each line has its own meaning. Fig. 10 shows how the lines are used in a drawing.

The *object line* is heavy. It stands out so the workman can see the *exact shape* of the object.

The *hidden parts* that cannot be seen are represented by the *hidden object line*. This is a broken line which is lighter than the object outline and is composed of one-eighth inch dashes. The length of these dashes never varies in properly made drawings.

The *dimensions* of an object (such as length, width, thickness, diameters of holes, and the radii of arcs) are described by means of a very fine line with an arrowhead placed at each end. The figure representing the size is placed in the middle of this line. This line is called the *dimension line*.

The *extension line* is slightly heavier than the dimension line, but lighter than the *object line*. It is placed at the end of the dimension line and refers the workman to the part of the object being dimensioned. It extends to the object but is never connected with it.

All holes are located by *center lines*. They are fine broken lines of very short and long dashes.

Dimensions and Sizes

In arithmetic you were taught that inches could be represented by placing two ″ after a numeral; and that feet could be shown by placing one ′ after a numeral. This is true in working drawings. Two feet would be shown as 2′; two feet and six inches would be 2′-6″. If all measurements are given in inches, the marks are usually omitted.

Many objects are so large that it is impossible to draw them full size on paper. They must be drawn small enough to be placed on a sheet of paper, but in exact porportion. The object is then drawn to *scale*. The scale is marked on the drawing. *Full-size* drawings are exactly the same in size as the object itself. *Half-size* drawings show the object in half its size. *Quarter or fourth-size* drawings represent the object in one-fourth its full size. The dimension numbers in a drawing never change, but are shown as though the drawing were full size. Besides those mentioned there are many other sizes of scale drawings. The scale is shown by a notation on the drawing.

A Problem

Study carefully the drawing in Fig 11. Following are questions that will help you to get the necessary information for making the object.

1. What is the scale? One inch equals what?
2. How many parts in the object?
3. What is the thickness? Width? Length?
4. How should the corners be made?
5. Are there any hidden edge lines?
6. Are there any holes?
7. If there are holes, where located?

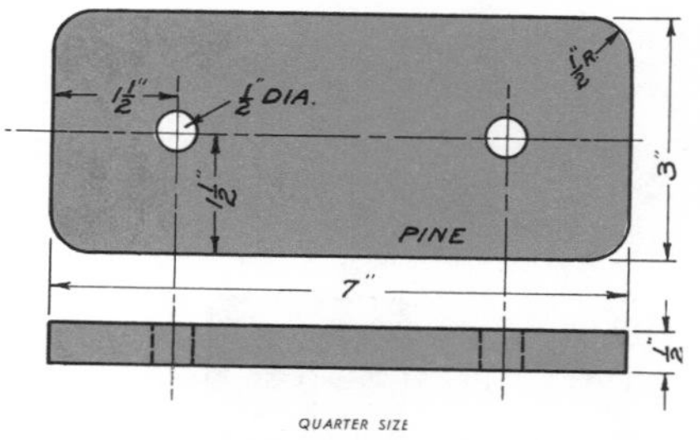

Fig. 11. Objects Often Drawn to Reduced Scale

8. What is the size of the holes, if any?
9. What is the purpose of the center line?
10. What kind of material should be used?

Your instructor may assign another drawing for you to read. Write the data taken from the drawing in your notebook or answer the questions he will ask in order to determine whether you have read the drawing properly.

Questions

1. Does a working drawing provide all the necessary information for the construction of a project?

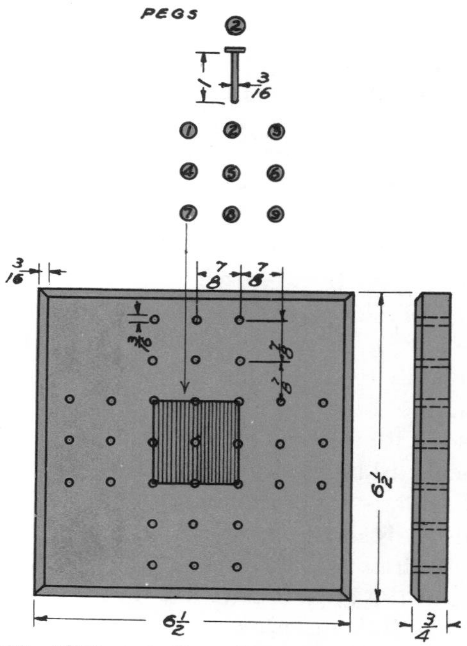

Fig. 12. All Parts in Exact Proportion in a Scale Drawing

2. Why is the working drawing called the universal language?
3. How many views are usually shown in a working drawing?
4. What are conventional lines?
5. Describe the object line and its use.
6. Describe the invisible line and tell where it is used.
7. What is a dimension line?
8. How are reference lines used?
9. How is four feet six inches indicated?
10. How would you dimension a circle?

UNIT 4

Calculating Board Measure

1. The board foot is the unit of measure of wood. In its simplest form, it is a piece of wood 1″ in thickness, 12″ in width and 1′ in length. In other words, it is one foot square and one inch thick, or 144 cubic inches (12″ x 12″ x 1″). One board foot may be 2″ x 6″ x 12″ or 1″ x 6″ x 24″.
2. Boards less than 1″ in thickness are always figured as though they were 1″ thick, but the price is usually less per board foot. For example: a piece of wood ¾″ by 12″ by 12″ is said to be one board foot. Also, a piece ¼″ by 12″ by 12″ is considered as one board foot. When the stock is over one inch in thickness, the additional thickness is taken into account. For example: stock 1½″ x 12″ x 12″ contains ½ more than a board foot or 1½ board feet. Plywood is sold by the square foot. A standard sheet, 4′ by 8′, contains 32 square feet.
3. For long pieces or figuring lumber in quantity, use the following formula to figure board measure: Thickness in inches (never less than 1 in.) x width in inches x length in feet ÷ 12 = Board Feet.

   Use this formula for long pieces:

   $$\frac{T'' \times W'' \times L'}{12} = \text{Board feet.}$$

   Use this formula to figure short pieces:

   $$\frac{T'' \times W'' \times L''}{144} = \text{Board feet.}$$

Illustrations

1. What is the board measure of a piece of wood 1″ x 8″ x 10′? Substitute in the formula and you have $\frac{1'' \times 8'' \times 10'}{12}$.

   By cancelling and clearing the formula, the answer is found to be 6⅔ board feet.

2. What is the board measure of a piece of wood ½″ x 8″ x 10′? In this case ½ is considered as one inch. Substitute in the formula and you have $\frac{1'' \times 8'' \times 10'}{12}$. By cancelling and clearing the formula, the answer is 6⅔ board feet.

3. What is the board measure of a piece of oak 1¼″ x 8″ x 10′? In this case, take into account the extra ¼″ thickness. Substitute in the formula and the problem is $\frac{5'' \times 8'' \times 10'}{4 \times 12}$. Cancelling and clearing the formula gives the answer: 8⅓ board feet.

Problems

Here are some practical problems. Can you solve them?

1. How many board feet in a piece of oak 1″ x 4″ x 12′?
2. How many board feet in a piece of pine 1″ x 10″ x 20′?
3. How many board feet in 6 pieces of oak 1″ x 8″ x 12′?

4. What is the cost of a piece of walnut 1″ x 6″ x 8″ at 40¢ per bd. ft.?
5. What is the cost of a piece of pine 1″ x 10″ x 18′ at 42¢ per bd. ft.?
6. What is the cost of a piece of pine ¼″ x 6″ x 14′ at 42¢ per bd. ft.?
7. What is the cost of 15 pcs. of plywood ⅛″ x 18″ x 4′ at 15¢ per sq. ft.?
8. How many board feet in a piece 2″ x 4″ x 10′?
9. What is the cost of 6 pcs. of oak 1½″ x 8″ x 10′ at 42¢ per bd. ft.?

UNIT

5 Making a Bill of Material

A bill of material lists all the necessary information for obtaining the exact kinds and amounts of materials needed for the completion of your project. It should have columns for (1) number of pieces, (2) description, (3) kind of material, (4) size, (4) board feet or other unit, (5) price per unit, and (6) cost.

Making a bill of material offers experience in the reading of drawings, in dimensioning, in ordering lumber and in figuring costs of lumber and other materials.

Procedure

1. Study a working drawing and list each part needed for the completed project.
2. Prepare a list of all pieces giving the exact dimensions as shown on the drawing. Allow extra stock for joints where needed. List each kind of wood. For example, if walnut and pine are used in the project, list them separately.
3. Study the drawing carefully for hardware needed and make a complete list. Determine the kind and size of nails and screws. Consult the catalogs covering these items for information regarding sizes and descriptions.
4. Estimate the number of board feet of lumber.
5. Determine the unit prices of lumber and other materials.
6. Figure the cost of the project by adding all unit prices. Go over the figures twice to make sure there are no errors or omissions.

Bill of Materials for Contemporary Desk Chair

No. Pcs.	Size (Th. x W. x L.)	Description	Material	Bd. Ft.
2	⅞ x 3 x 33	Back legs	E	1.37
2	1 ⅝ x 1 ⅝ x 16	Front legs	E	.89
2	¾ x 2 ¼ x 15 ⅞	Side rails	E	.55
1	¾ x 2 ¼ x 15	Front rail	E	.26
1	¾ x 2 ¼ x 13 ¼	Back rail	E	.24
2	¾ x 1 x 16⅛	Lower braces	E	.22
1	¾ x 1 x 13	Lower brace	E	.09
1	1 ¾ x 1 ½ x 13	Lower back	E	.36
1	1 ¾ x 5 x 17	Back	E	1.17
4	¾ x 2 x 4	Corner braces	S	.22
1	½ x 17 ½ x 17 ½	Seat board	P	2.25

Material Code: E—Walnut, Oak, Pecan, Birch; S—Ash, Maple; P—Fir plywood.

Questions

1. What is a bill of material and what should it contain?
2. Is it necessary to read and understand a working drawing to be able to make out a bill of material?
3. Where can standard available sizes of materials be found?
4. In what order should lumber dimensions be listed?
5. How can the total cost of a project be estimated?

UNIT 6

Ordering Lumber from Your Dealer

1. Examine your bill of material and determine the amount of lumber needed.
2. Decide whether you are to purchase the lumber in the rough or milled. *Milled* means that a board has been planed smooth to size in a planer.
3. Prepare a list of the pieces desired giving the following information:

   (a) Kind of wood
   (b) Number of pieces
   (c) Size of each
   (d) Grade FAS (Best grade in hardwood). Select A or B (Best grades in softwood).
   (e) Rough or milled
   (f) Kiln dried (K. D.) or Air dried (A. D.)
   (g) Rough (Rgh), Surfaced two sides (S2S), or Surfaced four sides (S4S)

Examples

Walnut—4 Pc. 1″ x 8″ x 16′—FAS.—Rgh.—K.D.
Walnut—8 Pc. 1″ x 8″ x 12″—F.A.S.—K.D.—S2S.
Walnut—6 Pc. ¾″ x 6″ x 12′—FAS.—K.D.—S4S.

4. Calculate the number of board feet and the costs.
5. When buying lumber from a dealer:

   (a) Present to him your list of pieces.
   (b) Check his figures on the number of board feet and his costs with the figures that you made in step 4. These should agree. If they do not agree, determine the reason for it.
   (c) Have an understanding about terms. Should there be cash with the order (C.W.O.) or cash on delivery (C.O.D.) or a deposit with the order and the balance on delivery. Be sure to have a clear understanding on these points.

6. Give him your order if you are satisfied with agreements, and ask for a copy of the order. Be sure to read this copy and see that the written order agrees with your verbal arrangements. Save this copy. You will need it when material is delivered.
7. Upon delivery be sure to check everything to see that the order has been properly filled.

Problem

Ask your instructor to assign a drawing of a project from which you will make out a bill of material, calculate the number of board feet and costs and prepare an order.

UNIT 7 Your Tools

Without tools, our world would be an entirely different place. In fact, tools are used to make the machines that in turn make the tools with which we make things. This process is very complicated. Machines are tools also.

Special steel is used in making most good tools and great care is taken in the measurement of all the parts. Inaccuracies would result in poor tools and consequently, poor work. Improper use and careless handling of tools render them unfit for fine work.

The life of a tool, under ordinary conditions, can be indefinite. Older craftsmen are proud of the tools they have owned for many years. These are still as accurate and serviceable as they were the day they were bought. The equipment in your shop will do accurate work for years and years if it is used properly. When tools are kept in a damp place they should be wiped occasionally with an oiled cloth so as to prevent rusting. If you get a tool wet, wipe it dry and apply a little oil with a cloth.

The equipment in a school shop is for your use. It was placed there by your parents and other taxpayers with the expectation that you would take care of it. When it is necessary to buy tools to replace those that have been misued, the cost may result in higher taxes.

The first important thing to remember, in the school shop or at home, is that there is a place for every tool and every tool should be kept in its place. Don't throw chisels or auger bits carelessly together or against each other in a way that will cause the sharp edges to be nicked. The teeth of the saw will easily get battered if you lay it down on other tools. A screw driver will not work satisfactorily in driving screws if you use it for prying things. If you pound a chisel with a hammer instead of with a mallet, the chisel cannot last long. Tin snips must be used only on sheet metal. Special cutters are used in cutting wire and small bolts. Keep tools clean at all times.

You will wish to cooperate in the care of the tools and equipment. Being a good citizen has real rewards in personal satisfaction. This is so important that part of your grade will be determined by your attitude in the shops.

Questions

1. Why should wet tools be cared for before being put away?
2. How long will good tools, well cared for, last?
3. Why should a person in school for three or four years want tools to last for a longer period?
4. Name five ways to help maintain the shop equipment.
5. Can you give three ways in which good bench tops can be maintained?

UNIT 8

Occupational Opportunities in Woodworking

Occupational Opportunities Related to Woodworking

Each step in the working of wood – from the tree to the finished article – offers job opportunities for every level of ability that people possess or can develop. Occupational opportunities are numerous, but they are always in keeping with one's training. Those who have had little schooling beyond the elementary grades must find work suited to their abilities and experiences. Considerable physical strength is an asset for some work in the logging and lumber industry. There are positions also that challenge the knowledge and skill of high school and college graduates and scientists.

Rates of Pay

Wages and salaries are always in proportion to the training and abilities of the individual. Some jobs require little training; and therefore the lower wages are paid to those who work at them. Some of these jobs are those involved in the logging process, in the handling of lumber, and in the making of boxes and crates. The wages paid vary in communities and with the different jobs. A willingness to become trained will eventually pay big dividends in increased income, even though the period of earning may seem to be a long time away.

Skilled Woodworking Occupations and Training

There are a large number of highly skilled occupations associated with the changing of lumber into finished articles. A highly skilled worker requires considerable training and does more than common labor. For example, the carpenter who builds houses is highly skilled; and so is the person who builds cabinets, furniture, or refrigerators. Training in shop work, mathematics, English, science, and social science are all essential for one to become a highly skilled worker. Of course, one can do without some of these subjects, but he would just get along on his job. He would always be in danger of being displaced by changes in the methods of doing a particular job. The training one gets in school enables him to study and understand changes as they come and thus be able to adjust to new situations.

Carpenters erect the wood frames of buildings including the flooring, partitions, layout rafters and install them, make doors and window frames and install them, do cabinet work and finish woodworking. The latter are called finish carpenters.

Another class of carpenters install heavy timbers in heavy construction such as trestles, docks, forms for special concrete on buildings and bridges. They work mostly with manufactured woods such as plywood and similar materials.

Training for carpentry is available in technical schools and by way of apprenticeship. A high school education, including woodshop and academic studies, is desirable for entrance to apprenticeship which usually includes four years of on-the-job training and related classroom instruction in technical courses.

Employment outlook is good and will continue for many years. There were 850,000 carpenters employed in the United States in 1967 and this number will increase gradually. The wages averaged $4.75 per hour in 1966 which means that good carpenters can be sure of $5.00 per hour or $40.00 for a working day.

A work week is 40 hours and overtime is paid time and a half and double time.[1]

This basic training of a practical kind, which one may obtain in a modern school, increases the opportunities for the ambitious person. Beyond the work in various woodworking occupations, there are more advanced kinds of work which pay higher wages. One can become a foreman and be in charge of a group of men.

Contracting is another step higher on the ladder of success. A contractor is the person who agrees to take responsibility for building a structure at a certain price. He hires skilled workers and laborers to do the work for him. Training is very important in modern day competition. The man who can plan and think, utilizing knowledge and skills learned in school and on the job, will be more successful than one who attempts contracting without such training. Some of the more successful contractors have college training. They have taken courses in architectural engineering, architecture, cost accounting, and materials of industry.

Wood patternmakers are skilled workers who do exacting work in wood. There are metal, plaster and plastics patternmakers also, but all patternmakers make forms used in making molds in which molten metal is poured to form metal castings in the foundry. The castings are usually later finished in other shops and become parts of finished objects of metal or plastics.

Technical school and high school cabinet making is of value in preparing to become a wood patternmaker. Use of various types of machine and hand tools in precise application is necessary in patternmaking because the work is very exacting. There were 18,000 persons employed in patternmaking in 1967 and the wages were $3.53 to $4.23 per hour plus fringe benefits.[2]

[1] Bureau of Labor Statistics, U. S. Department of Labor: Washington, D. C., 1968-69. Bulletin No. 1550, pp. 327 ff.

[2] Ibid. pp. 549 ff.

[3] Ibid. p. 204.

Professional and Scientific Opportunities

Architecture is a professional occupation comparable to law, medicine and engineering. An architect plans and designs buildings of all kinds utilizing the most modern, artistic and scientific methods and sees that all plans and specifications are followed.

An architect has advantage if he has had training and experience in various technical construction occupations and schooling in subjects such as drafting and woodworking before he undertakes the study of architecture in college. He should know the work of the various skilled workers on a building under construction, including carpentry, cabinetmaking, masonery and plumbing, and be able to recognize when the work is properly done. If one plans to become an architect, courses in technical work should be included with academic preparation in high school or technical school. Such courses are basic as are the various academic studies in high school and college.

In 1967, there were 32,000 architects in the United States and they earned well over $25,000 per year. Employment opportunities are on the increase and likely will continue so with the growth in volume in non-residential construction. Usually a commission of 6% is paid for architectural services.[3]

There are splendid opportunities in the wood industries for those who are willing to specialize in science. From the chemical laboratories come paper, the first byproduct of wood. Related to paper in production are various composition woods and insulating materials for which there is a wide commercial demand. Rayon and cellulose acetate are byproducts of wood created originally in the chemical laboratories. Movie films were once forest trees. A change here or there in the chemical formula representing wood pulp may supply almost anything from a shirt collar to paints. Only the chemical research worker can do it.

From wood, by way of the chemical laboratory, come charcoal, alcohol, creosote and tar; acetic, oxalic, pyroligneous, and many other acids; acetone, naphthalin, paraffin.

In fact, these are only a small sample of the many things research workers have created from wood. There could be listed pages and pages of things made from the cellulose of trees; and there are many more things yet to be discovered. Opportunities in the future for chemical research workers are as good as they have been in the past.

The principal wood-using industries have carefully planned programs of research which involve forest conservation, wood utilization and manufacture of their various products. Opportunities are numerous for those who have interest and training in the woodworking and related scientific fields. Wood has at present wider commercial and industrial uses than any other material. There are even greater possibilities of increasing and extending the use of wood through research. The young men and women of the future are offered a wide variety of careers in science and industry related to wood products.

Conservation Opportunities

Closely related to the activities leading to research in conservation are the activities of workers in forestry. See also Unit 74 for more information on conservation. Forestry is the scientific control of forest growth and harvest and wildlife protection. This involves the study of every phase of forest growth such as proper planting, care and control of disease, and forest harvest. The work is largely outdoors and it appeals to individuals who enjoy the wide-open spaces.

Training in a college of forestry is necessary for this work. It is interesting and fascinating because its study includes the whole study of lumber from tree growth to lumber production. In many instances, the experiences of rangers in the forest service have been the themes for story writers. There can be no more respected and healthy occupation than that of the forester.

There were 23,000 foresters in the United States in 1967. The government employed at least 8,000 of them and an equal number were employed by private industry. The latter were employed in pulp and paper manufacture and in logging and milling. Colleges and universities employed more than 1,000 foresters.

In 1966, forty-seven colleges and universities offered education leading toward the bachelor's degree or advanced degrees in forestry. Employment outlook is good for many years, and surely through the 1970's inasmuch as demand for forest products is on the increase. Plywoods and other manufactured woods are wood products that are in increasing demand and foresters are involved in various aspects of their growth and manufacture.

In 1967, a forester with a good college record could start at a salary of $6,451 a year. Advanced degrees commanded higher beginning salaries ranging from $9,000 to $12,000 a year. Opportunities for advancement are as good in this profession as in any other and the salaries are much higher than the foregoing and often include many fringe benefits. The working conditions for foresters in the field are inviting for those who like the outdoors. Even the foresters who work in private industry and in the universities enjoy the same working conditions as do workers in other professions.[4]

While you are working with wood, you are studying in an important phase of wood technology and it will be helpful to you in considering your choice of an occupation in another useful, pleasing and highly regarded profession.

And, too, whatever your choice of occupation, the hobby value, do-it-yourself, should be considered in any shop course when learning the various operations.

Questions

1. In the woodworking and allied industries what factors control the wage and salary scales?
2. Is the demand for workers in skilled occupations and college graduates on the increase or decrease?
3. How do the duties and wages of a foreman and a common laborer compare?

---

[4] Ibid. p. 50 ff.

4. Explain the work of a contractor.
5. In what ways is college training valuable to a contractor?
6. What does an architect do? What should his education be? Should he be a good judge of good craftsmanship?
7. What is the greatest byproduct of wood?
8. How do the commercial and industrial uses of wood compare with other materials?
9. What does a forester do? What should be the education of a forester and what are his opportunities?

SECTION

Two

Sawing Operations

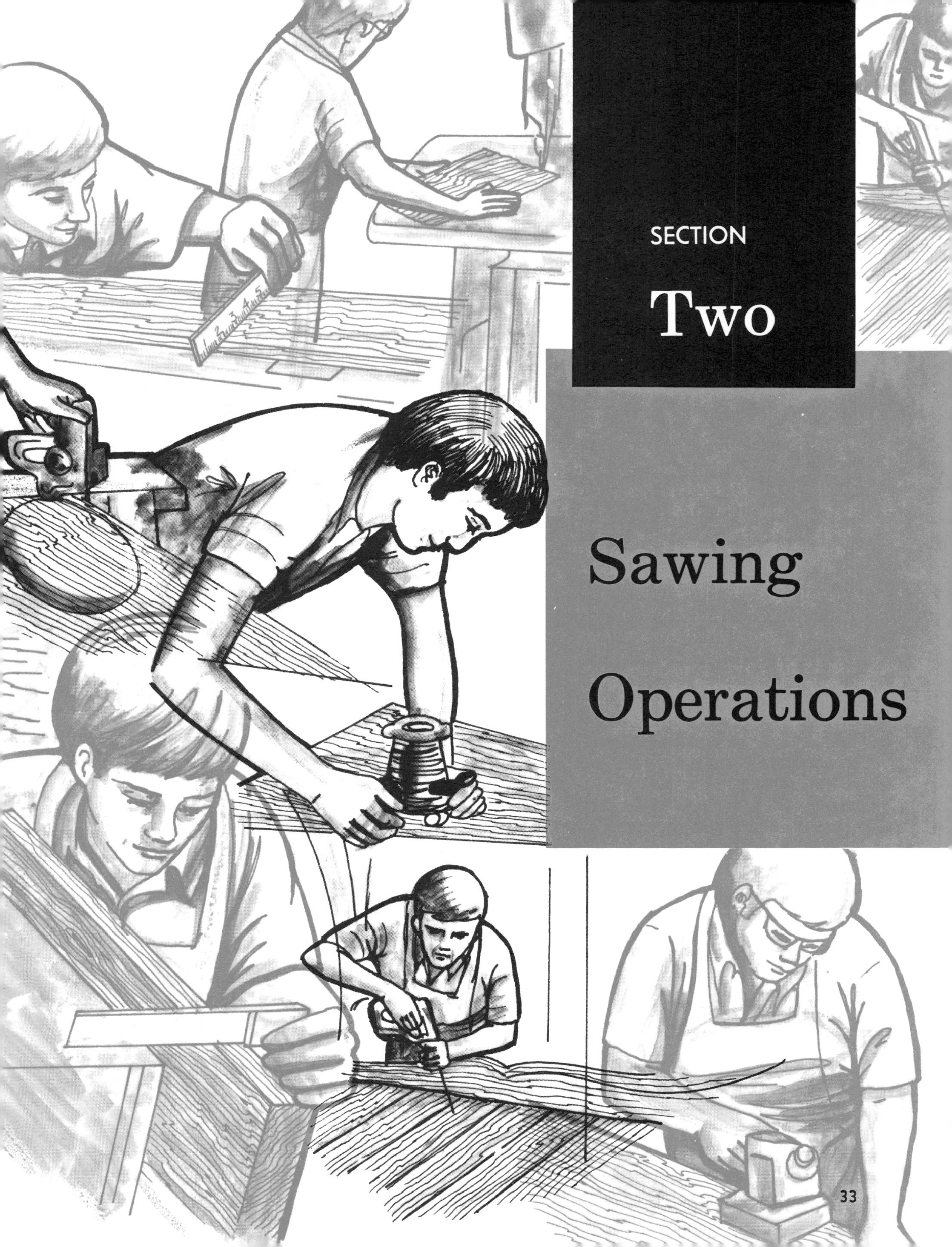

UNIT 9

How Saws Cut

In using the handsaw no doubt you have been surprised at the ease with which it operates. Especially is this true if you have developed some skill in sawing. At the start you probably found it hard to push. It may have had a tendency to get caught when pushed downward into the wood. However, after learning not to bear down and not to force the saw you found that it operated rather easily.

Kinds of Saws

Handsaws are of two kinds — crosscut and ripsaws. Examine Fig. 15, and observe the shape of crosscut and ripsaw teeth. Each tooth is filed to a sharp cutting edge. The crosscut saw is filed at an angle so the sides of the teeth are sharp and knife-like. The ripsaw is filed straight across so the points of the teeth are like a series of chisels. Crosscut saws are used to cut *across the grain,* ripsaws to cut *with the grain* of a board.

It is important that good steel be used in saws or the teeth would soon become dull or break. The better saws are made of the high grade steel and therefore slightly higher in price. Such steel is hard, but not too hard to be filed. The better grade saws can be easily distinguished by the clear tones they produce when held by the handle and tapped lightly with the knuckles.

Hand saws vary in length from 14 to 30 inches. The small crosscut saw is also called a panel saw and it varies from 14 to 24 inches in length. The saw which is technically, but not generally, called the handsaw is a crosscut and it is 26 inches long. The ripsaw is 28 to 30 inches in length.

Saw Teeth

Saw teeth are *coarse* or *fine* according to their size. This is described by the number of points per inch, Fig. 13. There is one more point to an inch than there are teeth. Crosscut teeth range in number from 6 to 12 points per inch and ripsaw teeth from 4 to 7 points per inch.

The teeth must be *set,* Fig. 14, to prevent the saw from binding. To set a saw, alternate teeth are bent so that the kerf (saw cut) will be a little wider than the blade of the saw is thick. Teeth that are properly set will lie in two rows parallel to each other. When the

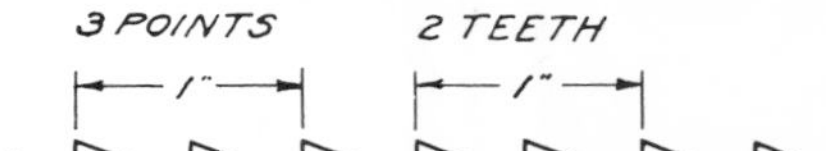

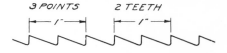

Fig. 13. Ripsaw Teeth

Fig. 14. "Set" of Teeth Provides Clearance for Blade

saw is held at an angle with the teeth up, a needle can be made to slide between the rows from the handle to the small end.

Crosscut Saws

Even though a crosscut tooth is like a knife, its cut is unlike that of a single knife edge. When the saw is in motion, the forward edges of the teeth cut the fibers, making two small furrows with a ridge between them, Fig. 14. This ridge is gradually crumpled by friction while at the same time a new one is being formed as the furrows go deeper and deeper into the wood.

Rip Saws

Ripsaw teeth are like two parallel rows of small chisels. At each forward movement of the saw the edge of each little chisel cuts off the ends of the wood fibers. Each tooth as it follows the other, cuts more fibers until finally the board is ripped.

Metal in Saws

While high-grade steel is used in making good quality wood saws, the teeth are not strong enough or shaped properly to cut metals. In fact, a stroke of a wood saw over metal will render the teeth practically useless until they are filed again. This means that you must be exceedingly careful with saws just as with other cutting tools. There is a certain desire on the part of everyone to preserve that which is good. To its owner, possession of a good saw not only is cause for satisfaction in itself, but it plays an important role in creating satisfaction in doing things well in woodworking.

Fig. 18. Marking Along the Length of Stock

Questions

1. Why are the teeth of a crosscut saw filed at an angle?
2. Why are ripsaw teeth filed straight across?
3. Why is high-grade steel used in saws?
4. How are saw teeth set and why?
5. How can the coarseness or the fineness of a saw be determined?

UNIT 10 Laying Out and Cutting Stock

One of the most important operations in woodworking is the proper laying out and cutting of stock. Each part of the project that you wish to make should be systematically laid out with a pencil and carefully checked with the drawing before cutting. By following these directions you will save time and be more certain to enjoy your work.

Laying Out

1. Be sure that the quality of the stock fits your needs. Examine it for knots and checks. If any appear, get other stock or plan your job so that the imperfections will be on the under or back side.
2. Check the stock to be certain that it is

of the required thickness and width for your needs.

3. The piece should be laid out so there will be as little waste as possible. Measure with a rule and mark the length and width of the piece. Be sure always that the rule is laid parallel with the edge of the board being measured.
4. Place the steel square at one of the points locating the length of the desired piece. Hold the tongue of square on the broad surface of the stock and at the same time hold the blade firmly against the edge, as in Fig. 16. Mark carefully along the tongue with a sharp pencil.
5. With the blade of the square on the face of the stock and the tongue across the edge at the line laid out in step 4, mark across the edge of the stock with the tongue as a guide, as shown in Fig. 17.
6. In laying out the width, mark lengthwise of the stock and gauge with a pencil and stick as shown in Fig. 18. A long straightedge would also be satisfactory to use in this step.
7. Check to make sure that all the markings conform with the drawing. Have your instructor check your work before sawing.

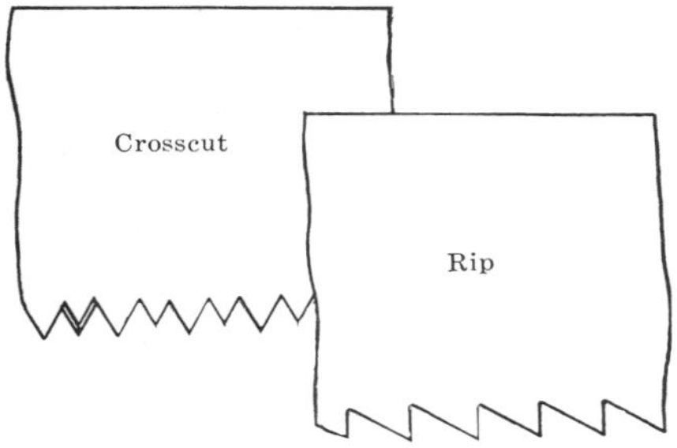

Fig. 15. Shapes of Crosscut and Ripsaw Teeth

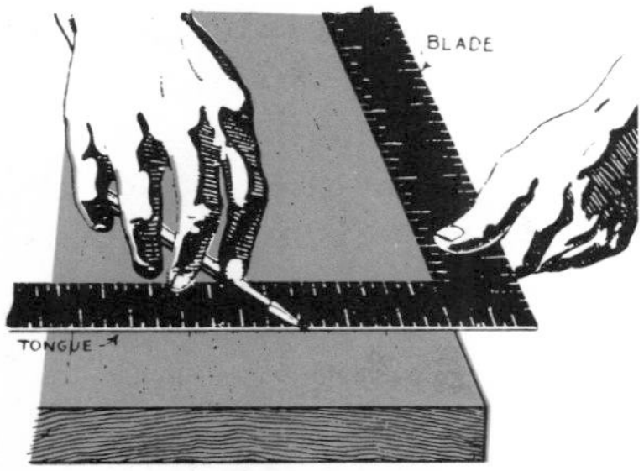

Fig. 16. Marking Across the Face of Stock

Fig. 17. Marking Across the Edge of Stock

Sawing

1. A crosscut saw is used to saw across the grain and a ripsaw to saw with the grain. A quick glance at Fig. 15 will enable you to readily identify the saw needed for each operation.
2. Place the board on a saw horse as shown in Fig. 19. Hold the saw in the right hand and extend the first finger along the handle as shown in Fig. 21. Study Fig. 19 for correct position for sawing and also the way in which to hold the

Fig. 19. Using Saw Horse for Ripping Stock

board. Grasp the board as shown in Fig. 19, and take a position so that an imaginary line passing lengthwise of the right forearm will be at an angle of approximately 45 degrees with the face of the board. Be sure the side of the saw is plumb or at right angles with the face of the board. Place the heel of the saw, Fig. 19, on the mark. Keep the saw in line with the forearm and pull it toward you to start the cut.

When sawing plywood, keep the good side up or towards you, and use a fine tooth saw exerting very little pressure. A saw with about twelve teeth to the inch will tear less than a saw with eight teeth to the inch.

Keeping the good side up, or towards you, protects from damage the finish side or the side to be exposed in the completed project. If you are cutting a long, thin piece of plywood, place a board under it to keep the plywood from bending while you saw. The edge of the supporting board should be close to the cutting line but not so close that you will cut it.

3. Take short, light strokes, gradually increasing the strokes to the full length of the saw. Do not force or jerk the saw. This only makes sawing more difficult. Take it easy. The arm that does the sawing should swing clear of your body so the handle of the saw operates at your side rather than from in front of you, Fig. 19.
4. Use only one hand to operate the saw. It may be a temptation to use both hands at times, but if your saw is sharp, one hand will serve you better than two. The weight of the saw is sufficient to make it cut. Should the saw stick or bind, it may be because (1) it is dull or/and poorly "set," (2) the wood may have too much moisture in it, or (3) you may have forced the saw and thus caused it to leave the straight line.
5. Keep your eye on the line rather than on the saw while sawing. Watching the line enables you to see just the moment that the saw tends to leave the line. Twist the handle slightly, and take short strokes to bring the saw back. See Fig. 20. Blow away the sawdust frequently so you can see the line.
6. Final strokes should be taken slowly. Hold the waste piece in your other hand so the stock will not split when taking the last stroke, Fig. 21.

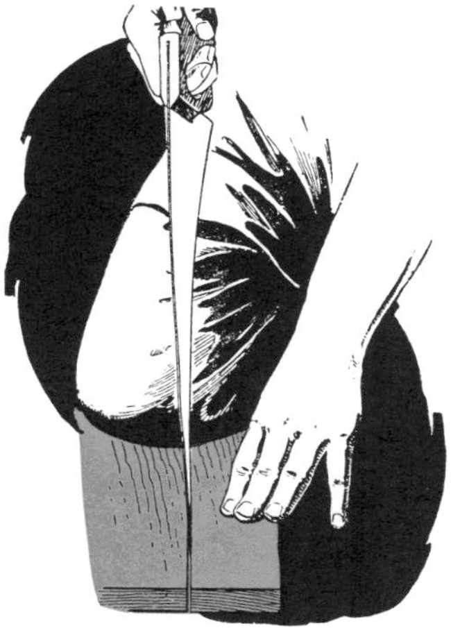

Fig. 20. If Saw Tends to Leave Line, Twist Handle Slightly

Fig. 21. Hold the End Piece so the Stock Will not Split

Fig. 22. Hold Short Pieces in the Vise

7. Short boards may be placed on one saw horse when sawing. Place long boards on two saw horses but do not saw so that your weight falls between them or your saw will bind. Your weight should be directly on one end of the board over one saw horse while the other end of the board rests on the other saw horse.
8. Short pieces are more easily sawed while held in the vise, Fig. 22. In order to rip short stock and keep the saw from sticking, it will be necessary to take a squatting position. The saw then takes an upward direction and works more easily.

Questions

1. What causes a saw to bind?
2. Why should the layout be checked before cutting?
3. What kind of saw is used in sawing with the grain?
4. To cut across the grain what kind of saw is used?
5. How do you distinguish between a crosscut saw and a ripsaw?
6. When sawing to a line should you watch the line or the saw?
7. Why should the final strokes in sawing be very light and slow?
8. What is a saw horse?
9. Why place the unfinished side of plywood down when sawing?

UNIT 11 Sawing with a Backsaw

The backsaw is so named because of the special piece of steel attached to the back of the blade. The blade is so thin that this reinforcement is necessary. The blade is thicker near the teeth than it is at the back and the backsaw cuts a very fine kerf. The word *kerf* means the groove made by the saw. For fine sawing, as in cutting joints, the backsaw is necessary. Do not use it for ordinary sawing. Preserve it for fine work.

1. Lay out the cutting lines with a sharp, hard pencil or with a knife. A common pencil is too inaccurate.
2. Hold the stock firmly against the bench hook with the left hand as shown in Fig. 23.
3. Hold the saw in the right hand with the middle part of the blade resting on the mark on the far corner of the stock as in Fig. 23 and Fig. 24. Place the thumb of the left hand against the saw as a guide and start sawing by drawing the

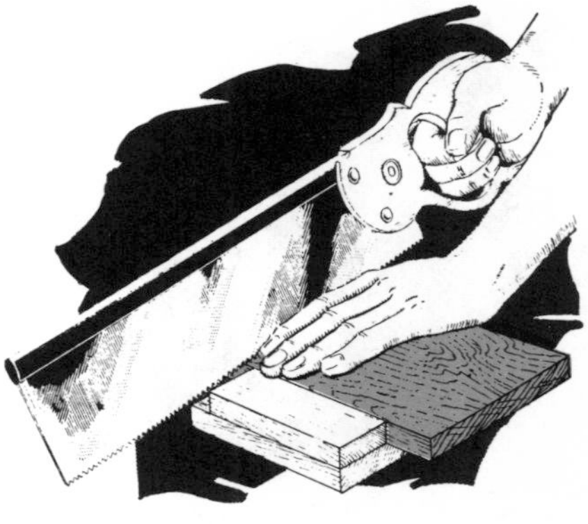

Fig. 23. Using the Backsaw

saw toward you. Take light strokes until the saw is well started.

4. Continue sawing and gradually lower the handle until the saw is level with the stock, as in Fig. 24. Be careful to see that the side of the saw is at a right angle with the top surface of the stock and that it follows the cutting line on the edges as well as on the face of the board.
5. Blow the sawdust away from time to time so you can see the line.
6. Never try to start sawing with the teeth of the saw resting on the full width of the board.
7. When very accurate work is required, as in cutting joints, the cut should be made just beside the line with the kerf in the waste stock, leaving no stock between line and kerf, Fig. 25.

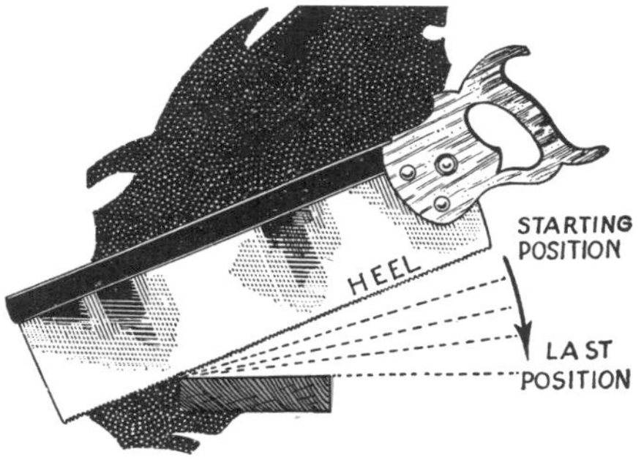

Fig. 24. Lower Handle Gradually after Starting Cut

Questions

1. How does the backsaw get its name?
2. Are the teeth of a backsaw larger or smaller than those of a crosscut saw? How many teeth are in an inch?
3. When should you use a backsaw?
4. Why make lines with a knife or a very fine pencil when the backsaw is used?
5. Should you start sawing with the saw resting flat on the board?
6. When accuracy is required, as in making joints, should the kerf be on the line or just outside in the waste?

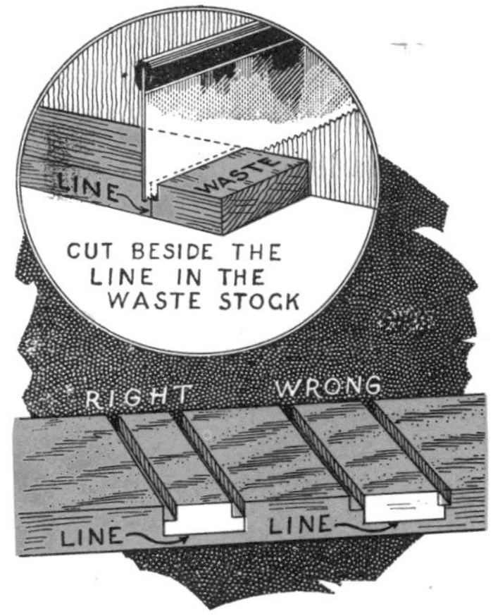

Fig. 25. Make Cut Beside the Line in the Waste Stock

UNIT 12

Resetting and Sharpening a Handsaw

It is not necessary to be an expert to reset and sharpen a handsaw. Follow carefully the directions given here, and you can do a fair job. Do not wait until your saw is in poor condition to reset and sharpen it.

Jointing a Handsaw

Jointing a handsaw means to level off the tips of the teeth and to touch up the teeth so they are the same depth and shape. When a saw is worn or has become dull by hard usage or carelessness, it should be jointed. However, saws will not need jointing at every sharpening.

When jointing, setting or filing a handsaw, a clamp of some type is necessary to hold the saw in place. A saw vise similar to the one in

Fig. 26 or a clamp made from wood can be used quite effectively.

1. Pass a mill file lightly along the points of the saw teeth, Fig. 27. Do this until all the points have touched the file.

Fig. 26. Saw Vise (Nicholson)

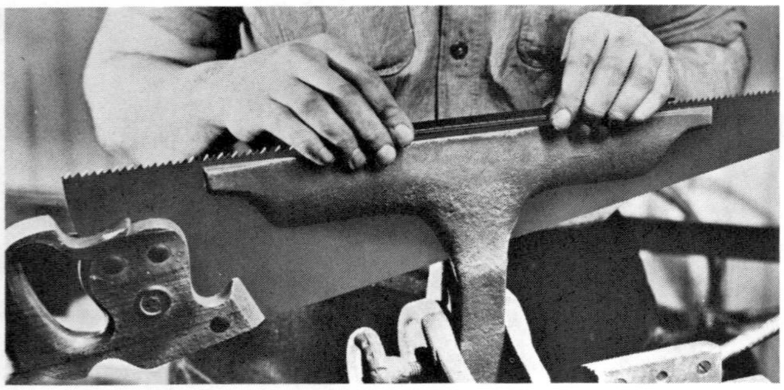

Fig. 27. Jointing a Saw (Nicholson)

Fig. 28. Tapered Triangular Saw File (Nicholson)

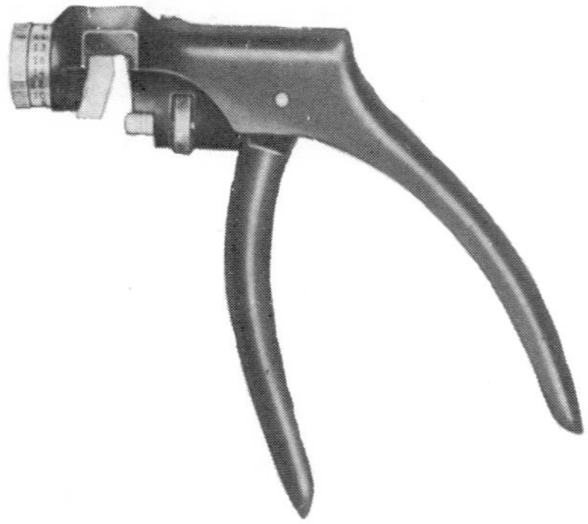

Fig. 29. Saw Set (Stanley)

2. With a regular or a slim taper triangular file, touch up or reshape the worn teeth. This is only a retouching operation, and not the actual filing of the saw.
3. The size of the file used will depend on the number of points to the inch of your saw. The taper file illustrated in Fig. 28 is most commonly used in the 6- and 7-inch lengths.

Resetting a Handsaw

The next step in sharpening a handsaw is to set or *reset* it. This means to bend the points of the teeth to the sides at the proper angle. A saw that is properly set will produce a saw kerf wider than the thickness of the blade and prevent the saw from binding.

1. Reset the teeth with a sawset, Fig. 29. The sawset can be adjusted to bend the saw teeth evenly to saw the desired kerf width.
2. Start setting from the small end or the toe of the saw, Fig. 26, setting or bending every other tooth to a distance of about half the thickness of the tooth.
3. Bend only the top half of each tooth, otherwise you may break the tooth.
4. When you have reset alternate teeth to one side, reverse the saw and reset the other teeth.
5. Both the hand crosscut and the hand ripsaw are reset in the same manner.

Sharpening a Hand Crosscut Saw

The teeth of a crosscut saw are knife-like and cut with their sharp edges and points, Fig. 30. When they are properly filed and shaped, they cut smoothly and evenly.

1. Fasten the saw in a saw vise for filing.
2. Start filing in the gullet next to the first tooth of the toe or small end of the saw, pointing the file toward the end.
3. Hold the file at an angle of 60 to 65 degrees when filing, as shown in Fig. 32. The filing guide attached to the filing vise can be a real help in keeping the file level and at the proper angle.
4. The file should touch evenly on the bevels of the two teeth, so both sides of the gullet are filed with the same stroke.

5. Make sure to keep the file level throughout the stroke.
6. Skip one gullet and file the next one. Continue with this procedure until every other tooth has been sharpened.
7. Reverse the saw, and start again at the toe of the saw, filing in the gullet to the right of the first tooth set away from you. The toe or small end of the saw should now point to the right.

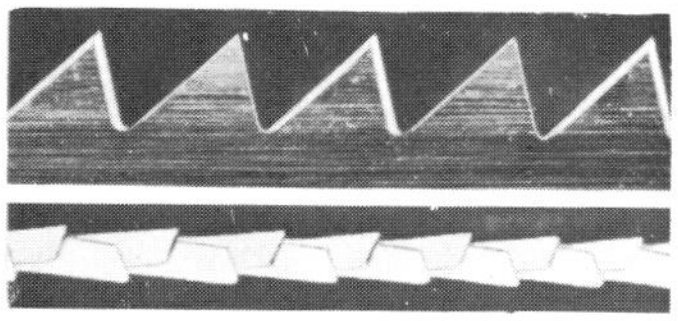

Fig. 30. Crosscut Saw Teeth (Nicholson)

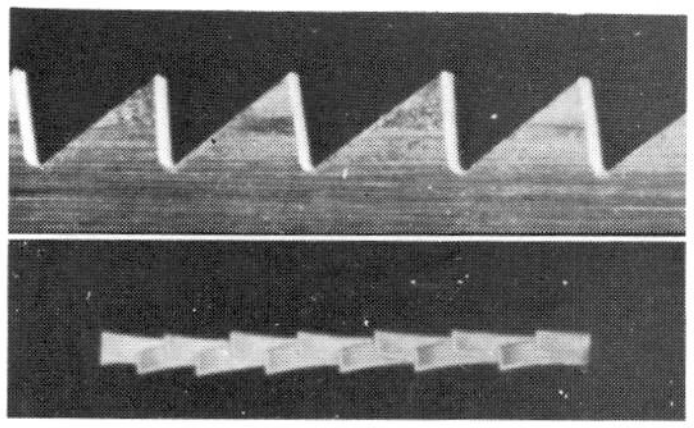

Fig. 31. Ripsaw Teeth (Nicholson)

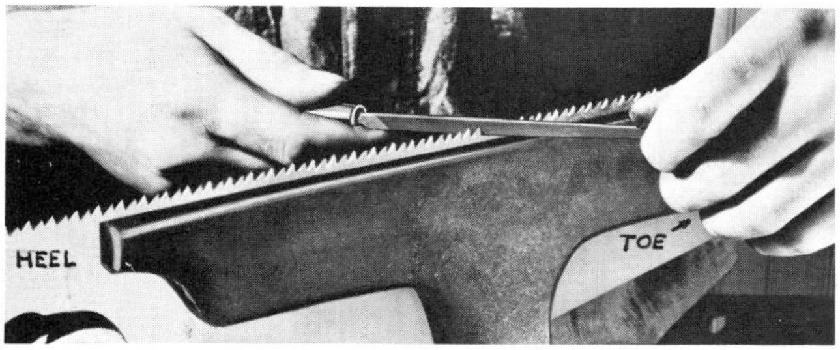

Fig. 32. File Crosscut at 60° (Nicholson)

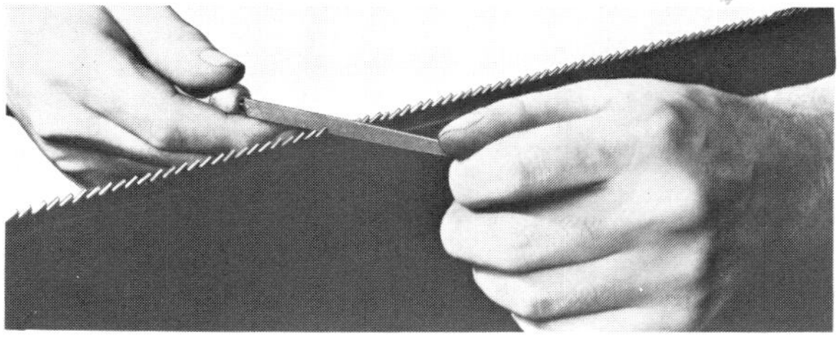

Fig. 33. File from the Narrow End of the Saw (Nicholson)

8. Continue to file every other gullet until side of the saw is completed.

Sharpening a Hand Ripsaw

Ripsaw teeth are like two parallel rows of small chisels, as shown in Fig. 31. The points of these chisel-like teeth do the cutting in a ripping operation.

1. Fasten the saw in a saw vise, as shown in Fig. 26, with the gullets of the teeth showing about $3/16''$ above the vise. The handle of the saw should be pointing to your right.
2. The teeth of a ripsaw are filed straight across or at an angle of 90 degrees with the blade.
3. File from the toe or narrow end of the saw in the gullet next to the first tooth, Fig. 33.
4. File every other tooth to a square edge by pushing your file straight across.
5. A little more pressure is applied on the long slant of the tooth than on the face of the next tooth when filing.
6. Continue to file in every other gullet until the handle is reached.
7. Reverse the saw so the handle points to your left this time.
8. Starting again from the toe or the small end, file every other gullet until you have completely filed the saw.

Questions

1. What is meant by jointing a handsaw?
2. Do all saws have to be rejointed when sharpened?
3. What is meant by setting a handsaw?
4. What tool is used in setting a handsaw?
5. What kind of files are used in sharpening handsaws?
6. What are gullets of a saw?
7. Are the teeth of hand ripsaws and crosscut saws sharpened in the same way?
8. How do the points on the ripsaw and the crosscut saws differ?

UNIT 13

The Circular Saw

The circular saw, often called the buzz saw or the table saw, is one of the most essential workworking machines in industry, the school shop, and the home work shop. For straight line sawing, the circular saw is a basic machine in any woodworking shop.

There are several manufacturers of circular saws and two main types of saws, but those shown in Figs. 34 and 35 are typical of the circular saws used in the school shops.

General Description

The main parts of a circular saw consist of (1) an arbor on which a saw blade is mounted, (2) a frame usually of cast iron, (3) a table, (4) a ripping fence, (5) a cut-off guide, and (6) a safety guard. The universal saw has a double arbor and is designed for heavy as well as light work. The rip saw blade is fastened to one arbor and the crosscut saw blade is fastened to the second arbor.

Fig. 34. Twelve-Inch Universal Saw (Oliver)

With the double arbor it is possible to change from a ripping operation to a crosscutting operation without changing the saw blade. When one saw blade is above the table and in motion, the other blade is below the table and does not rotate.

The size of a circular saw is determined by the diameter of the saw blade. The 10″ circular saw, Fig. 35, is often used in the home shop and junior high school shop. The 12″ universal saw, Fig. 34, is frequently used in the senior high school shop. For cutting angles, circular saws may be made with a tilting table or with a tilting arbor. The machine with the tilting arbor is very practical. It is safe, accurate, and convenient to use. The table is always level which makes it possible for the material to lie flat while sawing.

Circular Saw Blades

Circular saw blades are available in several sizes and gauges. The four most common types of saw blades are the rip, crosscut, planer, and the combination saw blades.

The Ripsaw Blade

The teeth on the circular ripsaw are coarse and are shaped for ripping with the grain of the wood. The teeth resemble the teeth of a hand ripsaw and are like a series of chisel points. See drawing *A*, Fig. 36. The circular ripsaw is intended for ripping, only.

The Crosscut Saw Blade

The circular crosscut saw is used for cutting across the grain of the wood. The teeth resemble the teeth of a hand crosscut saw with its knife-like points as shown in drawing *B*, Fig. 36.

The Planer Saw Blade

The planer saw is shown at *C* in Fig. 36. It may be used in cutting across the grain of the wood or in ripping. There are two kinds of teeth, cutting teeth and raking teeth. The cutting teeth cut the wood on either side of the cut, while the raking teeth clean out the wood filings.

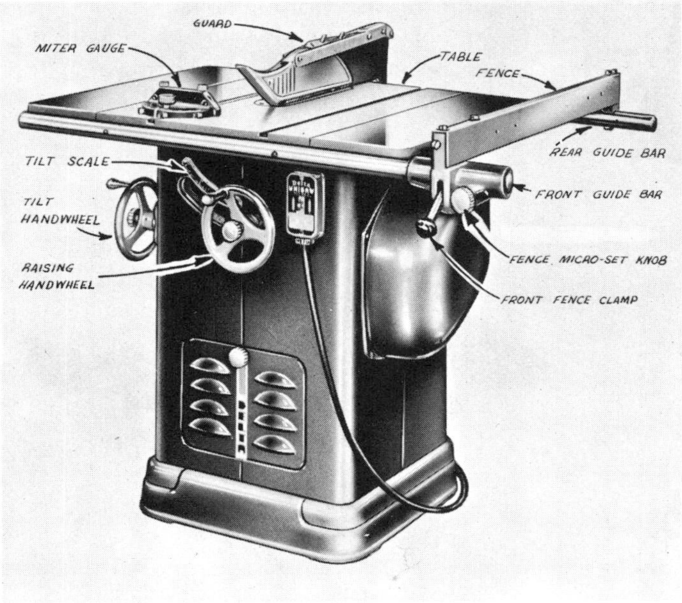

Fig. 35. Ten-Inch Circular Saw (Delta)

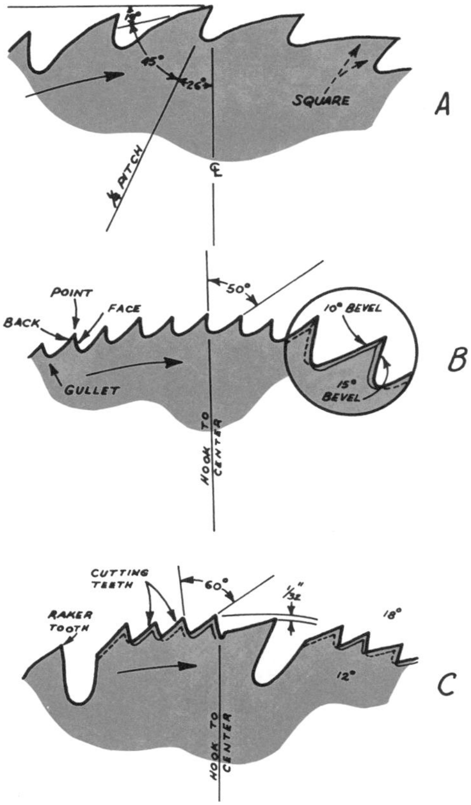

Fig. 36. Types of Circular Saw Blades

The Combination Saw Blade

The combination saw blade is designed for general use. It can be used for crosscutting and for ripping. This saw is similar to the circular rip saw, but the teeth are finer and beveled on the back so they will cut across the grain as well as with the grain.

Safety Instructions

1. As with all machines, the circular saw is safe to use if you follow directions. It can in no way reach out to hurt you. Injury can occur only if you get your hand in the machine.
2. Get permission from your instructor before using the saw.
3. Do not wear loose clothing, a necktie, or long sleeves.
4. Be sure the saw blade is sharp. Dull blades are dangerous.
5. Set the saw blade so it will be ⅛″ to ¼″ above the stock to be cut.
6. Stand to one side of the line of the saw when sawing.
7. Be sure that there are no scraps of wood on the saw table or on the floor around the machine when sawing.
8. When ripping wood, make sure the splitter guard is in place and the rip fence is locked in place. See Fig. 37.
9. Do not try to make adjustments while the machine is running.
10. Do not remove scraps of wood from the table until the machine has been stopped.
11. Do not try to saw warped or twisted stock.
12. Use a push stick for stock narrower than three inches.
13. Never saw freehand. Use the cut-off guide or the ripping fence.
14. Do not talk to anyone while working nor permit anyone to talk to you. Stop the machine if you must talk.

Fig. 37. Rigid-Type Splitter Guard

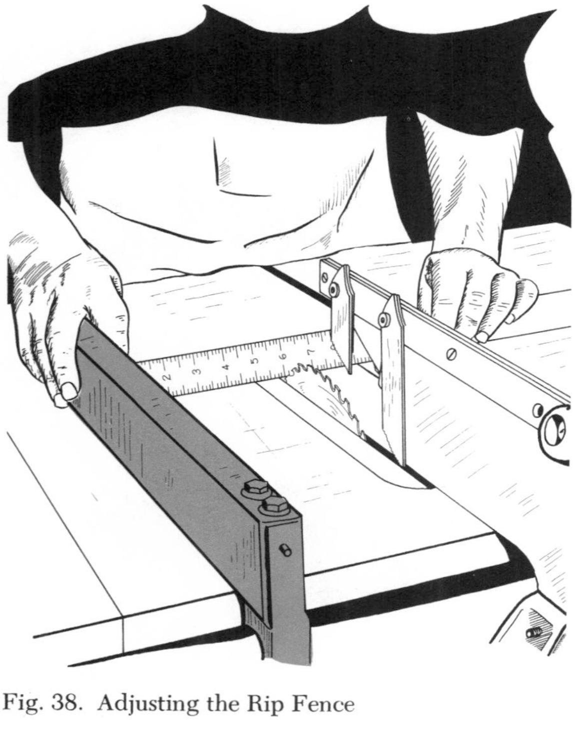

Fig. 38. Adjusting the Rip Fence

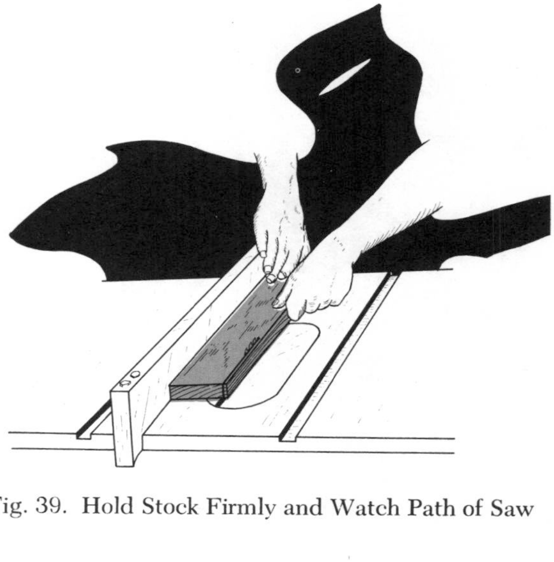

Fig. 39. Hold Stock Firmly and Watch Path of Saw

Plain Sawing

Rip sawing, crosscutting, and a few other fundamental standard operations are called *plain sawing operations.*

Ripping Stock

1. Making a lengthwise cut in a board is called *ripping.*
2. Adjust the rip saw blade to cut $\frac{1}{8}''$ to $\frac{1}{4}''$ higher than the thickness of a board.
3. Set the rip fence for a cut about $\frac{1}{16}''$ wider than the desired width of the stock, to allow for truing. Fasten the rip fence securely in place and recheck the measurement. See Fig. 38.
4. The ripping fence should be at right angles with the table top.
5. Make a trial cut with a piece of scrap stock.
6. Stand to one side of the saw and place the stock flat on the table top.
7. Start the machine and push the stock into the saw with the right hand while using the left hand to keep the working edge of the stock firmly against the fence. See Fig. 39.
8. Be sure to push the stock past the saw blade before letting go of the wood.
9. If the stock is less than 3″ wide, use a push stick as shown in Fig. 40.
10. In ripping long pieces, some kind of an outfeed table to hold the stock can be used as in Fig. 41. An assistant may receive the board as shown in Fig. 42. He should stand to one side and hold the board rather loosely. When starting to rip long pieces, the assistant may be needed to help align and hold the stock.
11. When sawing plywood with a power saw, follow the same procedure as in sawing with the handsaw. Keep the unfinished side down.

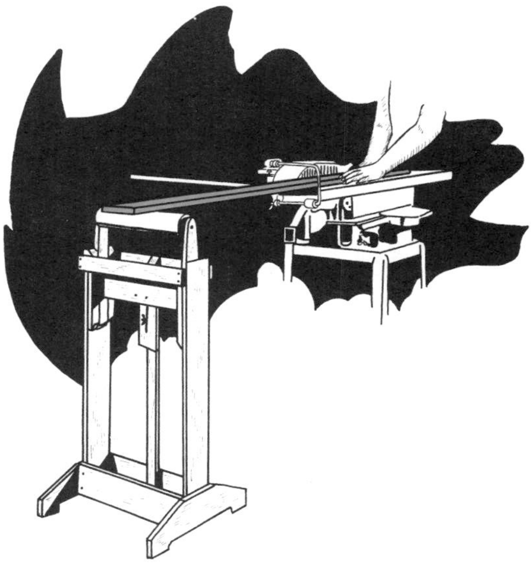

Fig. 41. Outfeed Table Useful on Long Pieces

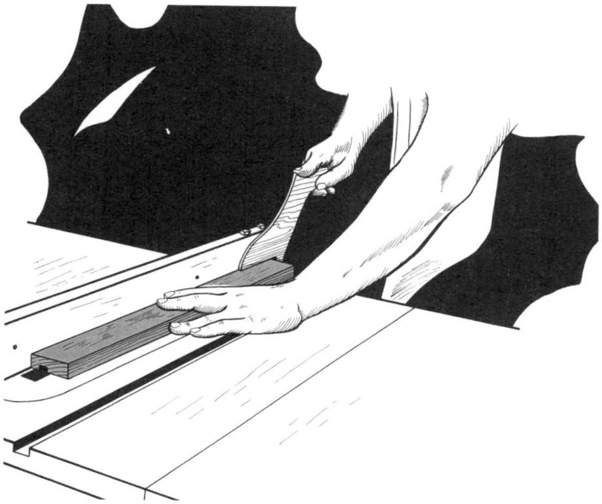

Fig. 40. Use Push Stick for Narrow Pieces

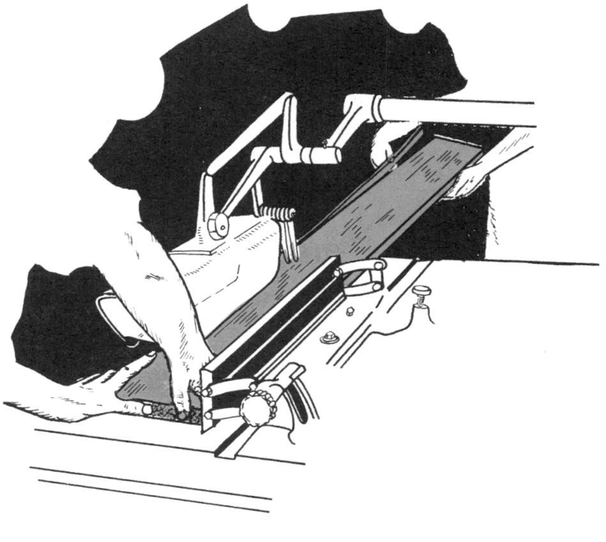

Fig. 42. Assistant Needed on Long Pieces

Crosscutting Stock

1. Trimming square ends and cutting stock to length are typical crosscutting operations.

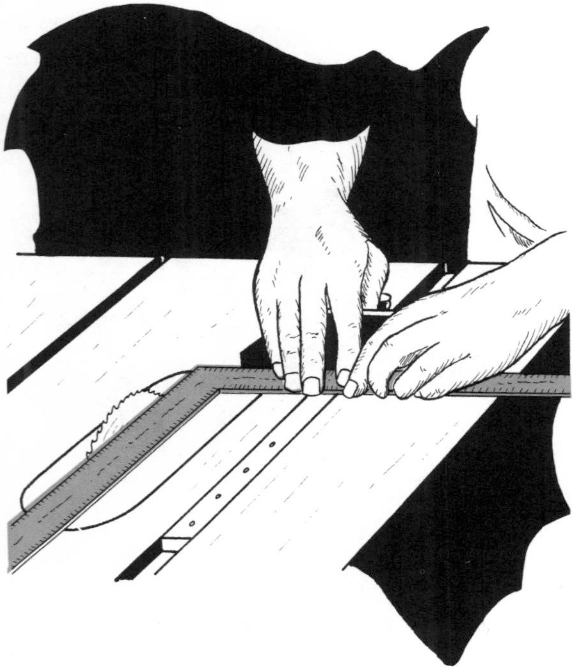

Fig. 43. Testing Guide for Squareness with Blade

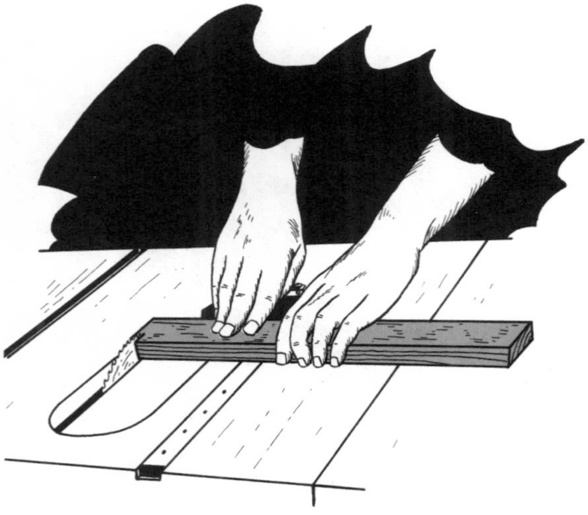

Fig. 44. Hold Stock Firmly Against Guide During Cut

2. Select a crosscut saw blade, *B*, Fig. 36, or a planer saw blade, *C*, Fig. 36.
3. Adjust the crosscut saw blade to be ⅛″ higher than the thickness of the board.
4. Test the guide for squareness to the saw with a steel square. See Fig. 43.
5. On the universal saw, the guide is held to the movable table with a special screw attachment.
6. Be sure you remove the pin that holds the table stationary when using the sliding table for crosscutting.
7. Hold the stock on the table and tightly against the guide.
8. A piece of garnet paper cemented to the face of the guide will prevent the stock from slipping or moving.
9. Start the saw; then move the stock with the guide forward against the saw blade. See Fig. 44.
10. On the 10″ circular saw the cut-off guide slides in a groove on the table top. A guide which slides in a groove is also provided on the universal saw.
11. For cutting duplicate pieces to length, fasten a clearance block against the ripping fence as in Fig. 45. Long pieces also may be cut to length by using a stop as shown in Fig. 46.
12. An iron clearance block, Fig. 47, or a wooden block that can be attached to the end of the ripping fence as in Fig. 45

Fig. 45. Cutting Duplicate Pieces with Clearance Block on Ripping Fence

should always be used in crosscutting with the circular saw. If you try to use the ripping fence without the clearance block, the stock is very likely to bind or kick back.

13. In order to cut long pieces, it will be necessary to remove the ripping fence and guard from the table.

Fig. 46. Cutting to Length with Stop on Cut-Off Guide

Fig. 47. Iron Clearance Block on Rip Fence

Questions

1. Do you need specific instructions to operate a circular saw? Give five safety rules.
2. How is the size of a circular saw determined?
3. Name three kinds of circular saw blades.
4. Why is a dull saw dangerous to use?
5. How far above the stock should the saw extend for ripping? For crosscutting?
6. Why should you not stand straight back of the saw blade when you are sawing?
7. Why use a splitter guard?
8. When should a push stick be used?
9. Is it advisable to try to rip stock that is warped?
10. Why should the floor be free of scraps and sawdust be removed from around the circular saw before starting to saw?
11. Under what conditions can the saw be used with the guard removed?
12. Is it wise to carry on a conversation with someone while you are using the saw?
13. When should a clearance or stop block be used against the fence?
14. What will happen if you try to use the fence for a stop block?
15. When should a stop rod be used?

SECTION

Three

Layout Operations

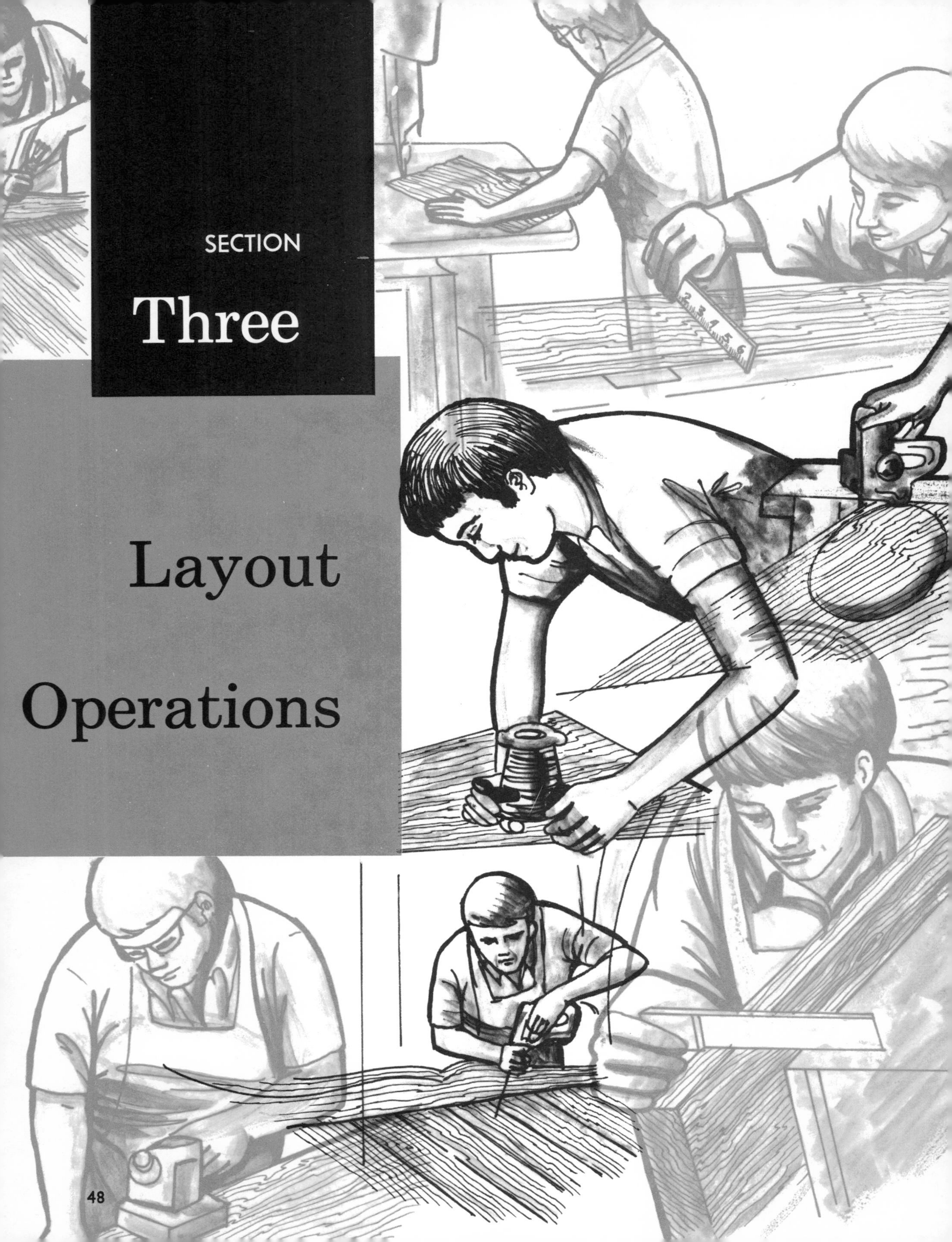

UNIT 14

Measuring and Dividing Spaces with a Rule

A rule is used to measure on rough stock and to lay out specified dimensions. You must be able to make accurate measurements in all shop work.

The foot and the inch are standard units of linear measurement in woodworking. The divisions along the outer edges show full inches, halves, fourths, eighths and sixteenths. You should know and be able to use these fractional measurements in your work.

Common Woodworking Rules and the Steel Square

1. The most common rules used in woodworking are the two-foot folding rule; the one-foot and the two-foot, one-piece bench rules; the zigzag rule; the steel tape; and steel square.
2. The two-foot folding rule is twenty-four inches long and hinged so as to fold twice. It is usually made from maple or boxwood, Fig. 48. This rule is not generally used in the shop because it is easily broken.
3. The one-piece rule, or bench rule, is most generally used in woodworking. Its divisions are similar to those of the two-foot rule, Figs. 49 and 52.
4. The zigzag rule can be obtained in various lengths. This type of rule is used in measuring long distances where slight variations in measurement are not important, Fig. 50.
5. The "pull-push" rule is a compact steel measuring tool which serves both as a rule and as a measuring tape. It is especially useful in measuring long distances and inside restricted areas where other measuring devices cannot be placed, Fig. 51.
6. The carpenters' steel square is made of metal with a 24-inch blade and a 16-inch tongue. It is commonly used to measure

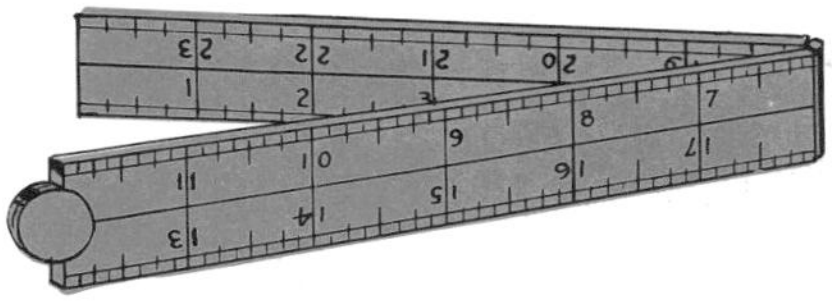

Fig. 48. Two-Foot Folding Rule

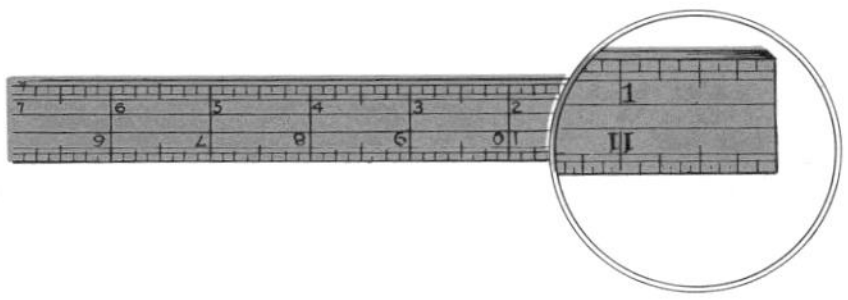

Fig. 49. One-Piece Bench Rule

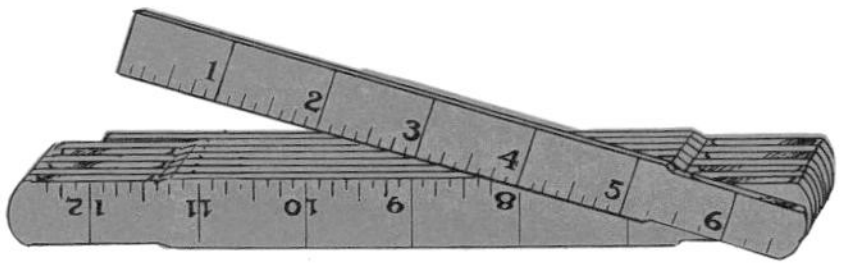

Fig. 50. Zigzag Rule

Fig. 51. "Push-Pull" Rule (Stanley)

stock, to square lines across stock, to test large surfaces for squareness and evenness, and to test for squareness when assembling. It is especially useful in laying out rafters and stairways in carpentry, Fig. 54. The tables that appear on the blade and tongue of the square are to help you solve many problems in woodworking and carpentry. The inch on the steel square is divided into halves, quarters, eighths, tenths, twelfths, sixteenths, and thirty-seconds.

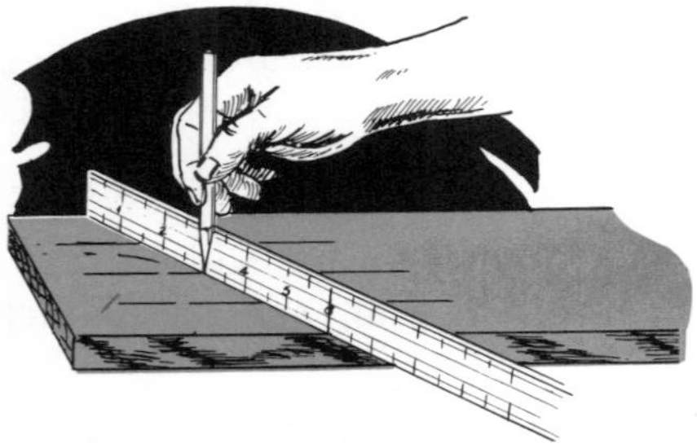

Fig. 52. Place the Rule on Edge when Marking

Fig. 53. Use Try Square for Marking, and for Testing for Squareness

Fig. 54. Steel Square — a Very Necessary Shop Tool (Stanley)

Measuring Short Distances

1. To measure distances less than the length of the rule, place the rule on edge as in Fig. 52. Mark with a knife, or with a hard pencil sharpened to a fine point, exactly at the graduation desired. For the most accurate measurement, the point of a knife is recommended. When you desire to measure several short distances in the same line, place the rule on edge and mark all points before moving the rule, Fig 52. A try square is often used to measure short distances, Fig. 53.

Measuring Long Distances

1. To measure long distances, use the zigzag rule, a short rule, steel tape, or a steel square. The longer the rule, the more accurate will be the desired measurement. A slight inaccuracy is possible each time a short rule is moved in making long measurements. Be sure to lay off the full length of the rule each time. Place it on edge and make fine layout marks.

Dividing a Board Into any Given Number of Parts

1. To divide a board into any given number of parts, place the rule on edge on the surface of the board at an angle as shown in Fig. 52, so that equal divisions can be laid off.
2. Mark the divisions, Fig. 52, and then through the points draw lines parallel to the edges of the board.
3. Example: A board is five inches wide. It is necessary to divide it into four equal parts. Place the rule on the board so that zero and the six inch mark appear on the edges. Hold the rule firmly in position and place marks at 1½″, 3″ and 4½″. Parallel lines drawn through these three points will lay off the board into four equal parts.

Questions

1. What are the most common measuring rules used in woodworking?
2. What are the standard units of measure

in woodworking?

3. Name the divisions along the outer edge of a common one-foot or two-foot bench rule.
4. Why place the rule on edge when measuring distances less than the length of the rule?
5. Is a long rule or a short one best for accurate measurements on long pieces?
6. How would you divide a board into a given number of equal parts?
7. Name three uses for the steel square.
8. What is the smallest division on a steel square?
9. When is the steel tape used to advantage over other rules?
10. Why is the steel tape more accurate for long measurements than a short rule?

UNIT 15

Gauging Lines with the Marking Gauge

The marking gauge is one of the tools which you will use frequently. It is used to mark lines parallel with the sides of stock. The spur, which is the part that makes the line, must be kept sharp with a file. The spur should be shaped like the point of a knife. In using the marking gauge proceed as follows:

1. Determine the desired dimension.
2. Set the marking gauge by holding it in the left hand with the first finger and thumb guiding the head as in Fig. 55. Hold a rule in the right hand and measure the desired dimension from the spur to the face of the gauge, Fig. 55. Holding the head in place with the thumb and first finger, set it firmly by turning the set-screw. After you have set the screw, test the setting by applying the rule again.
3. Hold one edge of the stock to be gauged in the left hand, with the other end against the stop of the bench, Fig. 57. Hold the gauge in the right hand with the first finger on the head and the thumb against the spur end of the beam, Fig. 57. Tilt the gauge slightly away

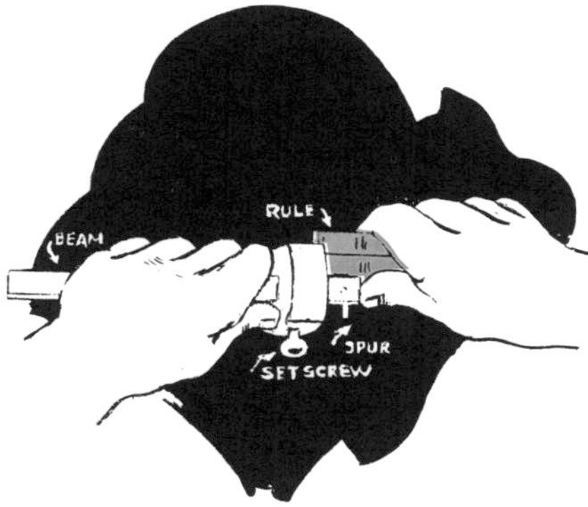

Fig. 55. Setting Marking Gauge

Fig. 56. Mortising Gauge

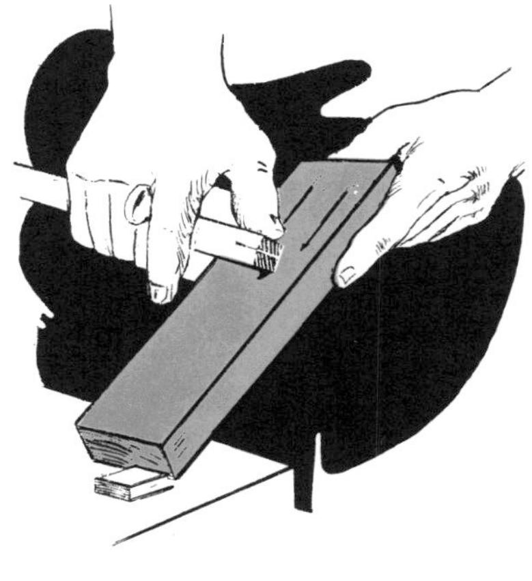

Fig. 57. Tilt the Gauge Slightly in Direction of Marking

from you, being careful to keep the face pressed firmly against the working surface of the stock. Push the gauge steadily away from you, making a light line just deep enough to be seen.

4. Do not use the marking gauge across grain or for laying out chamfers. It would leave marks that cannot be removed when the chamfer is completed.
5. The mortising gauge, Fig. 56, is a gauge which is useful in laying out mortises and tenons. It marks two parallel lines at the same time. One type is made of rosewood and has an adjustable screw in the end of the beam which moves one of the points up or down. The most recent type is the two-bar metal gauge.

Questions

1. For what purposes is a marking gauge used?
2. Why should the marking gauge not be used to mark across the grain of the wood?
3. Why should the spur of the marking gauge be kept sharp?
4. What is the final test of the setting of the marking gauge?
5. When using the marking gauge, how should it be held? Why should the pressure be light?
6. Is it necessary to practice gauging straight lines on scrap stock before using the gauge on your work?
7. What is a mortising gauge?

UNIT 16 Laying Out Curves and Dividing Spaces with Dividers

The dividers may be used in many ways in laying off circles, arcs of circles, and irregular curves. They may be used to take measurements from a rule as in Fig. 59, to take measurements from a drawing, to describe distances, and to divide a given space into a number of parts as in Fig. 62. The dividers are frequently used in laying out angles and to scribe where a marking gauge cannot be used.

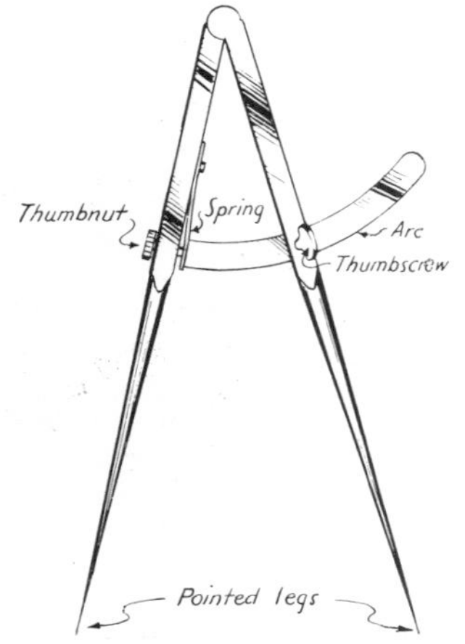

Fig. 58. Dividers

Trammel points are useful in laying out large circles, Fig. 63 and Fig. 63A. The points are fitted on a long, narrow, wooden bar or on a piece of strap metal. The points are clamped to the bar by adjustable screws and may be set to any desired dimension.

Laying Out Curves

1. Make sure the legs of the dividers are dressed to a fine point, Fig. 58.
2. Release the thumbscrew and with a rule set the dividers to the required radius, Fig. 59. When the proper setting has been made, tighten the thumbscrew. To adjust to a more accurate measurement, turn the thumbnut as necessary.
3. To strike an arc at a corner as in Fig. 60, measure from the corner of the stock along the two edges a distance equal to the desired radius. With a try square

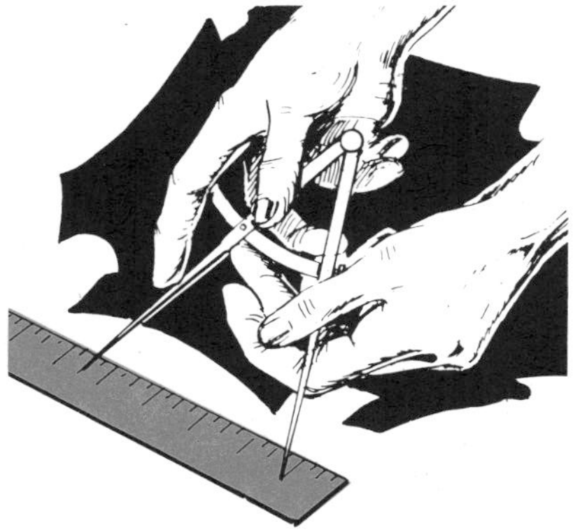

Fig. 59. Setting the Dividers

Fig. 60. Striking an Arc at a Corner

draw lines *A* and *B* being sure that the head of the square is firmly against each edge. The intersection of lines *A* and *B* will be the center for the arc.

4. Set the dividers with one leg on the intersection and test by swinging the dividers to the right and left to see if the center is located properly.
5. Swing the dividers from the left side of the board to the right, making a sharp but light line on the wood, Fig. 60.
6. In scribing a circle, hold the dividers in the right hand as in Fig. 61 while holding the board down with the left hand. Hold dividers so they slant in the direction in which line is drawn.

Dividing Spaces with the Dividers

1. To lay off a distance a certain number of times, set the dividers to the required measurements, Fig. 59.
2. Step off the measurement by turning the dividers first on one point and then on the other, Fig. 62.

Fig. 61. Tip the Dividers in the Direction of Movement

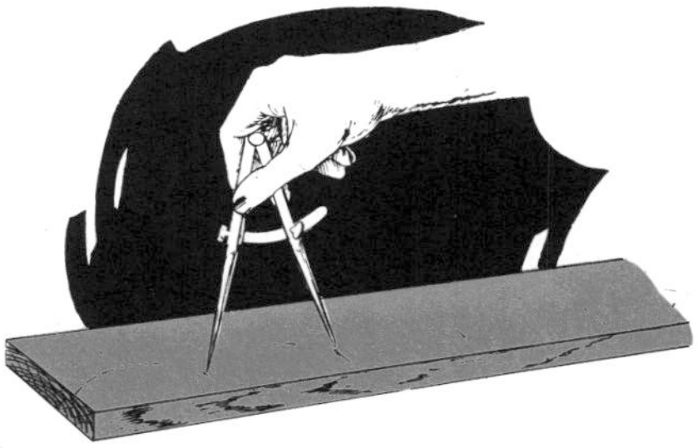

Fig. 62. Stepping off Spaces

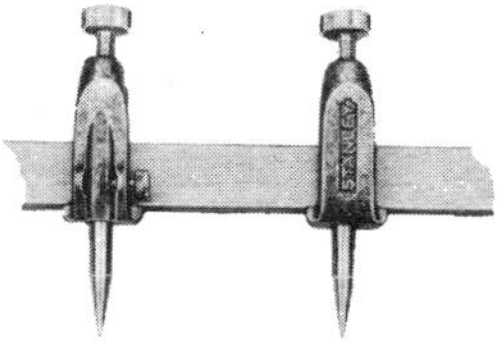

Fig. 63. Trammel Points (Stanley)

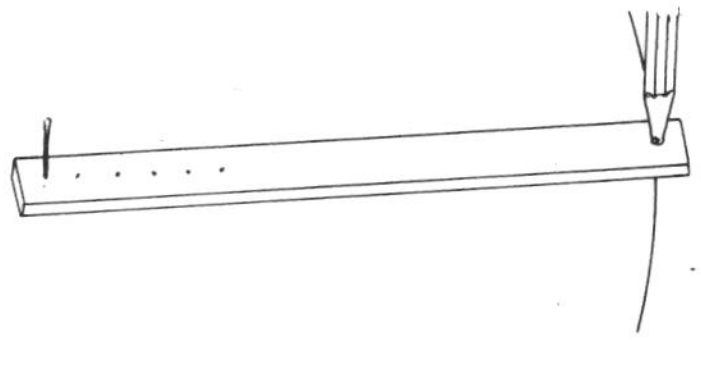

Fig. 63A. Using Trammel Points

3. Press the point very lightly into the wood, just enough to make a visible dot.

Questions

1. How are dividers used?
2. Why should dividers have fine points?
3. Explain how to lay out round corners.
4. Tell how to hold dividers while marking.
5. Should you hold the dividers straight up when describing a circle?
6. Why should the divider points not be pressed deeply into the wood?

UNIT 17

Transferring Designs

The selection of good designs and the designing of projects are important. Many beginners are so anxious to manipulate tools that they begin work without planning carefully beforehand. Take care in your work to see, in conference with your teacher, that your project is well designed. You will be much happier with your results if you give your best consideration to design before starting to work. A good-looking project requires not only good construction but pleasing design as well.

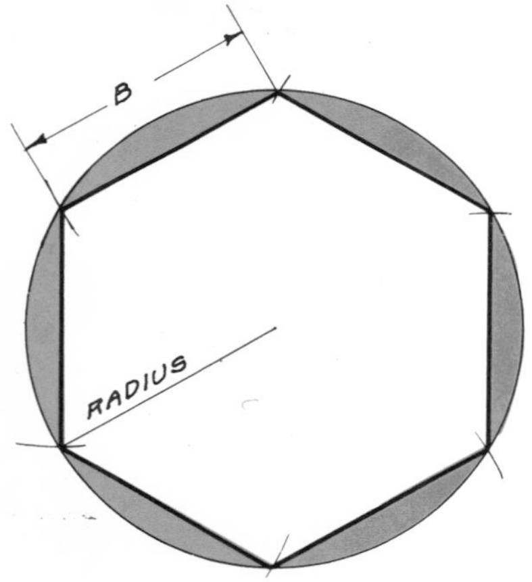

Fig. 64. Laying Out a Hexagon in a Circle

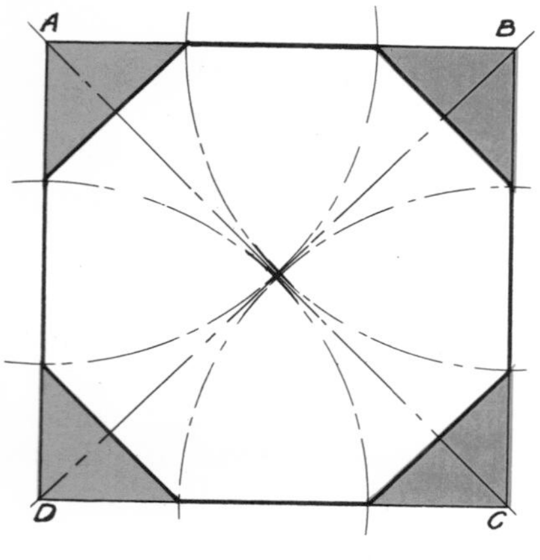

Fig. 65. Laying Out an Octagon in a Square

Every manufactured article has been carefully designed. In fact, in industry it is recognized that design is as important as construction. The good-looking articles sell best. That is why we can buy so many attractive devices for the home such as tables, lamps, chairs, magazine racks, and so on.

Many good project designs appear in magazines, and these are worthy of consideration. They are published for the benefit of the student as well as for the instructor and craftsman. Many of these designs are good and do not need change. Some are composed of irregular curves as well as geometrical curves. They may be transferred to your work by special methods. The ellipse, hexagon, and octagon are geometrical figures that sometimes appear in designs. They are usually laid out with compasses.

In order that you may be able to transfer designs from drawings, whether they include irregular or geometrical curves, the following methods are provided for your help.

Laying Out a Hexagon

1. A hexagon is a six-sided figure of equal sides and equal angles.
2. Draw a circle equal in diameter to the maximum distance across corners of the desired figure.
3. Determine length *B*. It is the radius of the circle, Fig. 64.
4. Set the dividers for distance *B*, and mark off this distance around the circle to locate six equally spaced points. See Fig. 64.
5. Connect the six points on the circle with straight lines.

Laying Out an Octagon

1. An octagon is an eight-sided figure of equal sides and equal angles.

2. Square the stock to required dimensions.
3. Draw diagonals *AC* and *DB* as in Fig. 65.
4. With one-half of *AC* as a radius and *A* as a center, draw an arc from side *AB* to side *AD*.
5. With the same setting, draw arcs with *B*, *C*, and *D* as centers.
6. Connect the end points of the arcs across the corners to complete the octagon.

Laying Out an Ellipse with a Trammel

An ellipse is an oval geometrical figure frequently used in woodworking. It has two axes (or diameters) of different lengths at right angles to each other.

1. The length of the major axis is represented by the letters *AB* and the minor axis by *CD* in Fig. 66.
2. On a narrow piece of drawing paper or cardboard, called a *trammel card*, mark off points *EF*, equal to *OD*, and *GF* equal to *OB*. Cut small sharp notches at points *F* and *G*.
3. The outline of the ellipse is made with the trammel card. Keep the trammel card with the point *E* always on the major axis, and point *G* always on the minor axis.
4. Hold your pencil point in notch *F* and continue to move the trammel until the ellipse is completed.

Laying Out an Ellipse with a String

1. This is one of the simplest methods of laying out an ellipse.
2. Lay out the axes *AC* and *DB* perpendicular to each other at the center *X*, Fig. 67.

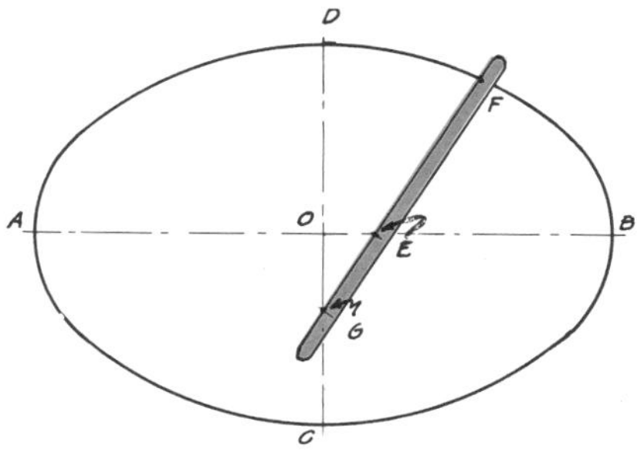

Fig. 66. Laying Out an Ellipse with the Trammel

3. With a compass set to a radius equal to one-half the major axis *AC* and with *D* as a center, draw arcs intersecting the line *AC* at *J* and *K*.
4. Insert a small brad at each of the points *J*, *K* and *B*. Fasten a string tightly around the three brads as in Fig. 67.
5. Take out the brad at point *B*. With a pencil held inside of the string loop, draw the ellipse.

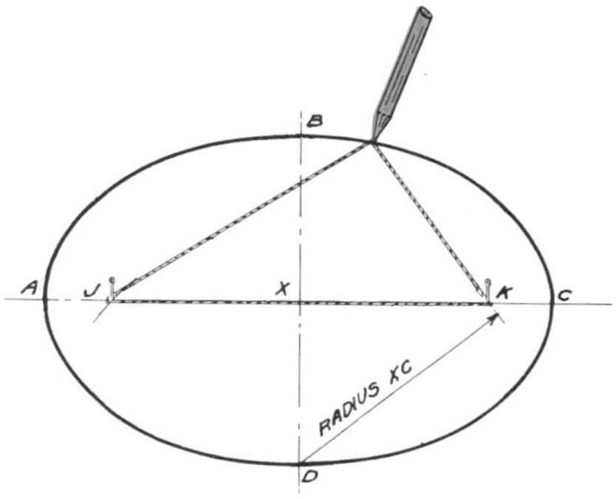

Fig. 67. Laying Out an Ellipse with a String

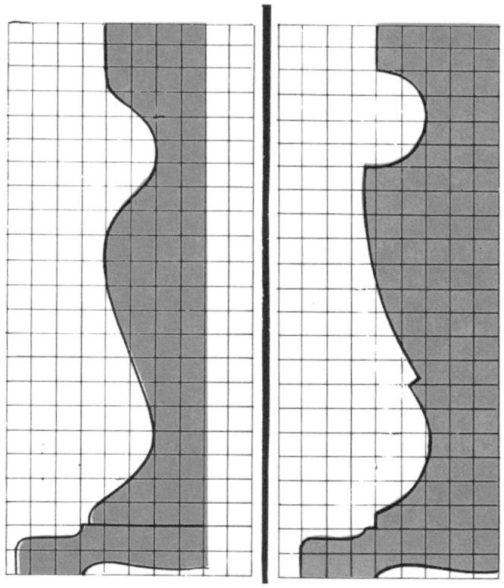

Fig. 68. Fig. 69. Squares on Design for Enlarging

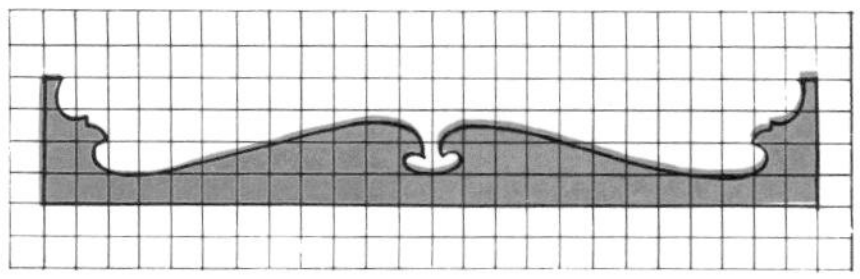

Fig. 70. Squares on Design for Enlarging

Laying Out Irregular Designs by Means of Squares

It is frequently necessary to transfer irregular contours from drawings to a project. Such designs are usually laid out in squares representing one-half inch or one inch. A design can be enlarged in the following manner.

1. Lay out on a sheet of heavy wrapping paper a number of one-inch squares corresponding to the number of squares in the original design. For an example, examine Figs. 68 and 69. Fold the paper carefully in the middle, for only one-half of the pattern will need to be drawn. Make sure that the original drawing is equal to one-half of the pattern.
2. Observe the points at which the curves cross the lines in the squares as in Figs. 68 and 69. Mark each square where the curves cross the lines.
3. With a pencil draw a freehand curve through the different points.
4. Study the enlarged drawing to see that it forms graceful curves. A pencil touch here and there will aid in producing pleasing curves.
5. With scissors cut the design on the curved outline. Open up the folded paper and place the full-size design on the surface of the wood and trace it with a pencil.
6. When a number of pieces of the same form are required, as in production work, a template should be made of tin or thin wood.

Questions

1. Define a regular hexagon.
2. Define an octagon.
3. Define an ellipse.
4. Name two methods of laying out an ellipse.
5. How may irregular designs be enlarged and transferred to materials for projects?

UNIT 18

Laying Out Duplicate Parts

It is frequently necessary to lay out a number of parts to the same dimensions or to mark the location of joints such as tenons, mortises, dadoes and gains.

1. To lay out duplicate parts, lay off on the working edge of one of the pieces the points which mark the location of the portion to be cut.
2. Lay the pieces together on the bench with all the edges up, keeping the working ends even with the aid of the try square as in Fig. 71.
3. Square lines across all the pieces at the points previously marked on one of the pieces, Fig. 72.
4. On each piece mark lines across the face with a fine sharp pencil. These lines correspond to the lines just made on the working edges.
5. When laying out duplicate parts, work as much as possible with the tool you have in hand before using another.
6. For duplicating the width, use the marking gauge for laying out.

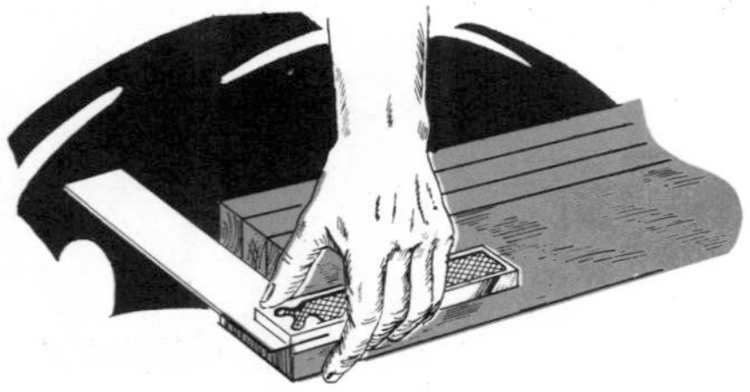

Fig. 71. Keep Ends Even when Laying Out Duplicate Parts

Questions

1. What are pieces or parts of a project that are alike called?
2. When laying out duplicate parts, why make all lines of one kind requiring a certain tool before starting with another tool?

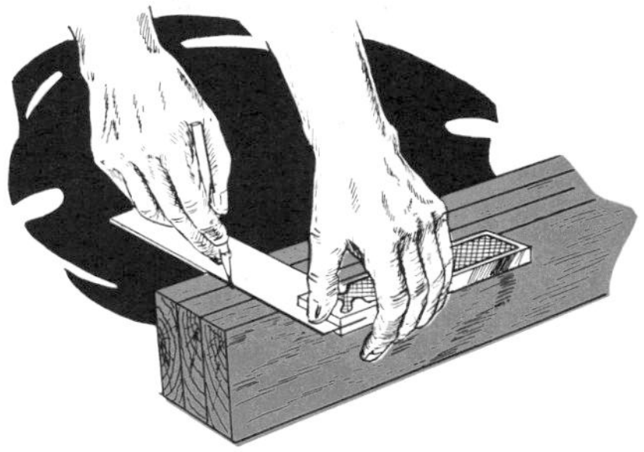

Fig. 72. Square Lines Across the Edges

UNIT 19

Adjusting and Laying Out with a Sliding T-Bevel

The sliding T-bevel differs from a try square in that it has a movable blade. There are two parts, namely, the beam and the blade. The blade may be set at any desired angle up to 180°.

The T-bevel, Fig. 73, is used in laying out work requiring angles.

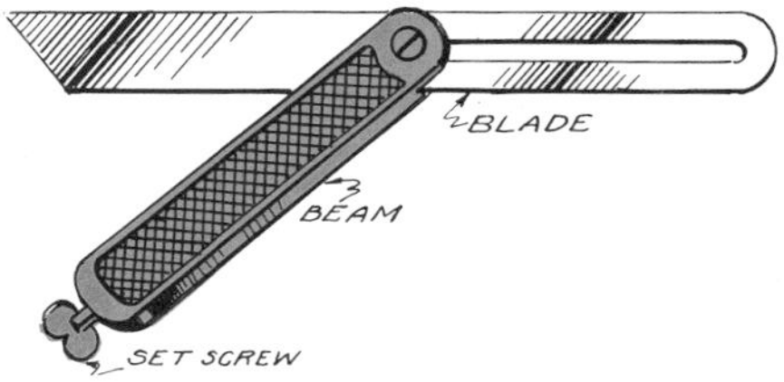

Fig. 73. Sliding T-Bevel

Adjusting a T-Bevel

1. To adjust a T-bevel, loosen the setscrew and slide the blade until the desired angle is obtained. Loosen the blade just enough so it will move with slight pressure and set it firmly when the desired angle is obtained. Fig. 74 shows the mechanism which controls the setting.

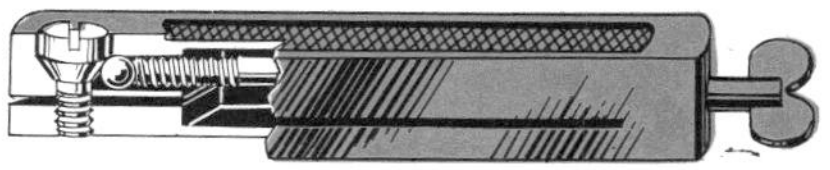

Fig. 74. Cross Section of T-Bevel Showing Control Parts for Adjusting

Setting the T-Bevel at 45 Degrees

1. The T-bevel is set at 45° by holding the blade at equal distances on the blade and the tongue of the framing square. Fig. 75.
2. The T-bevel can also be set to a 45° angle with the 45° triangle used in mechanical drawing.

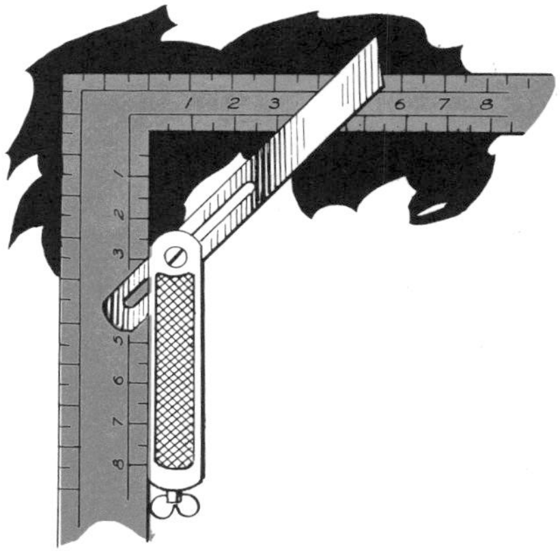

Fig. 75. Setting T-Bevel to 45° Angle

Setting the T-Bevel at 30° and 60° Angles

To set the T-bevel to approximately 30° or 60°, set the blade of the T-bevel at three

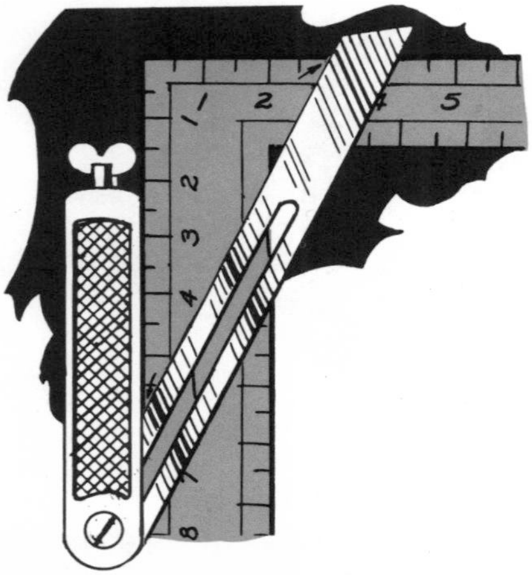

Fig. 76. Setting T-Bevel to 30° Angle

inches on the tongue and six inches on the blade of the framing square as shown in Fig. 76.

Setting a T-Bevel at any Desired Angle with a Protractor

1. The T-bevel may be set at any desired angle by using a protractor. Place the blade of the T-bevel on the center mark of the protractor with the beam against the base as shown in Fig. 78.
2. Set the blade of the T-bevel to the required angle and tighten the thumbscrew.

Laying Out Work

Fig. 77. Laying Out with T-Bevel

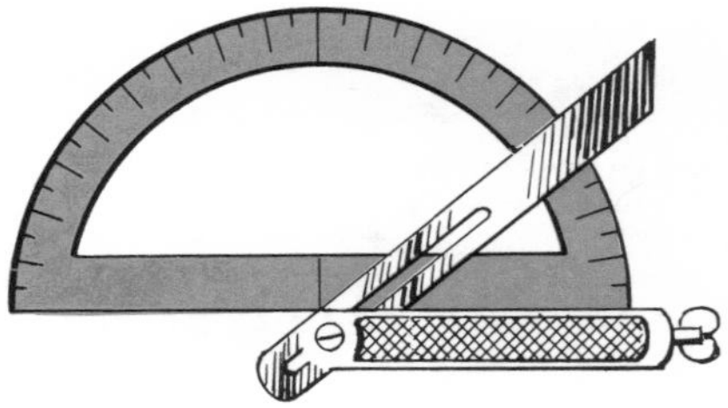

Fig. 78. Setting T-Bevel with Protractor

1. For laying out, hold the beam of the T-bevel against the working surface of the stock and mark along the side of the blade as shown in Fig. 77. Proceed in the same manner as in marking with a try square.
2. Hold the beam of your T-bevel tight against the edge of the wood and mark along the edge of the blade.

Questions

1. How would you set the T-bevel on the steel square to produce a 45° angle?
2. What tool other than the steel square can be used for setting the T-bevel at any angle?

SECTION

Four

Surfacing and Squaring Stock

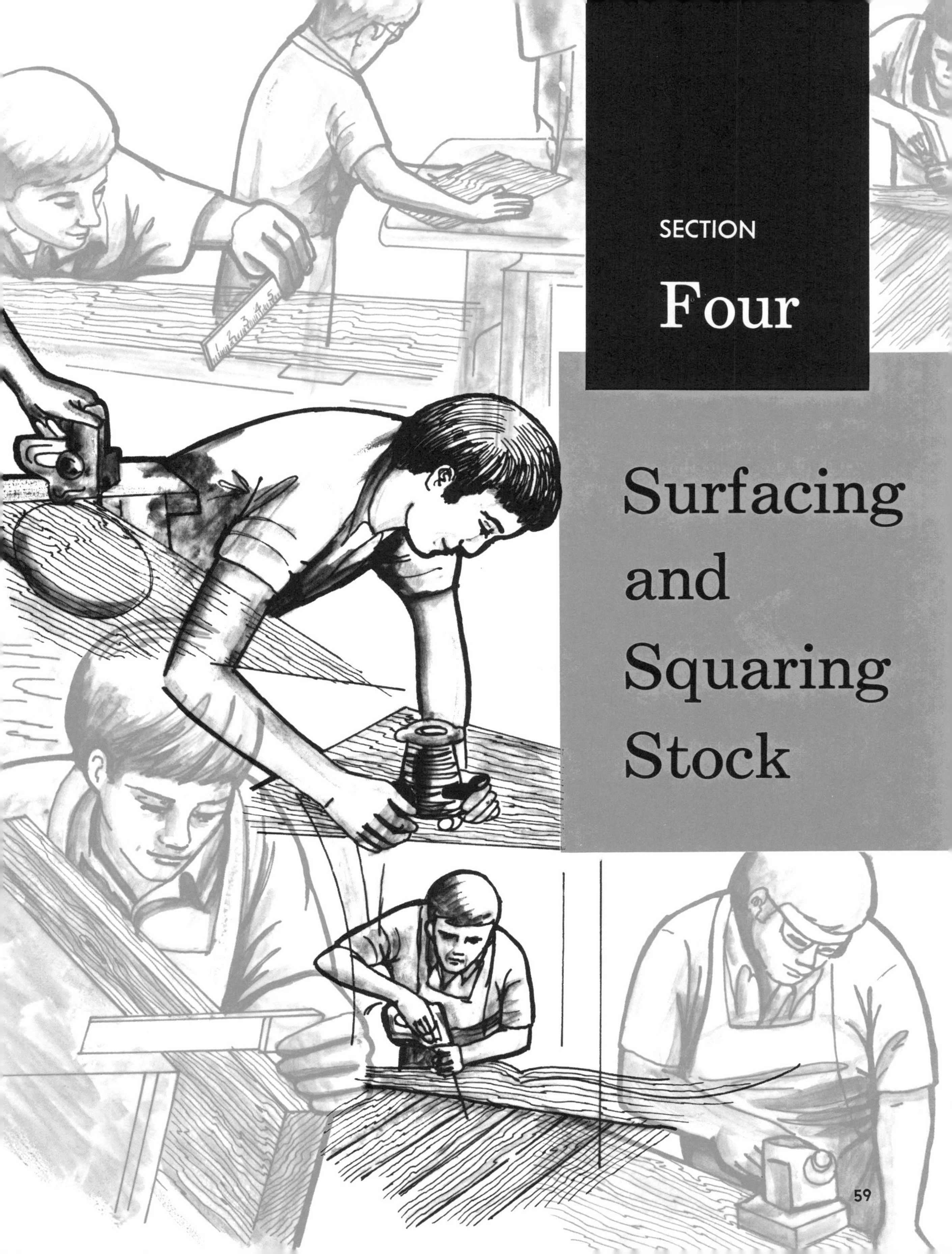

UNIT

20 Assembling and Adjusting a Plane

The jack plane is an all purpose plane. If necessary it can be used in place of any of the other planes. It is used a great deal for rough planing, smoothing surfaces, edges, and ends, and for squaring stock true to dimensions. If you learn to adjust and assemble this plane, you can adjust and assemble almost any type of plane. Fig. 79 shows a cross section of a typical plane.

The smooth plane, the junior jack plane, and the jointer plane are similar to the standard jack plane except in size. The smooth plane, which is the shortest, is ten inches in length, Fig. 80. The junior jack plane is next in size, and it is eleven and one-half inches long, Fig. 81. The jack plane is still larger, its length being approximately fourteen inches, Fig. 82. The jointer plane, which is the largest, is usually twenty-two inches in length though jointers are frequently made longer, Fig. 83.

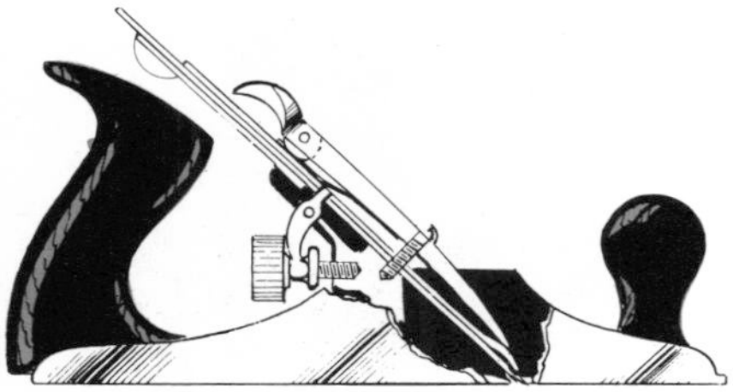

Fig. 79. Cross Section of a Plane

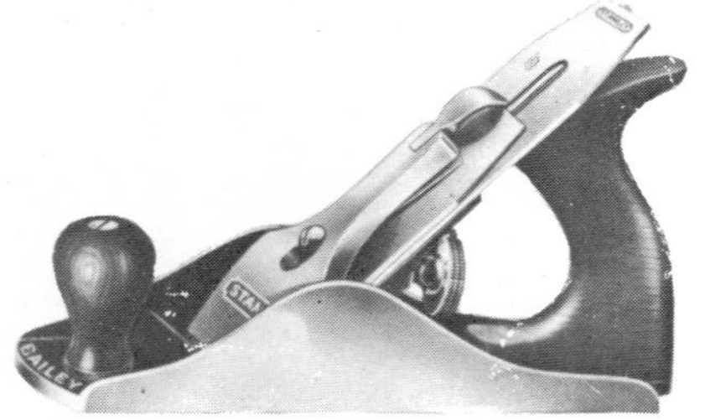

Fig. 80. Smooth Plane – Ten Inches Long

Fig. 81. Junior Jack Plane – Eleven and One-Half Inches Long

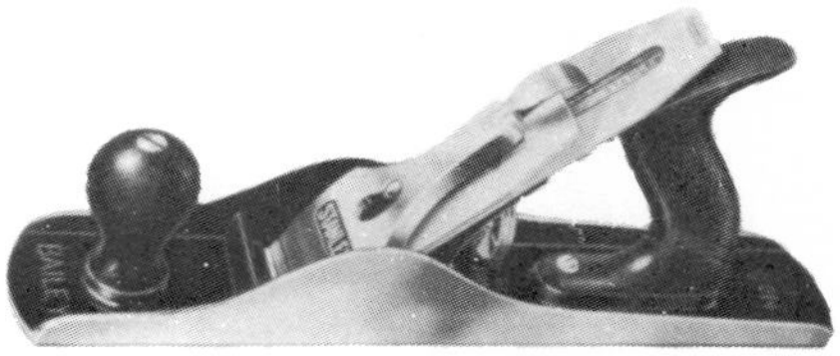

Fig. 82. Jack Plane – Fourteen Inches Long

Fig. 83. Jointer Plane – Twenty-Two Inches or More in Length

Fig. 84. Block Plane – Four Inches to Eight Inches Long

The block plane, Fig. 84, is the smallest of the planes, being from four to eight inches in length. All plane beds were originally made from wood, and the block plane was made from a single small block of wood. It is still called a block plane.

The block plane is essentially a one-hand plane, designed to fit the palm of the hand. It has hollows on the sides for thumb and fingers. A single plane iron is set at a low angle with the bevel up. The block plane is adjusted in the same manner as other planes except that some block planes do not have lateral adjusters. The block plane is sometimes used to plane end grain. The carpenter carries the block plane in his pocket for use when fitting mouldings, cornices, window trims, or end joints.

Assembling the Double Plane Iron

1. Never attempt to work with a dull tool. A dull tool is dangerous. It is hard to use and does poor work.
2. Hold the plane iron in the left hand, bevel down, with the plane iron cap crosswise in the right hand as shown in Fig. 85.
3. Slide the plane iron cap back and away from the cutting edge of the plane iron and turn it to the right until it is exactly parallel with the plane iron. Figs. 85 and 87.
4. Slide the plane iron cap toward the cutting edge until the edge of the cap is about 1/16″ from the cutting edge of the plane iron as in *B*. Fig. 86. This is the best adjustment for general work.
5. For very fine work and for planing burly and crossgrain stock, place the end of the plane iron cap about 1/64″ from the end of the cutting edge of the plane iron as in *A*, Fig. 86.
6. Be careful that the cap doesn't slip past the end of the plane iron and nick the

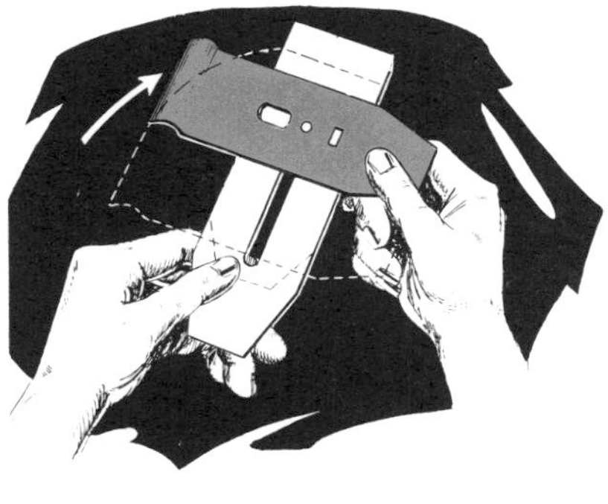

Fig. 85. Slide the Plane Iron Cap in Place, then Rotate

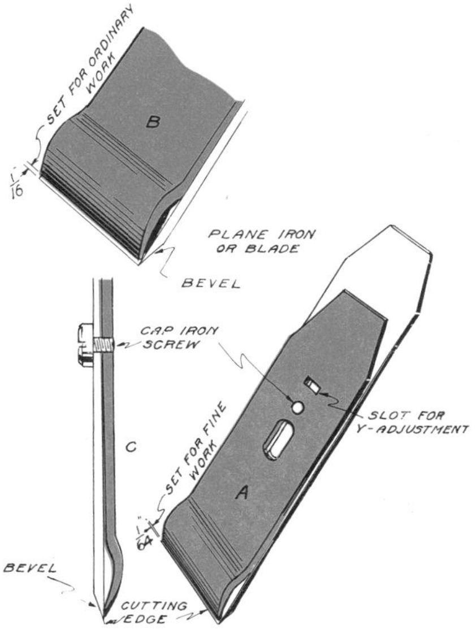

Fig. 86. Best Adjustment for Fine Work

Fig. 87. The Plane Iron Cap Should Parallel Cutting Edge

cutting edge. Keep in mind, too, that only the plane iron does the cutting. The cap iron serves as a shaving deflector.

7. Tighten the cap screw with a screwdriver. It is important that the cap screw be very tight so that the shavings will not catch between the cap and the plane iron and thus stop the progress of your planing. This assembled unit is called the double plane iron. If a screwdriver is not available, the lever cap can be used to tighten the cap screw, provided it is used with care.

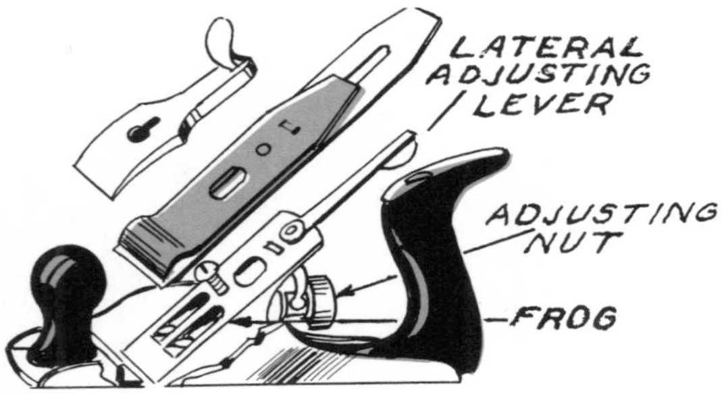

Fig. 88. Exploded View of Parts of Plane

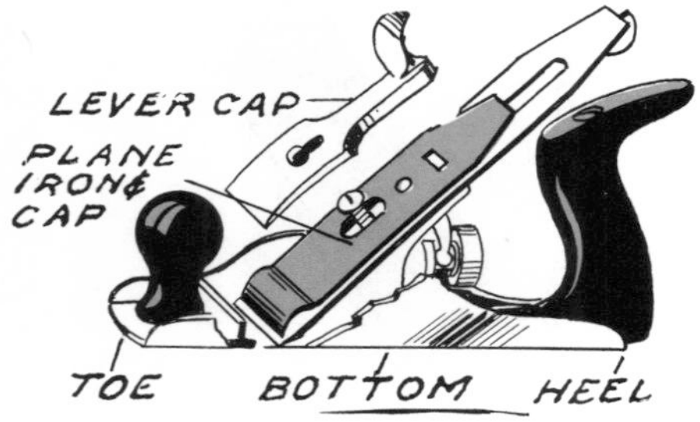

Fig. 89. Plane Iron and Plane Iron Cap in Place

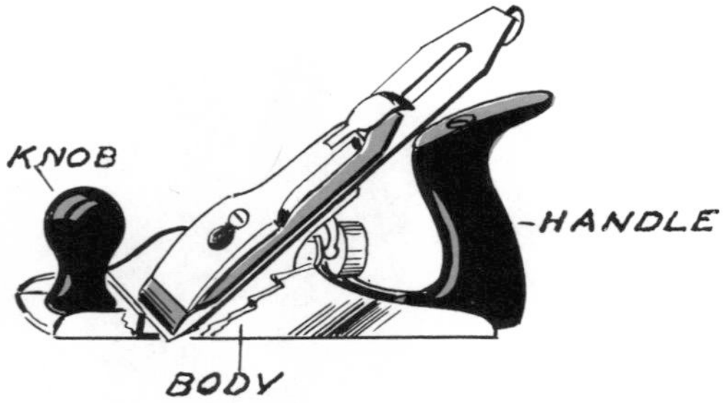

Fig. 90. Assembled Plane

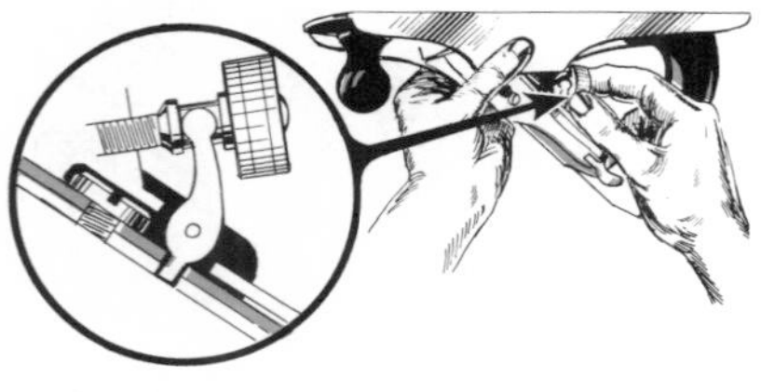

Fig. 91. Check Position of Plane Iron when Adjusting

Placing the Double Plane Iron in the Plane

1. Place the double plane iron with the beveled side down on the frog of the plane as shown in Fig. 88. Make sure that you slip the slot of the cap iron over the cap screw, keeping the plane iron on the under side. The screw of the double plane iron should fit nicely in the opening in the frog, Fig. 88.
2. Make sure that the end of the *Y* adjustment is placed correctly in the slot in the cap iron and that the lower end of the lateral adjustment is in the long slot in the plane iron.
3. Place the lever cap in position on the plane iron, permitting the cap to slide under the head of the cap screw. The cap screw in the frog should fit into the slot in the cap. Tighten the lever cap by pressing down on the lever. This should operate firmly but not so tightly that it needs to be forced. If it is too tight, you may break the lever cap. If it is too loose, it will not hold the plane iron in place. Make the correct adjustment by tightening or loosening the lever cap screw with a screwdriver. In Fig. 90 the parts are shown in place.

Adjusting the Plane

1. To adjust the plane correctly for planing, grasp the plane in the left hand with the bottom surface up, so the bottom or sole is level with the eye. Sight or feel with your thumb to determine whether the cutting plane iron is slightly projecting through the throat.
2. With the right hand move the lateral adjusting lever, Fig. 88, to the right or to the left until the cutting edge of the

plane iron is true, or parallel with the sole of the plane.

3. Turn the adjusting nut until the cutting plane iron slightly projects through the throat and above the bottom of the plane, Fig. 91. This adjusting nut forces the lug which controls the projection of the plane iron and the thickness of the shaving. Turning the nut to the right advances the plane iron for a heavier shaving. Turning the screw to the left withdraws the plane iron for a lighter shaving. Turn the adjusting nut between strokes until the cutting edge gives just the depth of cut which you need. Keep in mind always that thin, silky shavings are most effective in producing accurate work.

Questions

1. Give a brief description of the jack plane and its uses.
2. Describe the assembly and adjustment of the jack plane.
3. What is a smooth plane?
4. What is the purpose of the plane iron cap?
5. How is the double plane iron held together?
6. How far back from the cutting edge should the plane iron cap be set for ordinary work? For very fine work?
7. How would you adjust the cutting edge if not projecting evenly?
8. Is the bevel of the block plane set up or down?
9. Name some uses of the block plane.

UNIT 21

Surfacing and Squaring Stock with a Plane

Success in building a project in woodworking depends a great deal upon getting a proper start. A good start usually depends on the accuracy of the pieces to be made. It is therefore essential that a systematic procedure be followed. If a piece of stock is to be squared to certain dimensions of thickness, width, and length — six steps should be followed in the order here described.

It is not always necessary to completely square stock. Sometimes only one or two surfaces need planing. Other times it may be necessary only to plane to width. Or perhaps only an edge or an end need squaring without having to square the whole piece. Whatever surfaces of the stock need to be planed, the procedure is described here.

Remember, in order to square the piece to three dimensions, all six steps are to be used.

The try square is an important tool in woodworking, Fig. 92. It consists of two parts, the handle and the blade. The steel blade is from

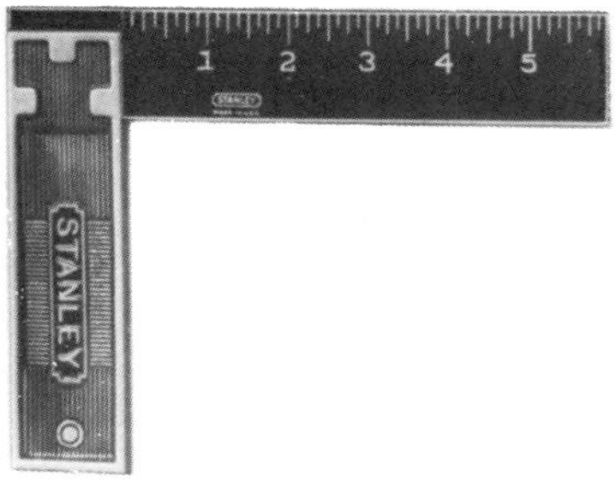

Fig. 92. Try Square (Stanley)

Fig. 93. Combination Square (Stanley)

four to twelve inches in length and is fitted to the handle to form a right angle. The handle may be entirely of metal or of a combination of metal and hard wood.

The principal uses of the try square are to test stock for squareness, to test surfaces for trueness, to square lines across stock, and to test for squareness in assembling.

The combination square with level, Fig. 93, is a very useful tool in all types of woodworking. The grooved steel blade is graduated in thirty-seconds of an inch. The handle is fitted with a spirit level glass. The combination square with level can be used as a straightedge, a marking gauge, a try square, and as a level. This square may be used in place of the try square for testing and laying out.

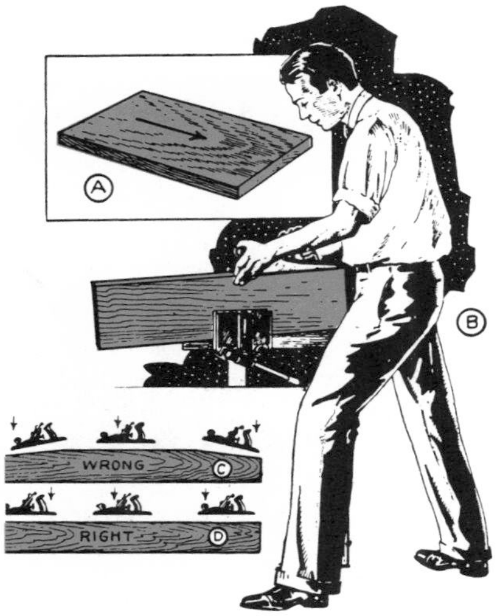

Fig. 94. Direction and Technique of Planing

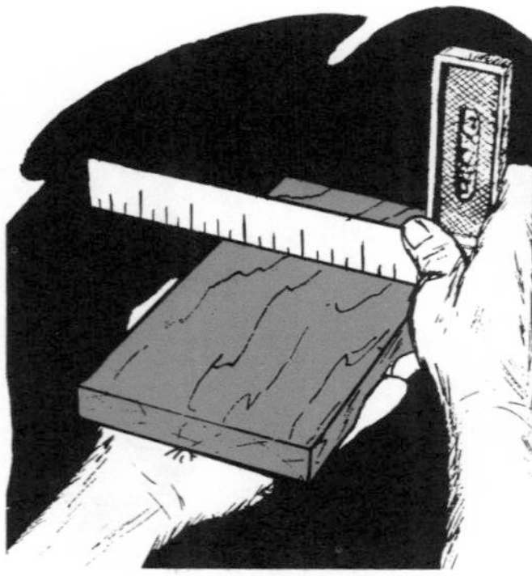

Fig. 95. Testing Planed Surface

Planing a Face True and Smooth

1. Select the best broad surface.
2. Examine the board for wind or twist by sighting across the surface for high corners. Mark the high corners, if any, and verify by turning the board over on the bench and rocking it on the high corners. Determine the direction of the grain on the edge and on the face of the board. Plane with the grain. The arrowhead in *A*, Fig. 94, shows the direction in which to plane. Place the end of the board toward which you will be planing against the bench stop.
3. Adjust the jack plane for a thin shaving. Grasp the handle in the right hand, with the knob in the left hand. Brace your feet firmly with the left foot ahead of the right as in *B*, Fig. 94. When starting the stroke, bear down on the knob at the front end of the plane. When the plane is well on the board bear down equally on both the knob and handle. As the plane begins to pass off the board, relieve the pressure on the knob, *D*, Fig. 94. This procedure will result in a true surface. The effect of wrong procedure is shown in *C*, Fig. 94.
4. Test the surface frequently with the edge of a try square, or other straightedge. Hold the board in the left hand and look toward the light, as in Fig. 95. Where light shows under the straightedge, the surface is low, and further planing is necessary where the straightedge touches the wood. Plane on these high places only and no more than is necessary. One thin shaving may frequently correct a slight error.
5. Mark this face so you will recognize it later. It is the *working face*.

Planing an Edge True with the Face

1. Fasten the board securely in the vise with the best edge up.
2. Grasp the plane as in planing a surface but hold the knob as shown in Fig. 96. Place the thumb of the left hand on the knob and allow the fingers to slide

against the face of the board. This will aid in holding the plane steady and keep the plane parallel with the board.

3. Take full strokes and get full width shavings. Keep in mind to press down on the knob at the beginning of each stroke and on the handle at the end of the stroke.
4. Hold the board in the left hand and sight down the edge to see that it is straight. Test with the try square by holding the beam snugly against the face and the blade on the edge of the board, as shown in Fig. 97. Where light shows under the blade, the edge is low. Further planing is necessary where the blade touches the wood. This should be done carefully because one thin shaving may be enough to correct the error. Work for a full width shaving the entire length of the board, and you will have little difficulty in getting a true edge.
5. Mark this edge so you will recognize it later. It is the *working edge.*

Planing an End True with the Face and Edge

1. If the end of the board is to be exposed, and if it requires a smoother surface than that left by a saw, it should be carefully planed.
2. Fasten the board securely in the vise with the best end up.

Fig. 96. Planing an Edge

3. Plane half the distance across the end and then turn the piece around in the vise and plane carefully from the other edge. This prevents chipping the corners, Fig. 98.
4. Hold the plane as in edge planing but at an angle with the side of the board as shown in Fig. 99. This gives a shearing cut across the wood fibers.
5. Test with the try square from the face and from the edge, Fig. 100. Plane carefully any high places that are found.
6. There is another way to plane end grain as is shown in Fig. 98A. Mark the exact end of the piece with a pencil on the side and on the edge. Cut a bevel at one end with the lower edge exactly even with the end mark. You can then plane

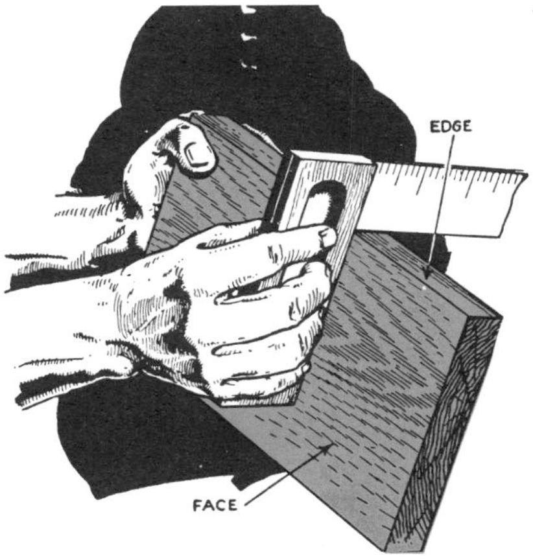

Fig. 97. Testing an Edge

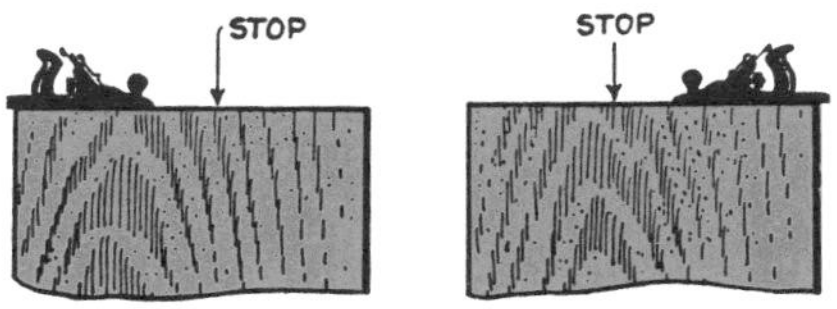

Fig. 98. Planing End Grain

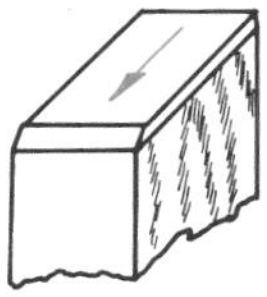

Fig. 98A. Bevel on Edge to Prevent Splitting when Planing End Grain all the way across in the direction of the arrow without splitting the stock. This is a quick but not the most accurate method.

Fig. 99. Block Plane – a Handy Tool

Fig. 100. Testing End with the Try Square

Fig. 101. Laying Out the Desired Width

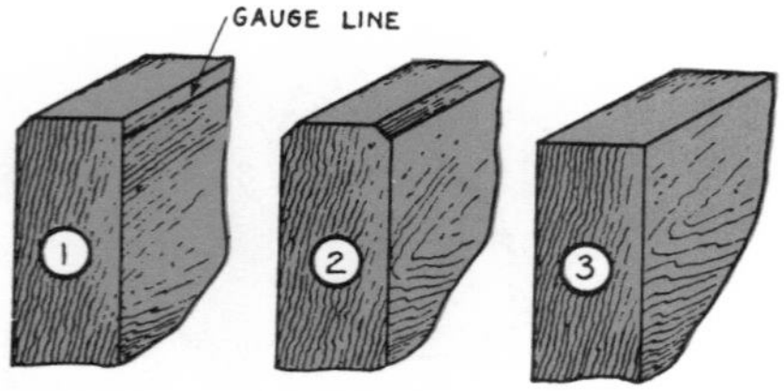

Fig. 102. Steps in Planing to Width

7. The block plane is especially useful on the end grain of narrow boards.

Cutting to Length

1. Measure the desired length from the working end. With a sharp pencil and a try square as a guide, score a line around the stock.
2. Place the stock in the vise and carefully saw off any waste. Leave about one-sixteenth of an inch of waste stock if the end is to be planed smooth. If you plan to cut a joint on the end of a piece, as in making tenons, it is only necessary to cut the end square with the saw.
3. It the end is to be smooth, plane to the line in the same manner as you planed the working end, testing it carefully from the working face and working edge with the try square, Fig. 100.
4. If the ends of a piece are not to be exposed in a project, it is not necessary to smooth the ends with a plane except to touch them up for squareness.

Planing to Width

1. With the marking gauge lay out the desired width on both broad surfaces of the stock, being careful to keep the head of the gauge against the working edge, Fig. 101.
2. Fasten the stock in the vise and plane to the middle of the gauge line in three steps as shown in Fig. 102.
3. Test from the working face with the try square as in Fig. 97. If you have been careful in planing to the middle of the gauge line, this edge should test true.

Planing to Thickness

1. Gauge the desired thickness on both sides and ends of the stock, being careful to keep the head of the marking gauge against the working face.
2. Place the stock on the bench against the stop, and plane to the middle of the gauge line in steps as shown in Fig. 102.
3. Test this surface with a straightedge.

If you have been careful in planing to the middle of the gauge line, this surface should test true.

Another Method

Ordinarily the procedure described will produce best results with little danger of spoiling work. A different order of squaring is used by some woodworkers. The order of squaring surfaces which has just been explained may be changed to a different order when found necessary. The steps are:

1. Working face.
2. Working edge.
3. Width.
4. Thickness.
5. Working end.
6. Length.

Questions

1. Name in order the six steps in squaring stock to dimension.
2. In using a plane, when should there be pressure on the knob? On the handle?
3. What is meant by the working edge?
4. How can end planing be done without splitting off the edges of the board?
5. To test the surfaces of a board for accuracy what tool should be used?
6. What is meant by wind or twist in a board?
7. Must all ends of pieces in a project be planed smooth? When may there be exceptions?

UNIT 22

Laying Out and Cutting a Chamfer

Examine Fig. 103 and observe how a chamfer differs from a bevel. A chamfer or a bevel *must not be laid out with the marking gauge.* Even if a light gauge mark is made, the mark will be too deep and it will remain after the chamfer is cut. When stain is applied, this unsightly mark will turn black and spoil the appearance of the work. For this reason the method of marking with a pencil as shown in Fig. 104 should always be followed.

Laying Out

The method of marking described here is used not only for laying out chamfers and bevels but also for laying out lines roughly for other work. In this manner lines can be gauged parallel to the edge on straight, irregular, or round stock.

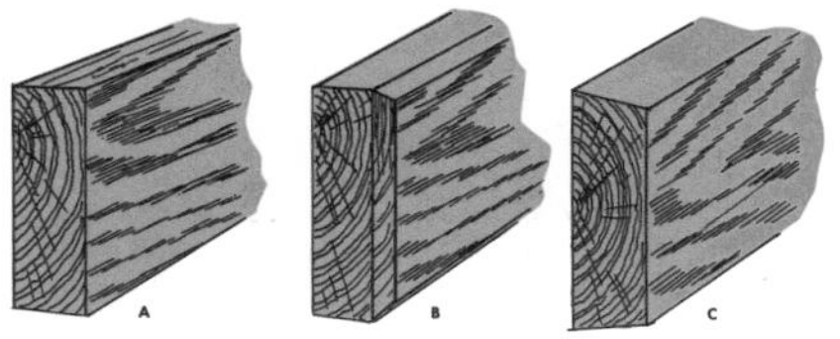

Fig. 103. *A*—Square Edge, *B*—Chamfer, *C*—Bevel

1. Determine the size of the chamfer from the drawing. The dimensions should be in proportion to the work. Usually $\frac{3}{16}$″ measured from the corner on the two adjacent sides will make a satisfactory chamfer.
2. Lay off the point through which the line, limiting one side of the chamfer, is to be drawn. Do this with the rule and pencil on the faces and edges of the stock. Fig. 104.

Fig. 104. Make Light Pencil Marks on the Face and Edge

3. Hold the stock firmly in the left hand, and place one end against the bench stop to steady it as in Fig. 105.
4. Place the point of the pencil on the mark and the middle finger against the edge of the stock, Fig. 105. Keep the fingers firmly together and against the stock, and with a free arm movement, draw a line the desired length through the point just marked. In this manner continue to draw lines along the face and edge of the stock, thus locating the limits of the chamfer.

Fig. 105. Pencil Gauge Through Marks

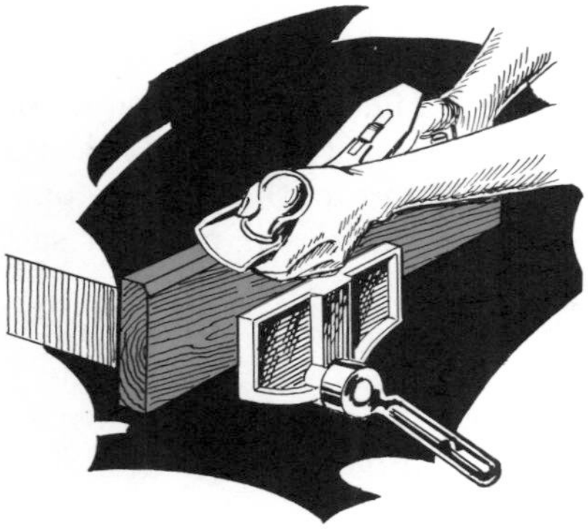

Fig. 106. Plane to Both Lines

Fig. 107. Test Planed Surface with the Blade of the Try-Square

Planing the Chamfer

1. Place the stock in the vise with the marked edge up and the marked face outward.
2. Hold the plane on the corner of the stock so that both sides of the strip being planed will be the same distance from the two pencil lines. Fig. 106.
3. Hold the plane steady with the fingers of the left hand under the plane and resting lightly against the work as shown in Fig. 106. Get the "feel" of the cut as you proceed. Each succeeding cut should be made exactly on the same angle as the preceding one. A good chamfer is one straight surface only and not several smaller surfaces each on a different angle.
4. Test the planed surface frequently with a straightedge, or the blade of the square, to make sure that it has a true surface. Fig. 107. You will soon learn to determine whether the chamfer is properly made by examining it.

Chamfering End Grain

1. When chamfering end grain, hold the plane at an angle as indicated in Fig. 108 and "slice" across the work so the plane iron takes a shearing cut. This

Fig. 108. Take Slicing Cuts on End Grain

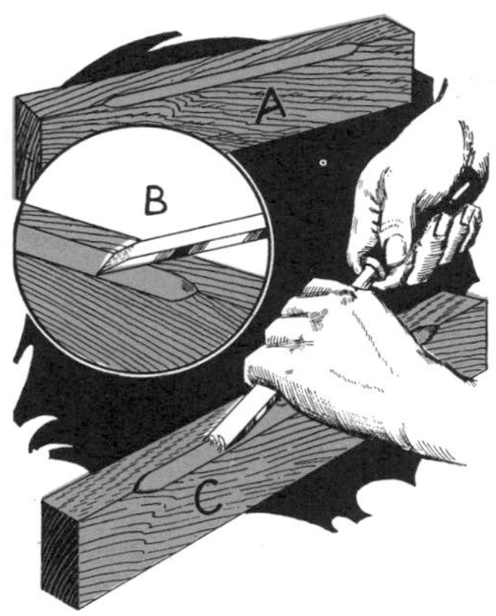

Fig. 109. Cut Stop Chamfer with Chisel

prevents the tearing of the grain. When chamfering all sides of a board, chamfer the sides first and the ends last to prevent chipping of the corners.

Cutting Stop Chamfers

1. A *stop chamfer* does not run all the way to the ends of the board. To cut a stop chamfer, as shown at *A* in Fig. 109, start the cut with a chisel keeping the bevel of the chisel down, as at *C*. If the chamfer is a short one complete it with the chisel by continuing the cut with the bevel down as at *C*, each time taking small shavings with shearing cuts. Watch the grain carefully so you do not cut into a cross-grained portion or you may cut below the line. Avoid cutting with the bevel of the chisel in the position shown in *B*, Fig. 109.
2. If the stop chamfer is a long one, it may be completed with the plane after the starting cuts have been made with the chisel.

Questions

1. Explain the difference between a bevel and a chamfer.
2. Why should chamfers not be laid out with a marking gauge?
3. Explain how to lay out chamfers by thumb gauging.
4. How is a chamfer tested for accuracy?
5. When chamfering all sides of a board, which sides should be cut first? Why?
6. What is a stop chamfer?
7. How are long stop chamfers cut?

UNIT 23

Scraping and Smoothing with a File

A file is used in woodworking to reduce or smooth surfaces that cannot be worked with a cutting tool. Files are of many kinds and shapes with teeth or serrations of various degrees of fineness. They are usually cut and finished diagonally across the surfaces, although some files are cut both horizontally and vertically across their surfaces. The most useful files to the woodworker are the medium and the fine flat file, Fig. 110, the medium and the fine half-round file, Fig. 111, and the round or rat-tail file, Fig. 112.

The rasp, Fig. 113, was formerly used to reduce stock, especially wagon tongues, axe handles, and other rough round projects; but it is now seldom used in woodworking.

Fig. 110. Flat File (Brodhead-Garrett)

Fig. 111. Half Round File (Brodhead-Garrett)

Fig. 112. Rattail File – Round and Tapered (Brodhead-Garrett)

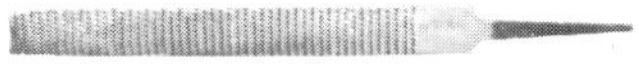

Fig. 113. Rasp File – Seldom Used in Woodworking (Brodhead-Garrett)

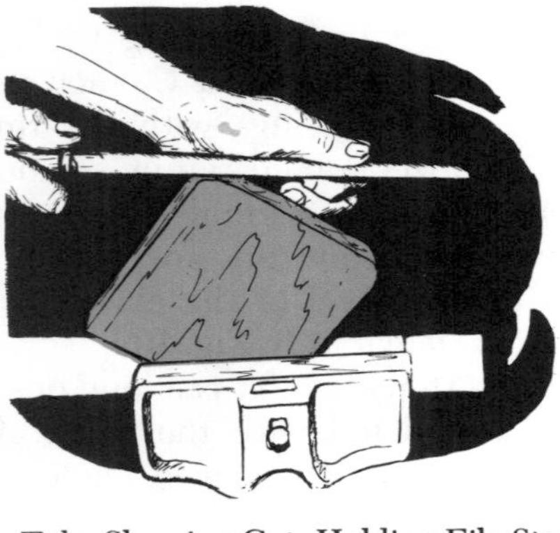

Fig. 114. Take Shearing Cut, Holding File Steady

Fig. 115. File Card (Brodhead-Garrett)

The *file card* or the file cleaning brush, shown in Fig. 115, is necessary to keep files in good condition. A file card should be used often when working with a wood file.

Roughing and Scraping Curves on Flat Wood Surfaces with a Medium Flat or Half-Round File

1. Clamp the stock in a vise. If a vise is not available, hold the stock in your left hand.
2. With a medium file, or half-round, Figs. 110 and 111, rough down the wood piece to a given line or close to the line.
3. This can be done by applying slight pressure on the forward stroke, making a slight shearing cut across the edge or surface of the wood, Fig. 114.

Smoothing an Edge or Curve with a Fine Flat or Half-Round File

1. Before attempting to smooth a curved surface, soften the edges of the stock with a fine flat or a fine half-round file.
2. File the surface by twisting the file slowly left and right until the proper fineness or smoothness has been acquired.
3. Work the surface to a smooth finish with 4/0 garnet paper around the file.

Smoothing an Inside Curve with a Rattail File

Some inside curved surfaces cannot be smoothed except with a fine rattail file, Fig. 112. For example, if you were making a series of letters, the inside curves of the "O" would be smoothed with a rattail file.

1. Soften the sharp edges of the curved surfaces with a fine rattail file.
2. With a light forward and backward movement and a left and right twist, file the inside curve fairly smooth.
3. Wrap a piece of 4/0 (150 mesh) garnet paper around the rattail file and complete the smoothing process by working again as in step 2.

Questions

1. What is a rasp?
2. What kind of files are essential in woodworking?
3. Is a file a cutting tool?
4. Where would you use a rattail file?
5. Can a file take the place of a cutting tool?

UNIT 24 Scraping with a Hand Scraper

Open-grained wood requires scraping before it is sanded. The smooth high portions of the stock must be scraped down to a level with the coarser low portions. All open-grained woods (such as walnut, mahogany, and oak) must be filled with paste wood filler and this cannot be done satisfactorily unless the surface has been scraped. Any burly or cross-grained wood can be smoothed with a scraper even when a plane iron will not make it smooth. It is important that the scraper be properly sharpened. Otherwise it will not work easily and effectively.

Sharpening the Scraper

1. Fasten the blade in a vise. File off the old burr by holding the file flat on the side of the scraper, as in *A*, Fig. 116.
2. File the edge of the scraper square with the face, *B*, Fig. 116, and cut the corners down slightly to prevent gouging, as in *C*, Fig. 116.
3. Whet the scraper on an oil stone by placing it alternately in a horizontal and vertical position, as in Figs. 117 and 118, until all the wire edge is removed. Take long steady strokes.
4. Hold the end of the scraper with the left hand so the cutting edge extends over the side of the bench, as in Fig. 119. Turn the arris (edge) slightly toward the side by stroking upward with the burnisher at an angle of about 85° with the face. Decrease the angle to about 75° while you gradually increase the pressure. Turn the burr until it just catches the fingers when drawn across the edge. Repeat on the other arris.
5. A burnisher is a small, round, smooth tool of hard steel.

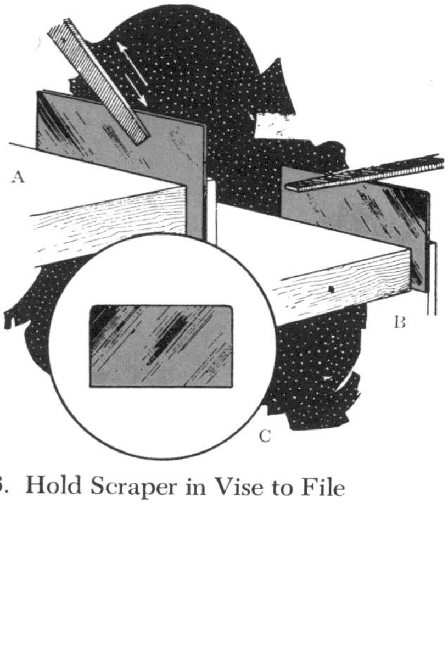

Fig. 116. Hold Scraper in Vise to File

Using the Scraper

1. Grasp the ends of the scraper with both hands with the thumbs pointing toward each other, as in Fig. 120. Tip the scraper away from you at an angle of 45° with the board, while also holding it at an

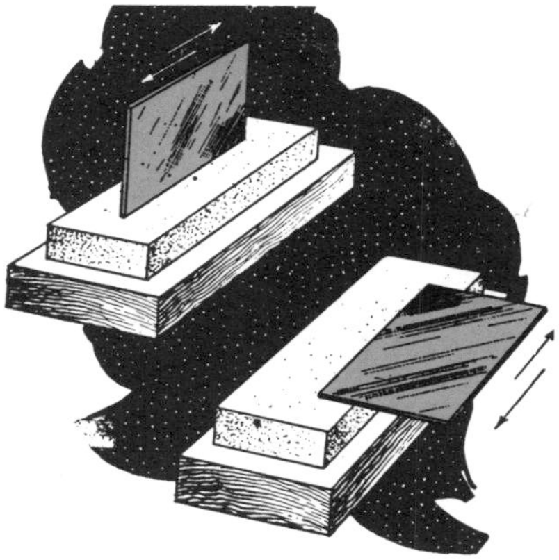

Fig. 117. Whet Scraper on the Oil Stone
Fig. 118. Remove the Wire Edge

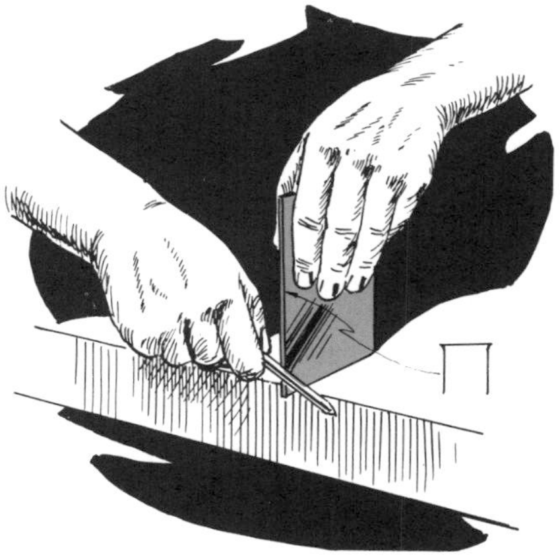

Fig. 119. Burnishing the Edge

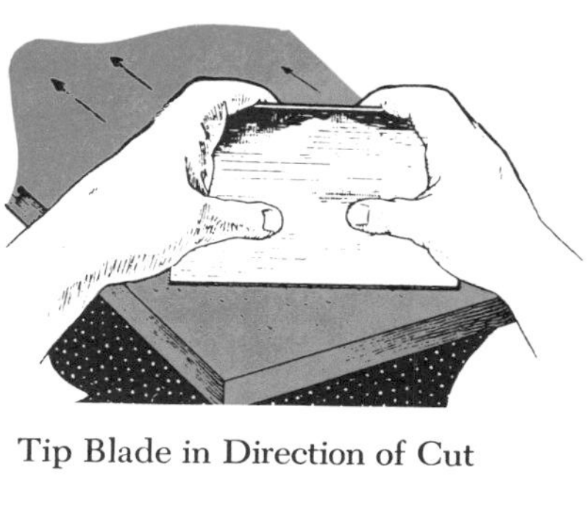

Fig. 120. Tip Blade in Direction of Cut

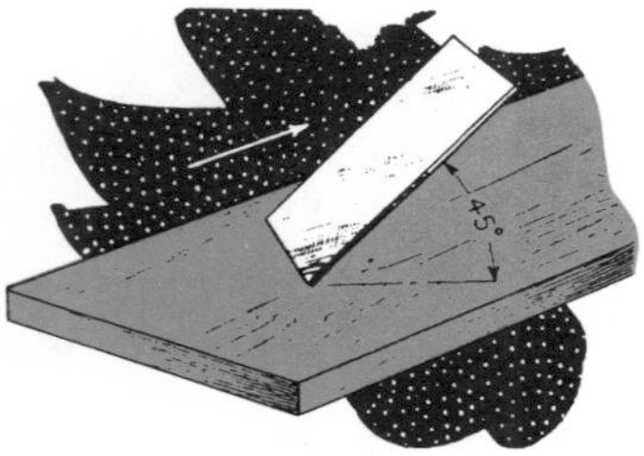

Fig. 121. Hold Scraper at Angle of 45°

Fig. 122. Scraper Holder (Stanley)

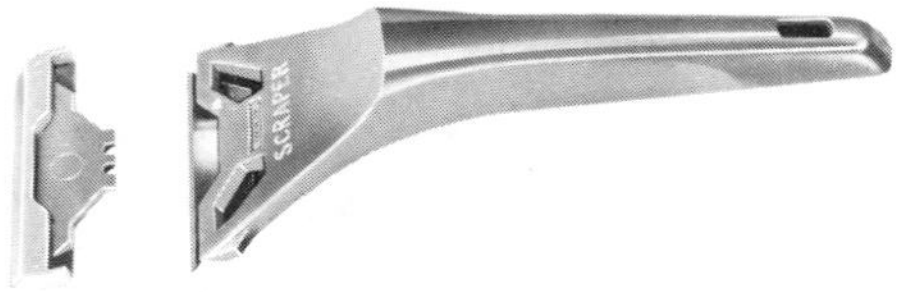

Fig. 123. Scraper Holder (Stanley)

angle with the direction of the stroke, Fig. 121. Push it away from you, changing the latter angle every few strokes.

2. It may be necessary at times to draw the scraper toward you. Grasp it as in pushing but tip the blade toward you instead of away from you.
3. Scraping can be made easier by using a scraper holder as in Fig. 122.
4. For light scraping or scraping paint, the scraper in Fig. 123 is very useful.

Questions

1. Why do some kinds of wood require scraping before sanding?
2. Why should a scraper be of rather hard metal?
3. How should a scraper be held when being sharpened?
4. How are wire edges removed from a scraper after it has been sharpened?
5. How is the arris on the scraper turned?
6. At what angle should the edge be turned?
7. How should a scraper be held when in use?
8. Why can you not draw the scraper toward you with good results?

UNIT 25 Grinding and Sharpening Stones

Grinding and sharpening stones are used in sharpening edge tools and in smoothing rough parts in metalworking. These stones are known as *abrasives*. Other abrasives are sandpaper, emery cloth, emery dust, pumice stone and steel wool. The cutting action of an abrasive is similar to that of a plane or scraper. Each little grain cuts a minute shaving from the surface. Since there are so many grains and all of them are on the same level, they make the surface seem smooth. Grinding stones are hard and will plane or grind metal away.

Grinding stones when mounted on a shaft are called grinding wheels. They are fast cutting, and are used in coarse work. *Whet* stones and oil stones or *hones* are finer grinding stones, and they are used in the last step of the sharpening process.

Selecting the Stone

In the selection of grinding wheels and whet stones there are three things to be considered: *grain*, or the fine sand-like cutting particles; *bond*, or the glue-like portion that holds the grains together; and *pores,* or the spaces between the bonded grains. These three things effect the cutting quality of the stone.

Stones are *coarse* or *fine* according to the sizes of the grains and the pores. They are known as *hard* or *soft* according to the strength of the bond. If the grains adhere to the wheel and do not come loose, the stone is said to be hard. If the grains break loose quickly and thus allow the stone to wear away, the stone is said to be soft.

Types of Stones

There are two general kinds of grinding stones — the natural and the manufactured. Natural stones are quarried. Old fashioned grindstones and Washita and Arkansas stones are natural stones and they come chiefly from the Ozark Mountains. They are rather soft. They were used a great deal in earlier times but the harder manufactured stones are in general use today. The natural stones are preferred for grinding glass.

Manufactured Stones

The various types of manufactured stones are made by fusing certain materials in electric furnaces. One type is made from a mixture of coke, sand, sawdust, and salt. These, in combination, are placed in electric furnaces and subjected to a heat of 4,000 degrees Fahrenheit for a period of thirty-six hours. The resulting product, called *silicon carbide,* comes out in large masses of crystals. These crystals are crushed into grains and graded. They are then formed into grinding wheels and stones by mixing with materials known as *bonds.* For example, selected sizes of grains are bonded with flexible materials such as rubber and shellac in order to make a wheel that will not break when used in gumming saws. Manufactured stones are made for many other special purposes. They can be purchased in a wide variety of shapes, sizes and grits, and for any purpose.

Manufactured stones have been found to be superior to natural stones in three ways:

1. Standardization of grain, produced by sifting and grading of materials.
2. Uniformity of texture which is made possible by means of bonding.
3. Toughness and hardness which makes them wear slowly and remain sharp.

Classes of Stones

There are two classes of grinding stones. They are the *dry* stones and the *wet* stones. Dry stones are used dry and wet stones are used wet. While working with the latter stones, a *coolant* or liquid (water or oil) must be poured on the wheel or on the whet stone before it is used. The coolant lowers the temperature of the piece being ground, and it lifts the small particles of metal out of the stone so that they will not fill the pores. If these particles are allowed to settle and remain they cause the stone to be *loaded.* Such a stone becomes *gummy* and grease-coated and will not cut. The stone should be washed frequently with gasoline and the dirt should be wiped off with cotton waste or cloth. After the stone is used, it should be wiped off and a few drops of oil applied. It should be kept in a covered box when not in use.

Care of Stones

The wheel and stone should be kept true and even. This means that they should be used properly so the surface will wear evenly. The whole surface of the whet stone including the edges and ends should be used. Sharp edges or points may be whetted on the edge of the stone. To true up a wheel, hold a wheel dresser against the face while the grinding wheel is in motion. The high places are thus worn down until the wheel is again true. The whet stone can be trued by rubbing it on the concrete floor or on the sidewalk.

Whet Stones

Whet stones are made in various forms: flat, rectangular, square, round, diamond, and so on. They may be used in various ways. A *slip* stone, used in sharpening gouges, has two flat surfaces and two rounded edges. One edge is larger in radius than the other. Wheels are made in many shapes and for various kinds of work.

Questions

1. What are grinding wheels and sharpening stones called?
2. Name three important factors in the selection of grinding stones.
3. The coarseness or fineness of a stone depends on what?
4. What are the two general kinds of grinding stones called?
5. How are manufactured stones made?
6. From what kind of stone were the grindstones used by our grandfathers made?
7. What is the difference between the *dry* and the *wet* stone?

UNIT 26 Sharpening Edge Tools

Sharp tools make woodworking a pleasure. Dull tools not only make woodworking displeasing, but they also lead to accidents and poor work. It often seems to take too much time to sharpen a tool, especially when one is anxious to work with it; but much time is really saved through the effectiveness of the sharp tool. Learn to sharpen tools quickly and do it whenever necessary to maintain a keen edge.

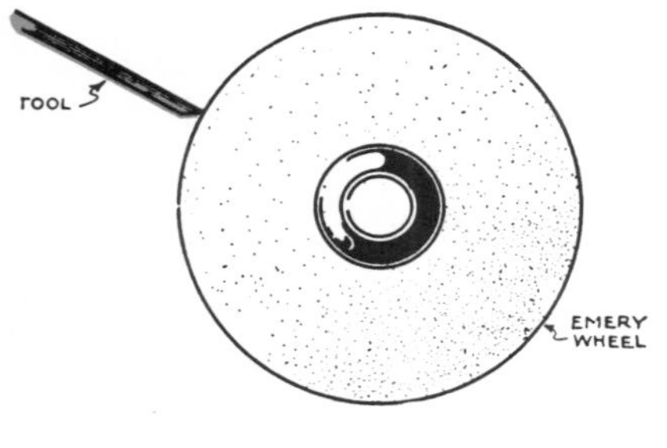

Fig. 124. Straighten the Cutting Edge on the Grinder

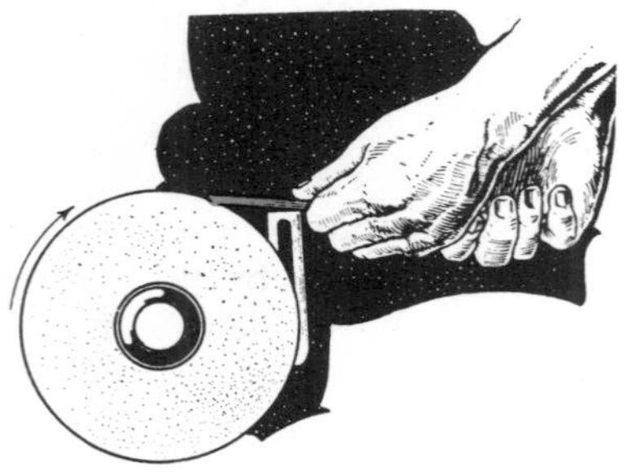

Fig. 125. Hold Blade Firmly Between Thumb and Index Finger

Grinding

1. Examine the edge of the tool to see whether it is sharp. If the edge is dull, a white surface will show on the cutting edge. The cutting edge should be square with the side of the blade. This should be tested with a try square.
2. Remove nicks and straighten the cutting edge by placing it carefully against the grinder as in Fig. 124. Test it for squareness with the try square after grinding.
3. If a special tool holder is not provided, hold the tool firmly between the thumb and index finger of each hand as in Fig. 125. A tool holder is provided on the grinder in Fig. 126.
4. Lay the tool on the tool rest as in Fig. 125, permitting the tool to come in contact with the grinder gradually.

Fig. 126. Grinder Hone and Tool Holder (Atlas Press)

5. Check the position of the tool on the tool rest so you will obtain the proper level. It is probable that the existing bevel is all right. On plane bits and chisels a 25 to 30 degree angle is about right. The bevel should be from 2 to 2½ times the thickness of the blade.
6. Exert light pressure and slide the tool from right to left across the face of the grinder as shown in Fig. 127.

NOTE: **Dip the tool in water frequently to prevent it from becoming overheated.**

7. After the tool has been removed from the stone to dip it in water, great care must be taken to replace it on the grinder again so as to keep the same bevel. This can be done by "feeling" it carefully into place.
8. Continue grinding until a wire edge appears on the edge of the tool.
9. The blade of a chisel should be ground so it is straight across. A plane iron to be used for smoothing, rather than for truing and squaring, should be ground so it is convex as shown at *A*, Fig. 132. For squaring, however, it should be ground straight across with the ends rounded off slightly as in *B*, Fig. 132.

Whetting

1. Clean the surface of the oilstone with waste.
2. Scatter a few drops of oil on the surface of the stone.

Fig. 127. Move Blade Across Wheel from Right to Left to Right Again

3. Place the bevel flat on the stone as in Figs. 128 and 129.
4. Move the tool back and forth as in Fig. 128, being careful to move your hand through a plane parallel to the surface of the stone. Avoid a rocking motion.
5. Remove the wire edge by placing the back of the blade flat on the stone as in Fig. 130; then move it forward. Keep it flat on the stone.

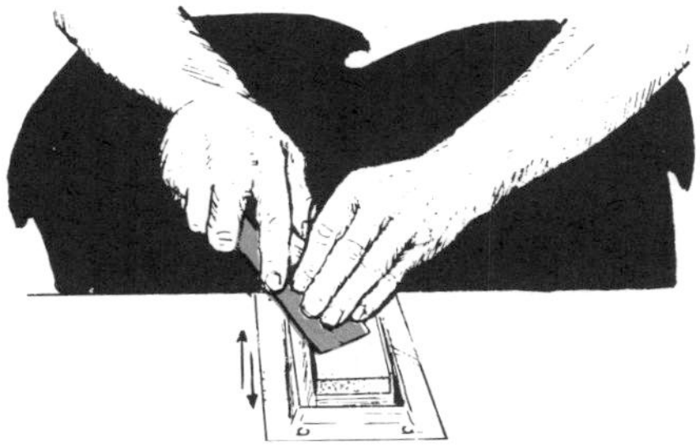

Fig. 128. Keep Bevel Flat on the Stone When Whetting

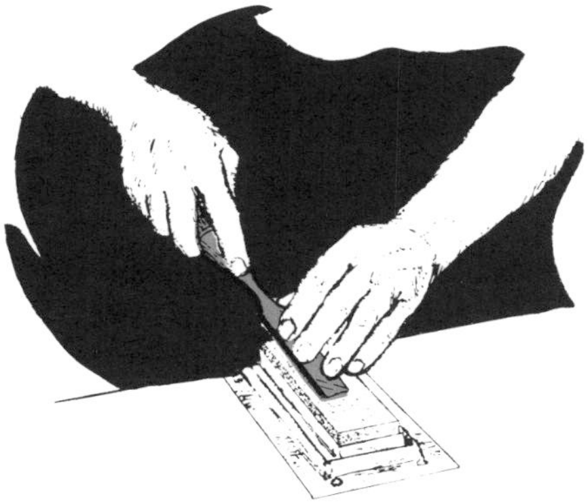

Fig. 129. Sharpening a Chisel

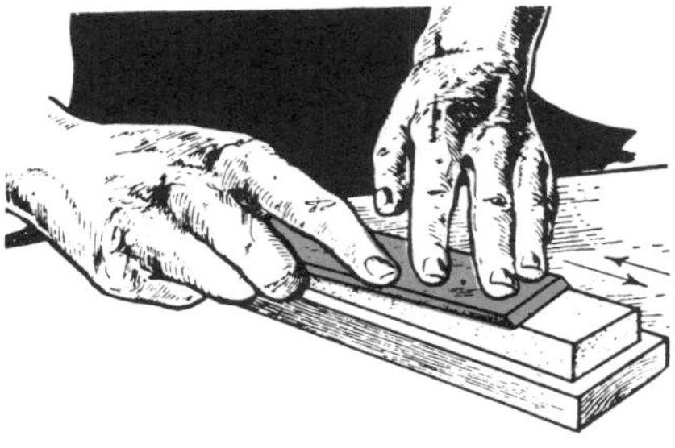

Fig. 130. Removing Wire Edge

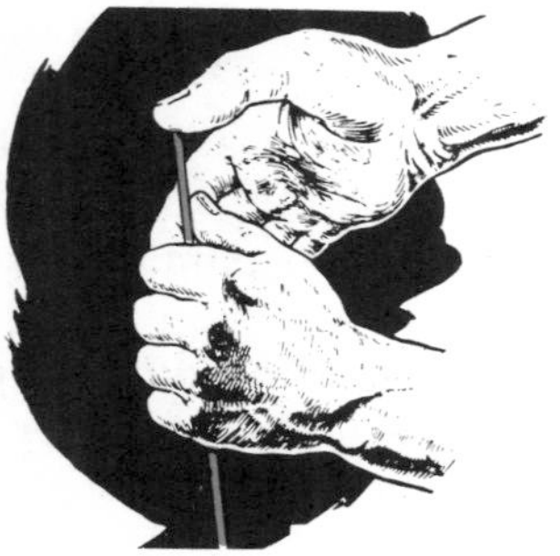

Fig. 131. Testing for Sharpness – Only Slight Pressure Necessary

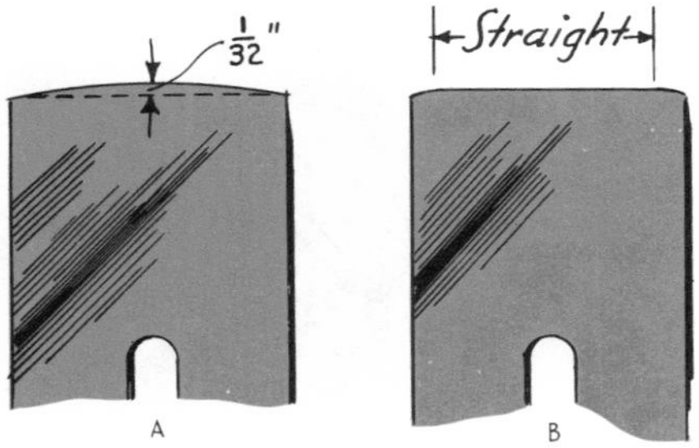

Fig. 132. Shape of Plane Iron – *A* for Smoothing; *B* for Squaring

6. Continue as in Figs. 128 and 130 until the wire edge is entirely removed, then test for sharpness as in Fig. 131.

CAUTION: Be careful when testing. Only slight pressure is necessary.

7. To sharpen a jackknife, proceed as you would with other edge tools, but, of course, you would not hold the knife as in Fig. 125 when grinding. Your hand would be at the side of the stone.

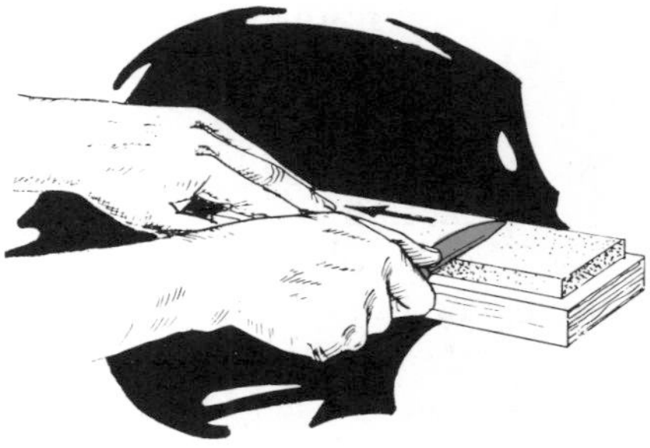

Fig. 133. Whetting a Jackknife

8. Whet it, Fig. 133, as you would whet a chisel by working it on the stone on one side and then the other.

Questions

1. Are plane irons and wood chisels beveled on one or two sides?
2. At about what angle should a plane iron be held when whetting?
3. Why lay the back side of a plane iron flat on the oilstone for a few circular strokes?
4. Give two reasons why all cutting tools should be sharp.
5. What is a simple way to test the squareness of the cutting edge of a plane iron?
6. How can overheating be avoided when grinding cutting tools?
7. When should you stop grinding an edge tool?
8. What should be used on the stone when whetting a tool?

UNIT 27 The Power Jointer

The jointer is a power machine designed to speed up the planing of wood. Besides planing wood edges and surfaces, other operations can be performed, such as cutting rabbets, bevels, tapers, chamfers, and moldings.

General Description

The main parts of a power jointer consist of (1) a base, (2) front, (3) rear table, (4) cutterhead including three or four knives, (5) fence, (6) safety guard, and (7) one or two table adjusting handles. See Fig. 134.

Jointers are made in several sizes, but the two most common ones are the 6″ jointer which is used for light planing, and the 12″ size which is most often used for heavy planing.

The size of the jointer is determined by the length of the cutting knives. They are held tightly in place in the cutterhead with special screws. The cylindrical cutterhead revolves on ball bearings at a speed of from 3600 to 4500 rpm or more, depending on the size of the jointer. The knives are sharpened on special machines, to the same angles as are hand plane irons.

Rear Table Adjustment

The rear table, also called the outfeed table, must be exactly level with the knives of the cutterhead. See Fig. 135. On the small jointers, the handle at the rear table is used to adjust the table with the knives. This setting may be tested with a straightedge as shown in Fig. 135. Two try squares, one on each end of the knife, can also be used to check the setting.

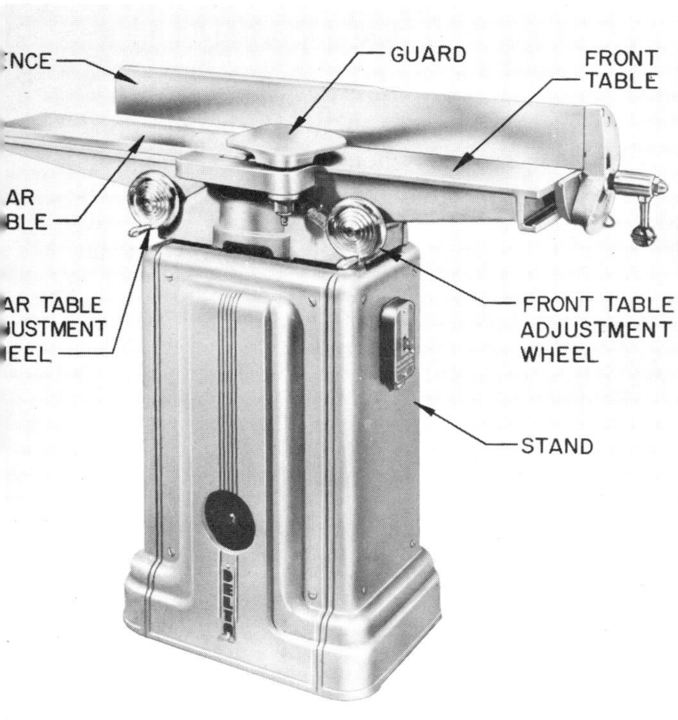

Fig. 134. Principal Parts of Jointer

Front Table Adjustment

The front table, also called the infeed table, is adjusted to the required depth of cut by lowering or raising the table. This is done by turning the adjustment wheel on the front end of the jointer. The scale and pointer attached to the front end of the front table will show the jointer setting. See Fig. 136.

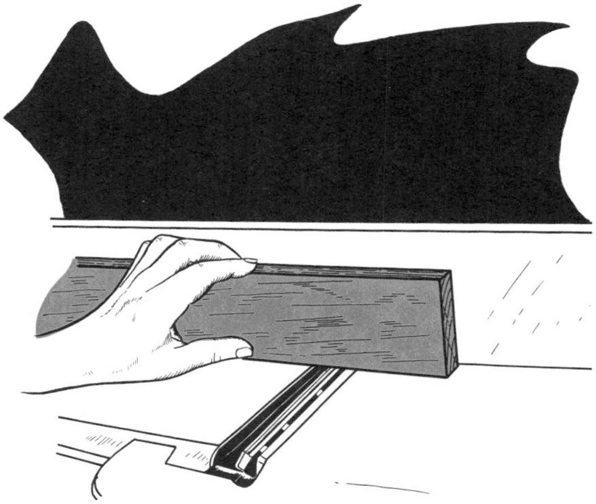

Fig. 135. Checking Rear Table Adjustment with Straightedge

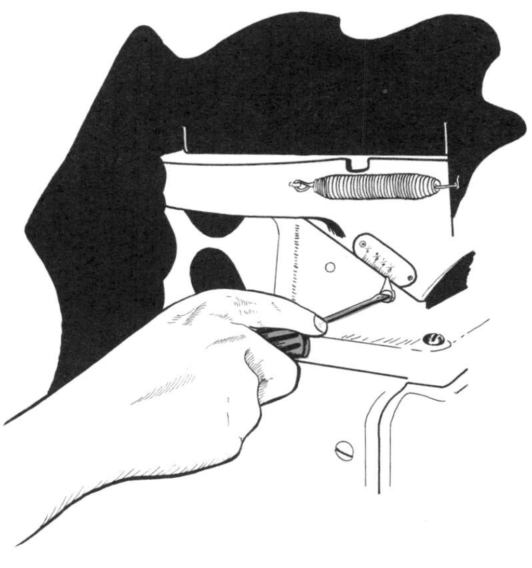

Fig. 136. Adjusting Depth of Cut Scale

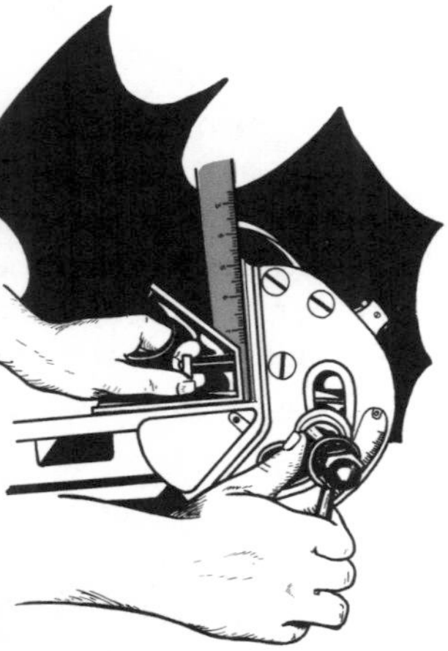

Fig. 137. Checking Fence for Squareness

Fig. 138. Hold Stock Firmly Against Fence and Table

Fence

The fence of the jointer is adjustable and can be tilted for cutting chamfers. It should be perfectly square with the table when jointing the edge of a board. Check for squareness with the try square, or the steel square as shown in Fig. 137.

Safety Guard

The safety guard on a jointer is an absolute *must* for your protection. It must be in place and adjusted properly when the jointer is in operation. See Fig. 137. Most states now have laws that require the jointer to be equipped with a safety guard.

Safety Instructions

1. The power jointer is safe to use if you follow safety instructions. As with all machines, it can in no way reach out to hurt you. You can be injured only if you get your hand in the machine. General safety instructions for woodworking machines apply in working with the jointer.
2. Get permission from your instructor before using the jointer.
3. Do not wear loose clothing, a necktie, or or long sleeves while using a jointer.
4. Keep the safety guard properly adjusted at all times.
5. Be sure that the jointer knives are sharp.
6. Take light cuts when learning how to use the jointer.
7. Do not try to plane stock that is shorter than 12″ long.
8. Stand to the left side when using the jointer.
9. Give the jointer all your attention when planing. Don't talk to anyone and don't look around when using the jointer.
10. Use a push block to finish planing flat pieces.
11. Do not make any adjustments when the jointer is in motion.
12. Keep the floor around the jointer free of scraps and shavings.

Jointing or Planing an Edge

1. Set the front table for about a 1/16″ cut with the table adjustment handle. See Fig. 134.
2. Make sure the fence is square with the table. See Fig. 137.
3. See that the safety guard is adjusted properly over the cutterhead.
4. Turn on the power. The jointer must be running at full speed before starting to plane.
5. Make a trial cut on one or two pieces

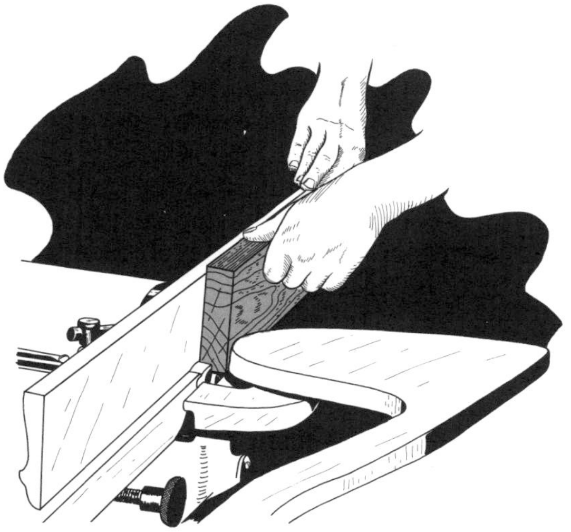

Fig. 139. Note Position of Hands in Jointing an Edge and Rabbeting

of scrap wood before planing stock for your project.

6. Place the working face of the wood to be planed against the fence. While holding the stock firmly against the fence, move it slowly forward. See Fig. 138. Check the edge of the stock for squareness with a try square. See Fig. 97.
7. The position of the hands as the board is pushed over the cutterhead is shown in Figs. 138 and 139.
8. When the stock rests solidly on the rear table, change the hand pressure from the front table to the rear table. At the same time keep the stock snug against the fence by exerting side pressure with both hands.

Planing Surfaces

1. Set the front table for a light cut, about 1/32″ or less.
2. See that the safety guard is in place and working properly.
3. Start the jointer and make a trial cut or two with a piece of scrap stock.
4. Select the truest face of the stock to be planed and lay it on the front table so the cut will be made with the grain.
5. Slowly push the stock into the cutterhead holding both hands flat on the stock on the front table.

Fig. 140. Use Push Block for Thin Pieces

6. Keep the stock flat on the front table as you push the stock to the rear table. Use a push block to finish the cut. Make sure that the push block is hooked firmly on the end of the board being surfaced. See Fig. 140. Do not attempt to surface a board without a pusher.
7. Do not attempt to surface stock that is shorter than 12″. Use a hand plane to surface stock under 12″ in length.
8. If the surface is slightly round or warped, hold the concave side of the board toward the table.

Cutting Rabbets

1. A rabbet is a groove sawed or planed on the edge of a piece of wood. Unit 45 tells how to lay out and cut a rabbet by hand.
2. To cut a rabbet with a power jointer, first lay out the size of the rabbet on the front end of the board to be rabbeted.
3. Move the jointer fence to the front edge of the table and set it to the width of the rabbet. Measure the width from the end of the cutting blade.
4. Lower the infeed table to the desired depth of cut. A rabbet deeper than 3/8″ may require more than one cut.
5. Make trial cuts on a piece of scrap stock until the desired cut is obtained. Reset if necessary.
6. When set, cut the desired rabbet on the project stock. See Fig. 139.

Chamfering and Beveling

1. Examine Fig. 103, and observe how a chamfer differs from a bevel. Lay out the chamfer or the bevel with a pencil and a rule.
2. Check the edges of the stock to be chamfered or beveled for squareness and straightness.
3. Adjust the fence of the jointer to the angle desired, which is usually 45 degrees for a chamfer.
4. A T-bevel, Fig. 73, may be used to set the fence at the proper angle to the table.

Fig. 141. Beveling May Require More Than One Cut

5. When the fence is set, make trial cuts on a piece of scrap stock.
6. Make the chamfers or bevels on the project stock. More than one cut may be necessary. See Fig. 141.
7. If you are chamfering the four edges of a board, make the end cuts first.
8. If you are cutting a bevel, several cuts may be necessary.

Questions

1. Do you need instructions to operate a power jointer? Give four safety rules.
2. What are the main parts of a jointer?
3. How is the size of a power jointer determined?
4. The adjustment of which table is made to determine the depth of the cut?
5. How should the rear table be adjusted in relation to the knives?
6. Name three different kinds of cuts that can be made with the power jointer.
7. Is a safety guard necessary?
8. What is a rabbet?
9. Why not plane short pieces of stock on the power jointer?
10. When should a push block be used?
11. Why are dull knives dangerous to use?
12. Where should you stand when using the jointer?

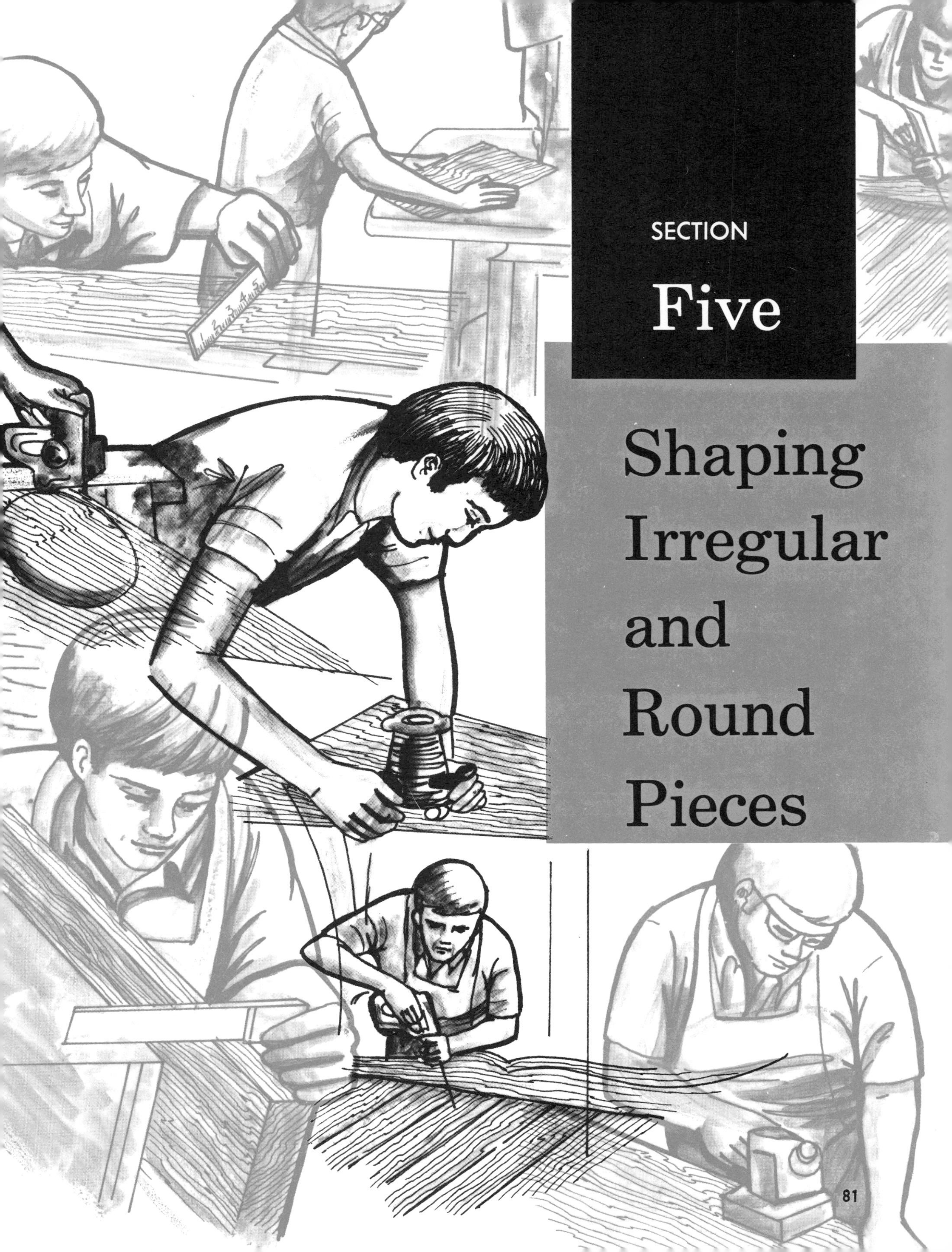

SECTION

Five

Shaping Irregular and Round Pieces

UNIT

28 Trimming with a Chisel

Chisels are essential cutting tools in woodworking. There are two general types of chisels, the *socket* chisel, Fig. 142, including the firmer chisel with reinforced handle, Fig. 143, and the *tang* chisel, Fig. 144. The socket chisel is more commonly used in woodworking. The firmer socket chisel with reinforced handle, Fig. 143, is a strong chisel especially for heavy cutting. The tang chisel, Fig. 144, has a slender blade and is mainly used for hand chiseling, such as paring. This chisel is made with a pointed end which fits into the handle.

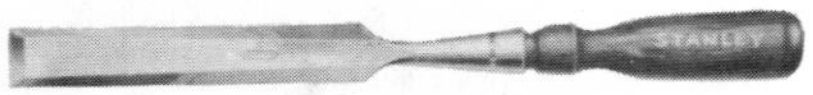

Fig. 142. Socket Chisel (Stanley)

Fig. 143. Firmer Chisel (Stanley)

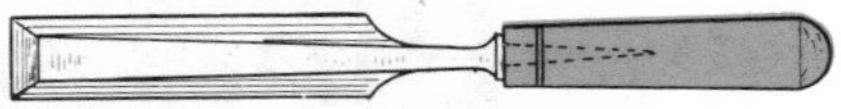

Fig. 144. Tang Chisel

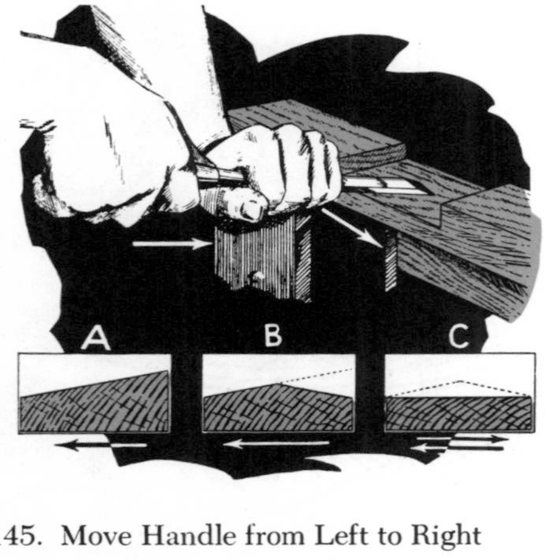

Fig. 145. Move Handle from Left to Right

The size of a chisel is determined by the width of the blade. The widths of chisel blades range from ⅛″ to 1″ by eighths and from 1″ to 2″ by fourths. Chisels may be purchased in either the standard lengths or in shorter lengths. The latter are called *butt* chisels.

There are many uses for chisels, but only the trimming procedures are shown here. Keep in mind that the chisel must be sharp.

Horizontal Trimming

1. Cut in the direction of the grain, and across the grain; never against the grain if it can be avoided.
2. Fasten the work securely in the vise or on the bench.
3. Grasp the chisel in the right hand, with the left hand holding the blade as in Fig. 145. Keep the flat side of the chisel against the stock.
4. Take thin shavings. Move the handle of the chisel from left to right as shown by the arrow in Fig. 145. To cut across the stock from edge to edge, trim half way from each edge and at the same time trim in an upward direction as shown in *A* and *B*, Fig. 145. Trim the center last as indicated at *C*, in Fig. 145. This prevents chipping the edges.

Vertical Trimming

1. Place the stock on the bench in order to trim across the grain or on end grain.
2. Hold the flat side of the chisel against the stock.
3. Grasp the handle of the chisel in the right hand with the thumb and fore-

finger of the left hand guiding the blade as shown in Fig. 146. The left hand should also steady the stock. Place a bench hook or piece of waste stock under the piece being cut to prevent marring the bench.

4. Place the shoulder on the handle and press downward moving the shoulder as the cut is taken so the blade takes a slice as shown by the arrow in Fig. 146.

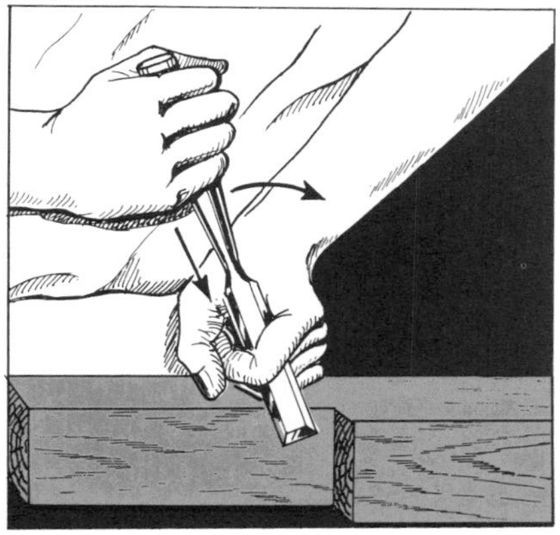

Fig. 146. Right Hand Holds Chisel, With the Thumb and Forefinger of Left Hand Guiding the Blade

Convex Trimming

1. Fasten the stock securely in the vise or on the bench.
2. Cut away surplus stock with the saw.
3. Grasp the chisel handle in the right hand and the blade in the left hand with the bevel up, Fig. 147.
4. Take a shearing cut by forcing the blade sideways as well as forward as shown by the arrows in Fig. 147.
5. Convex surfaces also may be trimmed vertically as shown in Fig. 146.

Fig. 147. Making a Shearing Cut on Convex Surface

Concave Trimming

1. Fasten the stock in the vise or on the bench.
2. Cut away the stock with a coping saw to within $\frac{1}{16}''$ of the mark.
3. Hold the chisel as shown in Fig. 148, with the bevel against the stock.
4. Take a thin shaving by applying pressure downward. At the same time, draw the handle toward you as shown by the arrow. The left hand guides the blade.
5. Trim with the grain only.

Fig. 148. Trimming Concave Surface

Questions

1. Why should small nicks in chisels be ground out?
2. How should a chisel be used when cutting across the stock from edge to edge?
3. What is meant by vertical trimming?
4. In convex trimming, is the bevel of the chisel toward the stock or away from it?
5. In concave trimming, is the bevel of the chisel toward the stock or away from it?
6. Name two general types of chisels.
7. What information about chisels is needed when purchasing?

UNIT 29

Doing Gouge Work

A gouge is a half-round, bevel-edge chisel. The bevel may be either on the outside or the inside of the curve. If the bevel is on the outside of the curve, it is called an *outside bevel gouge,* Fig. 149. If the bevel is on the inside, it is called an *inside bevel gouge,* Fig. 150. The outside bevel gouge is the most useful for general purposes.

The size of a gouge is determined by measuring the distance between the corners of the cutting edges. Gouges are sold in widths from ⅛″ to 2″ and they are ground to different bevels and curves. Small gouges of various sizes and curves are used in carving designs in wood. They are usually sold in sets. The large gouges are useful in gouging out model boat hulls.

Although the outside gouge may be used frequently, it is sometimes necessary to use an inside gouge. An inside gouge is usually used on deep, straight, curved openings and for cutting light concave outlines with the grain.

Fig. 149. Outside Bevel Gouge

Fig. 150. Inside Bevel Gouge

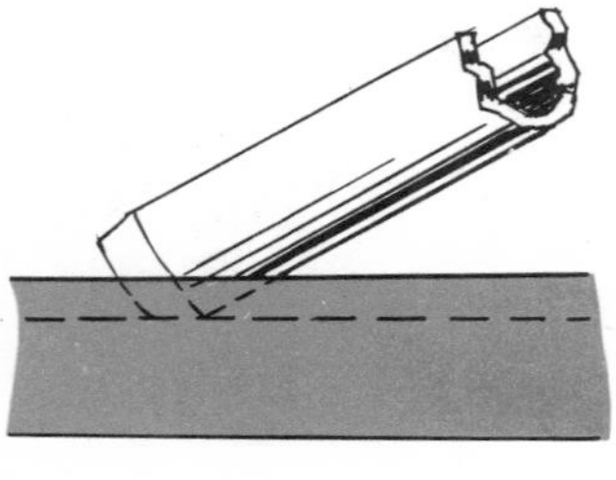

Fig. 151. Position of Outside Bevel when Cutting

Light Gouging with an Outside Bevel Gouge

1. Good examples of light gouging are found in carving a pen tray with an outside gouge, Figs. 152 and 153, and finishing the inside of a model boat hull, Fig. 154.
2. Place the stock in the vise or clamp it securely to the bench.

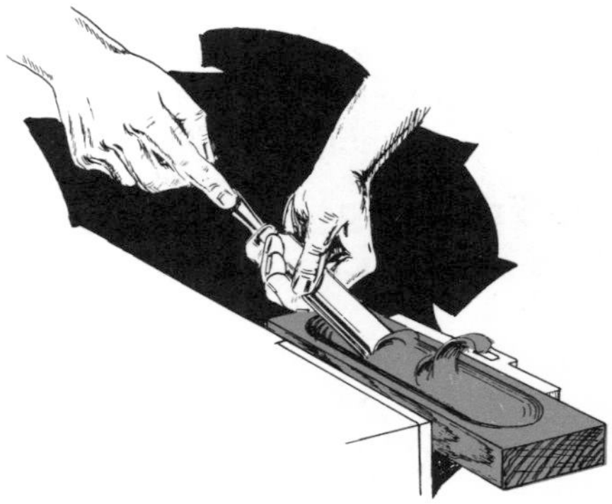

Fig. 152. Cutting with Outside Bevel Gouge

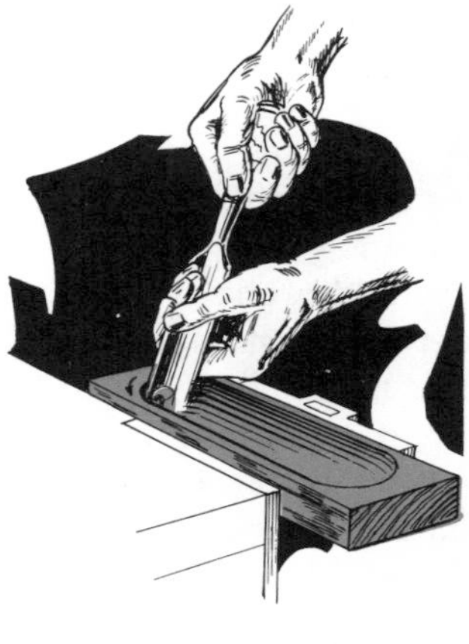

Fig. 153. Move Gouge in a Forward and Circular Motion

Fig. 154. Gouging the Hull of a Model Boat

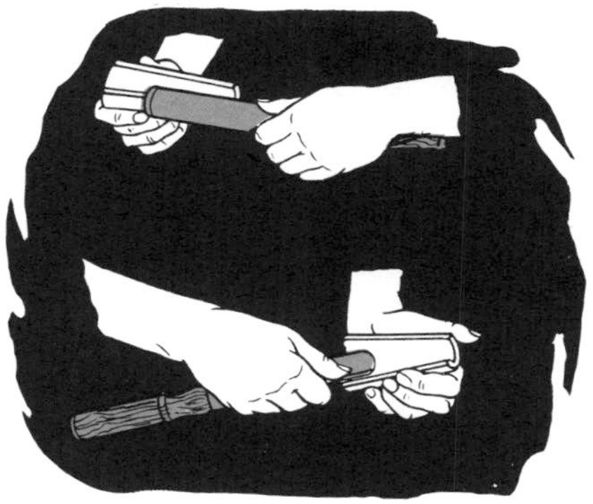

Fig. 155. Honing the Gouge

3. Hold the gouge with the handle in the palm of the right hand and guide the blade with your left hand as shown in Figs. 152 and 153.
4. Take long thin shavings to about the middle of the piece, then turn the piece around and work from the other end, Fig. 152. Fig. 151 shows the position of the bevel when cutting.
5. When shaping to a curve, move the gouge in a forward and circular motion. Fig. 153.
6. When nearing the line hold the gouge steadily in both hands and make sure it does not slip over the line.

Heavy Gouging with an Outside Bevel Gouge

1. Fasten the stock securely in a vise or clamp it to the bench. Fig. 154. An outside bevel gouge of good size for heavy work would be one inch or 1¼″ in width.
2. When gouging thick shavings, such as in gouging the hull of a model boat, hold the gouge in the left hand and drive with a mallet held in the right hand as shown in Fig. 154.
3. Until you know how the grain of the wood runs, take short cuts being careful not to cut too deep.

Sharpening the Gouge

1. In sharpening an *outside bevel gouge,* first grind it by rolling the gouge across the grinding wheel, somewhat as you do in grinding an ordinary chisel.
2. Finish sharpening the gouge with an inside round slip stone as shown in Fig. 155.
3. Roll the bevel while working it on the slip stone.
4. Slip stones are of various sizes. A stone that fits the curvature of the gouge should be used.
5. Remove the remaining wire edge by honing the inside of the gouge on the curved edge of the slip stone. Be sure to hold the stone flat against the gouge so another bevel will not be formed.
6. An *inside bevel gouge* can be ground on a narrow, round-faced emery wheel or on a special wheel for grinding gouges. Whet the gouge on the curved edge of the slip stone.

Questions

1. What is a gouge?
2. How do inside and outside gouges differ?
3. Which is more generally used?
4. Are long thin shavings or deep thick cuts used in light gouging?
5. How is the gouge forced along in heavy cutting?

UNIT 30

Forming with a Spokeshave

The spokeshave is really a short plane with handles at the sides, Fig. 156. The blade can be adjusted so that the thickness of the shaving can be controlled. It is effective in shaping and smoothing curved or irregular surfaces. It can be either drawn toward or pushed away from the worker. With a cross grain, it becomes necessary to use the spokeshave in both directions in order to follow the grain.

The blade of the spokeshave is ground and whetted in the same way that a plane iron is ground. Long fine shavings should be taken in using the spokeshave, as in using a plane.

The shaping of the outside of a model boat hull, Figs. 157 and 158, or a bow stave, Fig. 159, are typical examples of the use of the spokeshave.

Roughing

1. Make sure that the spokeshave is sharp. Even if it is only slightly dull, it will be very difficult to use. Be sure the blade is set so it projects evenly through the opening.

Fig. 156. Spokeshave

2. Fasten the stock in the vise so you will be working with the grain of the wood.
3. Adjust the blade just as you would adjust a plane blade for heavy planing. You may take a rather thick shaving on heavy work.
4. The spokeshave can be used effectively by pulling or pushing.
5. Keep the lower part of the spokeshave firmly against the wood. With a little practice you can "feel" the proper direction in which to go with respect to the grain.
6. It is sometimes necessary to push the spokeshave away from you, especially on a bow stave, boat hull, or on work of similar kind.
7. When pushing the spokeshave away from you, hold it firmly with the thumbs back of the bed near the sides of the blade. Hold the index finger in position at the front with the remaining fingers grasping the handle as in Fig. 158.

Smoothing

1. Make sure that the blade is sharp. Adjust it in the same way that you would adjust a plane iron for light planing.

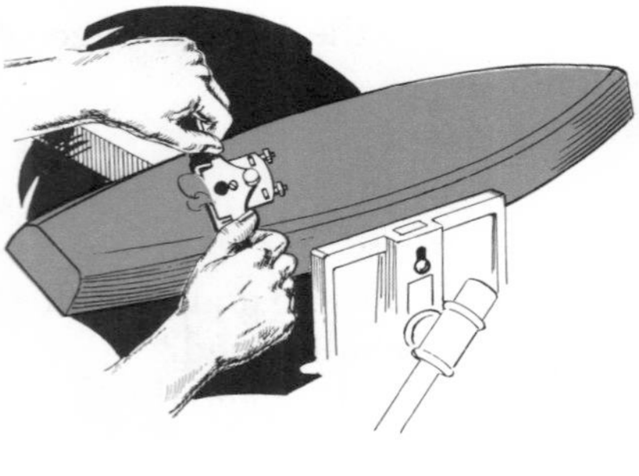

Fig. 157. Using Spokeshave on Outside of Boat Hull

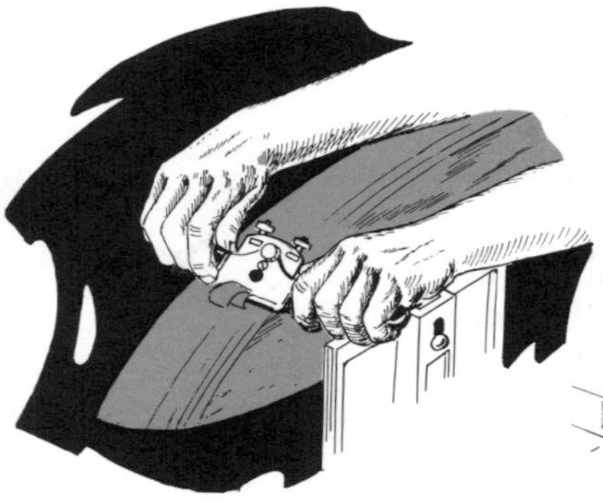

Fig. 158. Shaping by Pushing the Spokeshave

Fig. 159. Shaping a Bow Stave

2. Pull the spokeshave toward you and take a silky, thin shaving.
3. On short curves or on cross grain, push or pull the spokeshave sideways, taking shearing cuts. Just as in using a plane, you should see that the blade is adjusted in the frame so that it is exactly straight, and takes a shaving that is the same thickness its full width.

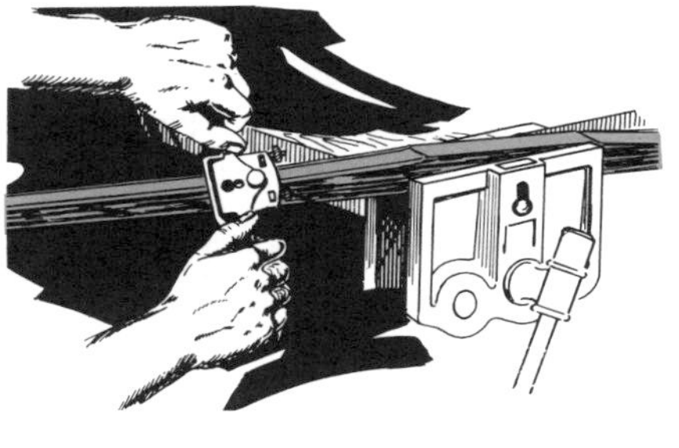

Fig. 160. Pull the Shave Toward You in Smoothing

Questions

1. How does the spokeshave differ from a plane?
2. For what is it used?
3. How is the blade of a spokeshave sharpened?
4. For heavy or light work, the blade is adjusted similar to what other tool?
5. Tell how to use a spokeshave.

UNIT 31

Shaping with a Wood Forming Tool

The *surform* (Figs. 161, 161A and 161B) is useful in shaping and trimming wood, tile, and plastic. It may also be used in forming copper, aluminum and brass. The hardened tool steel cutting blade has a large number of razor sharp teeth with each tooth set at a 45 degree angle. The shaving from each cutting edge or tooth passes through the blade, so the surform never becomes clogged. It is excellent for shaping model boat hulls, canoe paddles, gun stocks, and tool handles. For reasons of safety and because of its ease of handling, it has generally replaced the drawknife in woodworking.

Shaping with the File Type Surform

1. Use this tool in the same way as the half-round file shown on page 68.
2. Push the file across the surface at an angle, applying a light, even pressure, Fig. 161. Continue until the desired shape has been obtained. Finish with 2/0 and 4/0 garnet paper.

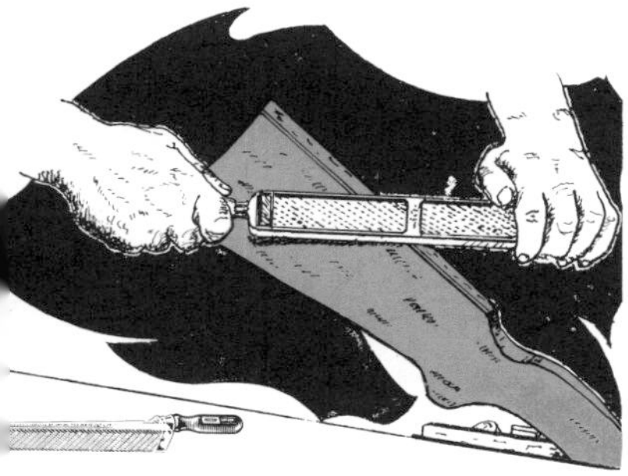

Fig. 161. Shaping with a File Type Surform

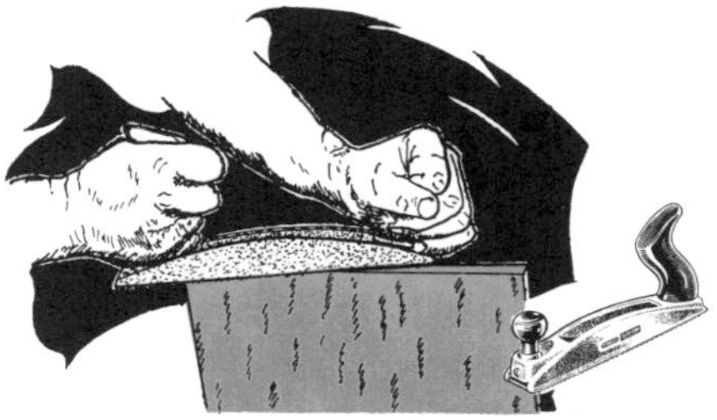

Fig. 161A. Shaping with a Plane Type Surform

Fig. 161B. Smoothing Inside Curves with a Round Surform

Squaring Stock with the Plane Type Surform

1. Use this tool as you would use the jack plane, Fig. 161A. Apply very light pressure.
2. Test with the try square from the face and edge as in Fig. 100, page 64. Surface the end until it is perfectly square and smooth.

Shaping and Smoothing Inside Curves with the Round Surform

The round surform, Fig. 161B, removes stock more rapidly than the common file.

1. Trim an inside curve by pushing the tool forward at an angle. Use light pressure and apply a left and right twist of the hand, Fig. 161B.
2. The trimming or shaping is done with the forward action of the tool only.

Shaping with a Perma-Grit File

The perma-grit file, Fig. 162, is very useful for shaping wood, plastic, and composition materials. It cuts in any direction—forward, backwards, sideways, and when moved in circles. The teeth, or grits, of this file are tungsten carbide, and stay sharp indefinitely. They are brazed to the steel with a copper bond. The tool supplements or replaces the regular woodworking file.

1. Use the coarse side to reduce the stock to shape and size, Figs. 162 and 163.
2. Use the fine side for smoothing, as you use a file. See Fig. 114, page 168.

Shaping with a Drawknife

A drawknife may be used when a great deal of wood is to be removed and when other tools cannot be used.

The drawknife consists of a long beveled blade with a handle on each end. It is used as shown in Fig. 164.

Questions

1. Name two types of surforming tools.
2. How is the perma-grit file constructed? The surform?
3. Compare the uses of the surform and the perma-grit file.
4. Under what conditions may the drawknife be used for shaping stock?

Fig. 162. Smoothing Wood with a Perma-Grit File

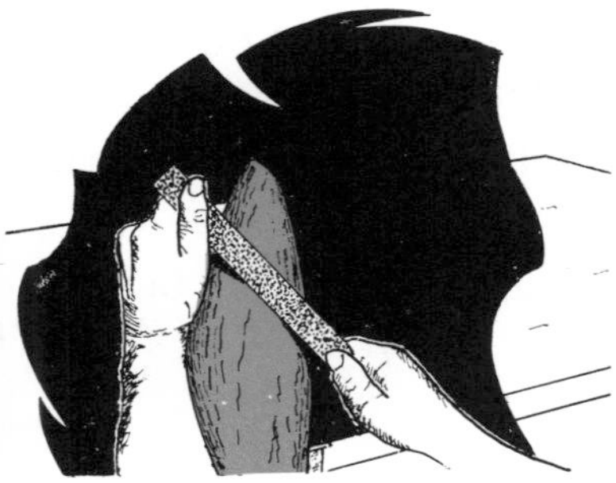

Fig. 163. Shaping Stock with a Perma-Grit File

Fig. 164. Shaping with a Drawknife

UNIT 32 Sawing Curves

The Coping Saw

The coping saw is a useful tool for cutting curves. It is especially necessary when shaping thin wood and in cutting sharp curves in thick wood. In toy making and in projects where outside and inside curves are so numerous that it is almost impossible to cut with other tools, the coping saw is indispensable. The one shown in Fig. 165 is practical because the blade can be turned in the frame.

Sawing Curves with the Stock Held in a Vise

1. Place the stock in the vise as shown in Fig. 166.
2. Adjust the blade of the coping saw so the teeth *point away from the handle.* Be sure that you hold the saw exactly in a horizontal position, Fig. 166.
3. With the coping saw properly adjusted, cut slightly outside of the outline. When the stock is held in the vise in this manner, both hands can be used as shown in Fig. 167.
4. Take short, quick strokes and apply very light downward pressure on the saw. When making sharp turns, work the saw back and forth without making special effort to go ahead, and at the same time, slowly turn the blade of the saw.
5. When using the coping saw to cut inside curves, it is necessary to bore a small hole at a convenient place near the line in the waste stock, Fig. 167. Insert the blade in the hole and proceed to saw.

Sawing Curves with the Aid of a Bracket or Jack

Another method of cutting curves with the coping saw is that in which a bracket is used as shown in Fig. 168. When a vise is not available, the bracket can be clamped to a box or table. This method is especially useful in coping saw work on summer playgrounds or in recreational centers where boxes or tables are used for work benches and where vises are out of the question.

1. When using a bracket for sawing, the *teeth of the blade should point toward the handle.*
2. Hold the blade exactly perpendicular to the stock at all times to insure a square edge and prevent breaking the blade.
3. Operate the saw up and down with one hand while holding the stock on the bracket with the other hand.
4. In order to follow the pattern or outline turn the wood rather than the saw, and at the same time be careful to apply only light pressure on the blade.
5. When making sharp turns, work the saw up and down without trying to go ahead, and at the same time, slowly turn the stock. Forcing the coping saw usually results in poor work and broken blades.

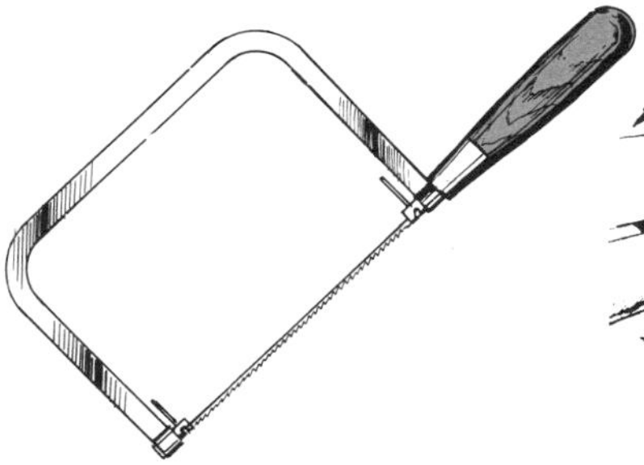

Fig. 165. Coping Saw

Fig. 166. Cut Slightly Outside the Line

Fig. 167. Sawing an Inside Curve

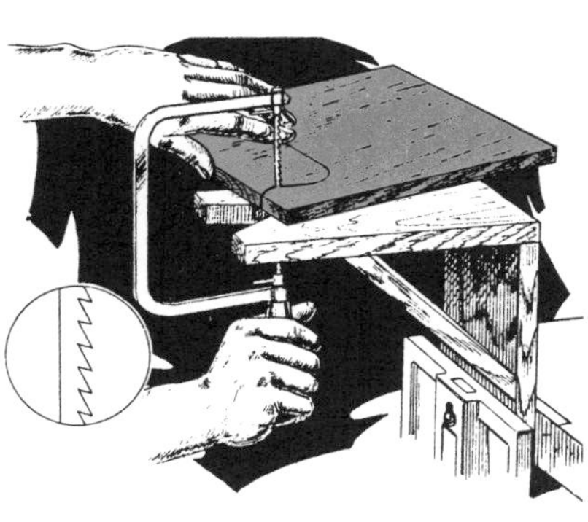

Fig. 168. Teeth Point Down when Using Bracket

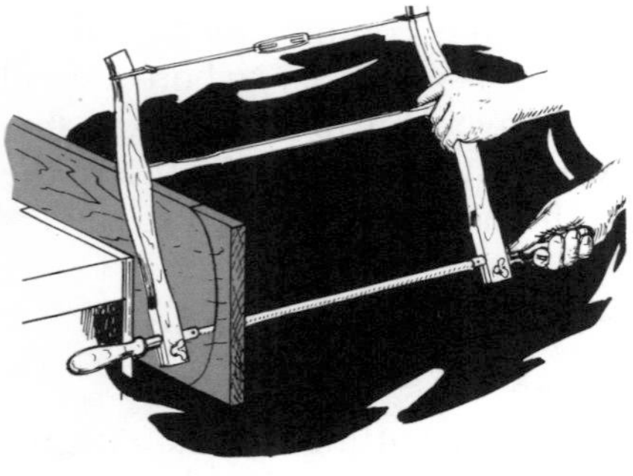

Fig. 169. Use Turning Saw in Cutting Thick Stock

Fig. 170. Compass Saw

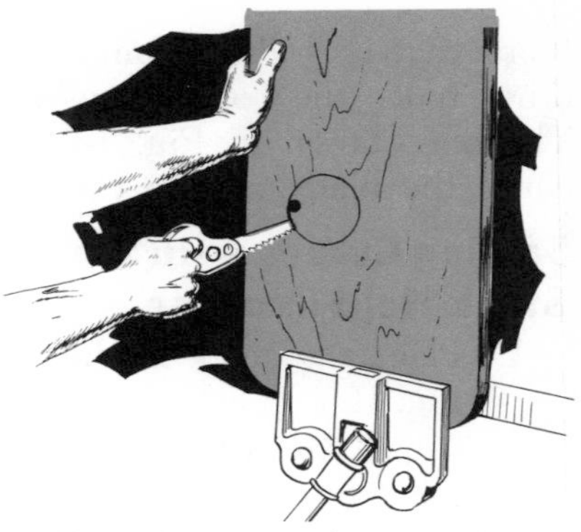

Fig. 171. Using Compass Saw

The Turning Saw

The turning saw is used in cutting curves on rather thick stock, Fig. 169. It has coarse teeth similar to those of a rip saw, and a handle is located at each end of the saw. When the stock is too thick to be cut with a coping saw, you should use the turning saw. It can be used for cutting inside straight lines as well as for curved ones. It is operated in much the same manner as a coping saw.

The Compass Saw

The compass saw is used in sawing inside curves. The blade, which tapers to a point as in Fig. 170, is shaped so that inside curves can be readily cut. Two or three blades of different sizes may be purchased with the standard compass saw handle.

1. Bore a hole in order that the blade may be inserted. The hole is bored in the waste stock.
2. Insert the saw in the hole and start sawing with short, quick strokes, Fig. 171. Do not apply downward pressure on the blade. Slightly twist the wrist as you cut around curves.
3. Use a small compass saw in very fine work or in sawing keyholes. A small saw of this kind is called a keyhole saw.

Questions

1. For what is the coping saw used?
2. Should the teeth point toward the handle or from it when the work is held in a vise?
3. How close to the line should you cut when using a coping saw?
4. How would you operate the saw when making sharp turns?
5. What is a turning saw and for what is it used?
6. Describe a compass saw and tell its special use.
7. What is a keyhole saw and for what is it used?

UNIT 33 The Jig Saw

The jig saw is useful in either the school shop or the home shop. It is a small machine that can be safely operated by boys in the sixth grade after they have learned to use the coping saw. The jig saw is used for cutting outside and inside curves and straight cuts.

General Description

1. A jig saw is usually mounted on a stand. However, some are of the portable bench type.
2. The motor on a jig saw is $\frac{1}{8}$ or $\frac{1}{4}$ horsepower and has bronze bearings that require oil lubrication or ball bearings lubricated with grease.
3. An important part of a jig saw is the driving mechanism, in which a rotary motion is converted into an up-and-down movement.
4. The upper chuck is attached to the lower end of a square metal rod which operates up and down inside of a metal tube or drum. This tube, clamped to the end of the arm, is provided with a tension spring, 2 in Fig. 172.
5. The lower chuck, which is fastened to the cross head, has three jaws to hold various saw blades, Fig. 173.
6. In Fig. 172, the guide post, *1*, is provided with a round guide plate, *2*, and steel roller, *3*. The guide plate has several slots of different depths and widths for guiding saw blades.
7. A hold-down metal spring, *1* in Figs. 174 and 176, is attached to the guide post to hold the stock securely.
8. There usually are two cone pulleys, one attached to the machine and one attached to the motor. These are connected by a V-shaped rubber belt. The speed of cutting is determined by the ratios of the pulleys. The usual three speeds vary from 700 to 1800 rpm.
9. Many types of blades can be used in a jig saw. They vary in length and number of teeth per inch.

Inserting and Adjusting a Blade for Cutting 1/4" to 3/8" Wood

1. Select a blade of medium size, similar to a coping saw blade.
2. Place the blade (with teeth pointing down) in the center of the jaws of the upper jaw chuck. Tighten the thumb nut by hand to support the blade. Do not use pliers.
3. Lift the lower chuck or plunger to its highest position.
4. Lower the tension head or tube until the lower end of the blade fits into the lower chuck or plunger. Tighten in place with the thumb nut, Fig. 173.
5. Adjust the guide plate until the desired slot is directly back of the saw, 2 in Fig. 173.

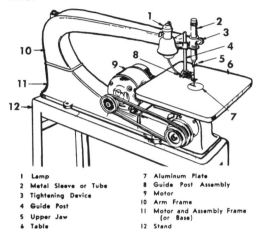

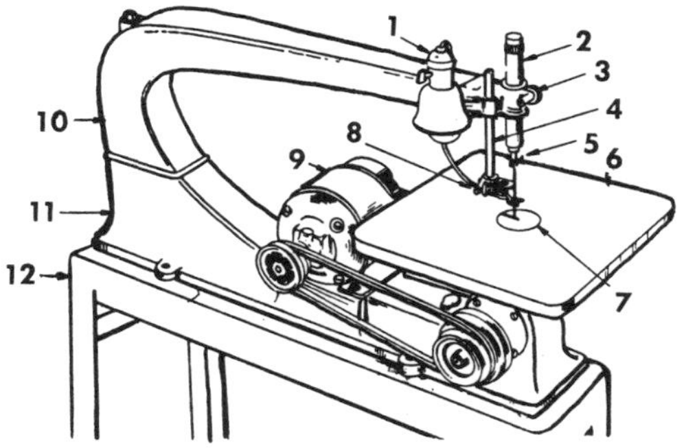

1 Lamp
2 Metal Sleeve or Tube
3 Tightening Device
4 Guide Post
5 Upper Jaw
6 Table
7 Aluminum Plate
8 Guide Post Assembly
9 Motor
10 Arm Frame
11 Motor and Assembly Frame (or Base)
12 Stand

Fig. 172. Jig Saw

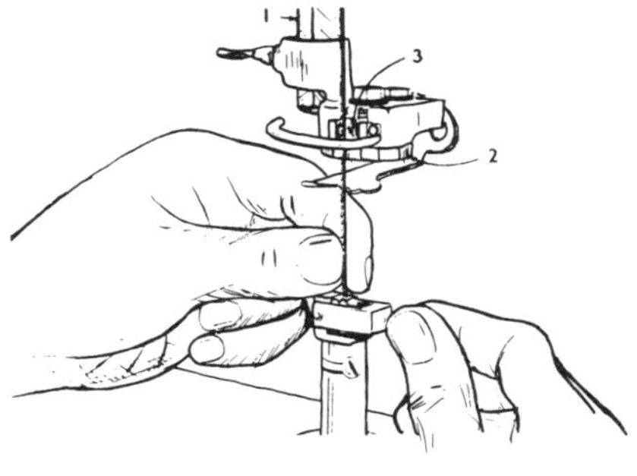

Fig. 173. Fastening Blade in Lower Chuck

Fig. 174. Hold-Down Spring Rests Lightly on Wood

6. Next adjust the guide roller. This metal roller should barely touch the blade, *3* in Fig. 173.
7. Lift or pull the upper head or metal tube upward about one inch to provide the proper tension. Experiment, moving the metal tube up and down until you are satisfied that the correct tension point has been reached.
8. Turn the machine by hand by pulling the belt to see that the saw blade works freely before turning on the power.
9. Adjust the hold-down spring next. It should rest lightly on the wood to be cut, *1* in Fig. 174.

Cutting with Saber Blades

Saber saws or blades are used to saw thick stock or hard wood. They are fastened to the lower jaws of the jig saw only, Figs. 173 and 174.

1. Although saber blades can be fastened in the lower jaws of the lower chuck as ordinary blades, it is best to fasten saber blades in the V cut between two of the jaws provided for this purpose.
2. On some jig saws, a special guide is provided below the table to guide the saber blade. On most machines, however, the circular guide plate serves as the main guide.
3. Because the saw blades are heavier and the teeth are larger, saber sawing is done much faster than ordinary jig sawing.
4. Much wider stock can be cut on the machine with a saber blade. The whole over-arm can be removed if much heavy cutting is planned.
5. An example of heavier cutting with the saber blade is shown in cutting 1″ stock for bookends in Fig. 174.
6. Parts for the jewelry box in Fig. 175 can be cut either with a regular jig saw blade or a saber blade.

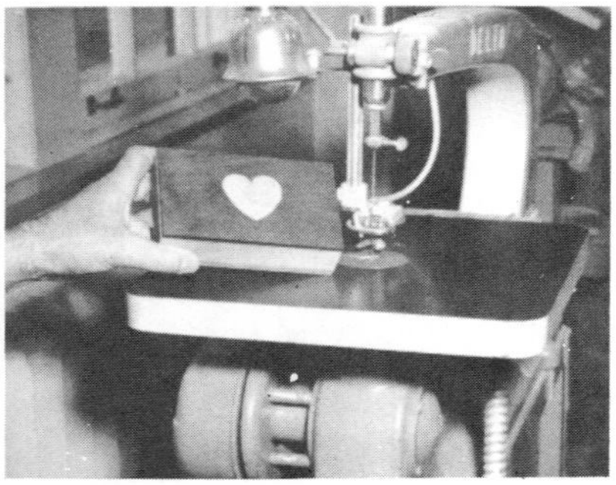

Fig. 175. Jewelry Box With Marquetry Top

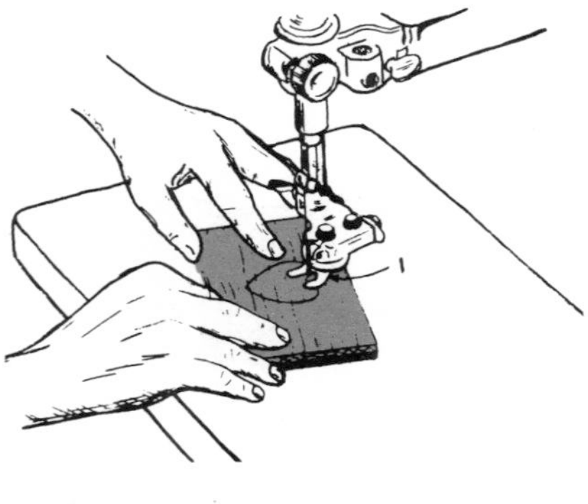

Fig. 176. Cutting Out Design

Sawing Simple Marquetry

1. One of the simplest ways of doing marquetry or inlay work is to use two pieces of wood of the same thickness, but of contrasting colors, such as pine and butternut or walnut and birch.
2. To make the cover for the jewelry box, fasten two pieces of contrasting wood together, with tape and glue.
3. First fasten the tape on one side of both pieces. Apply a bit of glue to the outside of the tape and then press the two pieces together.
4. Draw your design on paper and then trace it on the wood, preferably the light colored wood.
5. Bore a $\frac{1}{16}$″ hole at a convenient point on the outline of your design through both thicknesses of wood, Fig. 176.
6. Insert a fine blade of the jewelry type in the small hole in the outline and attach the blade to the upper and the lower jaws. Adjust the machine carefully to secure proper tension.
7. Tilt the table about two degrees and cut your design following the outline carefully. See heart design, Fig. 176.

8. To remove the pieces from the saw, loosen the upper thumb nut and raise the guide post and metal tube.
9. Insert and glue the dark design into the light wood and the light design into the dark wood, Fig. 176.
10. Marquetry and veneer material can be purchased in different patterns and thicknesses. It is also made in inlays of various shapes and designs.

Sanding with a Jig Saw

1. A jig saw can be easily converted into a sanding machine.
2. A sanding attachment is usually a part of jig saw equipment. This device consists of a metal drum which is fastened to a metal rod and held securely in the V jaws of the lower chuck, Fig. 177.
3. Special sandpaper tubings of various grades are available. The tubes are fastened to the metal drum by means of the special clasp provided with the sanding attachment.
4. It is a simple matter to construct various shaped sanding drums or devices.
5. Sanding with a sanding drum should be done with the aluminum throat plate removed. Use a low speed for best results.

Filing on a Jig Saw

1. A jig saw can be converted into a filing machine. Files of various shapes to fit a jig saw can be purchased.
2. These files are attached in the V jaws of the lower chuck in the same manner as the sanding drums are fastened, Fig. 178.
3. Many projects can be made of a combination of light metal and wood. The jig saw is useful in finishing metal decorative designs.

Questions

1. What advantages has the jig saw over other saws for cutting curves?
2. What do we mean by a jig saw?
3. Can a jig saw be operated safely by boys in the sixth grade?
4. What are the teeth on jig saw blades like?
5. What kind of a blade is best for heavy cutting?
6. What is marquetry work?
7. How can a jig saw be converted into a simple sanding machine?
8. How can files be attached for use on a jig saw?
9. How would you go about selecting a jig saw for your own home shop?

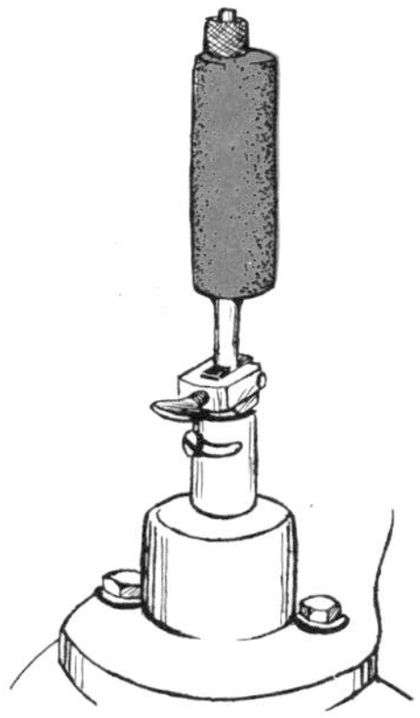

Fig. 177. Sanding Attachment

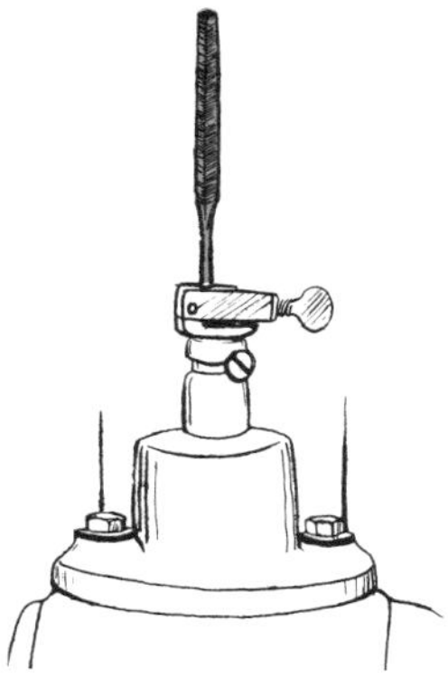

Fig. 178. Filing Attachment

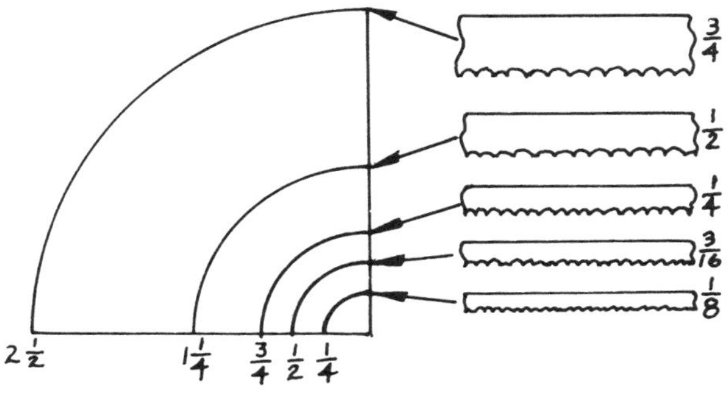

Fig. 178A. Band Saw Blade Widths

UNIT 34

The Band Saw

The band saw is used for sawing all kinds of curved work as well as making straight cuts. Several types of band saws are used in industry. Lumber mills use large band saws for sawing logs and planks into boards. The band saw you will use is a smaller type, which has a variety of uses, and is suitable for the home and the school shop. See Fig. 179.

General Description

All band saws operate in much the same way. The blade is made of flexible steel with teeth on one edge. When in use, the blade travels downward continuously through an opening in the saw table, with the teeth pointing toward the stock, so when you place the stock to be cut, keep the finish side up. The blade travels over two vertical wheels, one directly above the other. The top wheel may be adjusted up and down to secure the correct tension, or tightness of the blade. In order to make the blade track properly, the top wheel may be tilted.

The wheels and blade are enclosed in metal housings that serve as guards and leave only about six inches of the blade exposed. The blade will twist if used without controls, so guides are located above and below the table. See Figs. 179, 180, and 181. These guides also include blade supports which are especially hardened moving steel wheels. The back edge of the saw blade presses against these supports when the saw is in use.

The size of the wheels on a band saw denotes the size of the band saw. For example, if the wheels are 14″ in diameter, it is a 14″ band saw. This is the size often used in the home shop as well as in the school shop. Stock thicker than 3″ should not be cut on the 14″ band saw. The 30″ band saw is used in larger woodworking shops. The saw table is usually about the size of the wheels. In other words, one side of the table is equal in length to about the diameter of the wheel. The table must be at right angles to the blade when it is used for

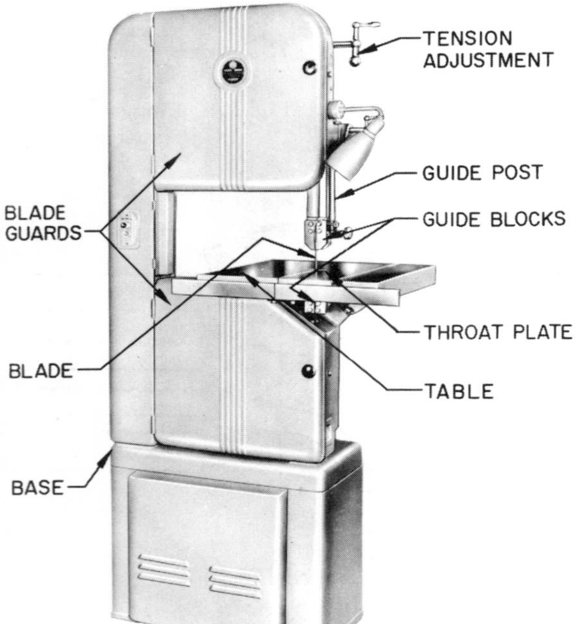

Fig. 179. Parts of the Band Saw

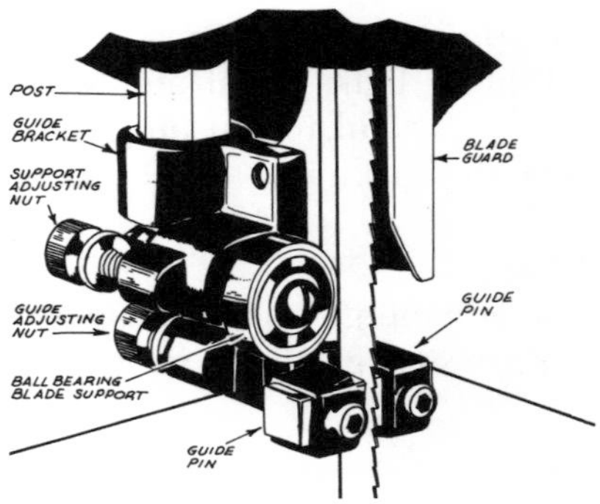

Fig. 180. Parts of the Upper Guide Assembly

straight cutting. This is checked with a try square as shown in Fig. 182.

Safety Instructions

1. As with all machines in the shops, the bandsaw is safe to use. It cannot reach out to hurt you. You can be injured only if you get your hand into the machine.
2. Make sure that the saw blade is properly tensioned and tracking on the wheels. The blade must be tight and it must trail properly so it will not come off. Your instructor will assist you to check this. Testing is done by moving the wheels *by hand.*
3. Accidents on bandsaws happen most often when the saw is improperly tensioned or when the saw is dull. Pressure in feeding stock into the saw need be only very slight. A dull saw requires extra pressure in feeding the stock with greater chance of the hand slipping into the saw.
4. Set the guide so there is a ¼″ clearance above the stock to be sawed.
5. Make sure there are no scraps of stock either on the floor or the table of the saw. A small block on the floor can cause a big accident.
6. Stand in front of the band saw when working, never at the side. See Fig. 183.
7. Allow no one to stand at the side while you work. If the saw blade should break, it will fly outward and could cause serious injuries.
8. Do not talk to anyone while working nor permit anyone to talk to you. Stop the machine if you must talk.

Fig. 181. Lower Guide and Table Tilt Control

9. If you hear a clicking noise, stop the machine. The blade may be cracked and if so, it must be replaced.
10. Do not wear loose clothing or a necktie while working with any power machines.
11. Rings, watch chains and wrist watches may be the cause of accidents. Take them off while working.
12. Do not attempt to remove scraps of stock or do cleaning while the saw is in motion. Stop the saw, then remove the stock or do any necessary cleaning.
13. Do not play around any machines.
14. Do not push stock through the saw after the power is shut off and while the saw is still in motion.
15. If it is necessary to stop sawing in the middle of a long cut, cut out through the waste stock. Do not attempt to back out, for the saw may come off the wheels.

Sawing Straight Lines

1. See that the machine is in proper operating condition with the saw tracking correctly and properly tensioned.
2. Test with the try square as shown in

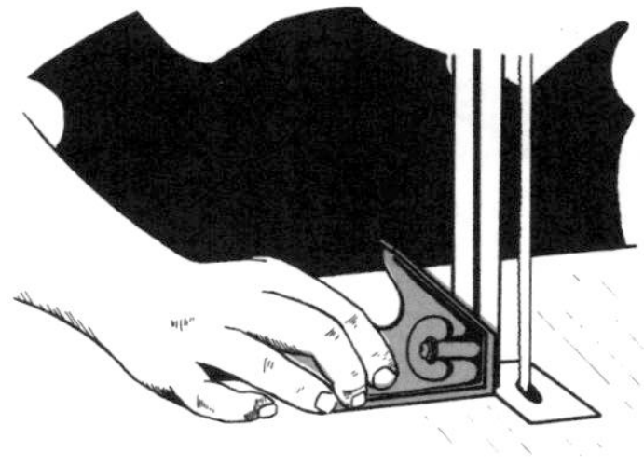

Fig. 182. Checking that Table Is at Right Angle to Blade

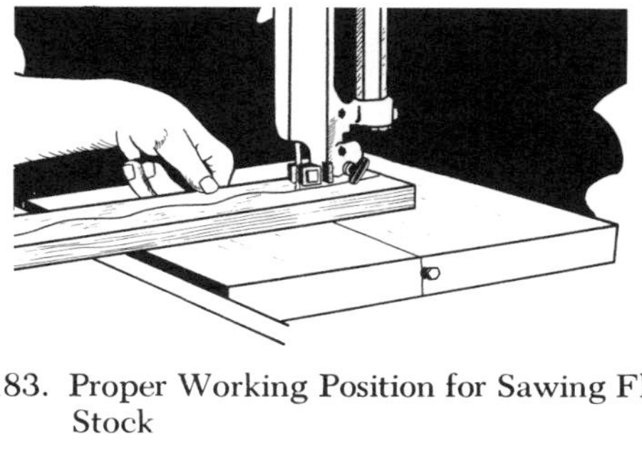

Fig. 183. Proper Working Position for Sawing Flat Stock

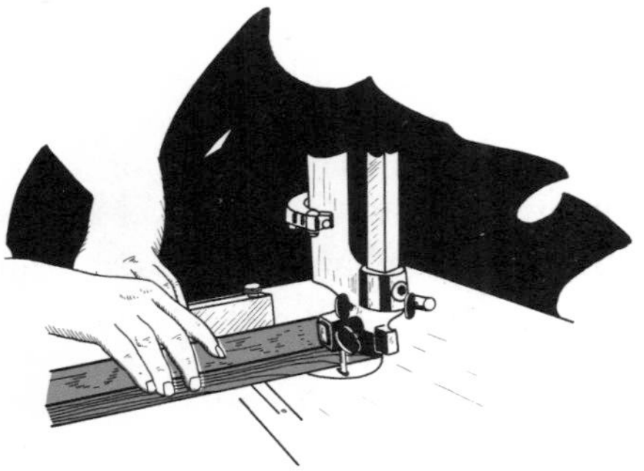

Fig. 184. Cutting Stock with Miter Gauge as Guide

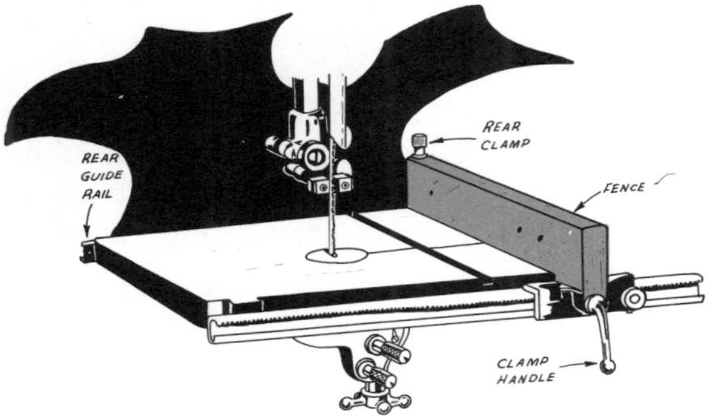

Fig. 185. Fence Adjusted for Use as Ripping Guide

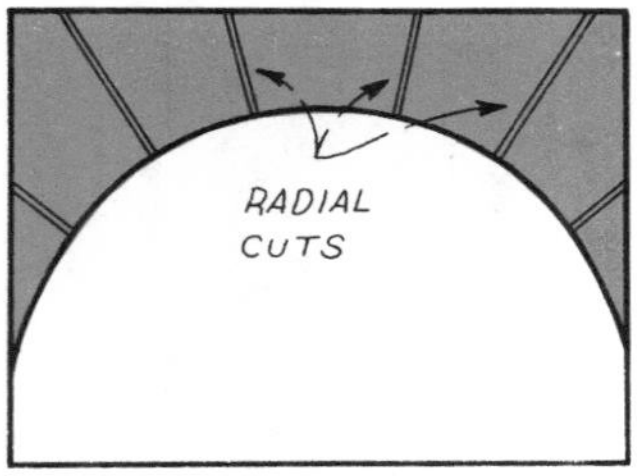

Fig. 186. Make Cuts to Line — Trim Away Waste Stock

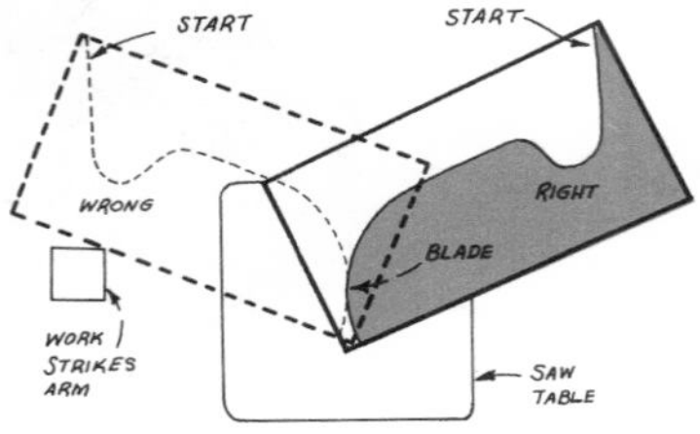

Fig. 187. Plan Sequence of Cuts Before Sawing

Fig. 182, to make sure that the table is at right angles to the blade.

3. Make sure that the saw is going full speed before you start cutting.
4. Take a position to the left of the stock that you are feeding into the saw. This will place you to the front left side of the table as in Fig. 183.
5. Feed the stock gently with the right hand and guide it with the left hand. If the saw is sharp, it will cut with very little assistance. Do not force or attempt to crowd the stock while cutting.
6. Cut in the waste stock, allowing just enough stock for trimming.
7. If the saw tends to pull away from the line when you feed the stock into the saw, something is wrong with the saw or you are not feeding it squarely. Ask your instructor to assist you. A dull, improperly tensioned saw blade will tend to lead away from a straight line.
8. Many kinds of straight cuts can be made accurately by using the miter gauge, Fig. 184 and the fence, Figs. 185 and 191. The miter gauge can be set so that any angle of straight line can be cut.

Sawing Curves

1. Sharp curves require a narrow saw. A ¼″ blade with about 8 teeth to the inch is satisfactory for most sharp curves.
2. Cut saw kerfs up to the line and then trim away the pieces of waste stock. See Fig. 186. You will be cutting a number of small pieces instead of one large one; thus you can better control the saw.

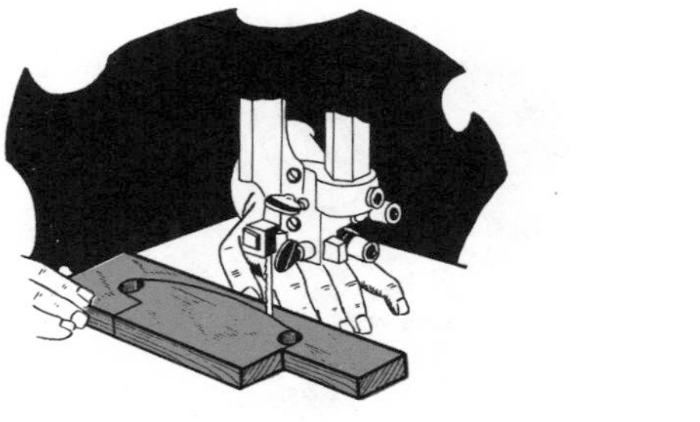

Fig. 188. Bore Holes for Sharp Curves

3. When cutting any curves, whether they are uniformly round or a combination of curves, plan ahead and visualize the path of the cut you are to make. See Fig. 187.
4. In cutting some types of curves including sharp inside corners, round holes should be bored at suitable places as in Fig. 188. The saw can then easily be used to cut the more gradual curves.
5. A good general principle to follow in cutting curved work is to rough out the stock as much as possible by cutting kerfs and removing waste stock, and then trim to the line.
6. Plan your cutting so as to save usable pieces of wood. This can be done by taking short cuts first, then you will not have to cut through large segments of stock. Study Fig. 189.
7. If you need two or more curved pieces exactly alike, the pieces of stock can be glued together and cut in one operation. Glue the pieces with paper between the surfaces. Apply the glue on each face and clamp until dry. Only the top piece will need to be laid out for duplicate sawing.

Making Beveled Cuts

1. Beveled cuts up to 45° can be made by tilting the table to the desired angle. See Fig. 190.
2. Make sure that the table is set at the proper angle by taking a test cut first. The angle can be cut in reverse from the one desired.
3. Once the table is set for the desired bevel, proceed as in making other straight cuts.
4. Do not leave the band saw as you used it. Return the table to its regular position for straight cutting. This applies to all special set-ups on the bandsaw.

Resawing

Resawing is the ripping of a thick board into two thinner boards. The bandsaw does this with considerable ease if the saw is sharp. A wide blade, ¾″ to 1″ with about 5 teeth to the inch should be used. Narrow blades, such as used in sawing small curves, do not produce results as good as does a wider blade. The saw must be under full speed before starting the cut.

1. Fasten the bandsaw fence to the table in such position as to allow for the desired thickness of the board to be removed from the thicker stock. See Fig. 191. For example, if you desire a one-half inch board, set the fence so there is one-half inch between the blade and the fence.

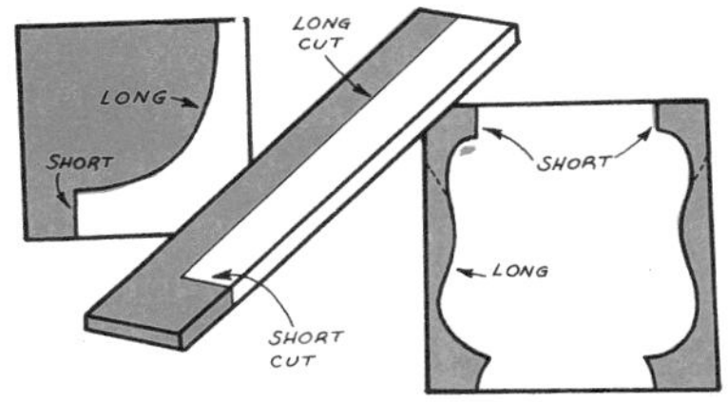

Fig. 189. Make Short Cuts First

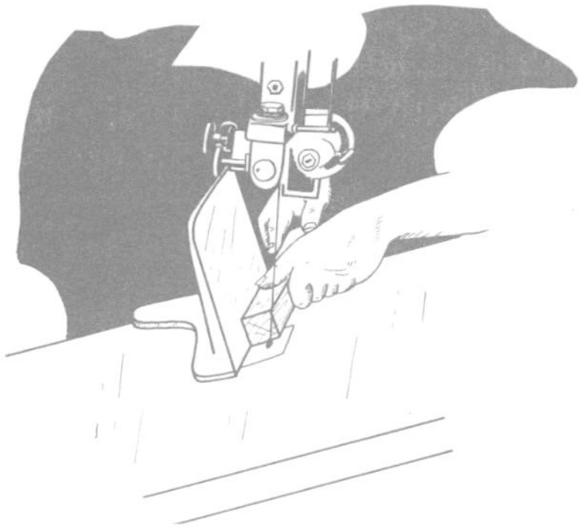

Fig. 190. Tilt Table for Bevel Cuts

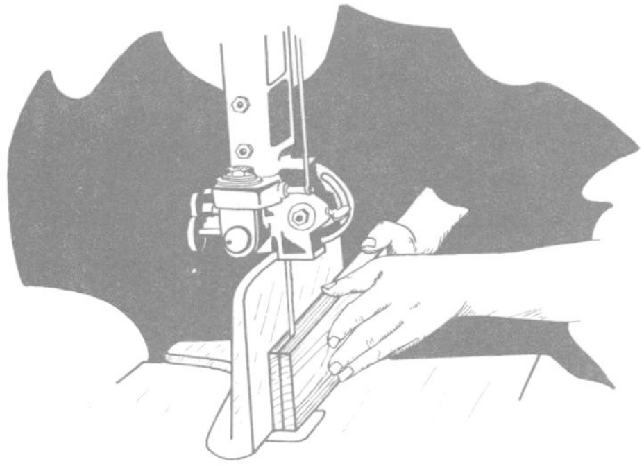

Fig. 191. Using Fence as Guide for Resawing

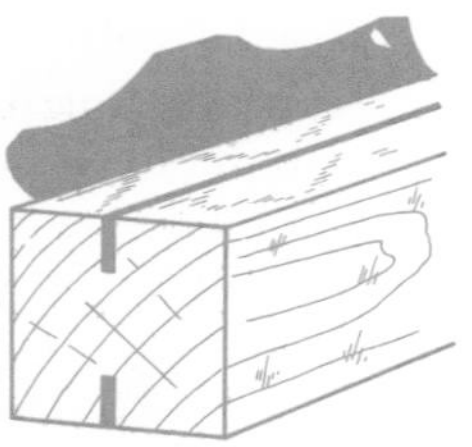

Fig. 192. When Resawing Thick Hardwood, Partial Cuts Can Be Made on Circular Saw

2. Square one edge with one face of the stock. Mark with a sharp pencil, opposite the working edge, the thickness of the board to be cut. This can be done by thumb gauging. See Fig. 105.
3. Test for the proper setting of the fence by cutting scrap stock. Adjust the fence if necessary and retest with another piece of scrap stock until the proper thickness is obtained.
4. Hold the stock on the table with the working edge down and the working face against the fence.
5. Hold the stock firmly against the fence with the left hand and feed it into the blade with the right hand without forcing. If the blade is sharp, very little pressure is needed.
6. As the stock nears the end of the cut, push the remainder with a stick so as not to get the fingers close to the saw.
7. When thick hardwood is to be resawed, kerfs can be cut on the circular saw as in Fig. 192. This provides an additional guide.

Questions

1. Is the band saw safe to operate? Give five safety rules.
2. Do the teeth on a band saw blade point toward the stock to be cut or away from it?
3. Why is a band saw provided with guides for the blade?
4. How is the size of a band saw determined?
5. What is the size of the band saw in your school shop?
6. What is the maximum thickness of stock recommended to be sawed on a band saw?
7. Would abrasive material placed on the floor in front of a band saw be helpful?
8. Why should anyone avoid standing in line with the wheels of the band saw while the machine is in operation?
9. How can you tell a cracked blade when sawing?
10. How much clearance should there be between the upper guide and the stock?
11. How are combination cuts made?
12. Why are holes bored on some kinds of band saw work?
13. How is the table set for bevel cuts?
14. What is the miter gauge? The fence?
15. What side of the stock should be down when sawing?

UNIT 35

The Wood Turning Lathe

The lathe is among the oldest of power machines. Wood turning combines hand tool work with machine work and it is one of the oldest crafts known. A simple turning lathe was used several hundred years before any other known woodworking machines.

Contemporary furniture includes comparatively little wood turning; however, turned parts seem on the increase in newer designs of furniture. Single pieces — such as lamp posts and bases, boxes, bowls, plates, table legs, and tool handles — will always be popular turning

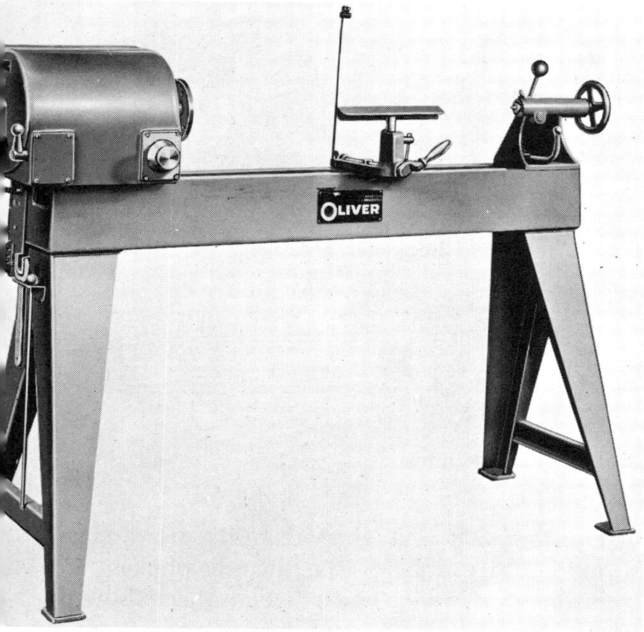

Fig. 193. Lathe with Direct Drive Variable Speed Motor (Oliver)

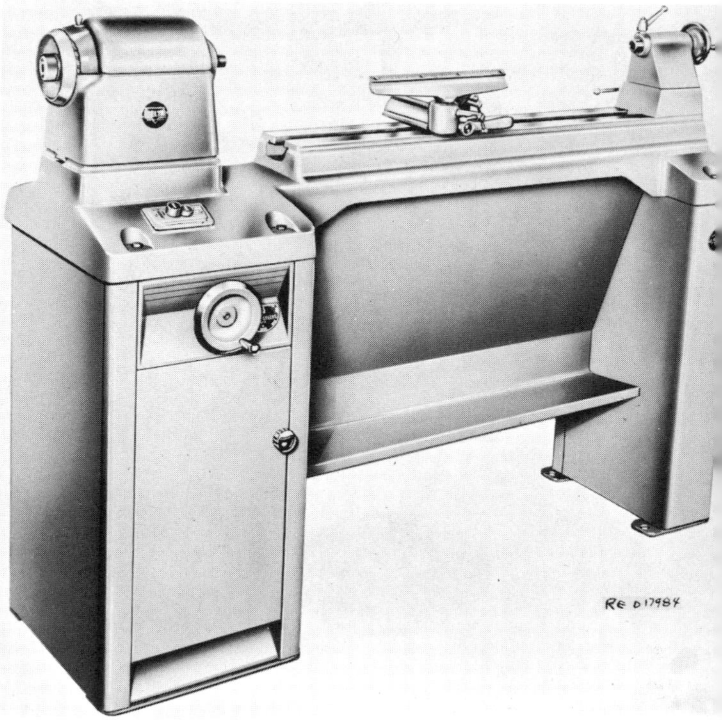

Fig. 194. Belt-Driven Lathe (Delta)

projects. Turning is not difficult and it is fascinating.

The modern wood turning lathe is available in several styles and sizes. The lathe with the direct drive variable speed motor, Fig. 193, and the lathe with the belted motor with step pulleys, Fig. 194, are typical. The size of a wood turning lathe is usually indicated by the largest diameter of stock that can be turned on it.

General Description

The main parts of a wood turning lathe are (1) the lathe bed, (2) headstock, (3) tailstock, and (4) the tool rest.

The *lathe bed* is a strong casting shaped like two "I" beams attached to a four-legged stand. See Fig. 193.

The *headstock* contains the driving part of the lathe and it is fastened to the bed with bolts. It consists of a hollow spindle that revolves on bearings. The spindle, or live center, is powered with a cone pulley and motor or by a direct drive motor. The cone pulley works with a countershaft arrangement, Fig. 194. On the direct drive motor lathe, Fig. 193, the

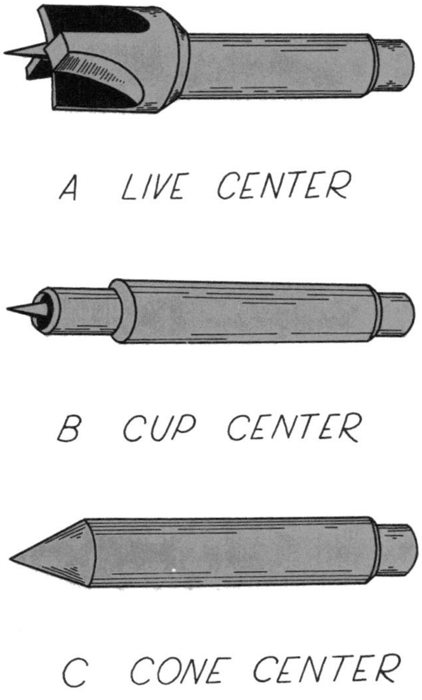

Fig. 195. Types of Centers

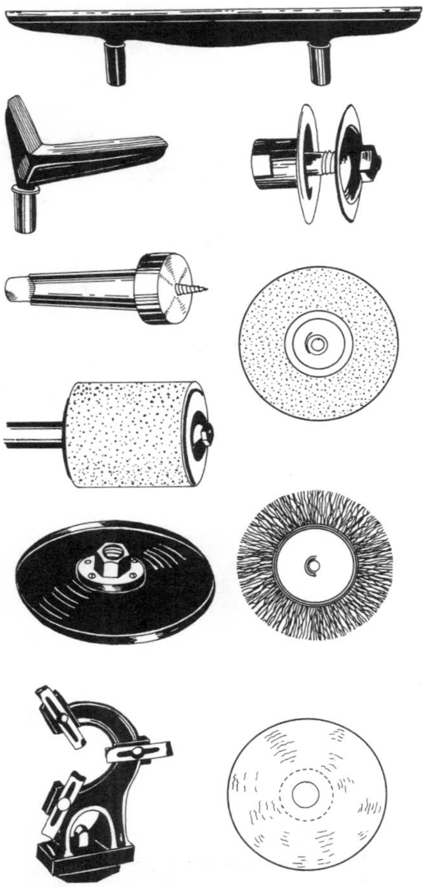

Fig. 196. Lathe Accessories

headstock is the motor. This type of a lathe usually has four speeds ranging from 500 to 3600 rpm. The live center, *A* in Fig. 195, fits into the hollow end of the spindle. The spindle is provided with threads on both ends to receive a face plate or screw chuck.

The *tailstock* assembly is made so that it can be fastened to the bed of the lathe at any desired point to accommodate the length of stock to be turned. It is clamped in place by means of a wrench located in the side of the tailstock nearest the operator. It contains a spindle that can be moved in and out by means of an end handwheel arrangement. The dead center is made to fit into the hollow end of the spindle. There are two kinds of dead centers, the cup center and the cone center, *B* and *C* in Fig. 195.

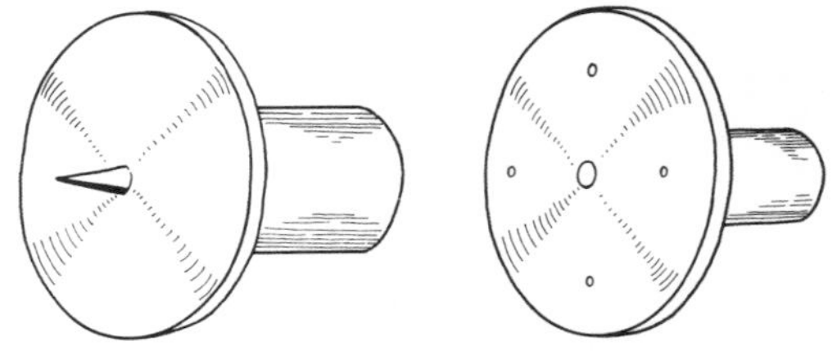

Fig. 197. Screw Chuck and Faceplate

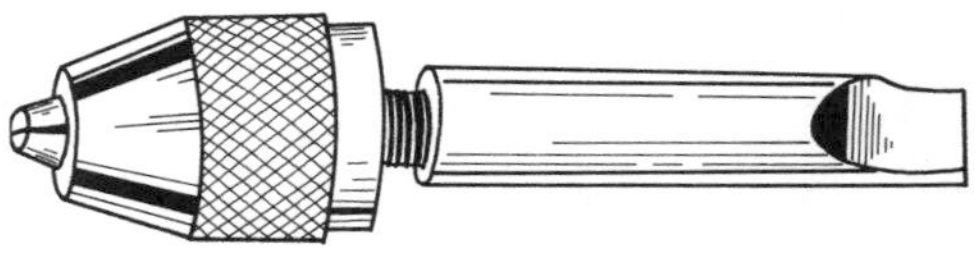

Fig. 198. Drill Chuck

The *tool rest* is T shaped and is used as a support and guide for the turning chisels. It is fastened in place with a clamp as shown in Fig. 194.

Accessories

The lathe may be equipped with a number of attachments or accessories such as lathe centers, faceplates, screw chucks, steady rests, drill chucks, sanding drums, sanding discs, grinding wheels, buffing wheels and right angle tool rests, Fig. 196. These are for special operations or for making turning easier to perform.

Lathe centers hold the stock in spindle turning. There are three types of centers, the spur or the live center, the cup center, and the cone center. See Fig. 195. The centers are tapered to fit in the hollow part of the spindles. The live center is made with four metal prongs and a center steel point. The prongs are driven into one end of the stock to be turned, Fig. 210. The cup and cone centers are called dead centers because they are locked in a stationary position and do not turn with the stock. The cup center is considered more accurate than the cone center for most spindle turning.

The *faceplate* is an iron disc that is threaded to the live spindle. Faceplates are available in several diameters to accommodate various kinds and sizes of stock. See *B*, Fig. 197.

The *screw chuck* is a small faceplate with a screw center. It is used for turning small pieces, *A*, Fig. 197. A grinding wheel, wire brush, or a buffing wheel attachment can also be held in place and be used on the screw chuck.

The drill chuck, which has a tapered center, can be used on both the live spindle and the tailstock spindle, Fig. 198. The drill chuck is a very handy drill or bit holder for drilling and boring in wood.

The *steady rest* is a necessary support in spindle turning of long pieces. See Figs. 196 and 199. The rest controls vibration and can be clamped to the lathe bed at any desired point.

A *sanding disc* may be attached to the live center of the lathe for sanding a good many flat parts and curved shapes of stock. The disc can be made from a piece of soft wood and mounted on a faceplate. Figs. 200 and 201 show operations that can be performed on the sanding disc.

The *sanding drum* is available in various sizes and it has many uses. It is attached to a special tapered shank. See Figs. 202 and 203.

Fig. 199. Steady Rest

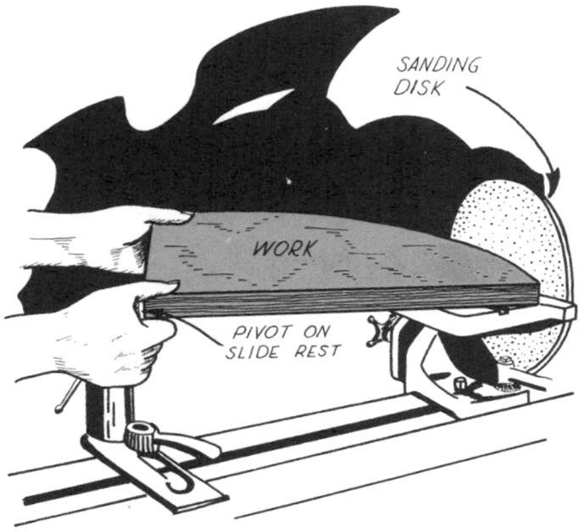

Fig. 200. Sanding Disk

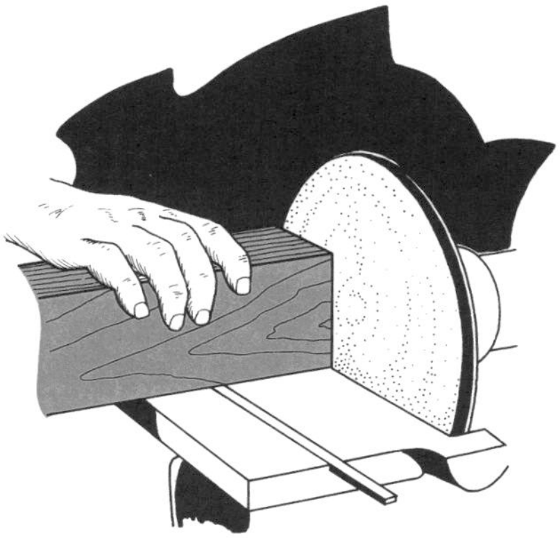

Fig. 201. Using Sanding Disk

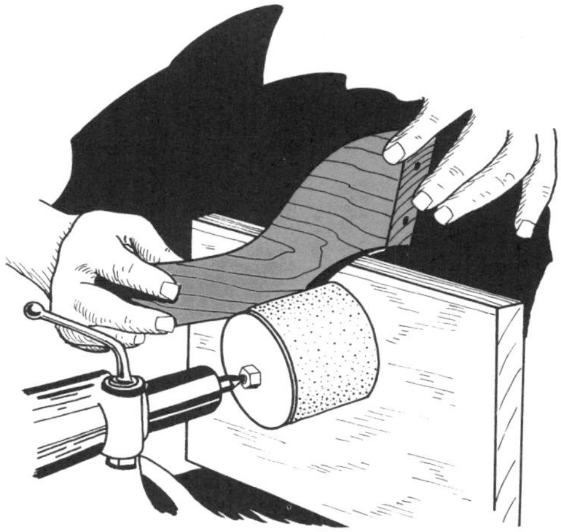

Fig. 202. Using Sanding Drum

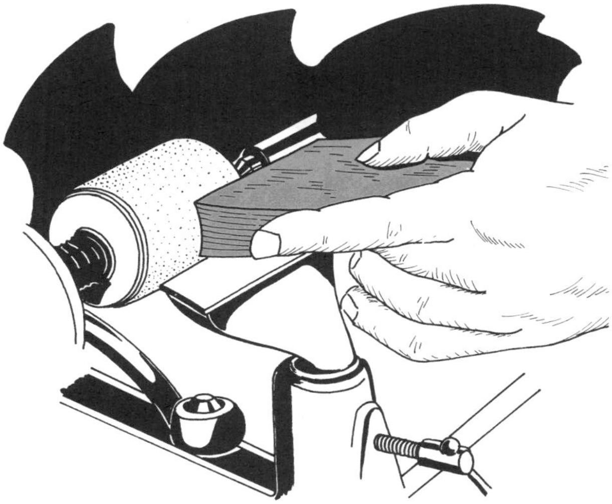

Fig. 203. Using Sanding Drum

Wood Turning Chisels

The chisels used in wood turning are of six standard shapes, Fig. 205. They are known as "tang" chisels and have long thick handles.

The *gouge* is a hollow roundnose chisel with an outside bevel. The large gouge is used primarily for making roughing cuts. The small gouge is used for cutting coves or small round grooves. Gouges come in widths from ¼″ to 1″.

The *skew chisel* is one of the most used cutting tools in wood turning. It is a double-ground, flat chisel with the end ground to an angle of 60 degrees with one edge. It is used to smooth cylinders and to cut shoulders, beads, vee grooves, tapers, and many other operations. The 1″ and the ½″ skew chisels are most used.

The *parting tool* is a V shaped chisel ground on two edges at angles of about 60 degrees. It is used for many operations, such as cutting off like a saw, for making straight cuts in faceplate turning, and making cuts to any required diameters. It is also a handy scraping tool.

The *squarenose, roundnose* and the *spear chisels* are all scraping tools. The squarenose chisel is like an ordinary hand chisel, but it is longer and heavier. It is used to smooth stock in spindle and faceplate turning. See *B* in Fig. 205. The roundnose chisel is like an ordinary hand chisel and is ground with a round end. It is beveled to an angle of approximately 45 degrees, *E*, Fig. 205. It is a scraping tool. The spear chisel is also called the diamond point and is used in scraping V cuts, corners and beads. It is ground to a sharp point and beveled on one side only. See *F*, Fig. 205.

Measuring Tools

The measuring tools in wood turning are the *rule, dividers, outside calipers,* and the *inside calipers.* See Figs. 206 and 207.

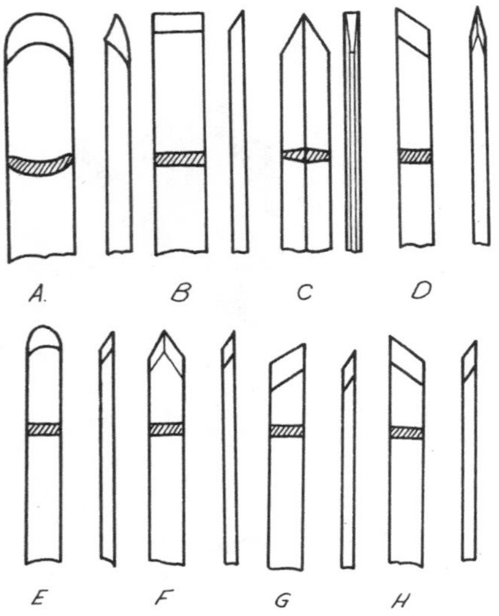

Fig. 205. Shapes of Wood Turning Chisels

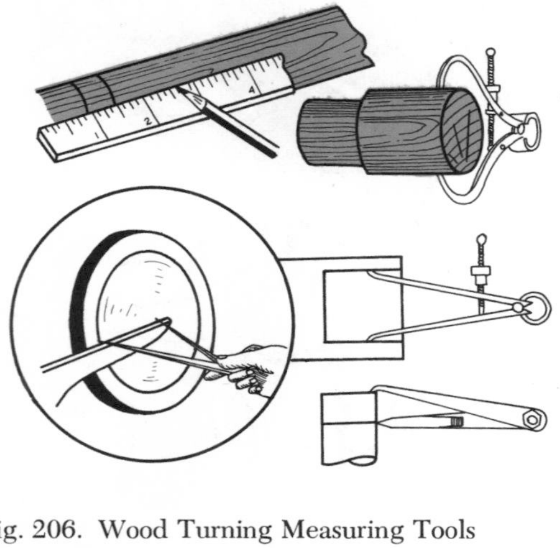

Fig. 206. Wood Turning Measuring Tools

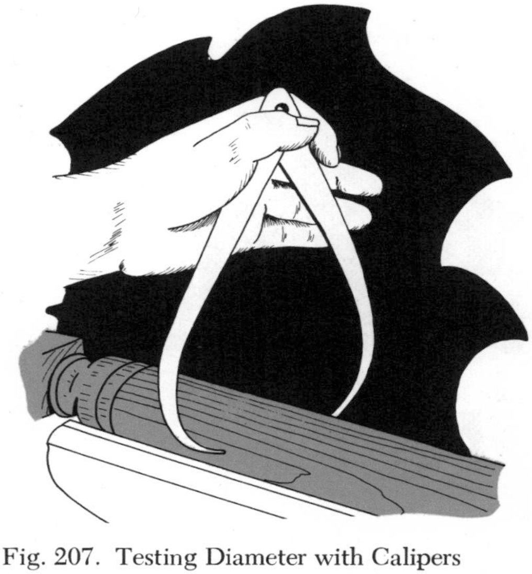

Fig. 207. Testing Diameter with Calipers

The *rule* is used in taking measurements in spindle and faceplate turning. The *dividers* are used in laying out circles and in stepping off measurements. The *outside calipers* are used in measuring the outside diameter of turned stock. The *inside calipers* are used in measuring the inside diameters of projects that are usually turned on the faceplate such as bowls, boxes, and picture frames.

Safety Instructions

1. The wood turning lathe can in no way reach out to hurt you. Injury could happen only if you do not follow safety instructions or if you are careless.
2. Get permission from your instructor before working at the lathe.
3. Do not wear loose clothing, necktie, or long sleeves when turning.
4. Keep the floor around the lathe free of scraps and shavings.
5. Don't talk to anyone or look around when working at the lathe. Give the lathe all your attention.
6. Do not try to adjust any part of the lathe while it is in motion.
7. Wear goggles for eye protection from dust and chips.
8. Tools must be sharp at all times. There is danger in working with dull tools.
9. Arrange your tools so they are readily accessible.
10. Adjust the rest so it is a little above the center of the stock.
11. Make sure the tool rest is smooth.
12. Do not stand in line with the stock in the lathe when turning on the power.
13. Make sure that the stock being turned is free of checks, knots, and splinters.
14. Revolve the stock by hand before turning on the power.
15. Make adjustments and take measurements when the lathe is not running.
16. Use only the hand wheel to stop the lathe or let the lathe stop without your help.
17. Place a leather washer on the live spindle before attaching the faceplate to the spindle. The washer will prevent the faceplate from locking with the spindle.
18. Faceplate turning on stock of large diameter requires slow speeds.
19. Be sure the stock is perfectly flat before fastening the faceplate to it.
20. Never screw a faceplate part way onto the spindle and then start the motor. A locked faceplate may be the result.
21. Hold wood turning chisels firmly in both hands when turning.
22. Remove the tool rest to do sanding and finishing on faceplate work.

Spindle Turning

Wood turning that is done between lathe centers (the live center and the dead center) is called spindle turning.

Centering and Mounting Stock

1. Any stock to be spindle turned should be square, and both ends should be square with the sides.
2. Suppose you start turning on a practice piece of white pine 1½″ x 1½″ x 10″.
3. Center the ends of the stock as in Fig. 208. With the combination square, mark a distance of less than half the width

Fig. 208. Locating Center with Combination Square

of the stock from each side. The true center will be in the middle of the small square.

4. You may use another method. Draw diagonal lines from corner to corner making the intersection of lines the center point.
5. After the ends have been marked, the centers should be clearly indented with a punch or dividers as in Fig. 209.
6. When turning hardwood, drill a small pilot hole about ⅛″ deep.

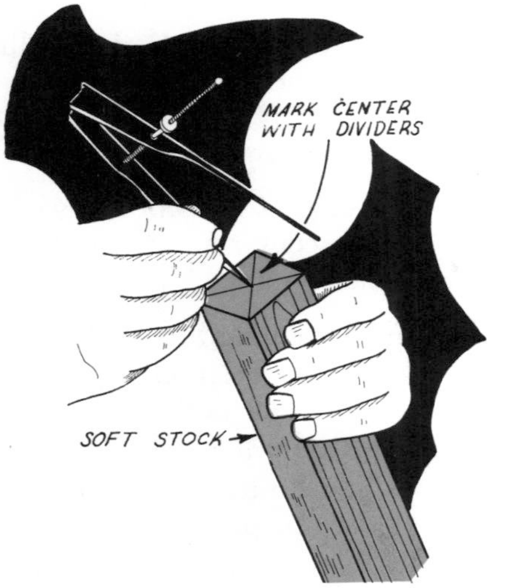

Fig. 209. Locating Center with Diagonal Lines

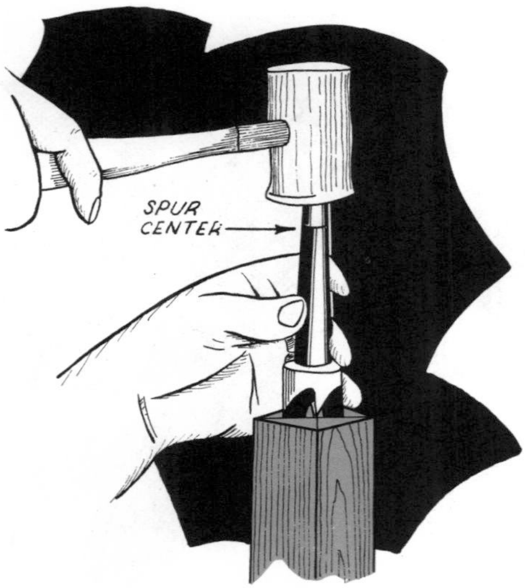

Fig. 210. Setting Spur Center with Mallet

7. With a back saw, make diagonal kerfs on one end of the stock to receive the live center prongs of the spur center shown in *A*, Fig. 195.
8. Remove the live center from the headstock spindle with the drive rod.
9. Set the prongs and center point of the live center into one end of the stock with a mallet as in Fig. 210.
10. Fit the stock in position on the lathe by first inserting the end with the live center in the headstock. Fasten the tailstock in position about 1½″ from the other end of the stock.
11. Fit the other end to the dead center by turning up the feed handle and tighten it.
12. Oil the dead center by placing oil on it after fitting the stock between centers.
13. Try to turn the stock by hand. If the stock is tight and difficult to turn by hand, turn the feed handle slightly back so the stock will turn easier. See that there is clearance between the stock and the tool rest.
14. Adjust the tool rest ⅛″ above the center of the stock and about ⅛″ away from the stock, Fig. 211.

Roughing a Cylinder

1. Start the lathe at low speed and let it run a few seconds so the wood fits the dead center.

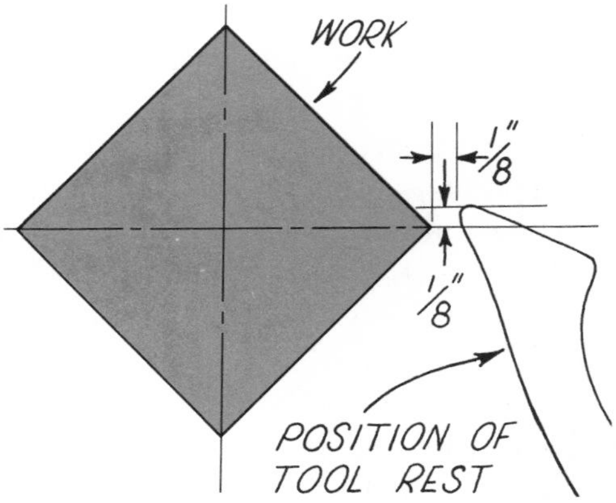

Fig. 211. Position of Tool Rest

2. The large gouge is used in roughing. Hold the gouge firmly in both hands with the right hand grasping the handle. The left hand should be holding the blade and at the same time touching the tool rest as shown in Fig. 212.
3. Start the cut about 2″ from the right end of the stock and work toward the end as shown in Fig. 212. Take just a little cut at first by making contact with the stock a little at a time.
4. As your left hand holds the blade firmly, it also controls the depth of cut as it slides along the tool rest.
5. Take the next cut about 3″ to the left of the first cut and work it to the right, Fig. 212.
6. Continue with a third and fourth cut until you have removed the stock to about 2″ from the live center.
7. At this point, turn the gouge in the opposite direction and make the final roughing cut toward the end.
8. Stop the lathe and readjust the tool rest as necessary to keep the tool rest ⅛″ from the stock.
9. Continue the roughing cuts until the cylinder is about ⅛″ larger in diameter than the desired dimension. In general, when turning, cut from the center towards the ends.
10. With the outside caliper, test from time to time for diameter measurement. See Fig. 207.
11. When the stock has been roughed to a cylinder, you are ready to smooth it with the skew chisel.

Smoothing with a Skew Chisel

Smoothing with the skew chisel is done after roughing with the gouge. There are two ways to smooth stock with a skew chisel. The simplest way is to scrape and it takes very little practice. The more difficult method is to cut instead of scrape. Cutting requires practice and is the method used by experienced wood turners.

Many wood workers use the scraping method especially if they only do occasional turning. Scraping is done by carefully holding the cutting edge against the cylinder and pressing lightly, thus removing a little stock at a time. Those who scrape say that it is accurate and the stock is sanded anyway so one cannot tell whether the piece was cut or scraped when it is finished.

There is satisfaction in learning the skill of the artisan wood turner and instruction is therefore provided. The skew chisel can be used not only in smoothing a cylinder but also in cutting beads, v-grooves, long tapers and square shoulders.

1. Before trying to cut with the skew chisel, practice laying the chisel flat on the wood cylinder as in Figs. 213 and 214.
2. Practice pushing the chisel forward at the same time taking a shearing cut as in cutting with a jack knife. Get the feel of the skew in relation to the stock before turning on the lathe.
3. Start the lathe and place the skew chisel on the stock starting 2″ from the live center. Hold the side of the chisel firmly against the tool rest. See Fig. 214.

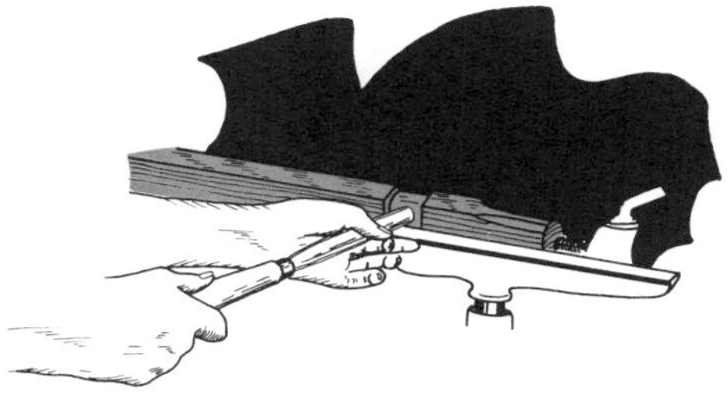

Fig. 212. Reducing Stock to Cylinder

Fig. 213. Practice Cutting with Skew Chisel

4. With the lathe in motion, push the chisel forward. Take a thin shaving. To increase the depth of the cut, raise the handle.
5. Cut with the center portion of the skew chisel. Lowering the handle will decrease the depth of the cut.
6. The skew chisel must be razor sharp in order to do a good job of cutting.
7. Practice cutting with the skew, even if it means spoiling a few practice pieces.

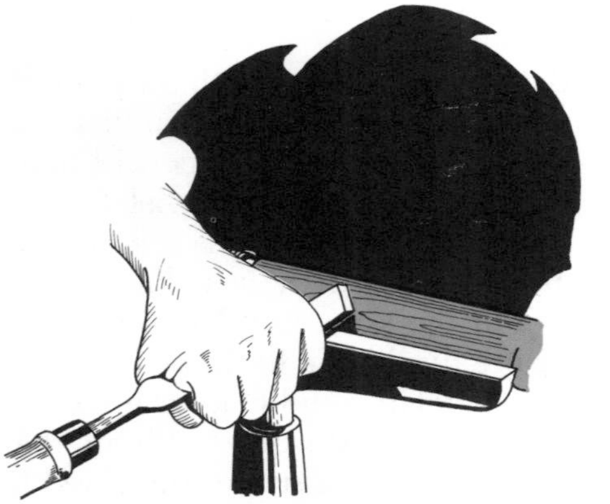

Fig. 214. Hold Chisel Firmly Against Tool Rest

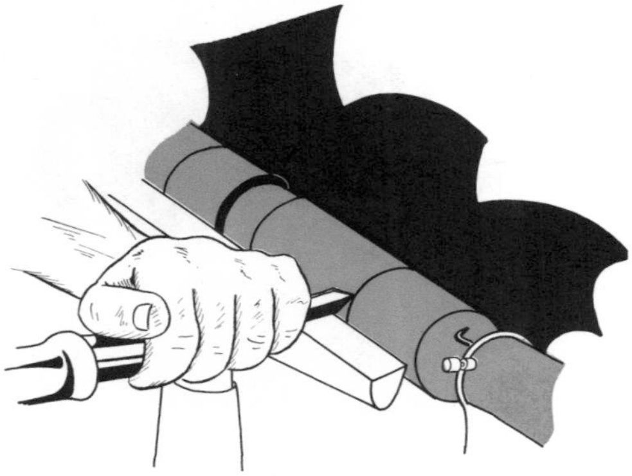

Fig. 215. Cutting with the Parting Tool

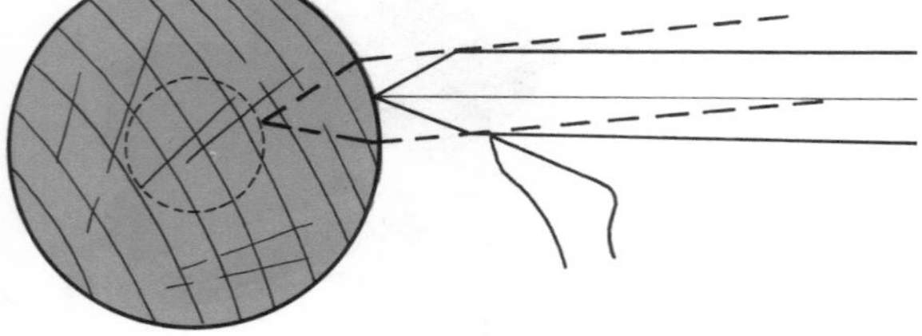

Fig. 216. Use of Parting Tool

Cutting Ends and Grooves

The parting tool is primarily a scraping chisel. It is used in cutting ends, and cutting grooves for setting depth of cut for a given diameter. See Fig. 215.

1. The parting tool is pushed into the stock as shown in Figs. 216 and 217 and therefore must be sharp at all times.
2. If one chooses to scrape, the parting tool is very useful and easy to use on other turning operations.

Squaring Ends

1. The end may first be scraped with the cutting tool and then finished with the skew.
2. The first step in squaring an end is to make an inclined nick cut with the toe of the skew chisel as shown in Fig. 218.
3. Direct the toe or point of the chisel toward the center of the stock, Fig. 219.
4. When cutting, hold the tool slightly away from the end surface, Fig. 220.

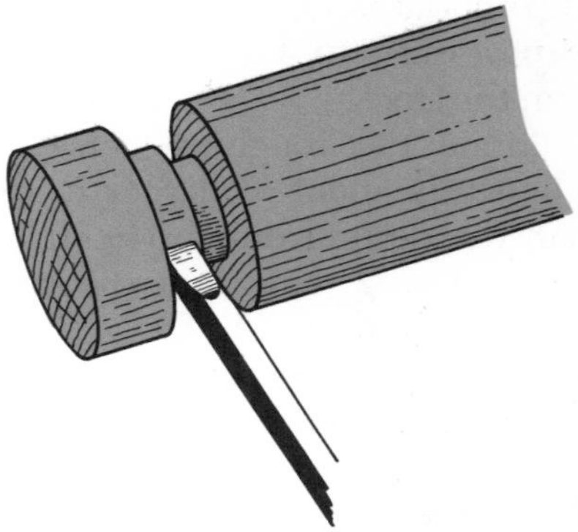

Fig. 217. Clearance Cut Necessary on Deep Cuts

Fig. 218. First Cut in Squaring End

Cutting Beads and Vees

1. Beads can be cut or scraped. In cutting beads, make a vertical light V-cut with the toe of the skew chisel at a point where the curved parts will come together. See Fig. 221.
2. Start the round part by placing the skew at a right angle with the cylinder as shown in Fig. 222.
3. Starting with the chisel flat, rotate the skew toward the heel in a series of steps shown in Figs. 222, 223, 224, and 225, cutting with the heel of the skew.
4. The cutting of beads with a skew takes practice, but the results obtained are well worth the effort.

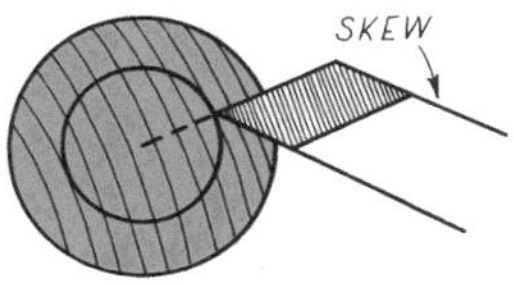

Fig. 219. Keep Chisel Directed Toward Center

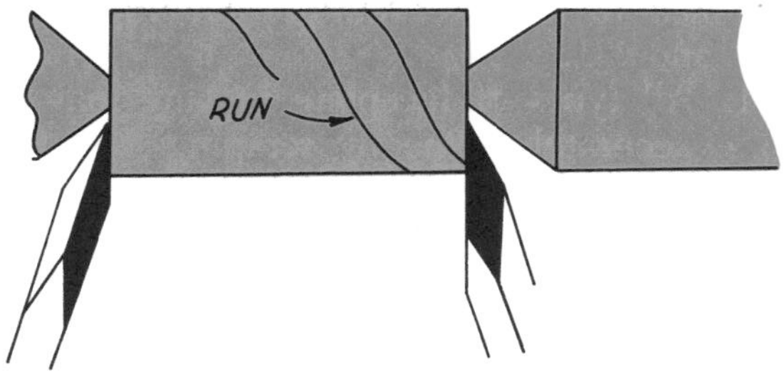

Fig. 220. Position of Cutting Edge in Squaring End

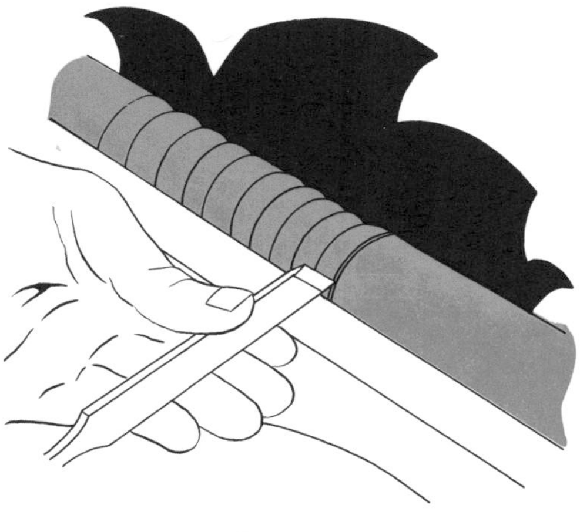

Fig. 221. Cutting Beads

Fig. 222. Beginning Position in Cutting Beads

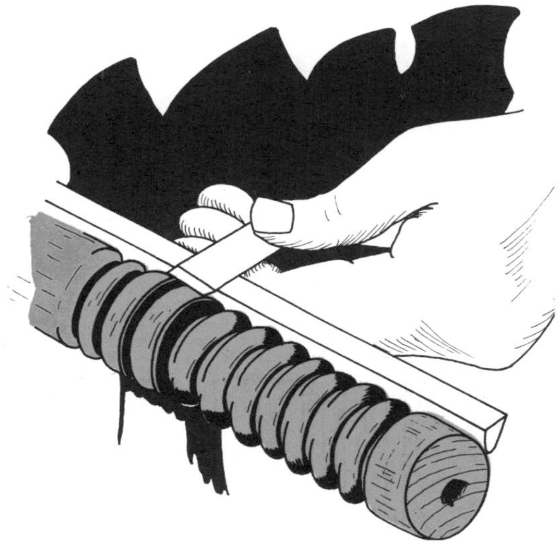

Fig. 223. Rotate Skew Toward Heel

Fig. 224. Top View of Skew Cutting

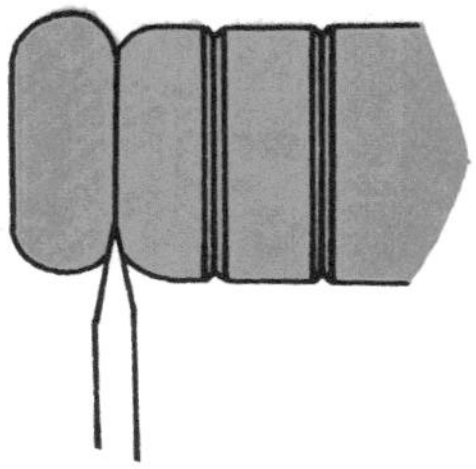

Fig. 225. Completing the Bead

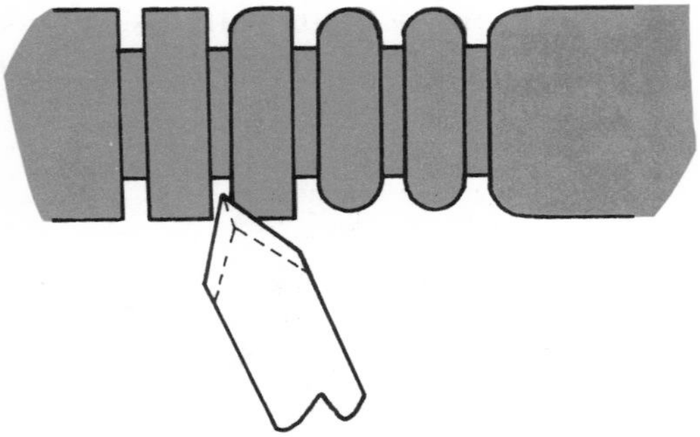

Fig. 226. Scraping Method of Forming Beads

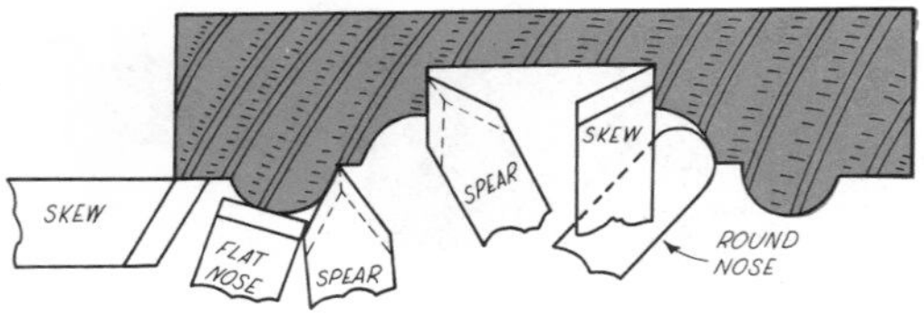

Fig. 227. Scraping Cuts in Faceplate Turning

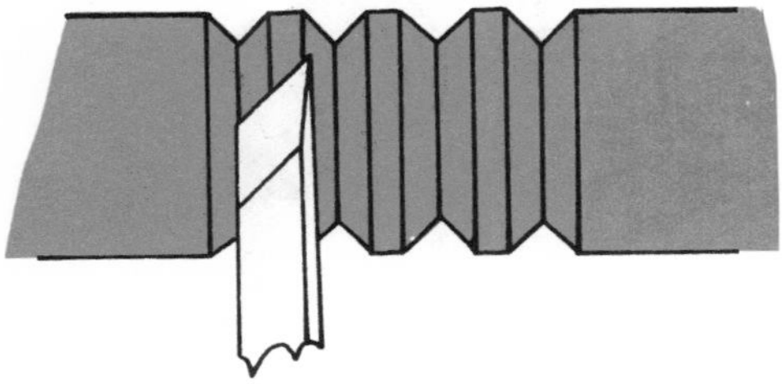

Fig. 228. Cutting Vees with Skew Chisel

5. You may scrape beads or round edges with the spear point and the flat-nose scraping tools. See Figs. 226 and 227. This is quite easy and requires little instruction.

Making V Grooves

1. Push the heel of the skew chisel into the wood without rotating it as shown in Fig. 228.
2. Make one-half of the vee at a time taking two or more cuts to obtain the right shape.
3. The spear point, Fig. 227, may be used to scrape a V-groove.

Faceplate Turning

If the stock cannot be turned between centers as in turning a cylinder, it must be turned on a faceplate. In faceplate turning the stock is fastened to a faceplate, a screw chuck, or a holding chuck which is in turn fastened to the live spindle. See Figs. 229, 230, and 231.

1. All types of faceplate turning may be accurately done by scraping. See Fig. 227.
2. Bowls, plates and bases are examples of projects that are turned by this method.

Fastening Stock to Faceplate

1. Select a piece of stock with a flat surface and make a circle on it of the desired size.

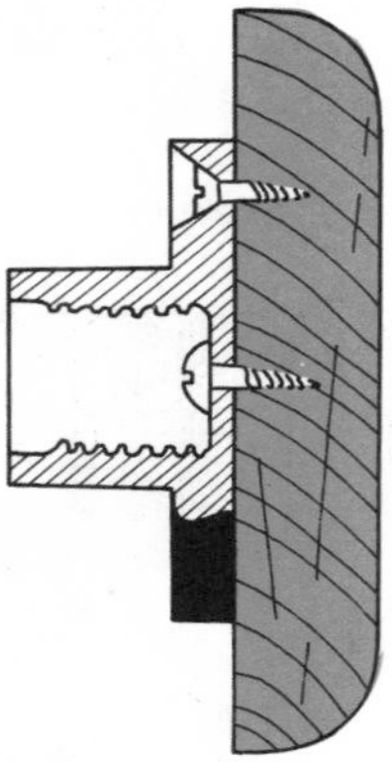

Fig. 229. Stock Mounted with Screws

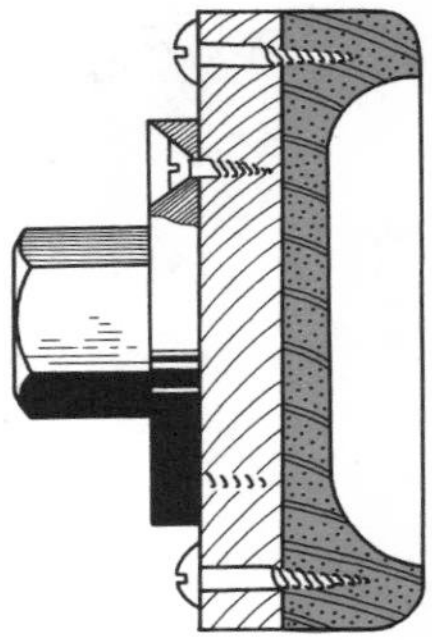

Fig. 230. Stock Mounted with Backing Block

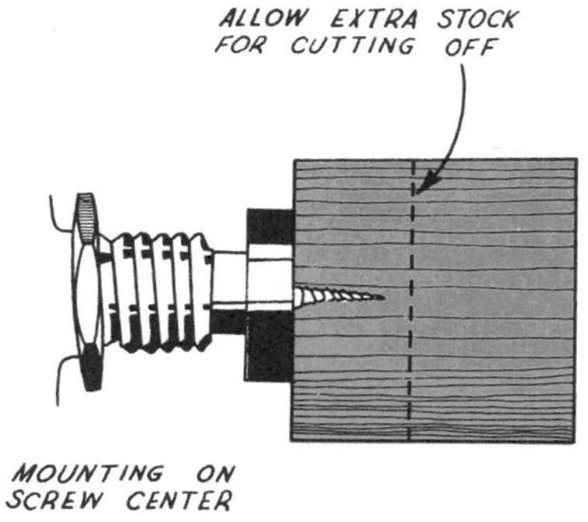

Fig. 231. Stock Mounted on Screw Center

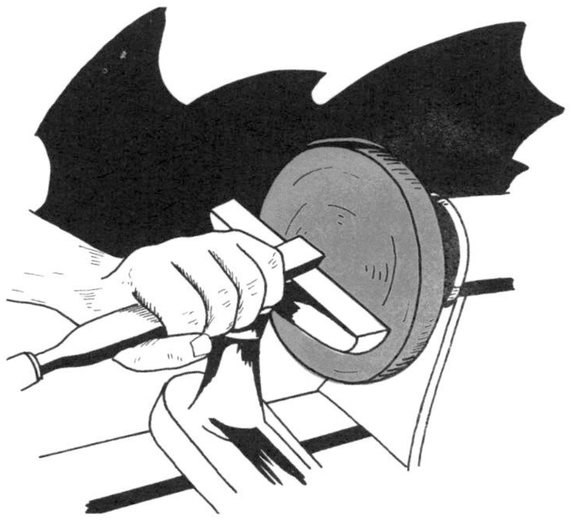

Fig. 232. Smoothing Face of Disk With Squarenose Chisel

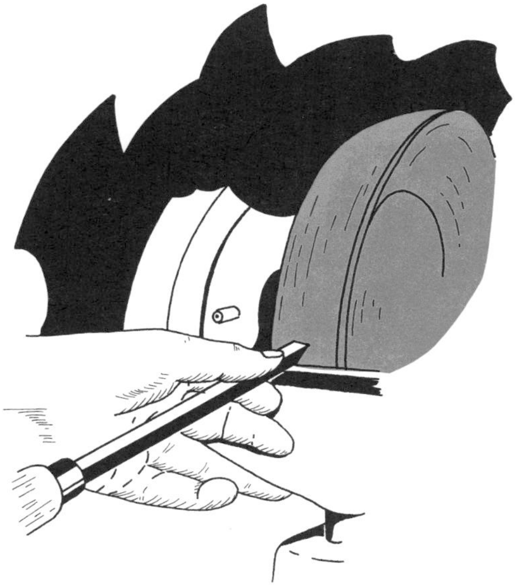

Fig. 233. Rounding Edge of Stock

2. Cut the stock a little larger than the marked circle with the band saw, jig saw, or hand saw.
3. Center the faceplate on the stock and fasten it with ¾″ flat head screws. See Fig. 229. If the screws may interfere in cutting, use a backing block as in Fig. 230. A simple and effective method of fastening a backing block is to glue paper between the pieces, applying the glue to both sides of the paper.
4. Fasten the faceplate to the spindle of the headstock.

Turning Procedure

1. Place the tool rest about ⅛″ away from the stock and turn the faceplate by hand to make sure of the clearance.
2. Start the lathe at low speed and shape the stock with the gouge.
3. Smooth the surface of the stock with a squarenose chisel. Fig. 232. This is known as facing-off, or making the surface flat and even.
4. If you choose to turn a bowl or a project that requires outside turning, turn the outside part of the stock with a roundnose chisel as shown in Fig. 233.
5. Turn the inside with the parting tool and the roundnose chisel, Fig. 234.
6. In turning the inside part of a bowl or a similar project, the stock is usually fastened to a holding chuck as shown in Fig. 235.

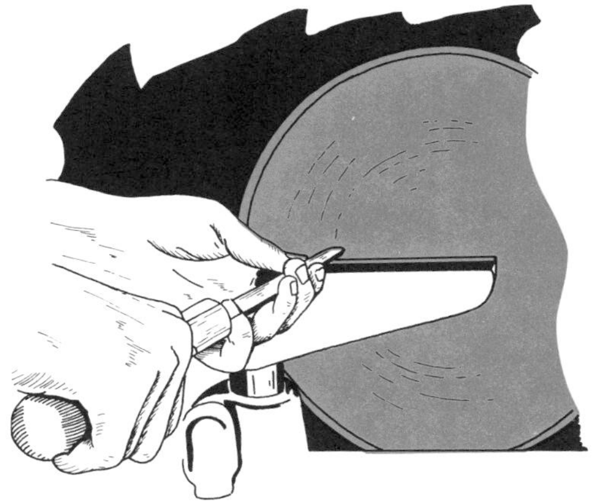

Fig. 234. Turning Bowl with Roundnose Chisel

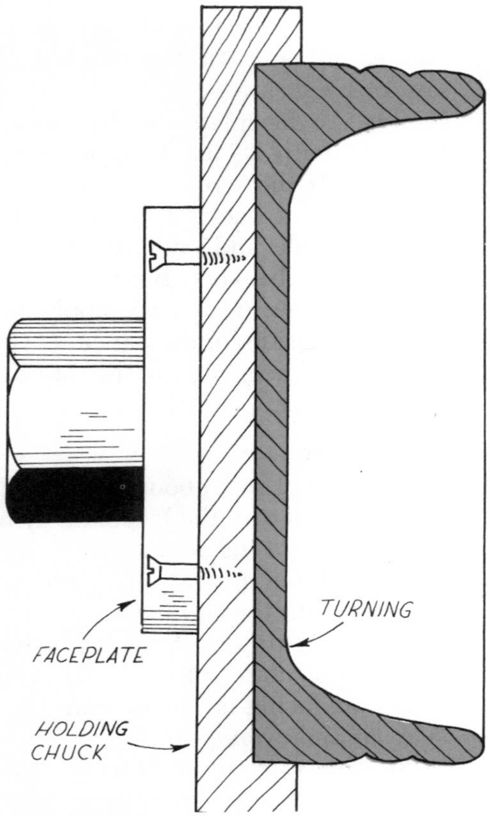

Fig. 235. Chucking Partially Turned Piece

Questions

1. Give five safety rules for the wood turning lathe.
2. Why be careful about the clothing you wear when operating a lathe?
3. The live center is attached to what part of the lathe?
4. Name four important parts of a lathe.
5. How close to the stock should the tool rest be secured?
6. Is it always necessary to lubricate the dead center and center point?
7. What determines the size of a wood turning lathe?
8. Why use sharp tools at all times?
9. Name four necessary lathe accessories.
10. Name five essential chisels used in wood turning.
11. Should you try to adjust any parts of the lathe while it is in motion?
12. Name two important operations performed with the skew chisel.
13. What are some of the measuring tools used in wood turning?
14. What kind of chisels are used in faceplate turning?
15. What is a holding chuck?

SECTION

Six

Cutting Holes

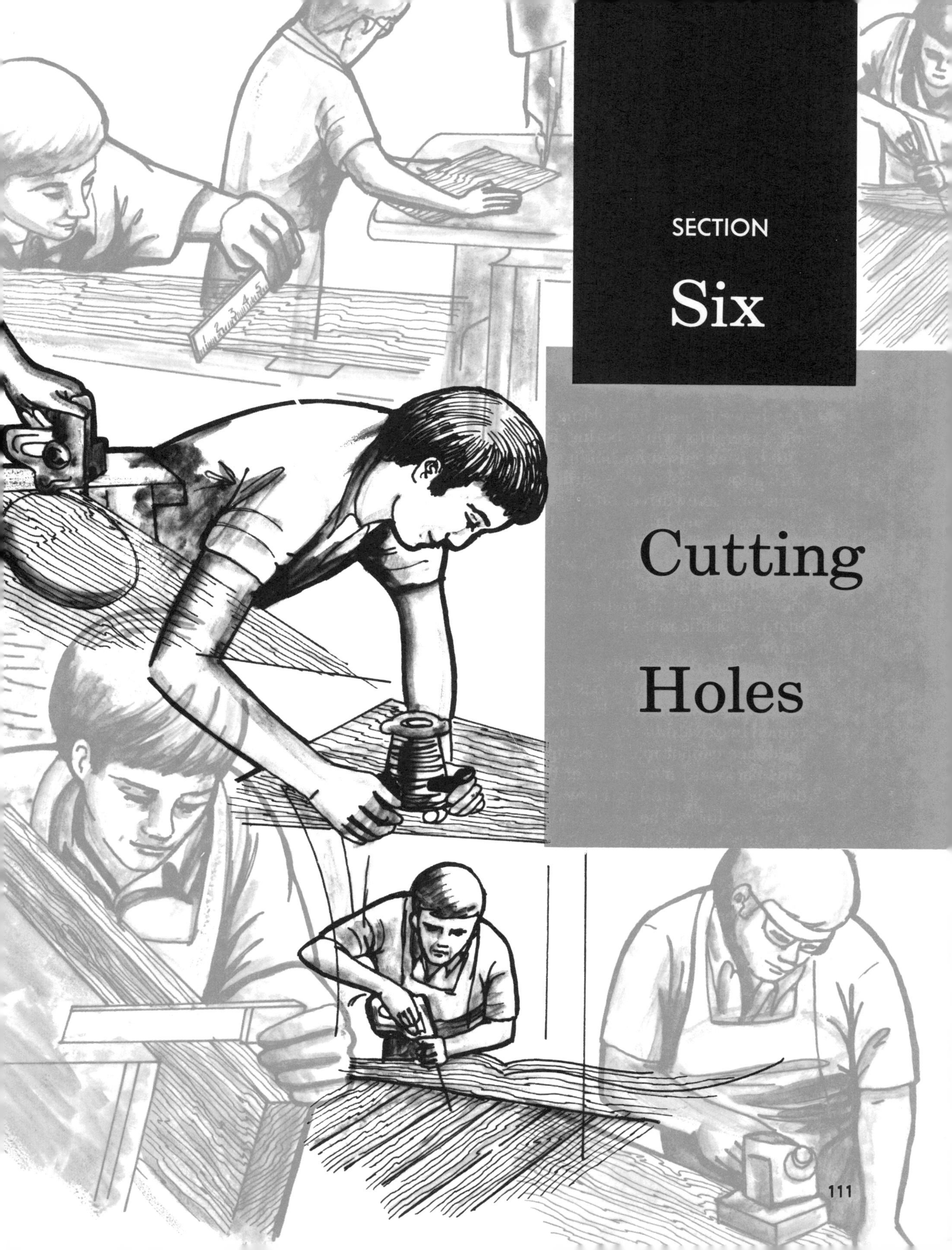

UNIT 36

Boring Holes

It will frequently be necessary to bore holes with a brace and bit. It is important that the hole be bored straight and that the bit does not splinter the wood on the opposite side.

The Brace

1. The brace is used for holding and turning auger bits while boring holes, Fig. 236. It is also used for holding and turning various other tools — drills, countersinks, and screwdriver bits.
2. The size of any brace is indicated by its *sweep* or *swing*, that is, the diameter of the circle that the handle makes while in motion, Fig. 236. A ten-inch sweep means that the diameter of the circle that the handle makes while in motion is ten inches.
3. The ratchet brace differs from the ordinary brace in that it has a device by means of which the handle may be turned backward in narrow spaces where the brace cannot make a complete turn. This backward movement of the handle does not move the bit. Forward motion, however, forces the bit ahead. There is a device on every ratchet brace for adjustment for this action, Fig. 236.

The Auger Bit

1. The auger bit is used in woodworking, Figs. 239, 240, and 241.
2. The shank of an auger bit may be either round or square depending on the brace used. The square shank is most common, Fig. 244.
3. Auger bits are sold singly or in sets of thirteen ranging from one-fourth of an inch to one inch in size.
4. Auger bits have a number stamped on the shank or on the tank. This indicates their sizes in sixteenths. A bit with the figure eleven stamped on it will bore a hole $1\frac{1}{16}''$ in diameter. It is a No. 11 bit. A bit with the figure eight on the shank is a half-inch bit and will bore a half-inch hole.
5. The screw point is the part of the bit

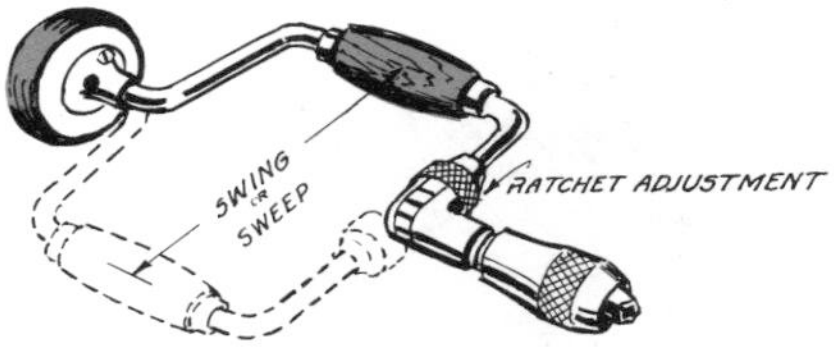

Fig. 236. Brace

Fig. 237. Bore Until the Point Shows on Other Side as at *A*, then Bore From the Other Side as at *B*

that touches the wood first. It draws the bit into the wood, *A* in Fig. 237.

6. The two spurs touch the wood just before the screw point reaches its full depth. They cut the outer edge or the circumference of the chip before the chip is lifted by the cutter.
7. Next come the cutting lips of the bit. These follow the spurs into the wood and cut the chips, starting them outward.
8. The throat of a bit is located just above the cutting lips. From the throat the chips go along the "twist" and then out to the surface.

Filing an Auger Bit

1. Before starting to use an auger bit, make sure that it is sharp.

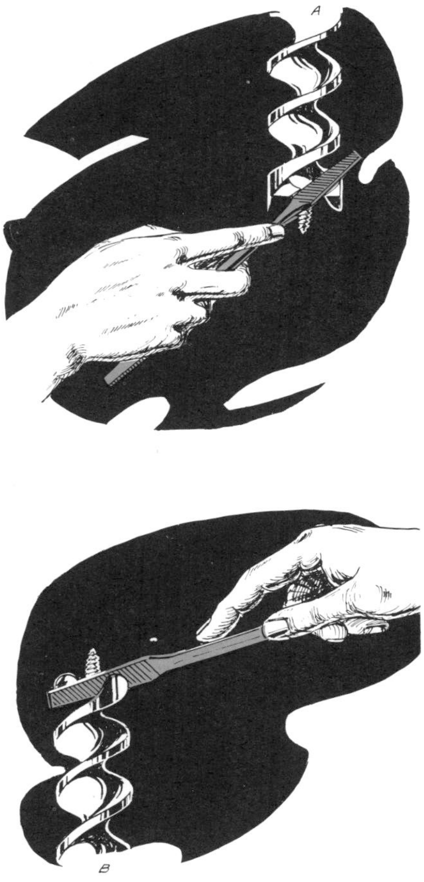

Fig. 238. *A* – File the Lips on the Upper Side
B – File the Spurs on the Inside First

2. An auger bit should be sharpened with a special file as shown in Fig. 238.
3. Do not attempt to file a bit unless you have received the proper instructions for doing it.
4. A bit file is shaped like a double-end canoe paddle. The ends only can be used for filing. The edges of one end are smooth, but the sides have teeth for filing. The edges of the other end have teeth for filing, but the sides are smooth.
5. File the spurs of the bit on the inside first as shown at *B*, Fig. 238.
6. File the lips on the upper side as shown at *A*, Fig. 238.

Horizontal Boring

1. Most boring is done horizontally. Fasten the bit in the brace by opening the jaws wide enough to receive the shank. This is done by holding the chuck firm while turning the handle to the left. Then tighten the jaws about the bit by turning the handle to the right.
2. Locate with two intersecting lines the exact position of the hole to be bored. Center-punch this position with a nail or scratch awl.
3. With the bit on the mark, start to bore by holding the knob with the left hand against the chest or stomach. This helps you give proper direction to the bit, Fig. 239.
4. To bore straight, you should sight a

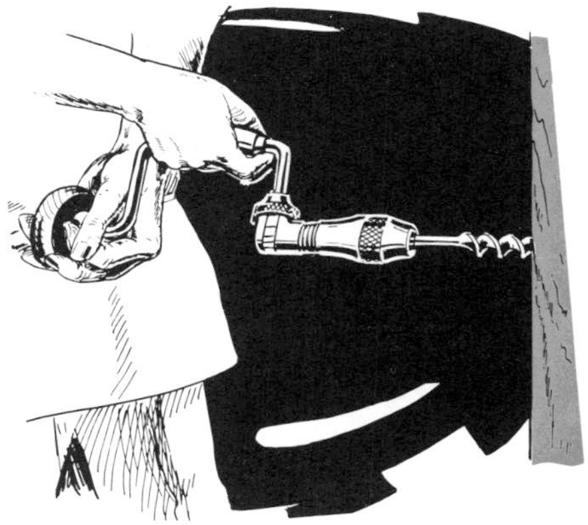

Fig. 239. Horizontal Boring

few times at the start and then after the hole is well started. Someone could help to check for accuracy while you are boring. For a guide, place a bench rule flat on the top surface.

5. Turn the handle and at the same time apply very little inward pressure on the knob. The bit draws itself inward.
6. Bore until the point reaches the bottom of the hole. Turn the brace slowly, watching or feeling for the point as in *A*, Fig. 237. As soon as it comes through, stop.
7. Reverse stock and bore through from the other side, *B*, Fig. 237, and the result is a clean straight hole.

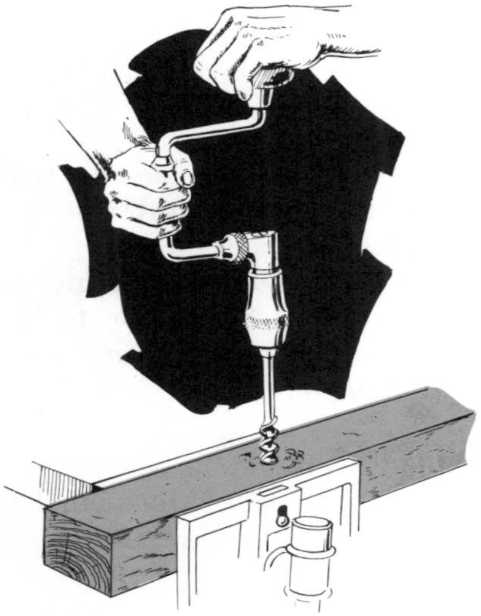

Fig. 240. Vertical Boring

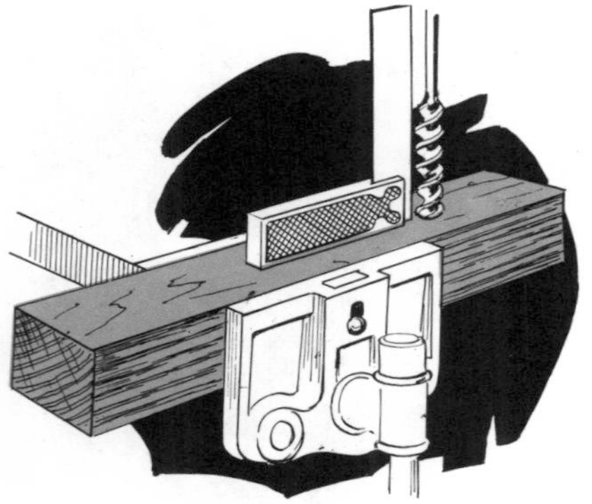

Fig. 241. Using Try Square as a Guide in Vertical Boring

8. Be careful not to put pressure on the bit when it is almost through, or the wood will split on the opposite side as shown at *C*, Fig. 237.
9. Should it be necessary to bore the hole from one side only, clamp a scrap of wood to the back of the stock to prevent splitting when the bit goes through.

Vertical Boring

1. Vertical boring is usually done on square stock when the hole is not to go through. In vertical boring the brace may be held steady by holding the handle as shown in Fig. 240.
2. While boring, change the position of the body several times in order to sight the bit from different directions.
3. If necessary, place a try square in position on the stock near the bit to guide you in boring straight, Fig. 241.

Boring to a Given Depth

1. One method of boring to a desired depth is to turn the brace until the lips are just about to cut the wood. Measure with a rule the distance from the chuck of the brace to the surface of the wood.

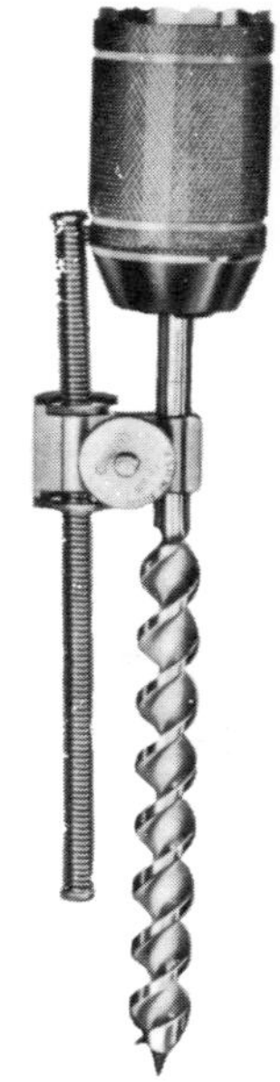

Fig. 242. Depth Gauge (Stanley)

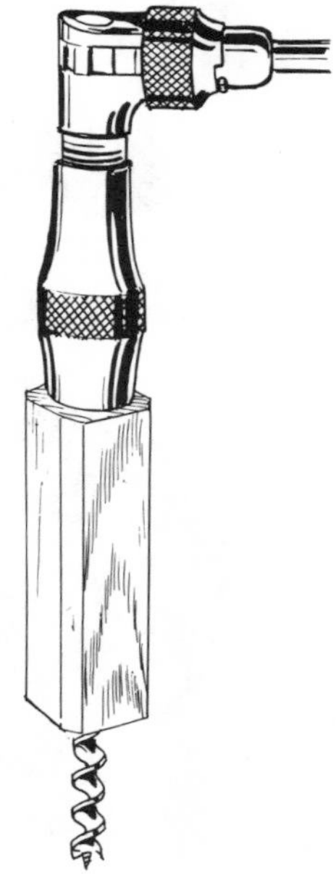

Fig. 243. Block Used for Depth Gauge

2. Turn the brace until the required depth is reached by checking the rule measurement.
3. A second method of boring to a desired depth is to use a depth gauge. Such a gauge may be used when several holes are desired the same depth. In Fig. 242 is shown an adjustable depth gauge that can be used on auger bits of various diameters.
4. You can easily make your own gauge by using a piece of wood with a hole bored lengthwise through the center as shown in Fig. 243.

Boring Large Holes

The *expansive bit,* Fig. 245, is a useful tool for boring large holes. It has a screw point, spurs, and lips like the auger bit. It is manufactured with various size cutters to bore holes from ½″ to 4″ in diameter.

1. The expansive bit has a special movable spur or cutter with gears cut on one edge. This edge fits into the threads of the adjusting screw.
2. To adjust the expansive bit for a desired size, loosen the clamp screw which holds the cutter tightly in place.
3. Slide the cutter along until the desired line on the scale corresponds with the center mark on the clamp. Each division on the scale represents $\frac{1}{16}$″.
4. When correct setting has been reached, tighten the clamp screw to hold the bit firmly in place.
5. Test the bit by boring in a piece of waste stock. Bore in the same manner as with an auger bit, from one side of the wood only, because the center of the hole is cut away before the outside of the hole.
6. Clamp a piece of waste wood to the back of the stock to prevent splitting.

Special Boring

The *forstner bit,* Fig. 246, can be used to do boring operations that cannot be done with the auger bit. It has no screw point, but is centered by a sharp edge around a circular rim. A hole can be bored to any depth without

Fig. 244. Square Shank Bit

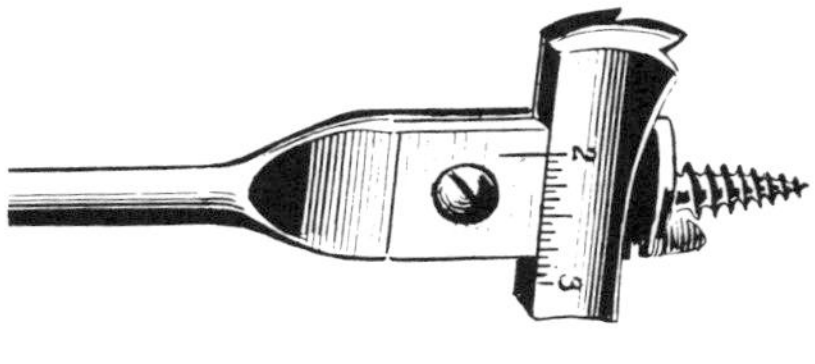

Fig. 245. Expansive Bit has Movable Cutter

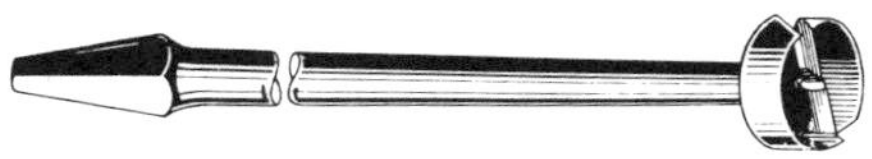

Fig. 246. Forstner Bit

breaking through. The forstner bit will bore a hole into the wood at almost any angle. Large holes can be bored over small holes if desired. The forstner bit will bore holes without splitting the wood. Holes of irregular shape can be made by using various sizes of forstner bits. These bits are made in sizes ranging from ¼″ to 2″, and are numbered in sixteenths, the same as auger bits.

1. Mark a circle with a pair of dividers the size of the hole desired. Center the bit carefully on the line provided.
2. Boring from one side of the stock only gives best results.
3. A piece of waste stock should be clamped to the back of the board to prevent splitting.
4. A depth gauge, Figs. 242 and 243, can be used with the forstner bit when holes must be a specified depth.

Questions

1. How are sizes of braces estimated?
2. What is meant by the words "sweep" or "swing"?
3. How do bits range in size? How are sizes indicated?
4. What tools besides the bit can be used in a brace?
5. What is a depth gauge? Tell how to make a simple one.
6. What do you mean by vertical and horizontal boring?

UNIT 37 Drilling Holes

Often small holes need to be drilled for screws, nails, and bolts. Holes less than ¼″ in diameter are usually *drilled* with a hand drill or automatic drill. Both of these drills hold the drills or bits by means of a chuck. Such drills give greater speed for drilling than the brace. The hand drill is also helpful for coil winding in radio and electricity and for twisting bow strings.

Wood Boring Drills and Twist Drills

1. Drill bits can be purchased with either the round or the square shank, Fig. 248.
2. The square shank bit is used in a brace, while the round shank is adapted to the hand drill and automatic drill, Figs. 247 and 249.
3. Round and square shank bits for drilling metal or wood may be purchased in sizes which increase by 64ths of an inch. The size of a bit is usually marked on the shank.
4. Round shank bits can also be purchased in sizes indicated by numbers ranging from 60 to 1. The number indicates the wire gauge of the drill – the *larger the number,* the *smaller the drill.*
5. Unlike the auger bit, the twist drill has neither screw point nor spurs. Light pressure is needed to force it into the wood.
6. Twist drills can be sharpened on a grinder.

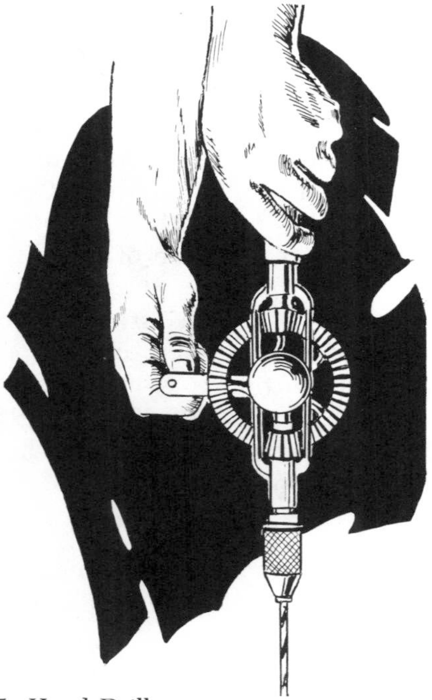

Fig. 247. Hand Drill

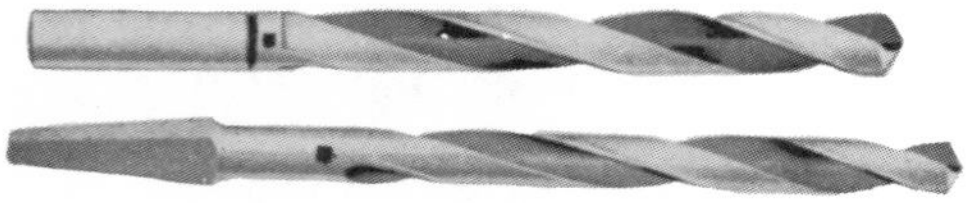

Fig. 248. Square Shank and Round Shank Drills

Drilling

1. It is easy to drill with a hand drill or an automatic drill. Sight for direction and be sure to hold the hand drill steady and press lightly on the handle while turning the crank, Fig. 247. When releasing pressure on the automatic drill,

Fig. 249. Automatic Drill, Often Called Push Drill (Stanley)

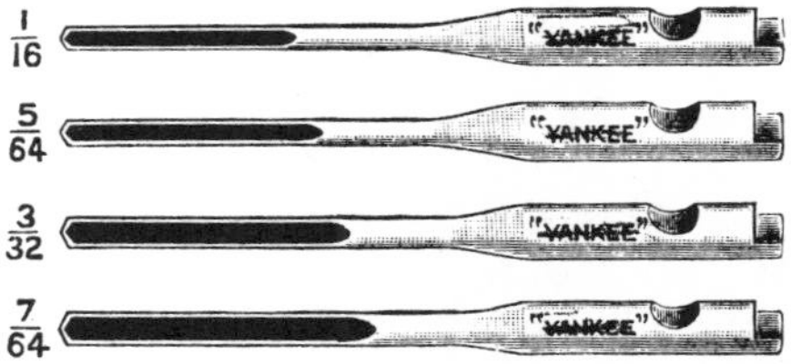

Fig. 250. Drill Bits Increase in Size by 1/64 Inch

you should be careful not to pull the hand so far back that the drill will be withdrawn.

Questions

1. How are holes less than ¼″ in diameter usually drilled?
2. Does a hand drill or an automatic drill require pressure?
3. When fastening with screws, is it necessary to drill holes for them?
4. Why should care be exercised in releasing pressure on the automatic drill?
5. How do you sharpen a twist drill?

The Drill Press

UNIT 38

The drill press has many uses and is a very important machine. Metal, as well as wood, can be worked on the drill press. The common woodworking operations that are performed are boring, shaping, routing, sanding and mortising. Drill presses can be obtained in a number of sizes and designs. In Fig. 251 is shown an often used type of drill press.

General Description

The drill press consists of four main parts: (1) the head, (2) the column, (3) the table, and (4) the base. See Fig. 251. The main part of the head is the spindle which turns in a vertical position. It is enclosed in ball bearings at both ends of a part called the quill. The quill and spindle are operated downward by the feed lever.

The column is a polished steel shaft which is fastened to a sturdy iron base. The table can be moved up, down, tilted, or swung to one side.

Speed and Power

There are cone pulleys on a drill press so that several speeds can be obtained. The common speeds for drill presses in woodworking are 680, 1250, 2400, and 4600 revolutions per minute. A drill press is identified by its size, which is determined by the largest circular stock that can be held on the table while boring through the center.

Spindles

Several kinds of spindles are available for most drill presses. The spindles make the machine useful in performing a variety of opera-

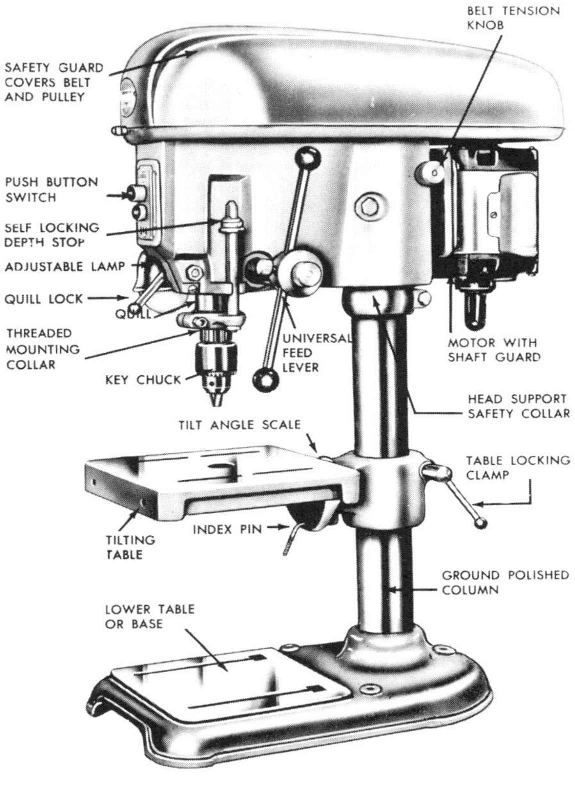

Fig. 251. Parts of a Drill Press

tions. The standard spindle is of ½-inch capacity with a chuck and key that will grip any one of several bits. See Fig. 252 for other spindles.

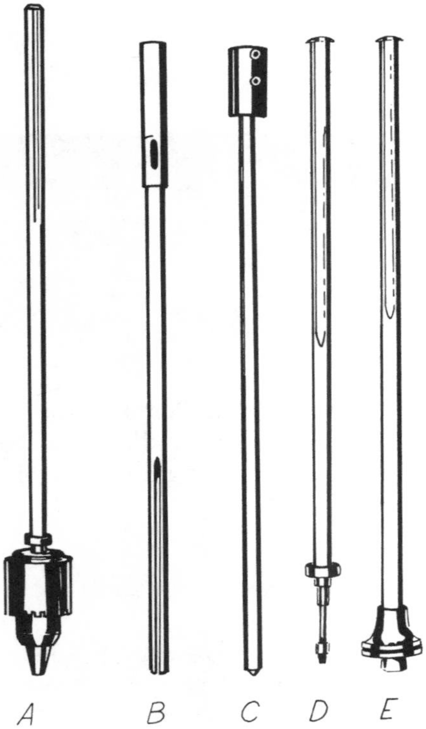

Fig. 252. Drill Press Spindles
A – Geared Chuck – ½″ Capacity
B – No. 1 Morse Taper
C – ½″ Hole
D – 5/16″ Threaded Spindle
E – ½″ Spindle with Flange

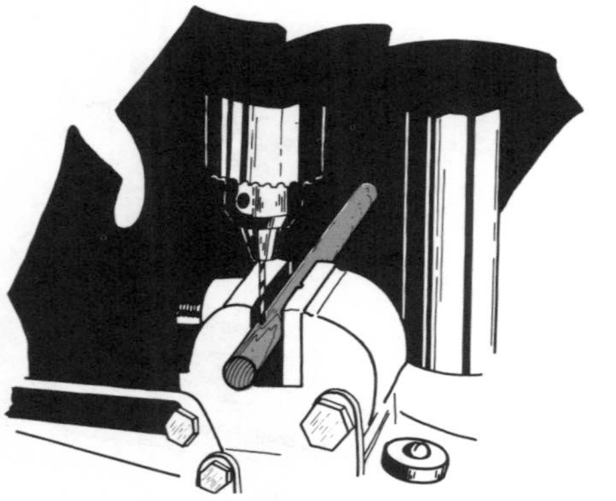

Fig. 253. Drill Press Vise

Attachments and Accessories

There are many attachments and accessories available for the drill press. Some of these are the foot feed, vise (Fig. 253), mortising bits and chisels (Figs. 254 and 255), sanding drums (Fig. 256), and the auxiliary wood table (Fig. 257). The wood table is necessary in doing shaping and routing operations, and in sanding.

Safety Instructions

1. As with all machines in the shops, the drill press is safe to use. It can in no

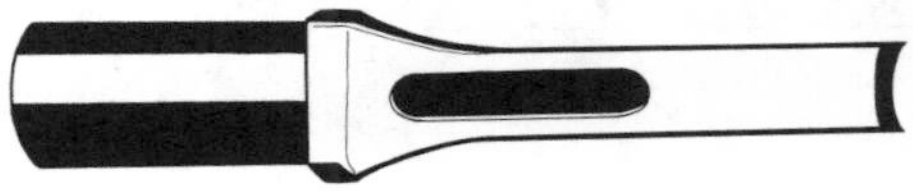

Fig. 254. Hollow Chisel for Mortising

Fig. 255. Hollow Chisel Bit

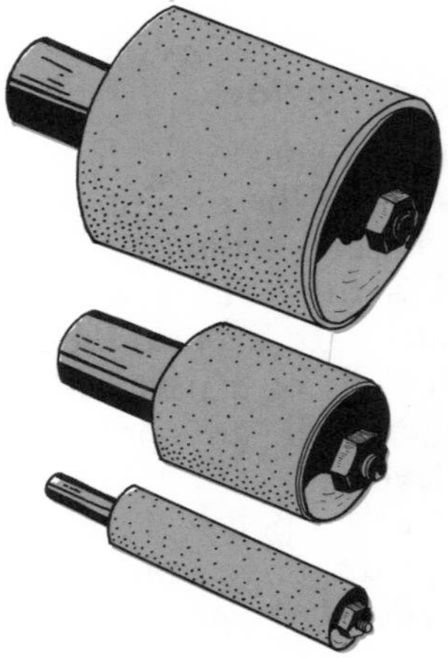

Fig. 256. Sanding Drums

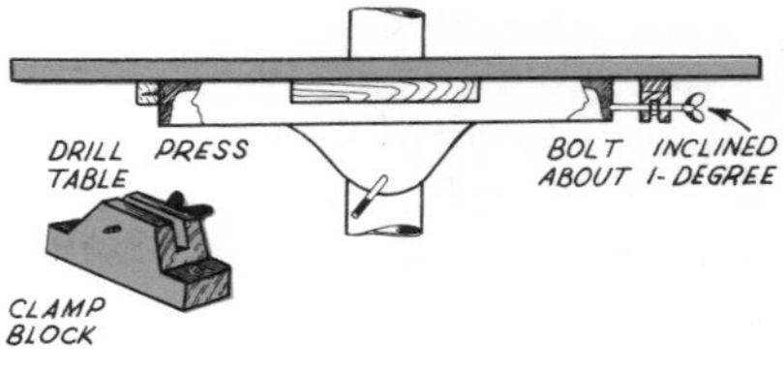

Fig. 257. Auxiliary Wood Table

way reach out to hurt you. Injury could happen only if you get your hand into the machine.

2. Get permission from your instructor before using the drill press.
3. Make sure that the chuck grips the bit tightly. Tighten it with the chuck key. Be sure that you remove the chuck key before starting the machine.
4. Do not wear loose clothing or a necktie while working at the drill press.
5. Do not talk to anyone nor permit anyone to talk to you while working. Stop the machine if you must talk.
6. Do not try to clean, adjust, or oil any part of the machine while it is running.
7. Make sure that the belt guard is in place.
8. Do not force a bit or a drill. Feed it carefully and slowly.
9. Do not attempt to hold small pieces by hand while boring. Hold small pieces securely in a vise. If the stock is too large for the vise, fasten it to the table with a clamp.
10. If the wood is hard and the hole is deep, reduce the speed of the machine.
11. Do not try to grab a piece of stock if caught by the drill bit. Quickly stand aside and turn off the power.
12. The operator is the only person allowed to start and stop the machine.
13. Hold the drill as you remove it from the chuck so it cannot fall and damage the bit.
14. Do not play in the shop or around machines. Always remember that machines do not know the difference between the stock you work on and human flesh.

Boring in Wood

The tools used to produce holes in wood are called bits. As a rule, you bore in wood but you drill in metal. In Fig. 258, the basic types of wood bits are shown.

Laying Out for Boring

1. Use the combination square for marking centerlines by holding the square in the left hand and the pencil in the right hand as shown in Fig. 259.

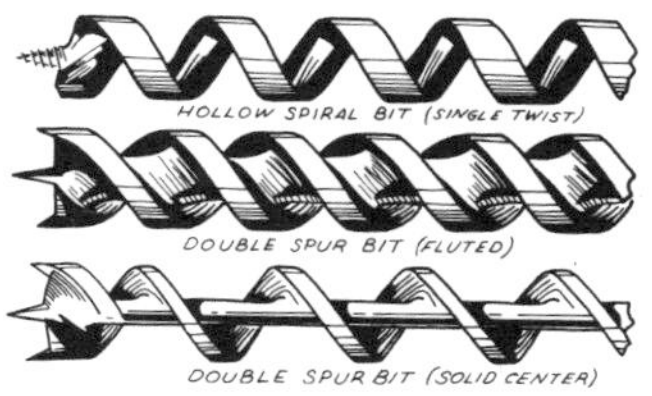

Fig. 258. Types of Wood Bits

Fig. 259. Marking Centerlines

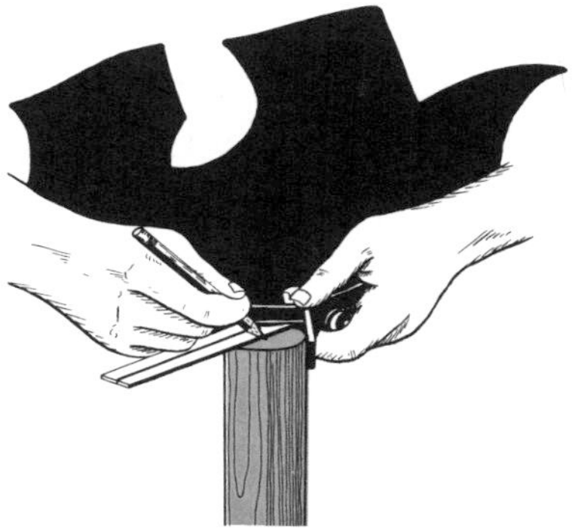

Fig. 260. Marking Center of Cylinder with Center Gauge

2. Use the combination square for centering the end of a cylinder as shown in Fig. 260.
3. The dividers may be used to set off the location of a series of holes equal distances apart. Fig 261.
4. The hermaphrodite calipers may be used to center a circle as in Fig. 262.
5. The combination square may be used to center stock on a circular end, Fig. 263.
6. Dowel holes must be center marked so the pieces to be fastened opposite each other come together exactly as desired. An accurate method of marking the

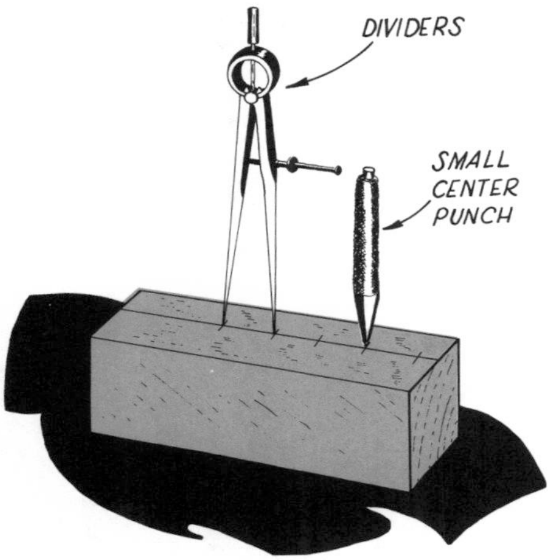

Fig. 261. Using Dividers to Locate Centers of Holes

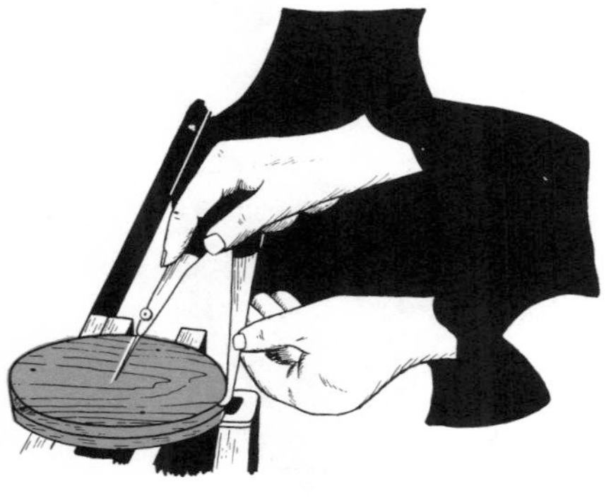

Fig. 262. Using Hermaphrodite Calipers to Find Center of Circle

Fig. 263. Using Combination Square to Locate Center

centers is to fasten two pins with heads in a block of wood as shown in Fig. 264. Press together the two pieces to be matched so the pin heads make dents, thus locating the centers for drilling the dowel holes.

7. There are other methods of matching dowel holes. A double pointed thumb tack may be used as in Fig. 264. A dowel pop may be used, but one hole must be bored first and the pieces are then pressed together to locate the center for the opposite hole.
8. After a center has been laid out with a pencil or scriber, it should be indented lightly with a center punch. Recheck the centers to make sure they are accurate, then deepen the punch mark with the center punch.

Boring Holes

1. Spur bits for boring holes up to ¾″ are shown in Fig. 258. Twist drills are used for drilling small holes up to ¼″. Make sure the holes have been properly laid out and center punched.
2. Place a piece of scrap stock called a base block under the stock to be bored to prevent splintering as the bit goes through the underside. Fasten the stock to the table with a C clamp. Be sure the stock is over the table opening before you start boring.

Fig. 264. Marking Centers with Pins

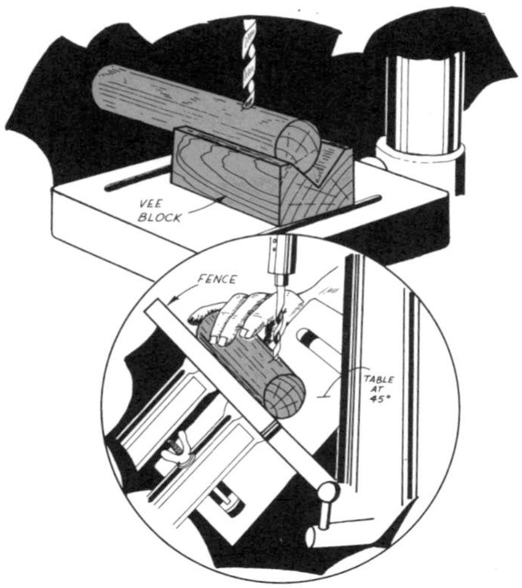

Fig. 265. Uses of V Block

3. If the hole is to have a fixed depth, there usually is a stop nut on the drill press which when properly set will serve to limit the depth of the hole.
4. Round stock to be bored may be held in place in a V block as shown in Fig. 265. The table may also be tilted to an angle of 45 degrees with a guide clamped to the table, instead of using the V block. Make sure the bit enters the highest point of the stock when it is held in position in the V block.

Mortising

1. A mortising attachment is available for the drill press, Fig. 266.
2. The hollow chisel bit, Fig. 254, is used with the attachment shown in Fig. 255. The bit fits into the hollow square chisel so that when the chisel enters the wood, the bit removes stock as in boring a hole and at the same time the sharp corners of the hollow chisel make the opening square.
3. The mortising chisel is attached to the quill. The bit is held in the chuck. The bit is inserted from the cutting end of the chisel. The shank is then fastened in the chisel holder. The spurs of the bit should project slightly below the chisel so as to prevent friction of the

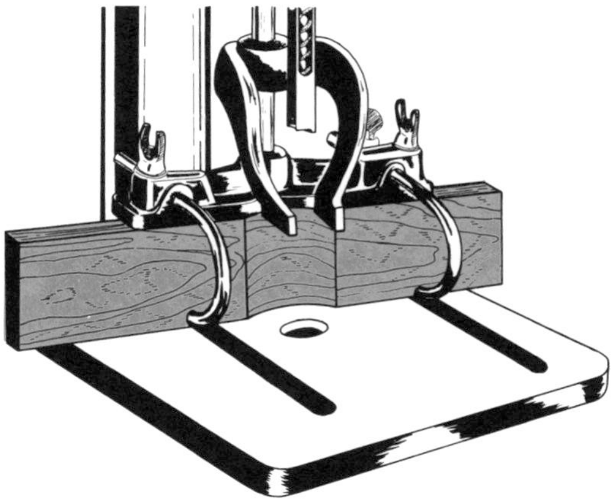

Fig. 266. Set Up for Mortising

bit against the cutting edges of the chisel.
4. The size of the mortise determines the size of the mortising chisel. A common size is 3/8 inch.
5. A fence attachment as shown in Fig. 266 is attached to the drill press table. There is a bracket that holds an adjustable holder as well as rods that hold the stock snug to the fence.
6. Stock to be mortised must be true and square on at least one edge and one face and the fence must be square with the chisel to make sure of exact cutting. The true face of the stock should be held against the fence with the true edge on the table.
7. Take the first cut carefully, then make a series of overlapping cuts until the mortise is completed.

Sanding

1. In Fig. 256 are shown sanding drums that are available for smoothing curved surfaces. They may be purchased in several sizes and grits for use on metal as well as on wood. Discs are also available for flat sanding.
2. The small size has a 1/2 inch shank which fits the 1/2 inch hole spindle. It should operate at about 1200 revolutions per minute (rpm). The larger sizes, with a

½ inch hole, are fitted to the spindle with a short piece of ½ inch rod. The three-inch size should be operated at about 1800 rpm.

3. Most drum sanding is done on the edge of stock. Sanding of irregular curves is done freehand as the stock rests flat on the table.
4. Fences, patterns, and other jigs may be used in guiding the stock in sanding several pieces one at a time to exact size and shape.

Questions

1. Is the drill press safe to operate? Give four safety rules.
2. Is the drill press used for boring or drilling holes only?
3. What are the four main parts of a drill press?
4. How is the size of a drill press given?
5. Name five attachments or accessories to a drill press.
6. How should a small piece of stock be held while boring?

SECTION

Seven

Joinery and Table Construction

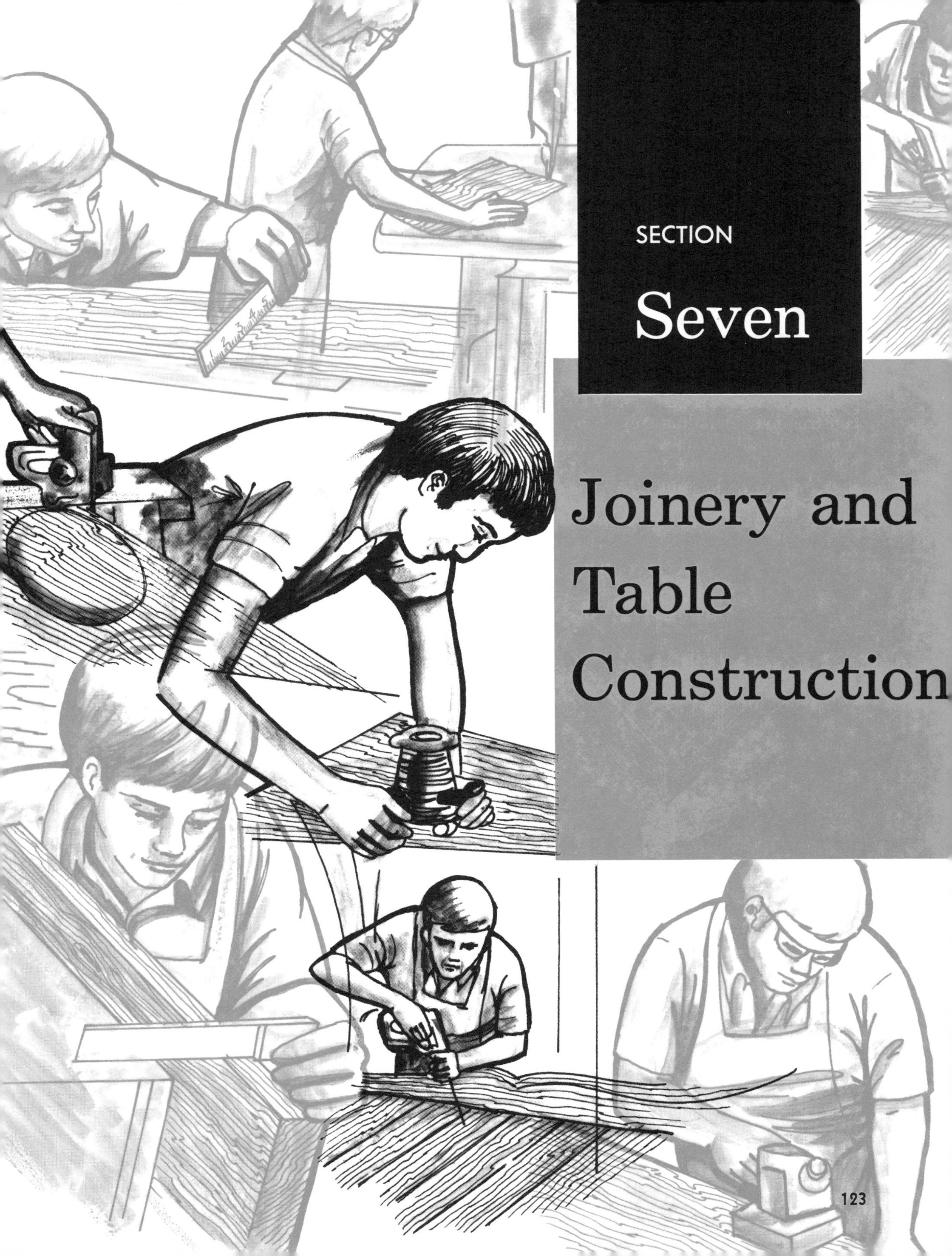

UNIT

39 Laying Out and Cutting a Dado Joint

A groove cut across the grain of a piece of wood, into which a second piece is fitted, is called a *dado.* The two pieces fitted together in this way are called a *dado joint,* Fig. 267.

Dado joints are used in many kinds of wood construction including plywood. They are used in window frames, book cases, drawers, and stepladders and there are many other uses for the dado joint.

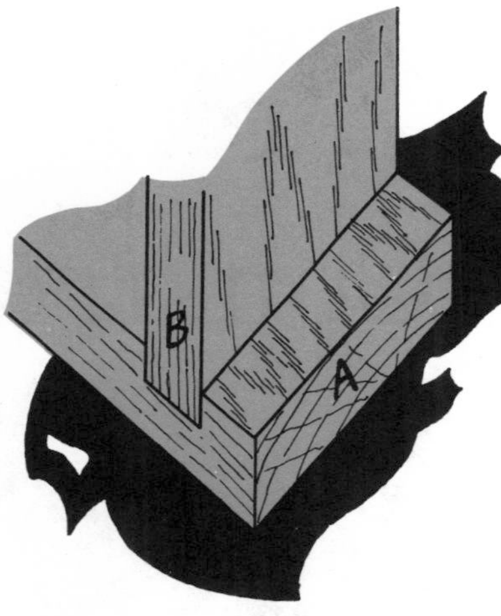

Fig. 267. Dado Joint – One of the Most Widely Used Joints

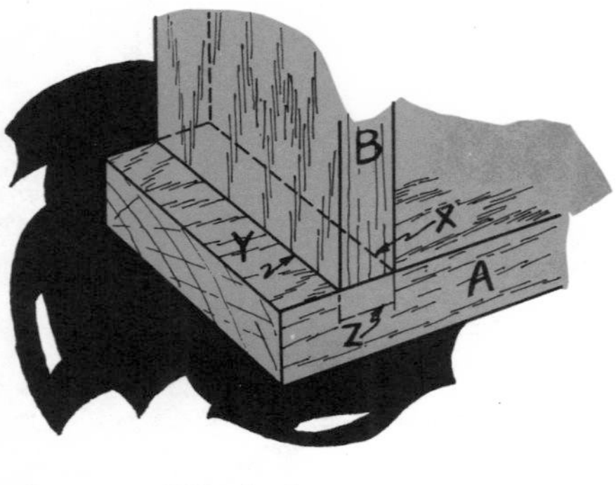

Fig. 268. Layout of Dado Joint

Laying Out the Dado

1. Square the pieces to be fitted.
2. Locate one side of the groove and square a line across the working face of member *A* as shown at *X* in Fig. 268. Continue the line across both edges.
3. Place member *B* so that one edge falls along line *X*. Mark the width of the dado by drawing line *Y* along the opposite side of member *B* as shown in Fig. 268. Continue this line across both edges with a fine pencil or a knife.
4. Set the marking gauge to the desired depth of the dado and score lines *Z*, Fig. 268, on both edges, keeping the gauge against the working face.

Sawing the Dado

1. Fasten the piece in a vise or hold it firmly against a bench hook.
2. Carefully cut the sides of the dado, being sure to saw along the lines in the *waste stock.* See Fig. 25.
3. Another way to saw a dado is to clamp a piece of wood on the outside of the dado at the center of the line to serve as a straightedge. Hold the backsaw tightly against the straightedge and saw.

Removing the Waste Stock with a Chisel

1. With a sharp chisel carefully remove the waste material as in cutting the groove for the cross lap joint shown in Fig. 281. Do not go below the gauge line, Fig. 269. Continue to trim and test until the dado is the required depth.
2. With a depth gauge, test to see that the bottom of the dado is the required depth.
3. If you have worked accurately, the parts

should fit snugly. If necessary, use a chisel to trim more stock from the dado, or use a plane to thin down the piece that should fit into the dado.

Removing the Waste Stock with a Router Plane

1. The router plane is a special tool used to cut dadoes to a uniform depth. The bit of the router is raised or lowered by loosening the *set screw* and turning the *adjusting nut*. Fig. 270.
2. To remove the waste stock, hold the knobs of the router with both hands and push directly forward from the body, as shown in Fig. 271.
3. Do not attempt to cut the full depth at one setting of the router. Make a shallow cut and re-set the cutter, continuing deeper until the bottom is reached.
4. When a number of dadoes are to be made, cut all of them to the same depth at one time, lowering the cutter after each time around.

Fastening the Joint

1. The joint may be fastened with glue and nails or screws. Glue used in connection with nails or screws strengthens the joint. If nails are used drive them at an angle, for the greatest strength.

Questions

1. In what kind of construction are dado joints used?
2. What tools are used in laying out a dado joint?

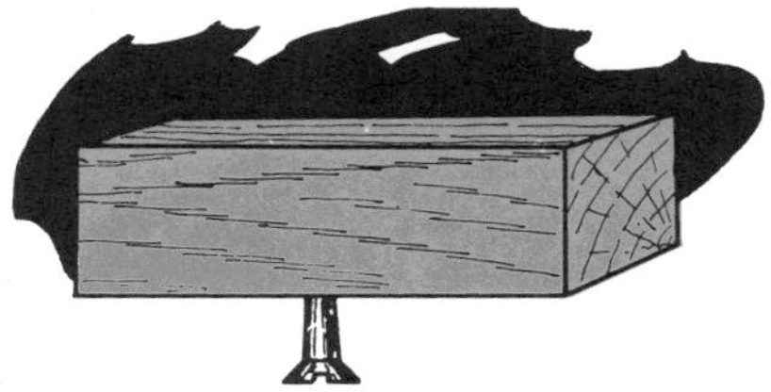

Fig. 269. A Shop-Made Depth Gauge

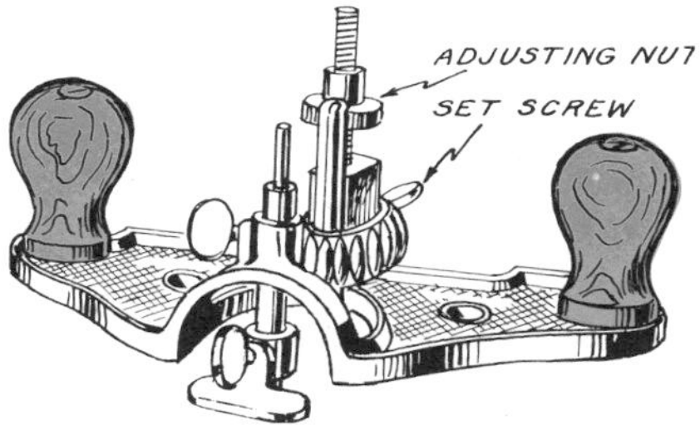

Fig. 270. Router Plane

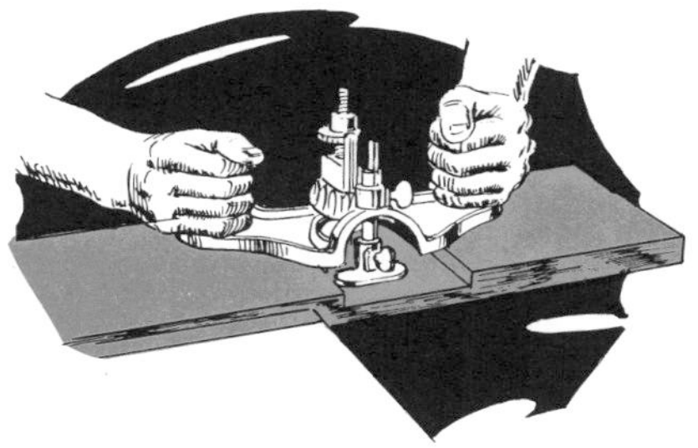

Fig. 271. Using Router Plane

3. What tool is used to test the accuracy of a dado joint?
4. What are the special values in cutting the dadoes with a router?
5. How are dado joints fastened?
6. If nails are used, how are they driven?

UNIT 40

Laying Out and Cutting a Rabbet Joint

The rabbet joint is used frequently in all woodworking including plywood construction. Good examples of this joint are to be found in cedar chests, table drawers, and in window and door frames. Modern furniture requires rabbet joints to secure strength and still maintain the proper form.

Making a Rabbet Across the Grain

1. In piece *A*, Fig. 272, a rabbet is cut across the grain. Make sure that the stock is square and true before attempting to lay out the rabbet. Mark the working face and working edge.
2. In *B*, Fig. 272, is shown a piece with its square end butted into a rabbet.

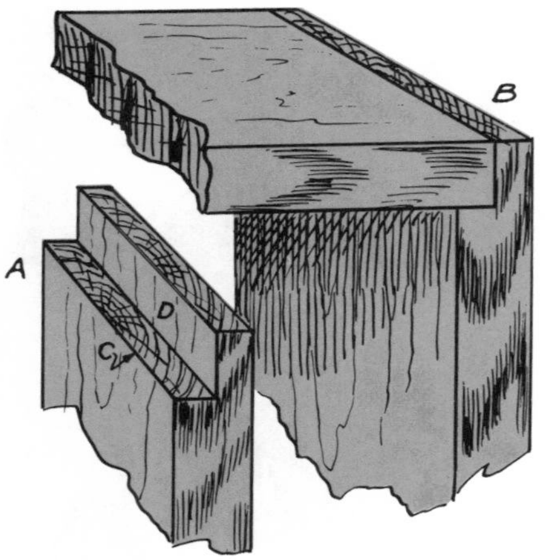

Fig. 272. Rabbet Joint

Fig. 273. Marking Depth with Sharp Knife

Fig. 274. Square Line Across the Surface

3. Mark the width of the rabbet by placing, or *superimposing,* one member on the other as shown in Fig. 273, or by measuring the exact thickness of the piece which is to fit into the rabbet. Make a light mark with a knife or a sharp pencil. Allow from 1/32″ to 1/16″ extra stock as shown at *A*, Fig. 273.
4. After removing the vertical piece, place the knife or pencil point on the mark. Place a try square against the marking tool you are using and square a line across the surface as in Fig. 274. Be sure that the handle of the square is snug against the working edge. Square lines down the edges also. These lines should be a little more than half-way down, or as shown in the drawing from which you are working.
5. Mark the depth of the rabbet with a marking gauge, Fig. 275. Be sure that you work from the working face of the board.

Cutting the Rabbet

1. Place the stock in the vise and cut the cheek, *D*, Fig. 272, with a backsaw or a fine tooth crosscut saw. Cut in the waste stock next to the gauge line.
2. Lay the piece on a bench hook or fasten it in the vise. Cut the shoulder *C*, Fig. 272, with a backsaw or a fine-toothed crosscut saw. Saw close to the line in the waste stock as shown in Fig. 25. Be careful not to saw on the wrong side of the line.
3. Finish the rabbet with a chisel as in Fig. 145, which shows how to use the chisel in cutting such a joint.
4. On wide pieces, use the miter saw or a crosscut saw to make the shoulder cut for the depth, *C*, Fig. 272, and the ripsaw to cut the cheek, *D*, Fig. 272.

Assembling and Fastening the Joint

1. The joint should be fastened with glue and finishing nails.
2. Place the rabbeted piece in the vise as in Fig. 276. Drive the nails through the butted piece while it lays on the bench.

Drive these nails just so the points come through the opposite side.

3. Apply the glue to the rabbet and the butted piece.
4. With the left hand hold this piece firmly in position as in Fig. 276 and drive the nails. Start the nails as far back from the end of the stock as possible and slant them so they penetrate the center of the rabbeted piece. Set the nails with a nail set. See Fig. 355.

Making a Rabbet with the Grain

1. It is often necessary to make a rabbet on the edge of a board as in Figs. 274 and 275.
2. This type of rabbet can be cut by hand with either a rabbet plane or combination plane. Either plane may be adjusted to the width and depth of the cut.
3. Cutting with a power saw is the most effective and easiest way of making rabbet joints.

Fig. 275. Mark Depth with Marking Gauge

Fig. 276. Fasten with Glue and Finishing Nails

Questions

1. What is a rabbet joint and where is it used?
2. What are some advantages in the use of the rabbet joint?
3. How is the width of the rabbet marked?
4. How and with what tool is the depth of the rabbet joint marked?
5. What tools are used in cutting the rabbet joint?
6. How are rabbet joints fastened?

UNIT 41

Laying Out and Cutting a Cross-Lap Joint

There are many kinds of lap and notched joints. The cross-lap joint is seldom used except in millwork. It is a variation of the middle half-lap joint. All half-lap joints are quite similar and constructed somewhat as shown in Fig. 277 and 278.

Cross-lap joints are used in the construction of furniture and in the construction of frames and house screens. Carpenters use half-lap joints in house framing.

Laying Out

1. Square both pieces to be joined to the required dimensions.
2. In Fig. 277, the joint appears assembled, and in Fig. 278, it is shown with the pieces apart. Observe how the members fit.
3. On the working face of the bottom piece *A*, and on the surface opposite the working face of the top piece *B*, measure

from the ends one-half the length of each piece and make a mark. From these center marks, measure on each piece a distance equal to one-half the width of the piece and square a sharp fine line across the stock. Square only one line on each piece at this time.

4. Place one piece on the other so the edge of the top piece falls along the line squared across the other piece. Mark with a knife or a fine pencil, a point through which a line will be drawn for the other side of the groove, Fig. 279.
5. With the knife and try square, score a line across the piece through this point. Exchange the places of these two pieces and mark the second piece as you did the first one.
6. Hold the head of the try square against the working face and square these lines, *A* and *B*, Fig. 280, down both edges of the two pieces to half the thickness of the stock.
7. Set a marking gauge to a measurement equal to one-half the thickness of the stock and gauge fine lines on both edges as in Fig. 280, being careful to keep the head of the marking gauge firmly against the working face.

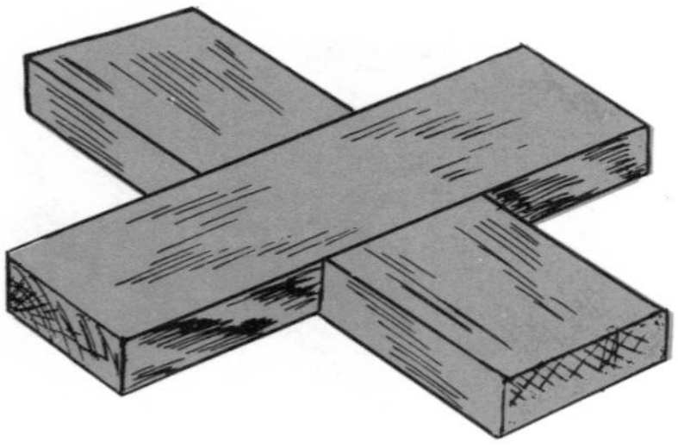

Fig. 277. Assembled Cross-Lap Joint

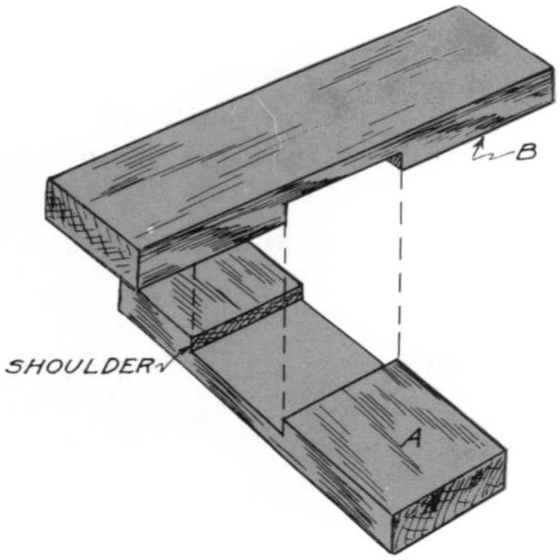

Fig. 278. Pieces of Cross-Lap Joint

Fig. 279. Mark Width of Piece

Cutting the Joint

1. With a backsaw cut the sides of the joint. Saw carefully along the lines in the waste stock. Try to "split" the knife line and do not cut below the gauge line.
2. In wide joints it is a good policy to make several saw kerfs in the waste stock to make the chiseling easy.
3. Remove the waste stock with a sharp chisel. Work from both edges, leaving the center rather high, as in Fig. 281 and 282.
4. Remove the remaining waste material, the high center portion, by carefully

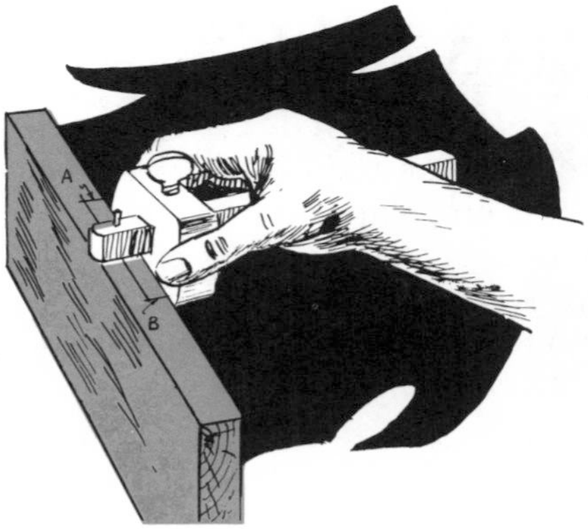

Fig. 280. Gauging Thickness with Marking Gauge

Fig. 281. Remove Waste Stock with Sharp Chisel

Fig. 282. Steps in Paring

paring down to the gauge lines, holding the chisel as shown in Fig. 283.

5. Test by putting the two parts together. Do not force them. If they do not fit together, mark the sides that cause the difficulty and carefully trim enough to make the pieces fit snugly.
6. Cross-lap joints may be fastened with glue alone or glue and small nails, or screws. Glue is most widely used in fastening such joints in furniture.
7. There are variations of this joint. For example, the end lap and the T lap joints (Fig. 325A) are made by following the same procedure as for the cross lap joint.

Fig. 283. Remove Waste Material to the Gauge Lines

Questions

1. In what construction are cross-lap joints used?
2. Why find the center of each piece in laying out cross-lap joints?
3. What tools are used in laying out the joints?
4. What tools are used in cutting the cross-lap joints?
5. On which side of the knife lines should you saw?
6. How are cross-lap joints fastened?

UNIT 42

Laying Out and Cutting a Mortise and Tenon Joint

Mortise and tenon joints are used in making good furniture, doors, window sash panels, and frames that require special strength. There are many kinds of mortise and tenon joints and a few of them are shown in Fig. 285. The blind mortise and tenon is used more than the others. The procedure is practically the same for cutting any one of these mortise and tenon joints. This method is quick and accurate.

The following method may be used in cutting any of the various mortises.

Laying Out the Mortise

1. Square the piece in which the mortises are to be cut. Mark the outside face of each piece.
2. Determine from your drawing the thickness and width of the mortise and tenon. If the drawing does not give the size, the following rules would be well to remember.
3. When $\frac{3}{4}''$ or $1\frac{3}{16}''$ stock is used for rails, a $\frac{3}{8}''$ mortise and tenon should be used.
4. The distance *C*, shown in *C* of Fig. 284, which is from the corner of the leg to the face of the rail shown by line *B*, should be $\frac{1}{8}''$ to $\frac{1}{4}''$ regardless of the thickness of the rails.
5. If $\frac{3}{8}''$ or $\frac{1}{2}''$ tenons are to be used, the distance *D* from the face of the rail to the tenon should be $\frac{3}{16}''$.

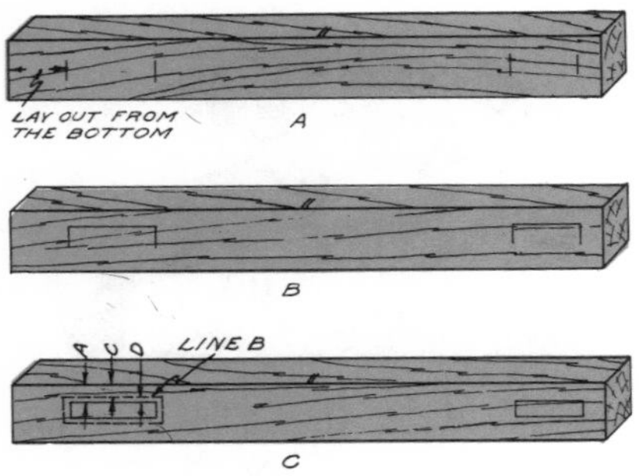

Fig. 284. Steps in Laying Out a Mortise

6. Lay out the ends of the mortises with the try square and a sharp pencil, measuring from the bottom of the legs, *A* in Fig. 284.
7. Set the marking gauge to distance *A*, shown in *C* in Fig. 284. Score from the working face between the two end marks for each mortise to be cut. If you wish to cut a $\frac{3}{8}''$ mortise, use a $\frac{3}{8}''$ chisel.
8. Add the thickness of the tenon to this setting and mark as before for all mortises, *C* in Fig. 284.

Cutting the Mortise

1. Select a chisel the same width as the thickness of the mortise to be cut. If you wish to cut a $\frac{3}{8}''$ mortise, use a $\frac{3}{8}''$ chisel. The mortise should be $\frac{1}{16}''$ deeper than the length of the tenon.
2. Hold the chisel firmly with a full grip in the left hand, keeping the bevel down as in Fig. 288.
3. Hold the mallet in the right hand and do not release it during the operation. Allow the second finger of the right hand to be free as a guide in placing the chisel as shown in Fig. 286.
4. Take a position behind the chisel so the sight will be directly in line with the mortise.
5. Place the chisel, bevel down, at the center of the mortise and take V-cuts one after another until the bottom of the mortise is reached, Figs. 288 and 289. Pry inward to break the shaving after driving the chisel to the bottom of each cut, Fig. 290.

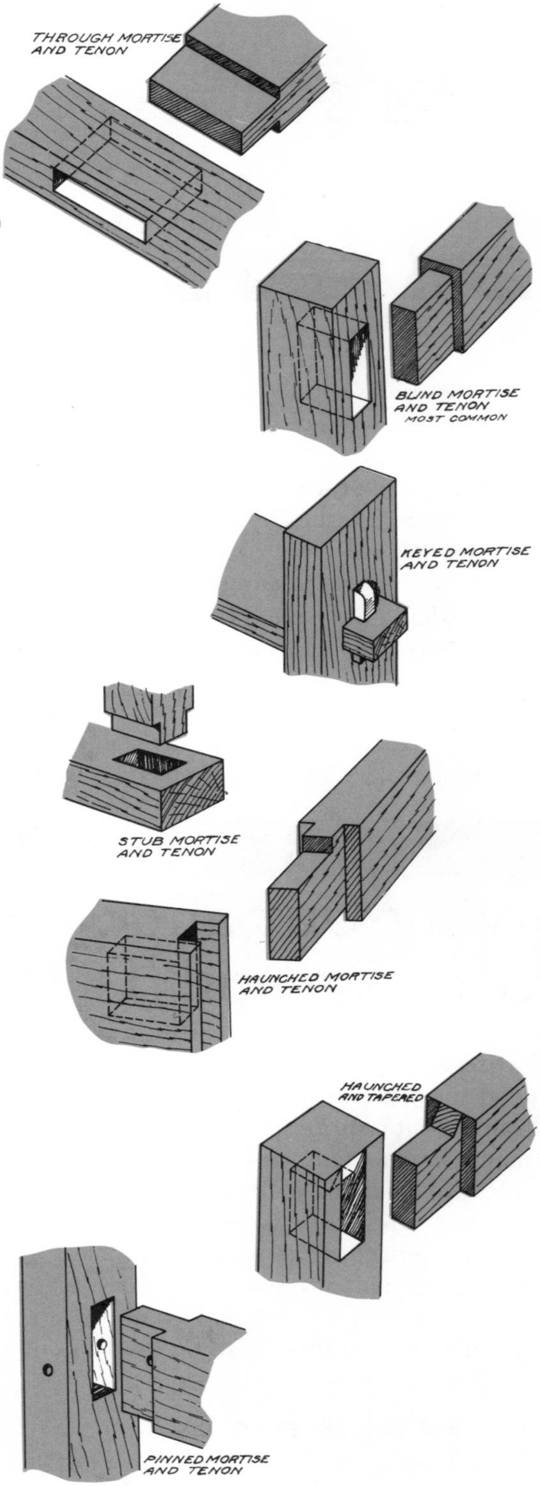

Fig. 285. Types of Mortise and Tenon Joints

6. Hit the chisel with solid blows, taking about 1/16″ for each cut in hardwood and about 1/8″ in soft wood. Be sure to keep to the line.
7. When the bottom of the mortise has been reached with the series of V-cuts, turn the chisel around so the bevel will be up and then make vertical cuts, Fig. 288. Proceed as before in using the mallet; each time breaking the shaving and placing the chisel in position with the second finger, Fig. 286.
8. Continue cutting, sighting carefully to keep the chisel straight. Sight sideways and endways before taking the last cut.
9. When making each cut, drive the chisel to the bottom of the mortise. After you have become accustomed to the procedure, work as rapidly as you can. Only one chisel is necessary.

Fig. 286. Adjust Chisel Position with Second Finger

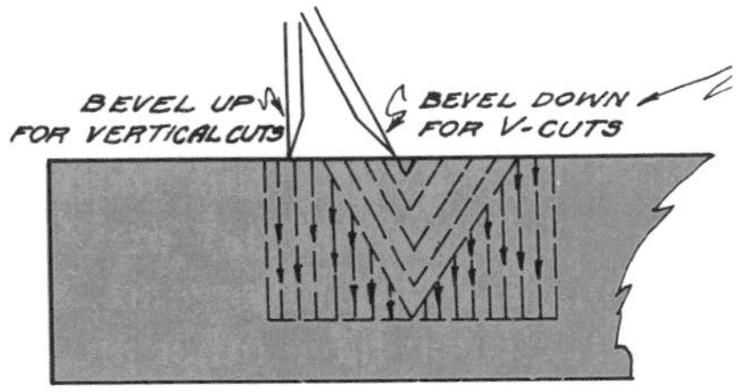

Fig. 287. Sequence of Chisel Cuts in Making Mortise

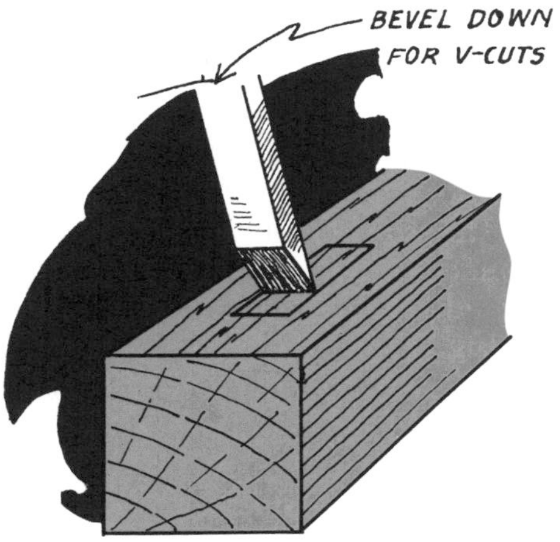

Fig. 288. Use 3/8″ Chisel for 3/8″ Mortise

Cutting Mortises by the Brace and Bit Method

1. After laying out the mortises, score a center line at the location of each mortise. This line will serve as a guide for boring the holes. This method may be used in hard wood.
2. With an auger bit the same width as the desired mortise, begin on the center line and bore holes close together to the full length and to the full depth of the mortise.
3. Use a depth gauge when boring.

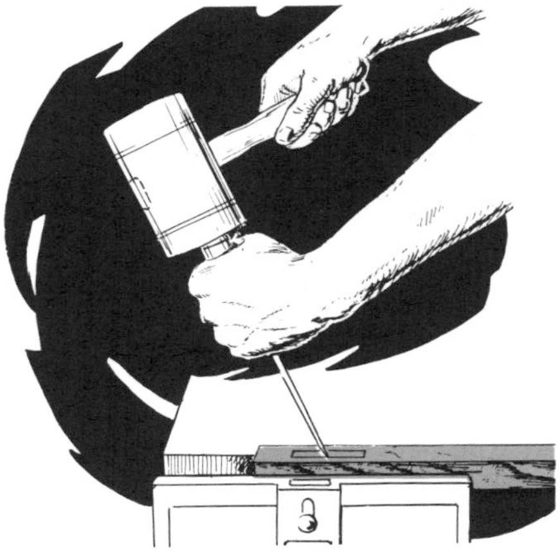

Fig. 289. Drive Chisel to Bottom of Each Cut

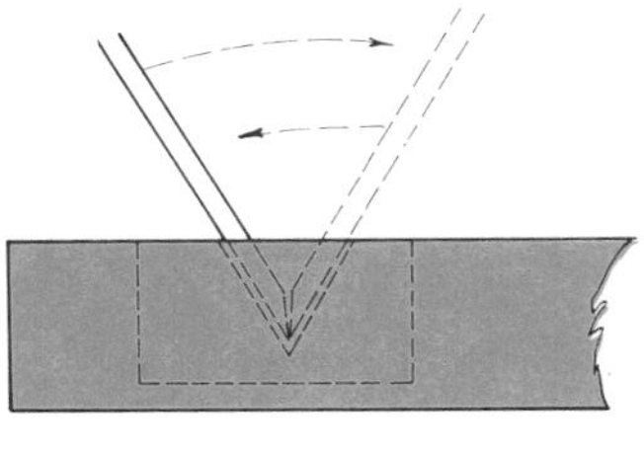

Fig. 290. Pry Inward to Break Shaving

4. Make sure that the holes are straight and perpendicular.
5. Clean and straighten up the sides of the mortise with a sharp wide chisel. Take care that you do not undercut when doing this or the mortise will be too big and will result in a loose joint. The method shown in Fig. 287 is considered the most accurate and the quickest method.

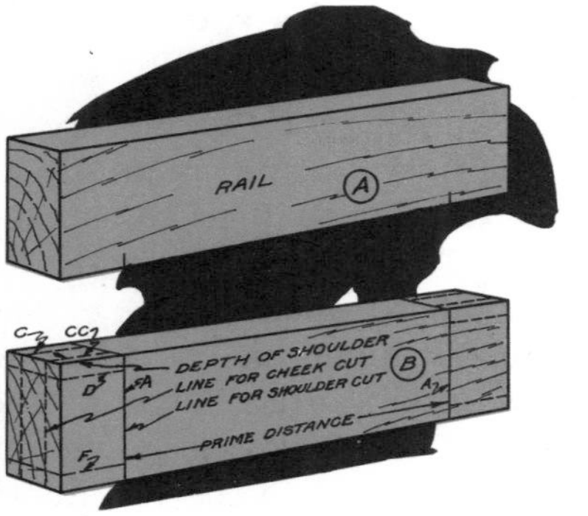

Fig. 291. Steps in Laying Out a Tenon

Fig. 292. Make Cut Diagonally in Waste Stock

Fig. 293. If Cut is Faulty, Reverse and Saw from Other Side

6. Use a chisel the width of the mortise to square the ends of the mortise.

Laying Out and Cutting a Tenon

A tenon should be about two-thirds as long as the thickness of the stock into which it is to fit. For example, if the leg is 1½″, the tenon fitting into it should be one inch long. To make sure of clearance, the mortise should be 1¹⁄₁₆″ deep.

In laying out joints remember that the working face and working edge serve as the base from which to measure, lay out, and test your work.

Tenons are cut on the ends of stock. In tables and doors the pieces that have tenons cut on them are called *rails.* The distance between the tenons, when they appear on both ends of a piece, is called the *prime distance,* Fig. 291. It is not necessary to finish the ends of rails when tenons are to be cut.

Laying Out the Tenon

1. From the drawing, determine the prime distance and the size of the tenon.
2. Begin at one end of the rail and lay off the length of the tenon. Mark this point with a knife. From this mark, lay off the prime distance and make another knife mark at the other end as in *A* in Fig. 291. If you have other pieces of the same size requiring tenons, lay them out by placing the first marked piece against the others and marking the points.
3. At each of the points, score a line around the stock with the try square and knife. Make clear-cut lines. Scratched lines will not do. Remember that the handle of the try square must be kept firmly in contact with the working face and working edge. This step will give you lines *A,* Fig. 291.
4. Set the marking gauge for the depth of the shoulder as shown in Fig. 291. With the marking gauge score a line around the end of the stock as shown by the broken line, *C,* Fig. 291. Be sure that you hold the head of the gauge snugly

against the working face. After scoring this line, score all lines on all pieces requiring the same depth of shoulder.

5. Add the thickness of the tenon to the first setting of the marking gauge and score line *CC*, being sure to gauge from the working face as before.
6. If you have a mortising gauge, you could set both points and carry out steps *4* and *5* together. If you need a tenon with four shoulders, repeat steps *4* and *5* by gauging from the working edge. This would give lines *D* and *F*, Fig. 291. Use only two shoulders whenever possible, Fig. 296. A four-shoulder tenon is unnecessary and serves only to hide a poorly cut mortise.

Cutting the Tenon

1. Fasten the stock securely in the vise as shown in Fig. 292. Cut in the waste stock with a backsaw or panel saw. Start on the corner nearest you and keep to the line. Continue making a diagonal kerf as shown by the broken line in Fig. 292. Watch carefully the waste stock to see that it remains the same in thickness at all points. Keep in mind that you should hold your head directly behind the saw when sawing so you can see both sides of the saw at once. This will help you to cut accurately. Blow the sawdust away frequently so you can see the line as well as the waste stock.
2. After cutting diagonally to the points as shown in Fig. 292. reverse the stock in the vise and repeat the sawing in step *1*. Stop sawing about 1/32″ from the shoulder line as shown in Fig. 293. If you have a number of tenons to cut, you will save time and become more proficient if you take all similar steps on all pieces at one time.
3. When one is cutting a tenon for the first time, the saw may tend to leave the line as in Fig. 293. If this occurs, stop immediately, reverse the stock, and saw again from the opposite edge. It will be necessary to saw to a point below the old cut before you can again saw from the edge from which you started.
4. Place the stock in the vise in position as shown in Fig. 294 and continue sawing. The two diagonal kerfs will serve as guides. Take it easy and do not force the saw.
5. To saw the shoulders, place the stock in the vise, or against a bench hook as in Fig. 295. Be sure to saw in the waste stock and follow the method as described

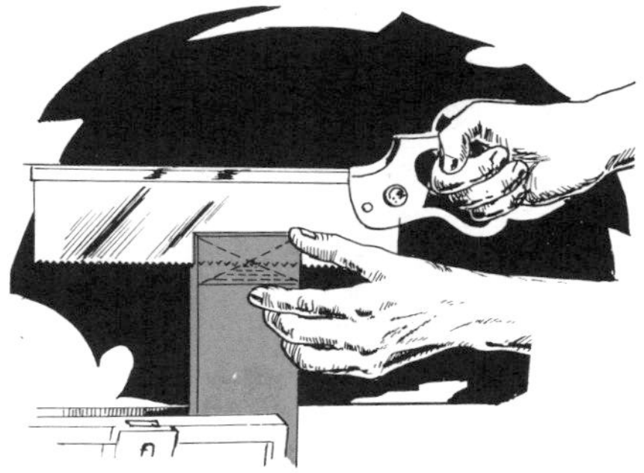

Fig. 294. Both Kerfs Serve as Guides

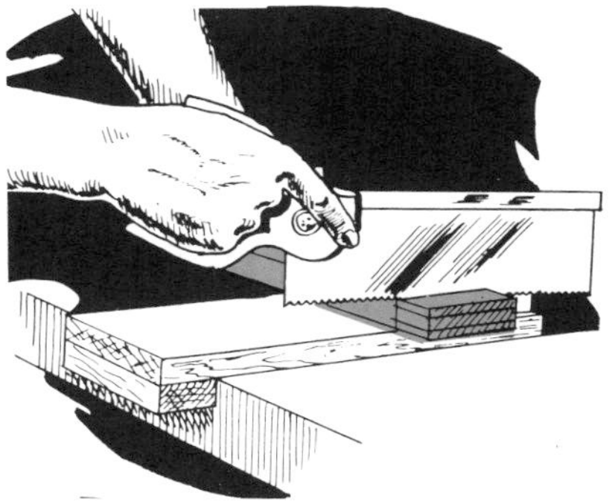

Fig. 295. Sawing Shoulders

Fig. 296. Chamfer Tenon Slightly

Fig. 297. Tenons of Rail Meet at Corner Post

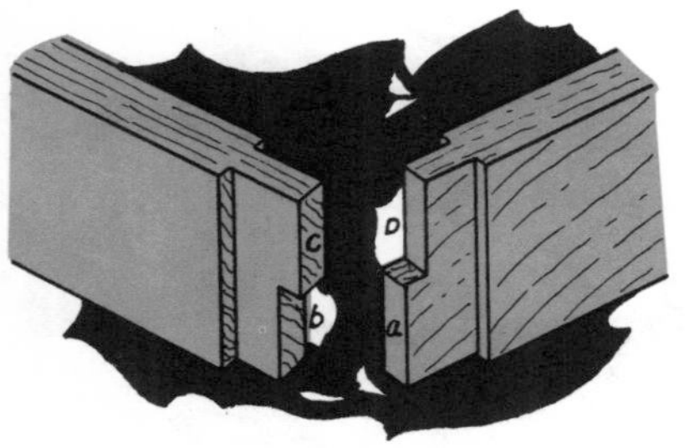

Fig. 298. Half Lap Tenons

in step *1*. Split the knife line leaving half of it to form the edge of a perfectly straight shoulder. Be sure to take plumb cuts leaving flat surfaces. Blow the sawdust away frequently so you can always see.

6. If you saw inaccurately at first, use a chisel to trim the surplus stock, but do not plan always to use a chisel for trimming. A tenon should be cut accurately by using only a saw.
7. Chamfer the end of the tenon slightly so it will fit easily into the mortise, Fig. 296.
8. When you put the tenon into the mortise, it should fit snugly, but not so snug that it must be forced by pounding. It should fit so that when it is withdrawn, there is a sound like that made by pulling a cork out of a bottle. Learn to make joints so you will not be required to cut and fit frequently while you are working.

Trimming Tenons for a Corner Post

1. When two rails come together in a leg as in the top rails of a table, Fig. 297, some clearance must be provided so the tenons will not interfere.
2. Cut from the end of each tenon a notch as shown in Fig. 298. One half of the width of each tenon should be cut so that it laps into the other. For example, when tenons meet at right angles, *A* fits into space *B* and *C* fits into space *D*.
3. Tenons may be cut at an angle of 45° on the ends so they fit in the corner post. Such trimming does not leave as strong a joint as does the foregoing.
4. If you are doing panel work, use the haunched mortise and tenon, Fig. 285.

Questions

1. Where are mortise and tenon joints used?
2. What tools are used in laying out a mortise?
3. When $\frac{3}{4}''$ or $1\frac{3}{16}''$ stock is used for rails, what size mortise and tenon should you use?
4. What kind of chisel is used for cutting the mortise?
5. In what position should one stand while cutting the mortise?
6. What is the brace and bit method of cutting a mortise?
7. When there are tenons on both ends of a rail, from what points are they laid off?
8. What kind of saw is used in cutting a tenon?
9. Is it necessary to finish the ends of rails when tenons are to be cut?

UNIT 43

Fastening with Dowels

The dowel joint is used frequently in plywood furniture construction. It is a good substitute for the mortise and tenon joint. Dowels are sometimes used in gluing edge-to-edge joints, in fastening the ends of rails to the legs in table construction and in frame construction. They are used always in patternmakers' split patterns.

Dowels are round pieces of wood usually made from such hardwoods as birch or maple, Figs. 299 and 300. They can be obtained in various lengths and in diameters ranging upward from ¼″. Spiral grooved dowels can be obtained in standard sizes, Fig. 301. Dowels that are 5/16″ in diameter are often used in making arrows in archery. Dowels for arrows can be obtained at a reasonable price from your lumber company.

Making an Edge-to-Edge Dowel Joint

1. Select enough boards so the total width, when the pieces are assembled, will be enough to allow for squaring to the desired dimensions. Joint these edges in the same way that you would plane a true edge.

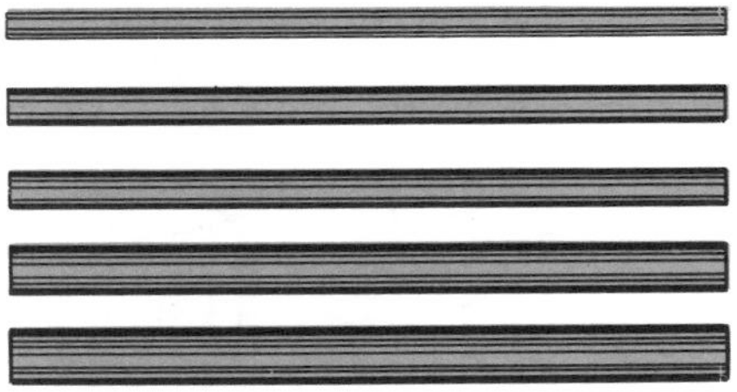

Fig. 299. Dowel Rods — ¼″ to ¾″ Diameter

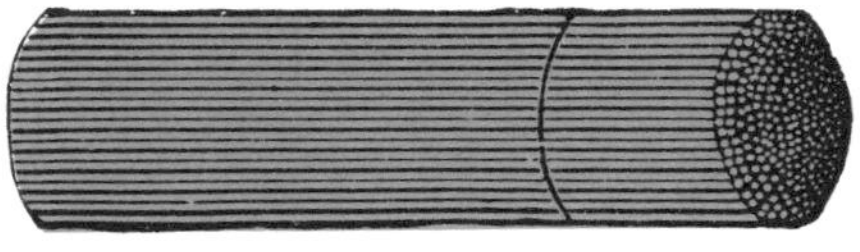

Fig. 300. Bundle of Dowels

2. Place the two boards in the vise as shown in Fig. 303, being careful to turn the marked surfaces out. These will serve as working faces. Determine the number and positions of holes for the dowels and square lines across the edges of both boards, *A*, Fig. 303.
3. Set your marking gauge to a distance equal to one-half the thickness of the boards. Gauge across the squared lines keeping the head of the marking gauge firmly against the marked faces, Fig. 303.
4. At each intersection make a small hole with the point of a nail set, nail, or awl, Fig. 305.
5. Dowels of ⅜″ diameter are usually used in boards ¾″ to 1″ in thickness. Larger dowels are used in thicker boards.

Fig. 301. Grooved Dowel

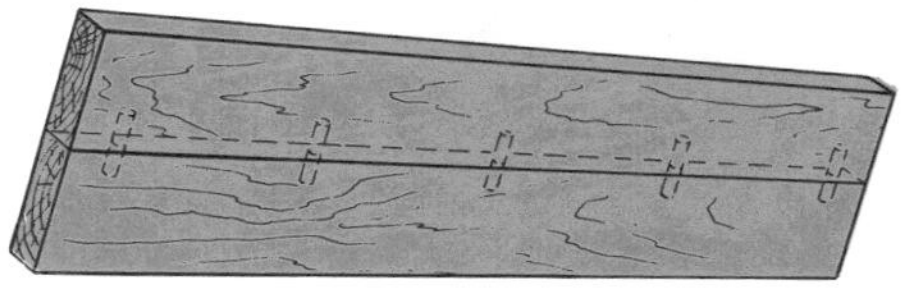

Fig. 302. Dowels in Edge-to-Edge Joint

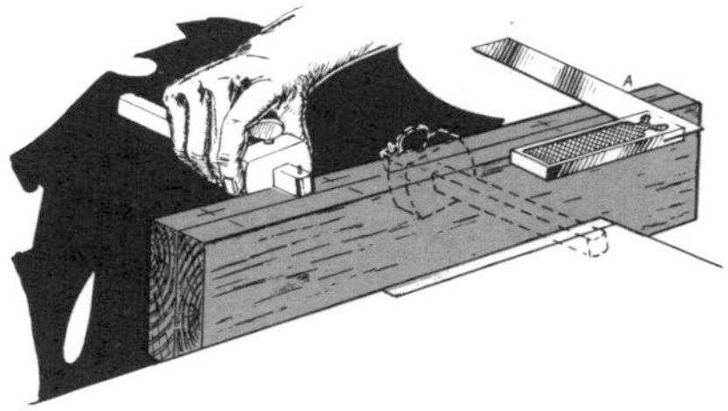

Fig. 303. Fasten Pieces in Vise, Marked Surfaces Up

6. Bore holes of proper size to a depth of about 1¼″, being careful to place the screw point of the bit in the hole at the intersection of the lines. Use a bit gauge to control the depth of the holes.
7. The adjustable dowel jig, Fig. 308, is useful in boring straight, accurate holes. If one is available, it will simplify the boring for dowel joints.

Fig. 304. Gauge Lines Across Ends of the Rails

Fig. 305. Mark Centers with Awl

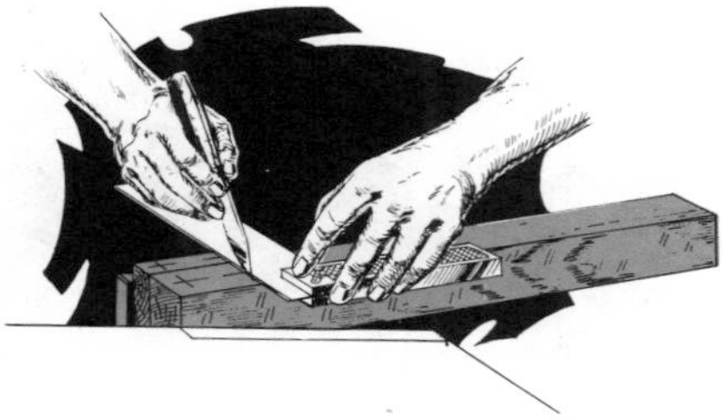

Fig. 306. Gauge Lines of Centers on Adjacent Sides

8. Cut dowels to a length ⅛″ shorter than the depth of the dowel holes. Chamfer the ends of the dowels so they will insert easily.
9. Assemble the joint to see that the dowels fit properly before applying glue.
10. Remove the dowels. Put glue in the holes in one piece. Dip the ends of the dowels in glue and drive them into the holes. Put glue in the holes in the other piece and on the joint edges, then assemble. The asembly is shown in Fig. 302.
11. Fasten the boards in clamps until the glue is set, Figs. 413 and 414.

Making a Rail and Leg Dowel Joint

1. Make sure that the rails and legs are squared to the required dimensions. On a table, the rail is the horizontal piece that fits into the legs.
2. Set the marking gauge to a measurement equal to one-half the thickness of the rails. From the working face, gauge a line across the ends of the rails, Fig. 304. The working face should become the outside, or exposed side, of the rail.
3. On these gauge lines locate the position of the holes for the dowels and square lines through these points across the ends of the rails. Make a small hole at each intersection.
4. Reset the marking gauge to a measurement equal to the distance from the face of a leg to a line of centers on each leg. This line locates the position of the

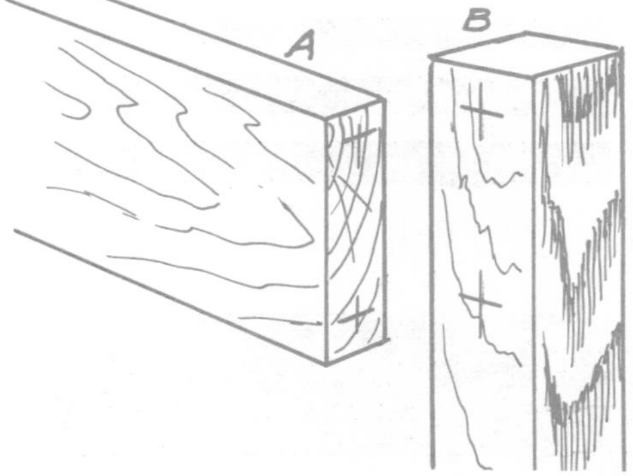

Fig. 307. Rail and Leg Properly Marked for Boring

dowels entering from the rails. The exact place for laying out the line of centers for the holes on each leg must be determined from your drawing.

5. If your drawing does not show where the holes should be on each leg, you can locate them by allowing ⅛″ from the face of the leg to the face of the rail and adding half the thickness of the rail to this measurement. This would be the setting for step *4*.
6. Gauge the line of centers on adjacent sides of each leg. Place the rail, which has been laid out, on a leg as shown in Fig. 305. Mark with an awl the centers for the dowel holes to correspond with those in the rails. These pieces may also be held in the vise and marked as shown in Fig. 306.
7. In Fig. 307 is shown a rail and a leg properly marked for dowel holes.
8. Bore the holes straight and to the required depth, being careful to start the bit exactly at the intersections.
9. Cut the dowels and place them as you did in making the edge-to-edge dowel joint, Fig. 309.
10. Assemble the joint to see that the holes are matched before gluing and clamping, Fig. 310.
11. Apply glue and clamp the joint firmly.

Making a Dowel Butt Joint on a Frame

1. In this type of butt joint, the parts of the frame are of the same thickness, Fig. 311.

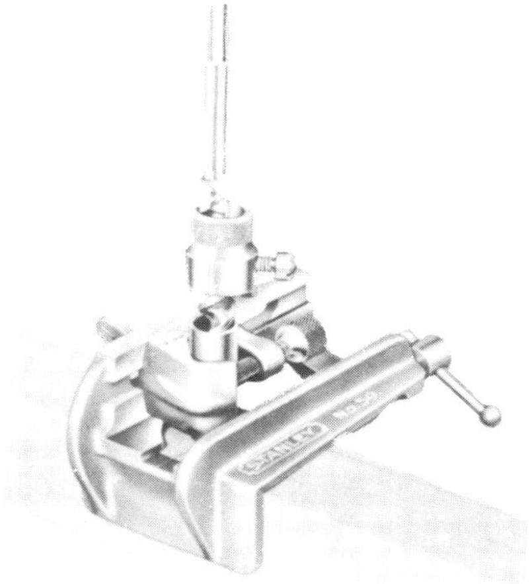

Fig. 308. Dowel Jig (Stanley)

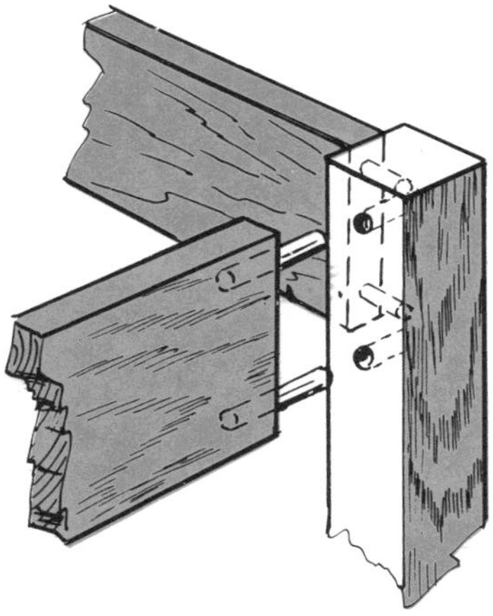

Fig. 309. Fitting Rail to Leg

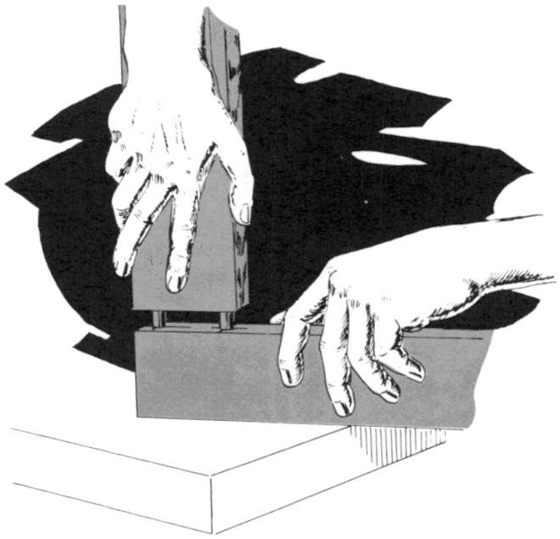

Fig. 310. Check Fit Before Gluing

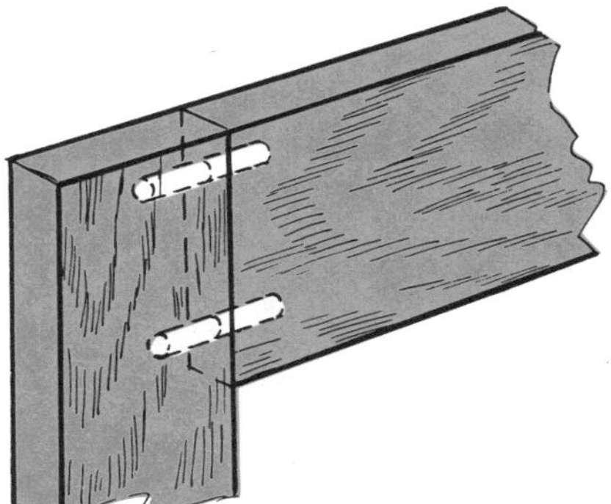

Fig. 311. Frame with Dowel Joint

2. Mark the joints to be jointed in the same manner as in laying out a rail, Figs. 304, 305, 306, and 307.
3. Be careful to bore the holes straight.
4. Test to see that the holes are matched as in Fig. 311 before assembling with glue and clamps.

Questions

1. Where are dowel joints used?
2. How should the length of the dowels compare with the depth of the holes?
3. What are dowels and in what sizes can they be obtained?
4. What is another common use of 3/8″ dowels?
5. What is an edge-to-edge dowel joint?
6. What size dowel would you use in boards 3/4″ to 1″ in thickness?
7. How can you drill dowel holes to a uniform depth?
8. What is a rail and leg dowel joint?

UNIT 44 Laying Out and Cutting Simple Miter Joints

A simple miter joint has its joining ends cut at an angle of 45 degrees and glued and nailed together. A good example of the use of the simple miter joint is in picture frame construction. The miter joint is used in many other kinds of wood and plywood construction, such as in boxes, floor borders, in ceiling and cornice work and in various molding constructions.

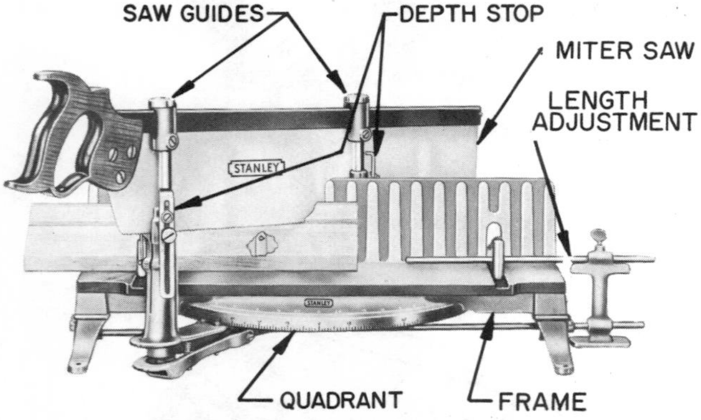

Fig. 312. Miter Box (Stanley)

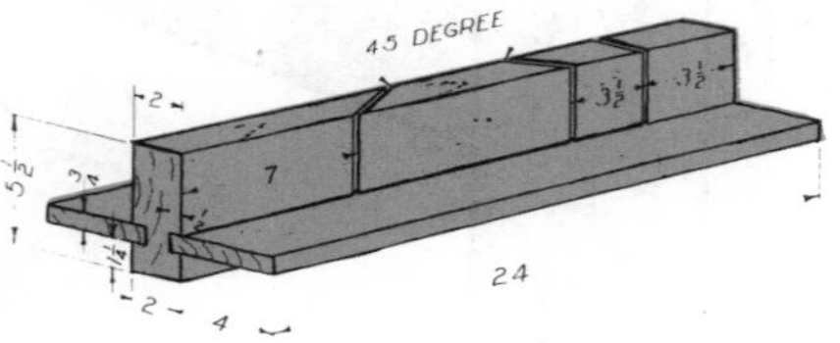

Fig. 313. Simple Miter Cutting Device

Miter Cutting Devices

A miter cutting device of some type is very essential in cutting accurate miter joints.

The Metal Miter Box

The metal or manufactured miter box, such as shown in Fig. 312, is a useful tool in a well-equipped shop. It will cut angles from 30 to 90 degrees. The swivel arm of this miter box usually has a tapered pin that fits in catches or holes on the under edge of the frame.

Fig. 315. Sawing with Miter Device

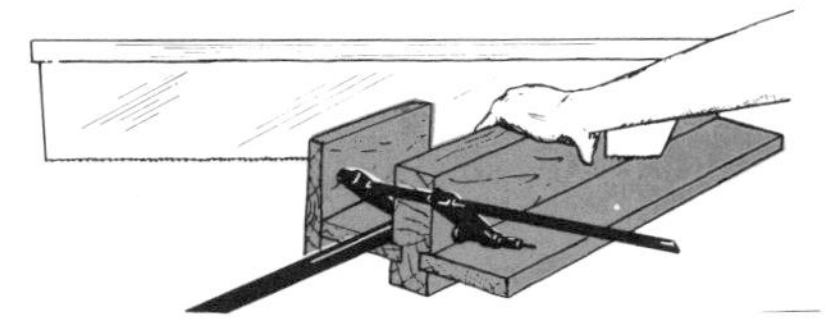

Fig. 316. Stock May be Held Securely with Clamp

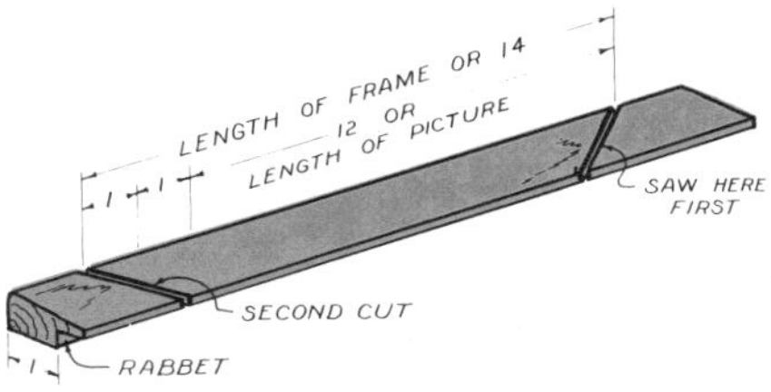

Fig. 317. Length of Picture and Length of Frame

It is equipped with a fine-toothed back saw selected from a series of miter saws ranging in size from 20″ to 30″ in length and from 4″ to 6″ in width. It is also equipped with adjustable stops for duplicating parts of equal lengths and with a graduated scale that gives the angle to the cut.

A Homemade Miter Cutting Device

The homemade miter device, shown in Figs. 313 and 315 is only one of many of such devices that can be constructed in the school or the home shop. It is so simple to construct that no shop should be without one. It should be accurately constructed from hard wood with special attention to marking and sawing the angle cuts of kerfs. Follow the detailed drawing in Fig. 313 to make this miter cutting device. Before you begin to cut, place a thin board of uniform thickness under the stock you are cutting to protect the base of the miter device.

Making a Simple Picture Frame Miter Joint

Picture frames are usually made from special picture moldings of various sizes and designs. Picture frame moldings can be purchased at many furniture and supply stores. It can be made easily by hand. Unit 47 tells how to make thumb molds.

1. Select or make a picture molding that will blend with the picture to be framed.
2. To determine the length of the picture moldings, measure the length of the picture or the glass and add twice the width of the molding – measuring from the back of the molding to the rabbet. This measurement is usually given on the back of the molding. Follow the drawing in Fig. 317 and determine the true length of the picture molding. This illustration is for a frame for a picture 8″ x 12″.
3. When measuring for miters make sure that the opposite sides of the frame are measured to equal lengths.

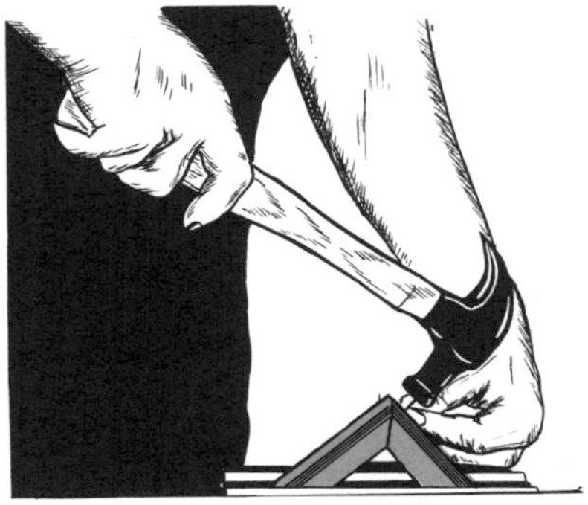

Fig. 318. Holding Pieces in Vise for Nailing

Sawing the Miter

1. When using a metal miter box, place the molding in the box with the rabbet face down, Fig. 312.
2. Hold the stock firmly against the frame of the box while sawing, Fig. 312. A hand screw or C clamp may be used to hold the molding to the frame if desired.
3. Gradually lower the saw until it barely touches the mark in the waste part of the stock.
4. Saw slowly, with uniform strokes and light pressure.

Assembling the Miter Joint

Several methods may be used in assembling miter joints.

1. A simple way to assemble a miter joint is to clamp its sides or members in a vise as shown in Fig. 318.
2. The clamping device shown in Fig. 319

is useful. It is homemade and can well be a part of every school or home shop. It serves as an ideal frame holder while gluing and nailing. Miter clamps of several types are available from tool and hardware manufacturers.

3. Apply glue to the ends of the mitered members and clamp them in the frame holders, Fig. 320.
4. Nail with fine brads as shown in Fig. 320.

Making a Slip Feather Miter Joint

A slip feather miter is a miter joint reinforced with a *spline*. A spline is a piece of thin wood, usually 1/16″ plywood, fitted into the assembled mitered pieces. This type of miter is well adapted to picture framing. It makes a strong, smoothly finished joint.

1. A simple way to cut the kerf for the spline is to use the assembling device shown in Fig. 321 or some similar device. Use a back or fine crosscut saw to saw the kerf.
2. Next, prepare a thin piece of wood, preferably 1/16″ plywood, and glue it in the kerf, Fig. 322.
3. Follow the same process in cutting the kerfs for the remaining corners.
4. Plane the spline even with the edge of the frame when the glue has dried.

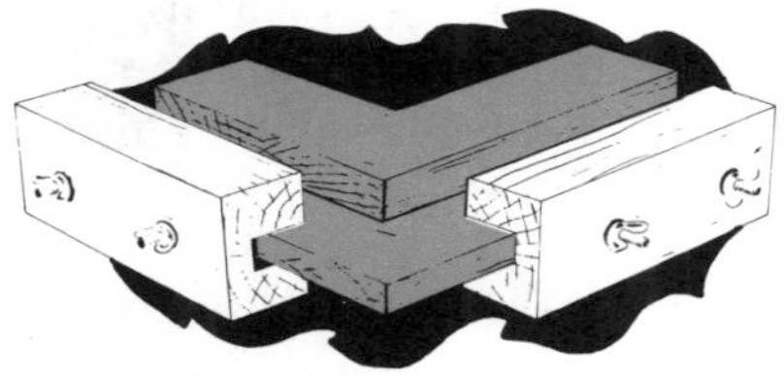

Fig. 319. Simple Miter Clamp

Fig. 320. Use Fine Brads in Assembling

Fig. 321. Sawing Kerf for Slip Feather Miter

Assembling a Miter Joint with Corrugated Fasteners

In the rougher types of miter and butt joint constructions, corrugated fasteners are often used. This is an easy and quick way of assembling frames in rough construction, such as temporary school stage scenery, theater displays, bulletin boards, and packing crates. These metal fasteners are sold in various sizes. Fig. 323 shows a saw-tooth fastener and a plain edge fastener.

1. Prepare and cut pieces to the desired length.
2. Add glue to the joint, if necessary, and clamp as shown in Fig. 319. Corrugated fasteners are usually applied without using a clamp or glue, Fig. 324.
3. Drive corrugated fasteners in each miter joint or butt joint across the grain of the wood, Figs. 324 and 325.
4. The metal fasteners should be driven flush with the surface.

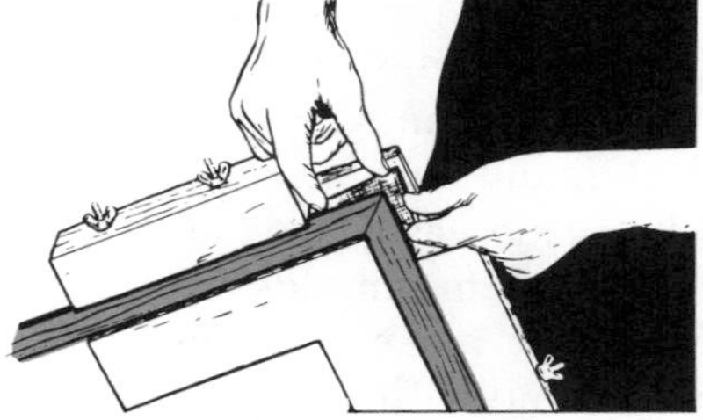

Fig. 322. Insert Thin Piece of Wood into Kerf

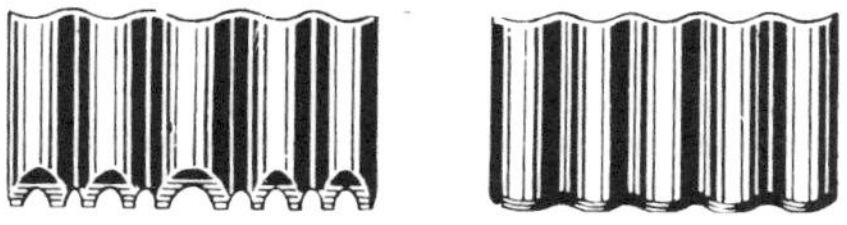

Fig. 323. Corrugated Fasteners

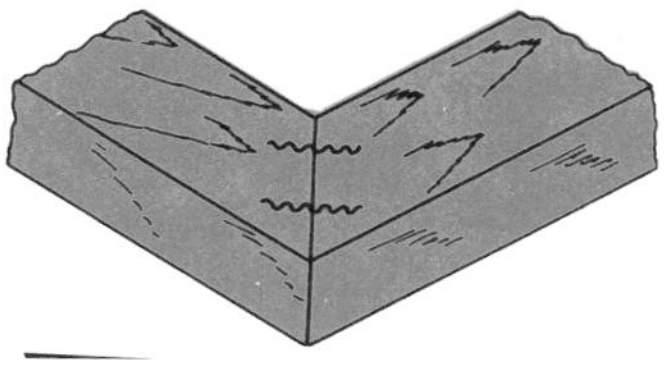

Fig. 324. Corrugated Fasteners on Miter Joint

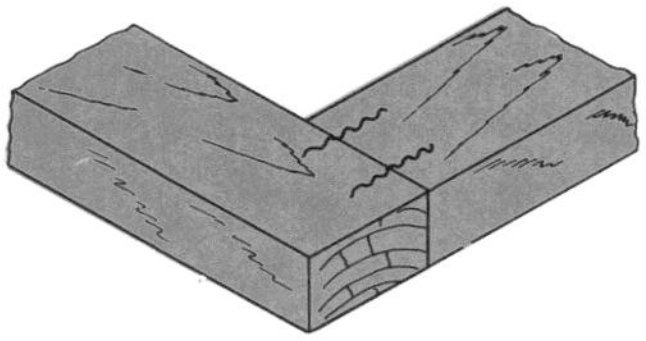

Fig. 325. Corrugated Fasteners on Butt Joint

Questions

1. In what kind of construction are miter joints used?
2. What angles can be cut in a metal miter box?
3. What kind of saw is most desirable in cutting a miter?
4. How is the length of a picture molding determined?
5. What are some of the methods used to assemble miter joints?
6. What is a slip feather miter joint? What is a spline?
7. How are corrugated fasteners used?

There are many more joints than those you have now learned to make and most of them are variations. A = butt, B = stop dado, C = box corner, E = corner rabbet, F = lap, T, G = dovetail slip, H = tongue and groove. The butt joint is fastened with nails or screws and glue or corrugated fasteners and glue. Others are glue joints.

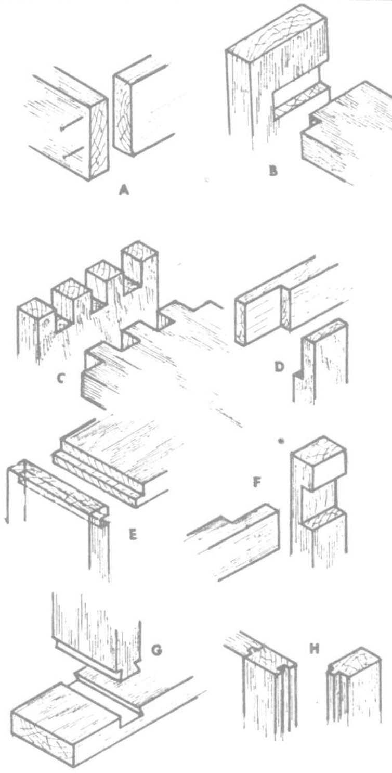

Fig. 325A. Variations of Joint Construction

UNIT 45

Making a Table Top

You may wish to make tops for tables, stools, and other furniture. Wide tops should be made from several narrow pieces. Molding boards, baking boards, and drawing boards are also made from narrow pieces. A wider piece made from several narrow ones is better than one single wide piece. When making a project requiring a large top, leave the top to the last so it will not lay around and warp while you work on the rest of the project. The stock for the top, however, should be selected first.

Table tops are often made of plywood and one piece is then used and the edges are finished as in Fig. 6.

Jointing the Stock

1. Select stock as free of wind and imperfections as possible, keeping in mind that the narrow pieces make the best top. Count out enough pieces allowing about ¼" extra for each joint. The sides that are free of all blemishes should be marked and used for the top surface.
2. Observe the nature of the end grain and arrange each piece so that the direction of the annual rings of one piece will be opposite those of the adjacent piece, Fig. 327. Place match marks on the face at adjacent edges to prevent confusion as in Fig. 327.
3. Plane the two edges of the inside pieces, *A*, in Fig. 327. The outside pieces, *B* in Fig. 327, need to be planed on what will be the inside edge only. Proceed as in planing a working edge and use the same methods of testing.
4. Place adjacent pieces together, edge-to-edge, Fig. 328, and test by holding them to the light. There should be no light seen through the joint at the ends and just a *trace* of light appearing at the center in joining two boards edge-to-edge. This is important and should be carefully observed. This is called a *spring joint*. Have your teacher carefully check this to see that the opening is not too wide.
5. When all edges have been jointed, put all pieces together on the bench and test for wind with a straightedge, holding the straightedge in different positions, diagonally as well as crosswise. If twist appears, it may be an indication of inaccuracy in jointing and the fault can be determined by testing each edge with the try square as in testing a working edge. Make corrections as in truing a working edge.
6. When all edges have been jointed, the pieces will be ready for permanent assembly with glue and clamps.

Fig. 327. Mark Edges for Proper Assembly

Fig. 328. Properly Jointed Edges

Gluing and Assembling the Stock

1. Place the pieces in position on two saw horses with the ends projecting from 6 to 8 inches as in Fig. 329.
2. Select bar clamps of proper length and adjust them to an opening equal to the width of the top. There should be a clamp for about every foot of length of top allowing one for each end. Have several of the largest hand screws at hand with the jaws opened to a distance a little wider than the thickness of the top.
3. Taking one piece at a time, apply glue sparingly to the edges, being sure no dry spots are left. There is no advantage in applying an abundance of glue. Work rapidly.
4. Return the pieces to position on the saw horses. Check the match marks.
5. Apply hand screws to the ends of the top to prevent buckling as shown in Fig.

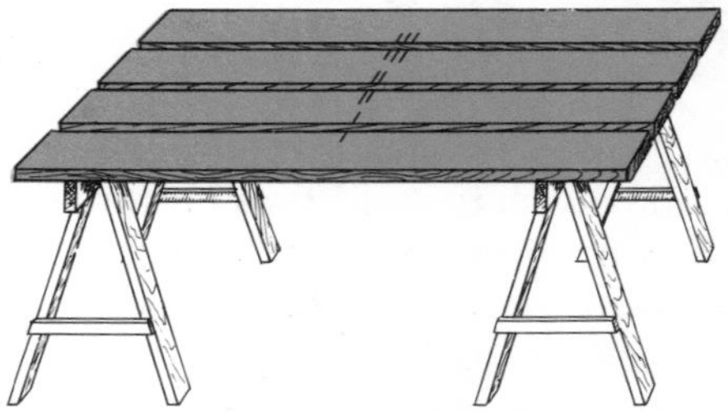

Fig. 329. Place Pieces in Position on Two Saw Horses

413. They should be adjusted evenly but not drawn too tightly. If the hand screws are too short, place a heavy strip of wood over and another under the ends and clamp securely with hand screws as shown in Fig. 414. Place pieces of paper between the strips and the top to prevent them from adhering.

6. Apply the iron clamps beginning at the center. See that the bar is touching the stock at all points and draw it tightly. It should be just tight enough to bring the matched edges of the pieces together without crushing the edges of the outer pieces near the ends of the clamps. Place clamps alternately on opposite sides at about one foot intervals with one at each end, and see that each clamp is drawn up in the same manner as the first.
7. Draw the hand screws up tightly, being sure to apply uniform pressure at all points.
8. When an extra wide top is to be made, it is advisable to assemble it in two sections and to handle them as two separate boards to be joined later into one piece.
9. Surplus glue should be removed as directed by the manufacturer of the glue being used. Some types are wiped off immediately, while others are allowed to dry and then removed with a chisel.
10. The clamps can safely be removed in a few hours, but only on the next day should work be continued.
11. Square the top as in squaring a board. The process of planing the surface is more extensive and requires more energy than does a small piece. The final smoothing, scraping, and sandpapering should be done after the top is fastened in place.

Questions

1. Will a single wide board warp as badly as one that has been made up by gluing several narrow pieces together?
2. Why should wide table tops and cedar chest lids not be glued together until ready to be used on the project?
3. Why should you note the direction of the grain and the annual rings in each piece?
4. For edge joints to be glued should there be just a slight trace of light between the pieces at the ends or in the center? Why?
5. Why should the bar clamps be placed alternately on opposite sides?
6. Before applying glue to edge joints, how can you test them for accuracy?
7. When should surplus glue be removed?

UNIT 46

Fastening a Table Top

Fasten the top temporarily to the rails with hand screws in order to hold the work firmly in place while applying the permanent fastening, Fig. 330. There are many ways to fasten tops but those described here are the most commonly used. Do not glue the top to the rails.

Fastening by Cutting Recesses in the Rails

1. One of the easiest and most effective ways to fasten table tops is by the recess method shown in Fig. 331.
2. Bore a hole at any angle in the top edge of the rail so the hole comes out on the

Fig. 330. Hold Top in Place With Hand Screws

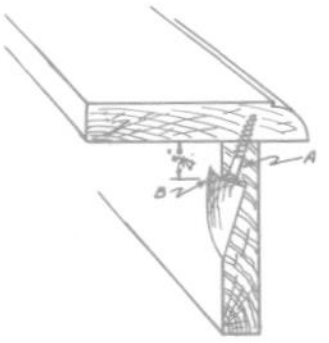

Fig. 331. Recessed Rail for Screw

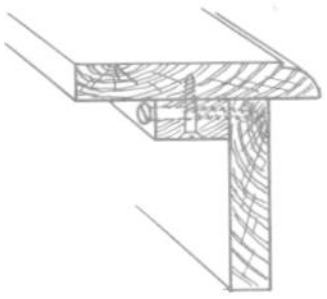

Fig. 332. Top Fastened with Wood Cleats – Not Best Method

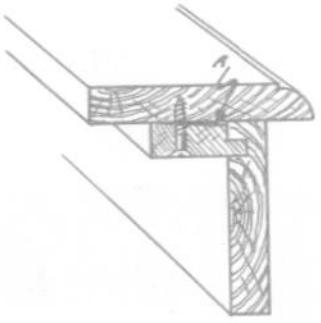

Fig. 333. Top Fastened with Rabbeted Blocks – Good Method

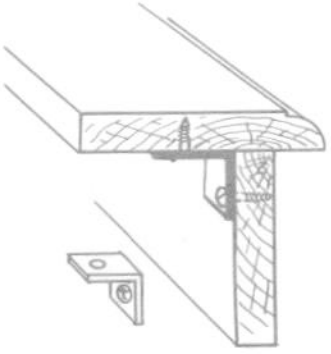

Fig. 334. Corner Irons Make Rigid Fastener

Fig. 335. Iron Table Top Fasteners Allow for Expansion and Contraction

Fig. 336. Sturdy, but Rigid, Fastener

inside face of the rail at a point about 1¾″ down from the top edge. This hole should be large enough to take a screw as shown at *A*, Fig. 331.

3. Cut the recesses on the inside of the rails with a ¾″ or 1″ inside ground gouge. Start each cut far enough down so you will leave a shoulder for the screw heads as shown at *B*, Fig. 331. Leave about ¾″ of stock through which to drive the screws. Place one hole near each leg and space the remaining ones about 12 inches apart if the top is large.
4. Use flat head screws of such length that they will penetrate half way into the top.

Fastening with Wood Cleats

1. To fasten with wood cleats, Fig. 332, bore holes through the cleats from two sides. Make the cleats ¾″ x ⅞″ and nearly as long as the rail. Some workers prefer to use a series of short pieces rather than long ones.
2. Use flat head screws to fasten the cleats to the rails and to the top of the table.

Fastening with Rabbeted Blocks

1. Cut grooves ⅜″ wide and about 5⁄16″ deep on the inside of the rails. These grooves should be about ½″ from the top, Fig. 333. This, of course, must be done before assembling. The grooves may be cut by hand with a chisel, with a special plane, or with a power saw.
2. Make the blocks with rabbeted ends and taper them slightly as shown at *A*, Fig. 333. The rabbeted ends of the blocks may be cut with a backsaw and made to fit loosely in the grooves.
3. Bore one hole in each block using a bit equal in size to the shank of the screw.
4. Fasten these blocks at intervals of about 12″, placing one at each corner, Fig. 330.

Fastening with Corner Irons

1. A satisfactory way to fasten a table top is to use small corner irons as shown in Fig. 334. Small irons of this kind can

be purchased or they can be easily made from strap iron.

2. Be sure to bore the holes for the screws first, if working with hardwood. Fasten these corner irons at 12″ intervals, placing one at each corner.

Fastening with Iron Table Top Fasteners

1. The iron table top fastener shown in Fig. 335 is used in the same way as the rabbeted block. It is made to fit in a groove on the inside of the rail.
2. Cut the groove before assembling the table.
3. Insert one end of the iron in the grooves and fasten the other end to the under side of the top with flat head screws. If working in hard wood, bore small holes for screws.
4. Another type of table fastener is shown in Fig. 336. Cut a groove on the top edge of the rail equal in depth to the thickness of the fastener. Flat head screws are used in holding these fasteners.

Questions

1. Why should table tops not be glued to the rails?
2. How should the top be temporarily held in place?
3. Name five ways of fastening on table tops and explain each.
4. What kind and what length screws are used in fastening on table tops?
5. When wood cleats are used, where should the holes be drilled in the cleats?
6. What size should the cleats be?

UNIT 47

Laying Out and Cutting a Thumb Mold

It is sometimes necessary to form the edges of a desk or table top as shown in Fig. 337. This is called a *thumb mold*. There are other shapes than the one shown, but the principle of laying out and cutting is much the same in all of them. A machine, if one is available, provides the ideal means of cutting this mold.

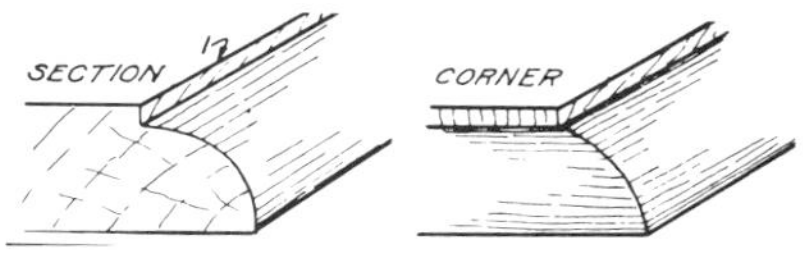

Fig. 337. Thumb Mold

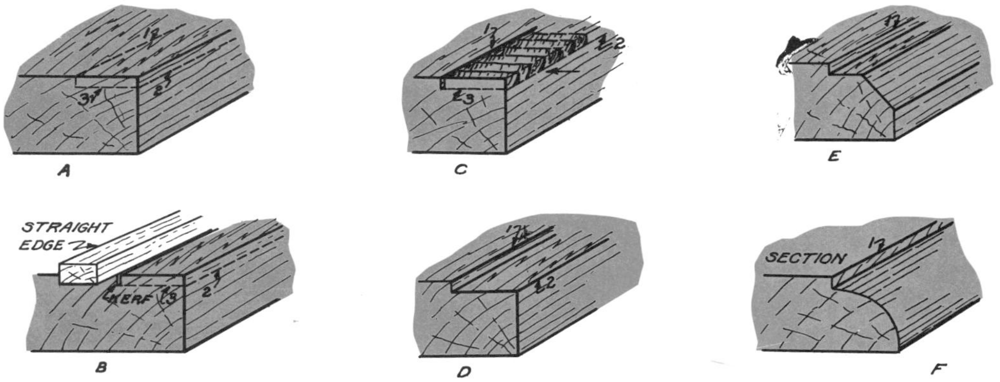

Fig. 338. Steps in Cutting the Thumb Mold – Other Edge Forms Shaped in Similar Manner

One need not refrain from making a mold because of lack of machinery, however. It can be made with hand tools.

Determine the dimensions from the drawing and proceed as follows:

1. Lay off by thumb gauging, lines *1*, *2*, and *3* in *A*, Fig. 338.
2. Clamp a straightedge on line *1* and use it as a guide to saw down to line *3* as in sawing a rabbet, *B*, Fig. 338.
3. Keep the straightedge in place. With a chisel as wide as the mold, and with the bevel down, chip the stock as shown at *C*. Take solid blows with the mallet.
4. Remove the chips by chiseling inward as shown by the arrow in *C*. Be careful to cut horizontally.
5. With a bullnose plane or a rabbet plane, shape the mold in steps as shown in *D, E, and F*. Keep in mind that the arris, line *1*, must be carefully preserved. In the absence of a special plane a block plane may be used. The block plane does not work well into the corners, however. The corners must be trimmed out with a chisel.
6. Having shaped the mold carefully with the plane, sand with No. ½ or 60 mesh sandpaper wrapped on a block.
7. Feel carefully with the fingers to see that there are no bumps or rough places. High places can be seen by holding the work toward the light.
8. Finish with No. 210 or 100 mesh sandpaper.
9. Observe how the corners are finished in *F*, Fig. 338. The side and end molds meet to form a straight line. This line can be made straight by perfecting the intersecting curves with sandpaper.

Questions

1. How should one sand end grain?
2. What two planes can be used for cutting thumb mold?
3. How can the corners of the thumb mold be trimmed out?
4. What equipment is finally used to smooth the thumb mold properly?
5. How may a guide be provided for the sawing to be done in making a thumb mold?

UNIT 48

Making a Simple Drawer Slide

1. Make from scrap stock two pieces ¾″ x 2″ and long enough to reach from the front rail to the back rail, *A*, Fig. 339, and *A*, Fig. 342. Carefully square one end of each piece. Cut two short pieces ¾″ square and 5 inches long, *B*, Fig. 339.
2. Bore holes and countersink for No. 7 flat head screws at points about ¾″ from each end of the short pieces. Be careful that these holes are bored and countersunk from the same side.
3. Size the squared end of the long piece, *A*, with glue.
4. Glue and nail one of the short pieces to the squared end of the long piece with two 6 d box nails, being careful that distance *a* is equal to distance *b* as in Fig. 339, and that the countersunk ends

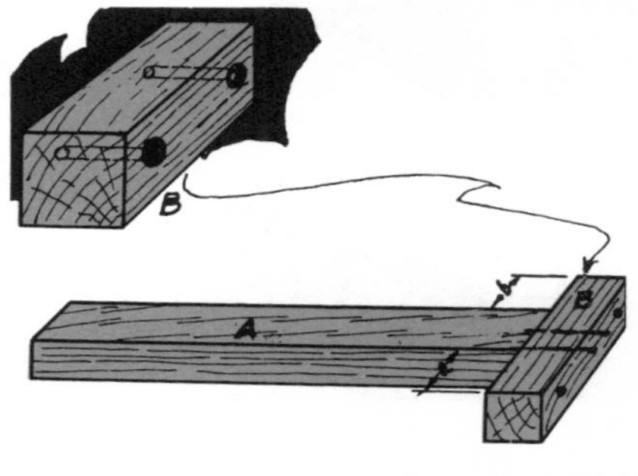

Fig. 339. First Stage of Assembly of Drawer Slide

of the holes are turned toward the long piece, *A*.

5. Hold the slide with end *X* against the back rail and place the other short piece on the slide as in Fig. 340. Mark along the side of the short piece to get the correct length for the long piece.

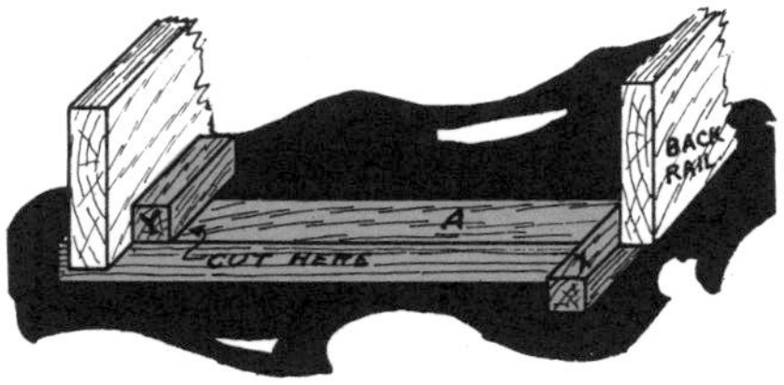

Fig. 340. Fitting Drawer Slide

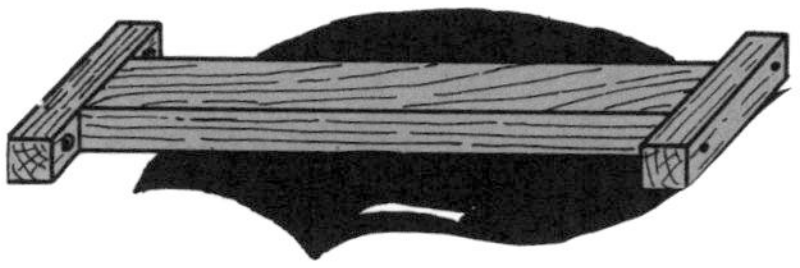

Fig. 341. Slide Ready to Install

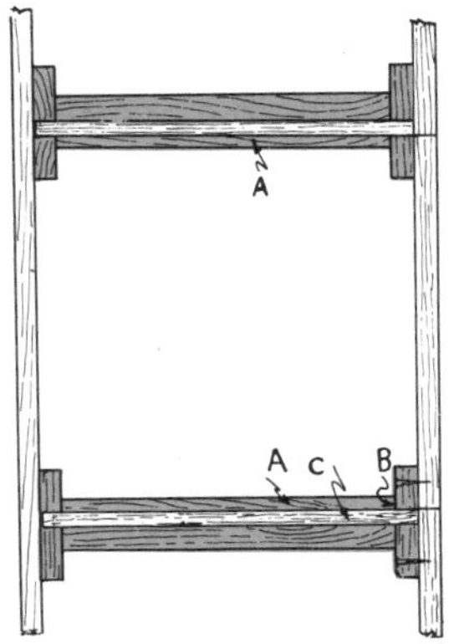

Fig. 342. Drawer Slides in Place

6. Cut piece *A* to the length as shown by the mark in Fig. 340 and nail and glue the short piece *Y* to the cut end, as shown in Fig. 341.
7. Clamp the assembled piece temporarily in place between the rails, having one-half inch of piece *A* extending inside the opening for the drawer, as at *B*, Fig. 342. Fasten the assembly to the rails with 1¼″ No. 7 F. H. B. screws.
8. Make another slide for the other side of the drawer.
9. Fasten with brads and glue a strip on each side ½″ from the inner edge of the long piece, as shown at *A* in Fig. 342. These strips will serve as guides for the drawer, and must be exactly the same distance apart at the back as they are at the front.

Questions

1. Should the ends of piece *A* be square?
2. Why should the countersunk side of pieces *X* and *Y* be to the inside of the table?
3. What kind of nails are used in assembling the drawer slide?
4. How may the assembled slide be temporarily held in place for fastening?
5. How is the slide fastened to the rails?

UNIT 49

Making and Fitting a Drawer

In making a drawer several kinds of joints are involved whether solid wood or plywood is used.

1. Before starting construction, make sure you understand all the dimensions and details of construction given in your drawing.
2. Select material for the front of the drawer that will match the material in the project. The grain should be selected for uniformity and should be similar to the grain in the other pieces that make up the front of the project. The wider and heavier grain, if any, should be placed toward the bottom.

3. A less expensive, close-grained wood, such as poplar, pine, or basswood, should be used for the rest of the drawer. Three-ply panel and hardboard are recommended for drawer bottoms because they are not affected by changes in temperature.
4. Square the sides to dimensions. Plane the front part of the drawer to size by fitting it snugly into the opening where it is to go.

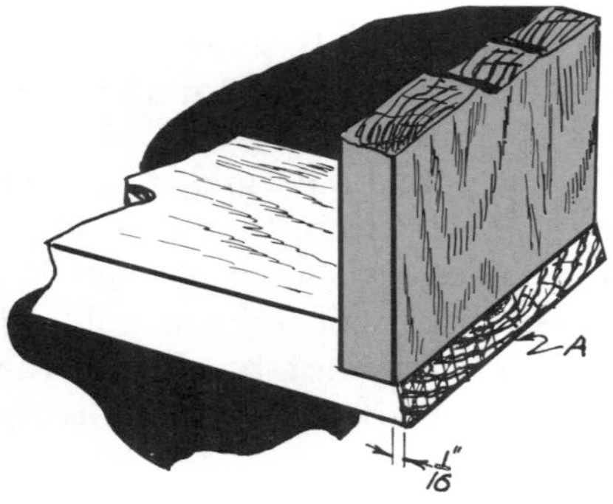

Fig. 343. Rabbet Joint at Front of Drawer

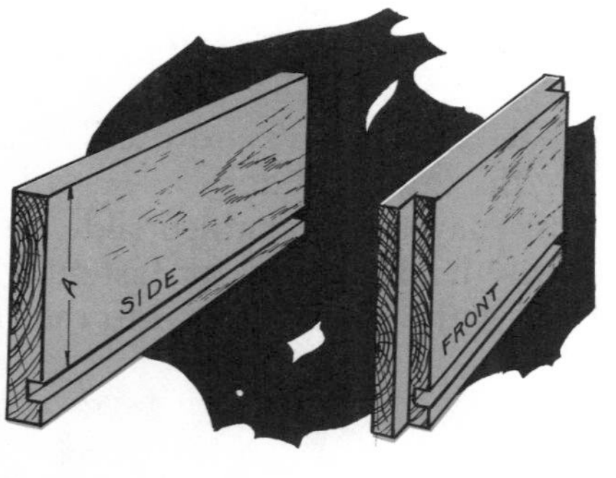

Fig. 344. Cut Grooves in Side and Front

Fig. 345. Laying Out Back Piece

5. Lay out and cut the rabbet for the front as in cutting a common rabbet joint, leaving a scant sixteenth of an inch extra at the end as shown in Fig. 343.
6. With a matching plane, cut the grooves in which to fit the bottom panel. These grooves should be cut into the side and front pieces as shown in Fig. 344, to a depth of $5/16$ of an inch. The grooves can also be cut very satisfactorily with a chisel of the proper width. The power saw is most convenient and can be used if it is available.
7. Determine the length of the back piece by laying it on the inside of the front piece as shown in Fig. 345, and mark it.
8. Take the measurement for the width of the back piece from the groove to the top of the drawer as shown in *A*, Fig. 344 and gauge and plane the piece to width.
9. Place the front part of the drawer in a vertical position in the vise, Fig. 276. Size the ends of the side pieces and the rabbet of the front piece with glue.
10. Apply another coat of glue to the other pieces and quickly nail a side piece in place with three six-penny box nails, being careful to have the grooves for the bottom piece exactly in line.
11. Turn the front piece around in the vise and glue and nail the other side piece.

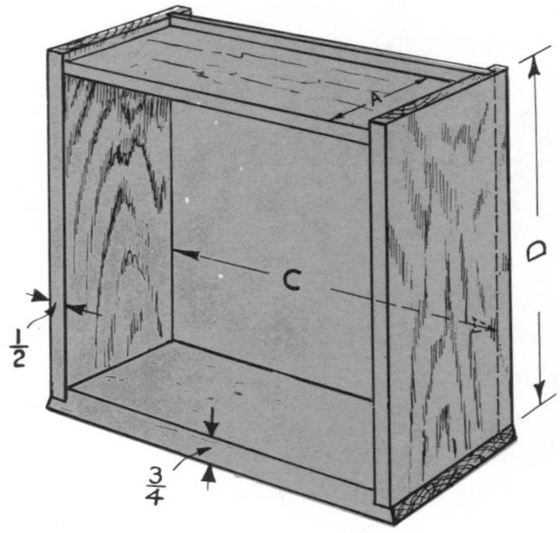

Fig. 346. Assembled Drawer

Fig. 347. Drawer Bottom Fits Grooves in Sides and Front

Fig. 348. Plane the Extra Stock on Sides to Slight Bevel

12. Place on the top of the bench resting on one side, the front and side pieces thus assembled, and nail the back in place with two six-penny nails, being careful not to obstruct the groove which is to receive the bottom panel.
13. Determine the size of the stock for the bottom of the assembled drawer. Measure the width at point *C* in Fig. 346, including also the depth of the grooves less one-sixteenth of an inch. Measure the length from the front to a point about one-half inch beyond the back, as shown at *D*, Fig. 346. The grain of the wood should be crossways of the drawer to allow for expansion or shrinkage. If you are using plywood or hardboard, the direction of the grain is not important.
14. Slip the bottom in place from the back of the drawer and drive a ¾″ brad into the bottom edge of the front, so that it will hold the bottom in place, Fig. 347.
15. Fit the drawer in the opening by planing it so a dime can be inserted around the sides and at the top. The space around the sides must be exactly uniform.
16. Plane the extra stock *A* in Fig. 343 to a bevel as shown at *A*, Fig. 348. The bullnose plane is very satisfactory for this step. If one is not available, use a block or rabbet plane.

Questions

1. What kind of joints are used in making a drawer?
2. What kind of material is usually used for the bottom of a drawer?
3. How is the bottom held in place?
4. What kind of joints are often used on the drawer front?
5. What size nails should be used on the front part of the drawer? The sides of the drawer?

SECTION

Eight

Common Assembly Operations and Materials

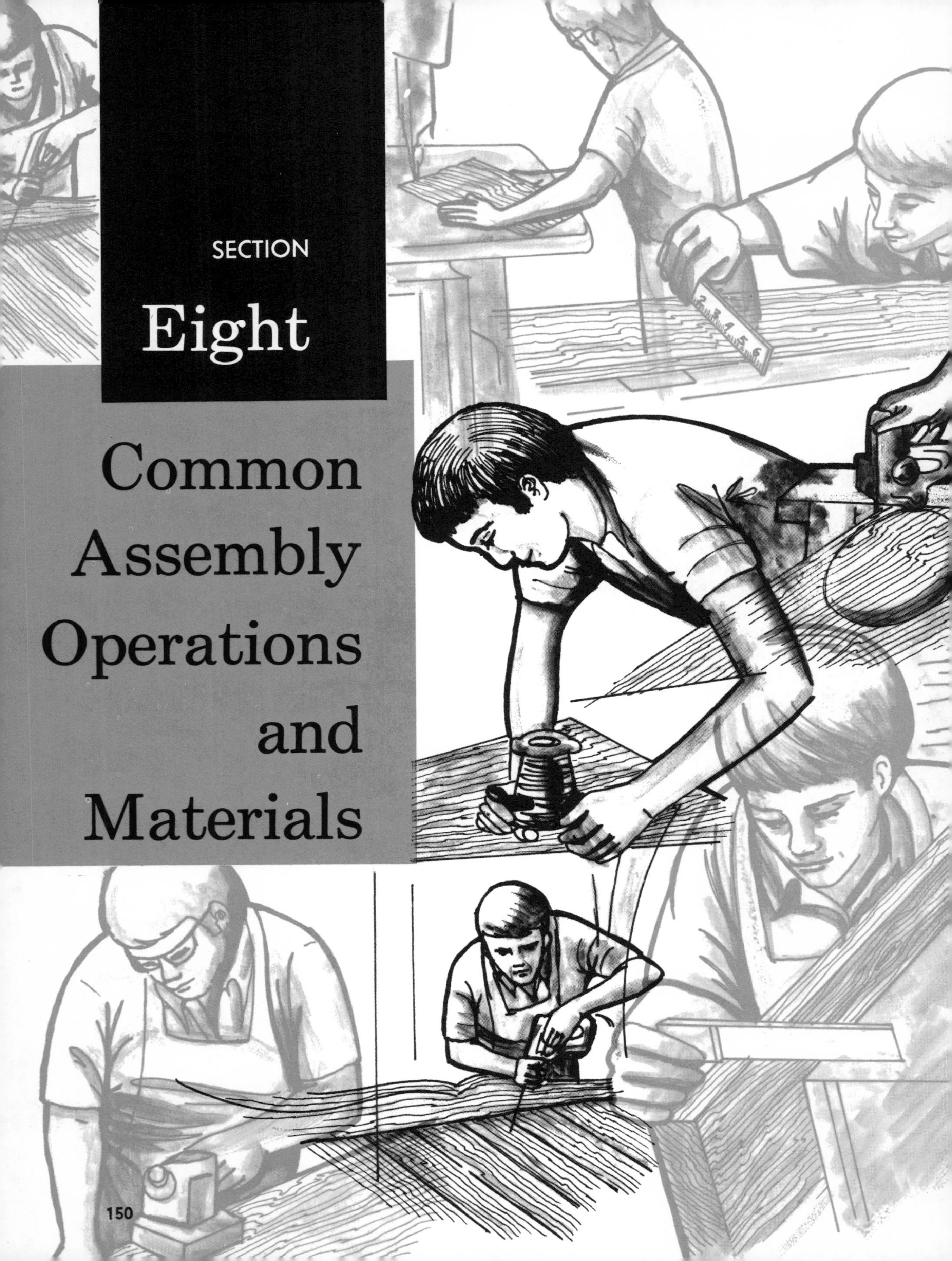

UNIT 50

Driving and Drawing Nails

You should know how to drive and draw nails properly. You will undoubtedly have use for a hammer and nails during your leisure time in doing repair work about the home or in building something for yourself from wood.

The *claw hammer* is the most commonly used tool for driving nails. The parts of a claw hammer are shown in Fig. 350.

Nails are without question the most common fastenings in woodworking. Most nails are made from steel wire and for that reason they are called wire nails. The nails which are most used are the *common, box, finishing* and *casing* nails. They are made in different sizes and for almost any purpose.

Finishing and casing nails are used in plywood construction in exposed places.

Driving Nails

1. Select the kind and size of nails best suited to the work. The drawing will help you to determine which nails to use. See unit on nails.
2. Hold the nail firmly between the thumb and first finger of the left hand as shown in Fig. 349. Place the point on the spot where you wish to drive it.
3. With the right hand, grasp the hammer handle firmly near the end. Fig. 350. Do not "choke" it by holding it near the head.
4. When starting to drive, give a slight tap to set the nail and then withdraw the left hand. With a full swing of the wrist and forearm drive the nail in as far as you want it to go.
5. Keep the face of the hammer smooth and clean. A sticky substance on the face of the hammer might result in bending the nail.
6. Make sure that you strike the nail squarely on the head. Keep your eye on the nail rather than on the hammer. If you strike the nail with a glancing blow, the hammer will either slip and dent the wood or it will bend the nail.
7. When driving a finishing nail leave a small portion of the nail to be driven home with a nail set.

Drawing Nails

1. Once a nail has been started at the wrong angle, do not attempt to change its direction, but pull it out and start again in another place.
2. When it is necessary to draw a nail, place a piece of wood under the claw of the hammer to prevent marring the stock and to keep the nail straight, Fig.

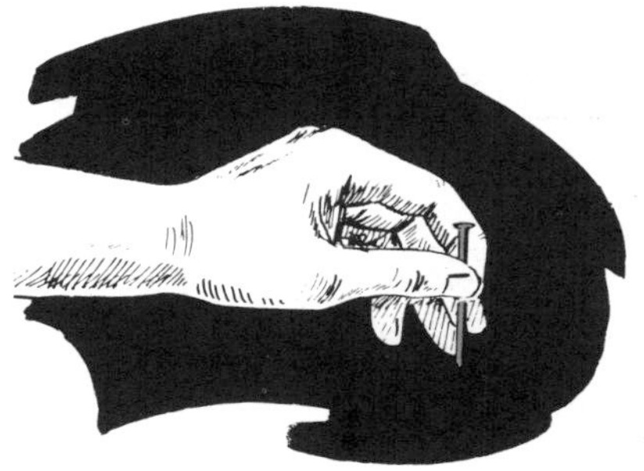

Fig. 349. Hold Nail Between Thumb and First Finger

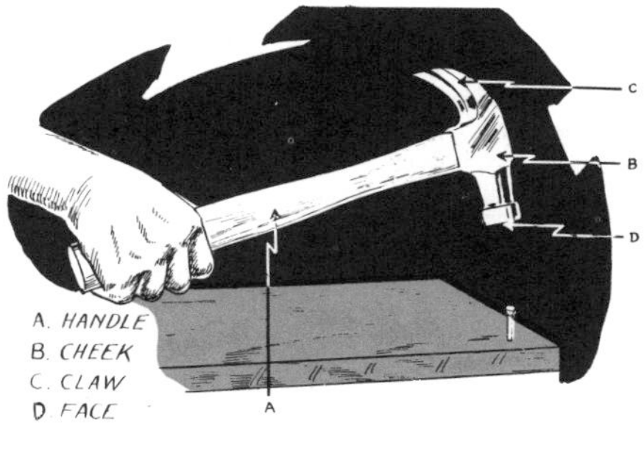

Fig. 350. Grasp the Hammer Near the End

351. Pull the nail by drawing the handle of the hammer toward you.

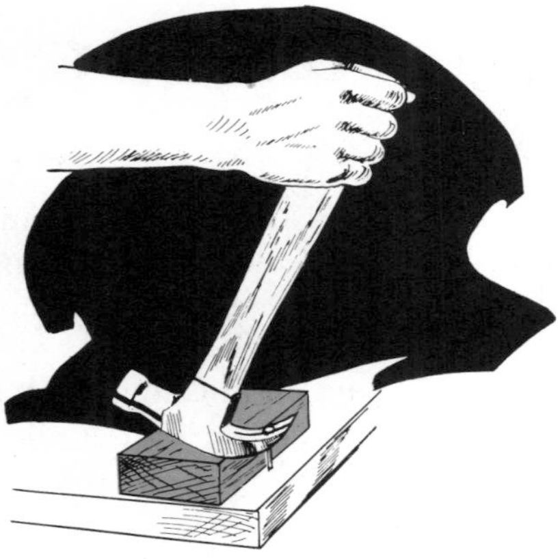

Fig. 351. Block Prevents Marring the Stock

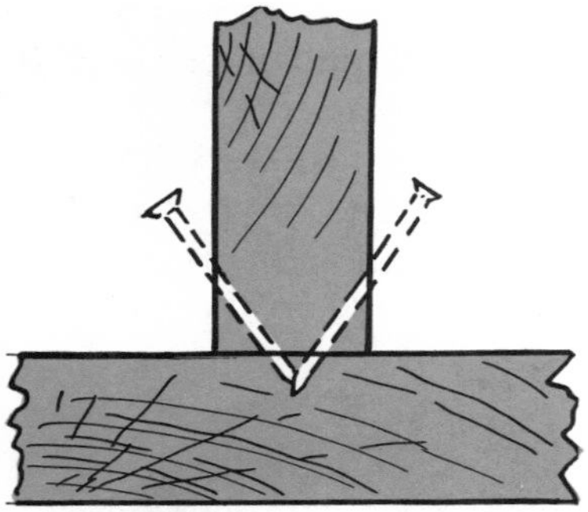

Fig. 352. Toenailing

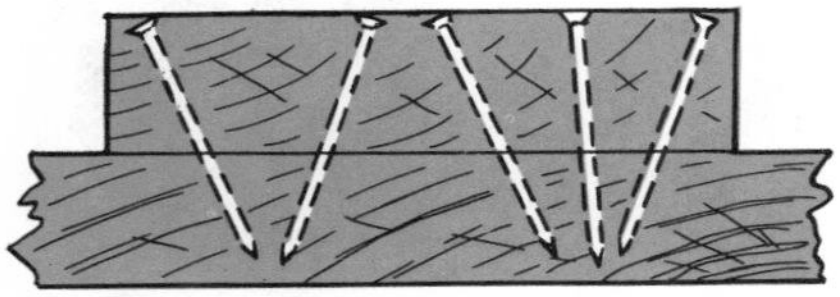

Fig. 353. Nailing at Angle Increases Holding Power

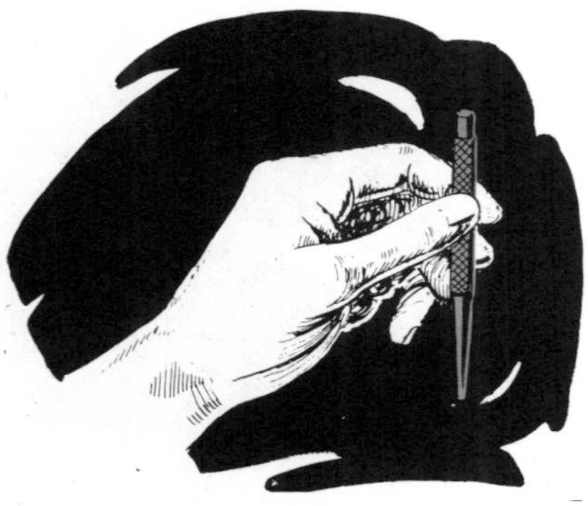

Fig. 354. Holding Nail Set

3. In drawing a long nail, a larger block should be used.

Driving Nails in Hardwood

1. One method of driving a nail in hardwood is to hold the nail very tightly between the first finger and thumb of the left hand while driving with the right hand. If the nail should bend, pull it out and drive a new nail in the same place.
2. Apply soap or wax to the nail to make it penetrate more readily.
3. Another way to drive nails in hardwood is to drill holes in the outside piece slightly smaller than the nails. Soap or wax on the nail will make the nail penetrate in the second piece more easily.

Driving Nails Diagonally

1. It is sometimes necessary to drive nails at an angle in order to obtain a stronger joint, Figs. 352 and 353.
2. Drive nails diagonally through one piece to toenail to another, as in Fig. 352.
3. Drive one nail straight and in the center of the board and then follow by driving the other nails diagonally as in Fig. 353.

Setting a Nail

1. A nail set is usually used to complete the driving of finishing nails, casing nails and brads. It is used to set nails below the surface of the wood, in fine cabinet work and interior house trim. The de pressions are filled with plastic wood so the nailheads are not visible.
2. Select a nail set with a point slightly smaller than the head of the nail.

Fig. 355. Keep Nail Set in Line With Nail

3. Hold the set firmly between the thumb and the first finger of the left hand as shown in Fig. 354.
4. With the hand resting on the surface of the piece, place the point of the nail set on the center of the nail head. With the third finger guiding the point of the nail set, drive the nail about ⅛″ below the surface, Fig. 355. To keep the set from slipping off the nail head, hold the nail set in line with the nail.
5. Common nails need not be set since they are used in rough carpentry or only in unexposed places in other woodwork.

Questions

1. Should the point of a nail set be larger or smaller than the head of the nail? Why?
2. Of what materials are most nails made?
3. Name the kinds of nails with which you are most familiar.
4. When driving a nail, should you keep your eye on the nail or the hammer?
5. Explain how to drive a finishing nail.
6. Name three ways of driving nails in hardwood.
7. What is the purpose of driving nails diagonally?

UNIT 51

How Nails are Made and Sold

Until the Colonial period the nails used in this country were forged by hand from wrought iron rods. In the early revolutionary days, the New England farmers were engaged in nail making as a profitable home industry. The war of the revolution brought on new economic demands and changes. One of these was the forced movement toward mass production in manufacturing. This marked the beginning of the making of nails by machines.

Early machine-made nails were of steel. They were really "cut nails"; they were cut from tapered plates. These nails were cut one after another from the edges of these plates. These early nails were tapered squares. The ends were blunt and the heads were square and much smaller than those of the nails now produced. These old square nails are still doing service in buildings erected in the early days of this country.

Modern Nails

Modern nails are made from harder steel than were those of earlier times. The superiority of modern nails is in the quality of steel, the uniformity of the body, the shape of the head, and in the pointing at the ends.

Modern nails are made from steel wire, which is made in special machines. A power-driven drum is mounted on a bench and the wire is wound into this drum after it is pulled through a special form called a die. This die is made of high quality steel, and it is perforated with holes that are gauged exactly to take a particular size of wire. These holes are tapered and the wire is started through the large end. The coil of wire from which the nails are to be made is placed on a reel. One end of the wire is passed through the die and fastened to the power-driven drum. As the drum revolves, the wire passes through the die.

The drawn wire is placed on a reel in front of each nail machine. One end of the wire is fed into the machine through a small hole in a vertical casting. From the opposite side of the machine there comes a stream of nails which drop into small iron containers. The head of the nail is formed by a hammer blow from a very powerful device which is operated by a cam. The pointing is done by a pair of dies having V-shaped cutting edges.

The nails are now ready for polishing. They are placed in a large tumbling machine where they are rolled and tumbled against each other and the sides of the tumbler. Sawdust is also placed in the tumbler in order to clean the nails thoroughly of grease and dirt.

The number of nail machines in a given factory varies. Factories with 250 machines in operation are common. Each machine can produce from 150 to 350 nails per minute depending somewhat on the size of nails. Three-penny nails are turned out at the rate of 350 per minute, and sixty-penny nails at the rate of 150 per minute. Nails are packed in kegs which hold one hundred pounds. These kegs are marked to designate the size and the kind of nails contained in the kegs. Nails are sold in any quantity by lumber yards and hardware dealers.

Kinds of Nails

There are many kinds of nails and each has its particular use. However, there are a few kinds that everybody should know. They are:

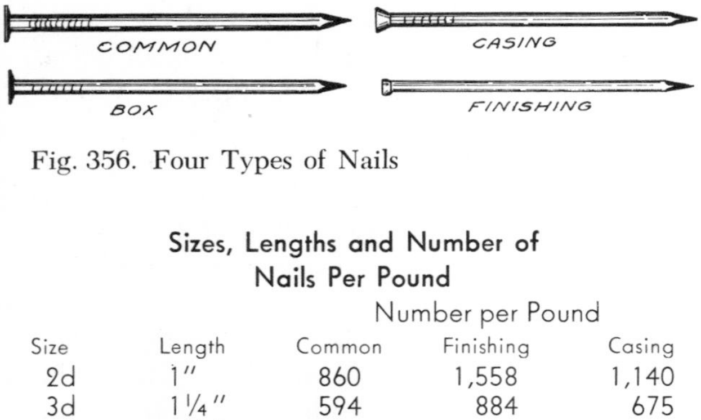

Fig. 356. Four Types of Nails

Sizes, Lengths and Number of Nails Per Pound

Size	Length	Common	Finishing	Casing
		Number per Pound		
2d	1″	860	1,558	1,140
3d	1¼″	594	884	675
4d	1½″	339	767	567
5d	1¾″	230	491	396
6d	2″	135	359	260
8d	2½″	96	214	160
10d	3″	63	134	108
12d	3¼″	52	120	99
16d	3½″	38	91	69
20d	4″	30	61	50
30d	4½″	23		45
40d	5″	17		35
50d	5½″	13		
60d	6″	10		

common nails, box nails, casing nails, and *finishing nails.* Fig. 356. The size of nails is specified by the term penny (d), prefixed by a number, such as 6d, 10d. They vary in size from 2-penny to 60-penny. The larger ones are called spikes.

It is interesting to know how the term penny (d) came into use. One theory is that the term had its origin in England and that it represented the price per pound in terms of pence. Another theory holds that in earlier times, nails were specified according to the weight of a thousand nails. Eight-penny nails weighed eight pounds to a thousand; four-penny nails weighed four pounds to the thousand. Whichever is true, we still buy nails according to the term penny: 4d, 6d, 8d, 16d, and so one.

Common nails are larger in diameter and they have wider heads than do other nails. They are used almost entirely in rough carpentry.

Box nails are not as large in diameter as common nails but they have wide heads. They are used in box construction and in certain types of carpentry where common nails would be too large.

Casing nails are used when large heads are undesirable as in blind nailing of flooring and ceiling. Casing nails are smaller in diameter than are box nails.

Finishing nails or wire brads are the most slender of all nails and they have the smallest heads. They are used in fine woodworking such as in the inside finishing of homes and in the blind nailing of furniture.

Questions

1. In the early period of our country how were nails made and by whom?
2. What led to making nails by machines during the revolution?
3. Describe the first machine-made nails.
4. From what are the best nails made to-day?
5. How and in what quantities are nails packed for shipment?
6. What nails are most in use today?
7. How are nails specified as to size?
8. Common nails are generally used for what kind of work?

UNIT 52

Fastening with Screws

A joint held with screws is secure and lasting. An important advantage in using screws is that the parts fastened can be taken apart without injury to them, and they can be readily assembled again.

Screwdrivers

The common screwdriver may be purchased with any length of blade from two inches to eighteen inches, Fig. 357. In the better screwdrivers, the blade is extended through the handle, and it has a flattened shank to which the handle is riveted.

The *screwdriver bit* is a screwdriver blade, the upper end of which has been forged to a square tapered shank like that of an auger bit, Fig. 358. This square shank makes it possible to use the bit in the brace in the same way that an auger bit is used. Screwdriver bits are usually five inches in length and from one-fourth to one-half inch in width at the point.

The *automatic screwdriver* can be operated more rapidly than can the common screwdriver, Fig. 359. It is made on the same principle as the *automatic drill*. There is a ratchet arrangement which makes it possible to drive in one direction and release in the other. The best of this type can be used to both drive and withdraw screws. It can also be locked to act as a plain screwdriver.

The special screwdriver shown in Fig. 360 has been designed to fit the recessed heads of Phillips screws. These special screws are used on nearly all automobiles, trucks, bus bodies, furniture, and many other assembled articles.

Before attempting to turn a screw, see that the screwdriver bit is properly ground to fit the slot. See also that the bit is as wide as the screw head. Grind the screwdriver square and flat at the point as shown at *C*, Fig. 361. It should be ground to fit snugly in the opening of the screw. A screwdriver which is improperly ground, as at *A* and *B*, Fig. 361, will slip out of the screw slot, damage the head of the screw, and mar the surface of the wood.

Screws

The common types of screws for joining wood, Fig. 362, are the flat head, *A*, the oval head, *B*, and the round head, *C*. The most common wood screws used are the steel flat head, and these are used when ornamentation

Fig. 357. Screwdriver (Stanley)

Fig. 358. Screwdriver Bit – Used in the Brace (Stanley)

Fig. 359. Spiral Ratchet Screwdriver (Stanley)

Fig. 360. Screwdriver for Phillips Screw (Stanley)

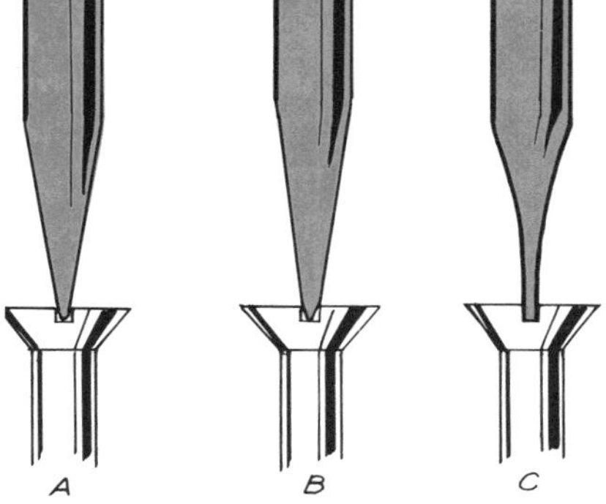

Fig. 361. Bit Should Fit Slot as at *C*

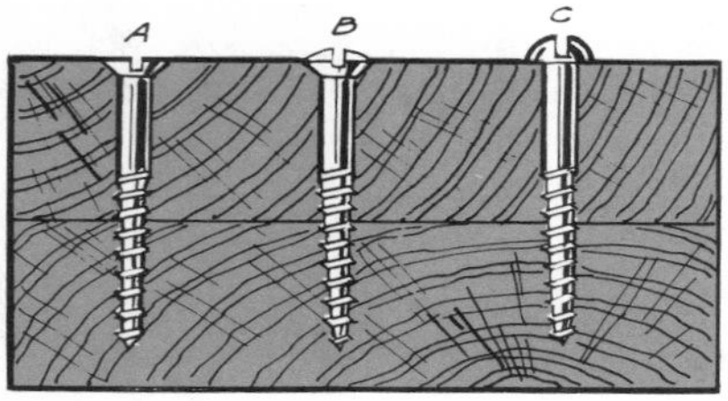

Fig. 362. Screw Heads

Fig. 363. Lay Out Positions of Screws

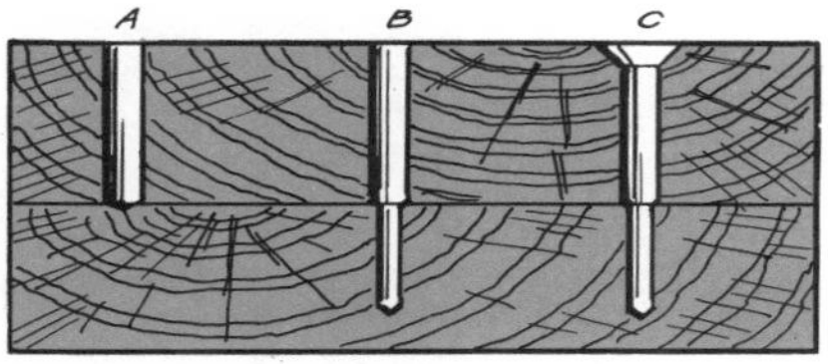

Fig. 364. Drill Clearance and Pilot Holes in Hard Wood

is not important. Oval head screws are used mostly in attaching hardware. Round head screws are used when ornamentation is desirable. See special unit on screws.

Fastening Soft Wood

1. Determine the kind, the diameter, and the length of screw you wish to use. The screw should penetrate the second piece about $\frac{2}{3}$ the length of the screw.
2. Lay out the positions of the screws from the edge or the end of the stock in a similar way to that shown in Fig. 363.
3. Drill the hole in the outside piece slightly smaller than the diameter of the shank of the screw, as at *A*, Fig. 364. Be sure to test for the proper size by drilling a hole in a piece of scrap stock.
4. It is not necessary to drill a pilot hole, as at *B*, Fig. 364, when working in soft wood. Make a starting hole with an awl in the second piece if it is difficult to start the screw. It is usually not necessary to countersink for the head of the screw when working in soft wood.

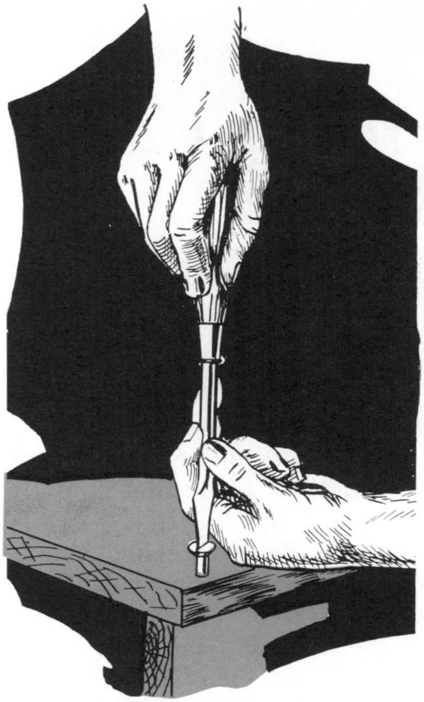

Fig. 365. Hold Screwdriver in Straight Line with Screw

5. To drive the screw, hold the screwdriver at right angles with the surface of the board and in line with the screw. While driving, guide the screw and at the same time hold the end of the screwdriver in the screw slot with the thumb and index finger of the left hand, Fig. 365.
6. Do not allow the screwdriver to slip out of the slot or it will mar the wood.
7. Stop turning the screw when it has been driven home. Continued turning may strip the threads which the screw has made in the wood.

Fastening Hard Wood

1. When fastening pieces of hard wood together, it is necessary to drill small holes in the wood for the screws. Brass and aluminum screws are soft and likely to twist or break if holes are not drilled.

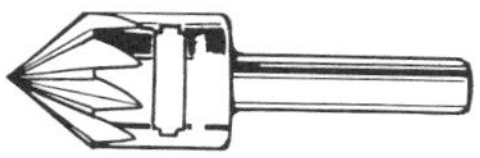

Fig. 366. Countersink

Fig. 367. Square Shank Countersink

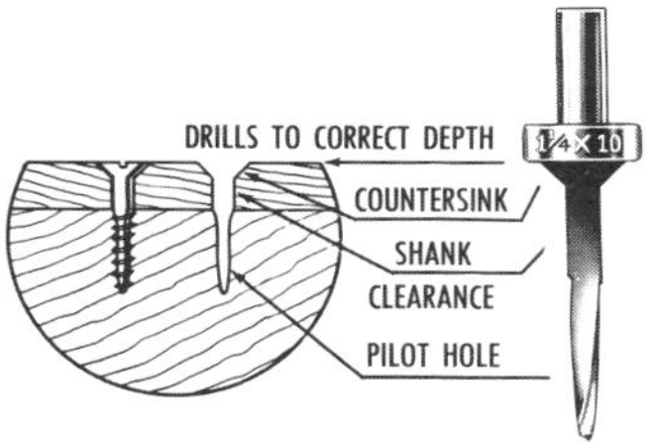

Fig. 367A. Screwmate

2. Use two sizes of bits or drills in boring screw holes in hard wood, Fig. 364.
3. Bore the hole in the outside piece first being sure that it is correct for the diameter of the shank, *A*, Fig. 364.
4. Bore the pilot hole in the second piece or bottom piece to a length equal to that of the screw thread and slightly smaller than the core or root diameter *B*, Fig. 364. If a pilot hole is not bored in the second piece, the screw may break or the stock may split.

   Specially ground bits, called *screwmates,* can be purchased. These bits are shaped to make the pilot hole and the shank hole at the same time.
5. Countersink for the head of either a flat head or an oval head screw.
6. Put soap or wax on the threads of the screw so it will drive easier.
7. On heavy work a long screwdriver permits more arm movement, resulting in more turning force.

Countersinking

1. To countersink, the hole is reamed out with a *countersink*, Fig. 367, so that the head of a flat head or oval head screw will be even or below the surface of the board, Fig. 362.
2. The countersink is fastened in the brace in the same way as an auger bit.

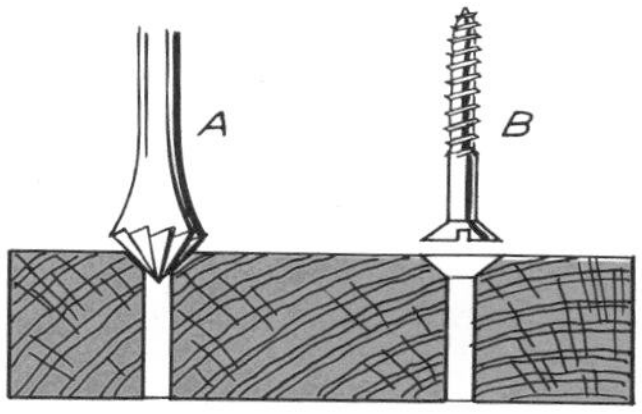

Fig. 368. Checking Countersinking

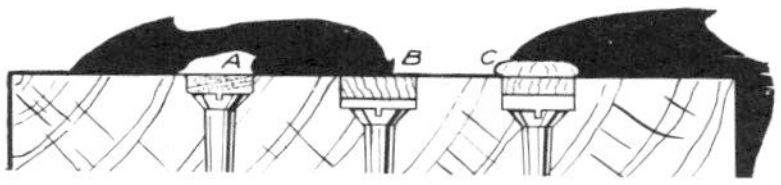

Fig. 369. Methods of Covering Screw Heads

3. Place the point of the countersink in the shank hole and ream out the hole as shown in Fig. 368.
4. Test the countersink hole by placing the head of the screw in it. The width of the opening should be slightly larger than the width of the head of the screw as in *B*, Fig. 368.
5. Do not countersink for round head screws.

Covering Screw Heads in Projects

1. The head of a screw is sometimes covered.
2. It can be covered with plastic wood as shown at *A*, Fig. 369. Plastic wood can be obtained in small tubes or cans in almost any color desired.
3. A wood plug cut with a special cutter can be glued in to cover the screw as in *B*, Fig. 369. Plane the plug even with the surface of the wood.
4. Ornamental wooden buttons can be used to cover screws. See *C*, Fig. 369. They are sold in various sizes and are finished in the common woods to match a project.

Questions

1. Should a screwdriver be sharpened to a chisel point?
2. Name the kinds of screws.
3. When are round head screws used?
4. How long should a screw be in comparison with the thickness of the stock used?

5. How large should the hole be for the shank of a screw?
6. Is it necessary to drill holes for the thread on screws?
7. What can be used on screws to make them more easily driven?
8. What is a countersink?

UNIT 53 How Screws are Made and Sold

Screws were at one time made by hand. A blank screw was forged on an anvil and threads were then cut with a file. Later the lathe was used in cutting these threads. The coming of machines and mass production included equipment for making screws. The screws made by these machines are more uniform and accurate in size than those made by hand. *Automatic screw machines* have been adapted for many other products requiring high rates of production and several machining operations.

Types of Screws

There are many types of screws available for various purposes, but the flat head, round head, and oval head are most common. There are other kinds of screws, but they are regarded as special.

Screws are made of steel, brass, bronze and copper. The most common are those made of steel and brass. Steel screws are the least expensive and are used for all ordinary purposes, but they should not be used on a job that is to be in contact with moisture. Brass screws are best for jobs to be subjected to continued dampness, as, for instance, in boat building or in general outdoor work.

Everyone should know how screws are specified and sold. The flat head screws are usually sold in the "bright" finish and the "round" head screws are sold in the "blue" finish. The *gauge* of a screw is a term used to specify the "shank", or diameter as measured under the head, Fig. 370. When buying screws specify them according to the length, gauge, shape, head and finish. For example, a 1½-inch number 8, flat head, brass screw is designated as 1½" No. 8, F.H.B. A round head screw this size would be written 1½" No. 8, R.H.B.

Selecting Screws

The selection of the kind and size of screw depends upon the job. Approximately two-thirds of the screw should enter the wood to which you are fastening. The proper kind and size of screw to use is a matter of judgment

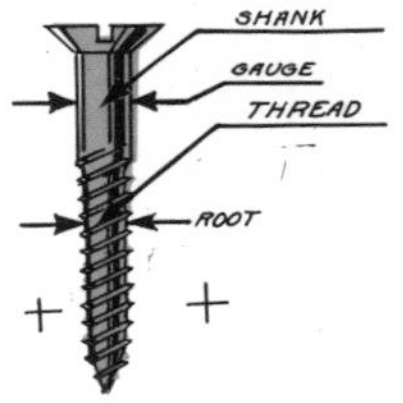

Fig. 370. Parts of a Screw

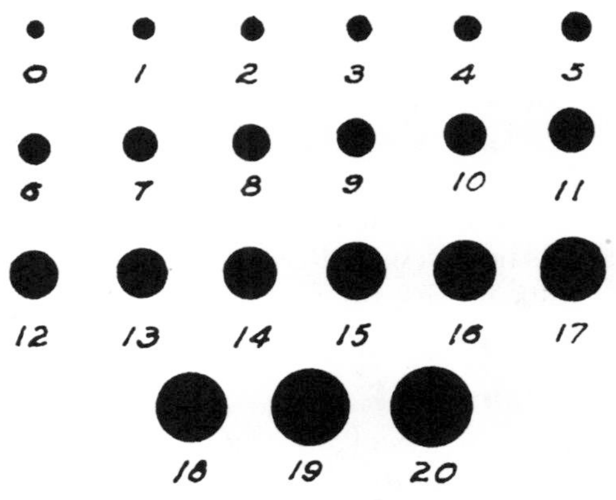

GAUGES	0-4	0-8	1-10	2-12	2-14	3-14	3-16	4-18	6-20
LENGTHS	1/4"	3/8"	1/2"	5/8"	3/4"	7/8"	1"	1 1/4"	1 3/4"
GAUGES	6-20	6-20	6-20	8-20	8-24	10-24	12-24	14-24	14-24
LENGTHS	2"	2 1/4"	2 1/2"	2 3/4"	3"	3 1/2"	4"	4 1/2"	5"

Fig. 371. Gauge Numbers of Screws

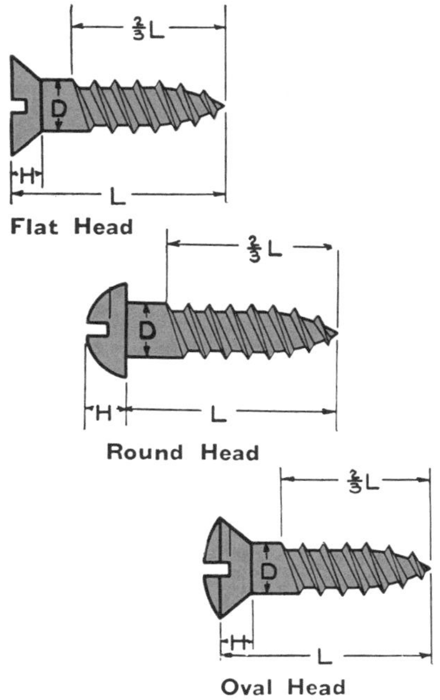

Fig. 372. Standard Dimensions of Wood Screws

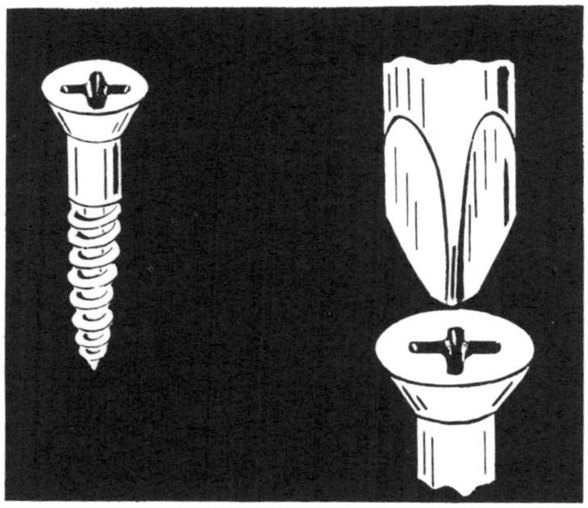

Fig. 373. Phillips Head Screws and Screwdriver Tip

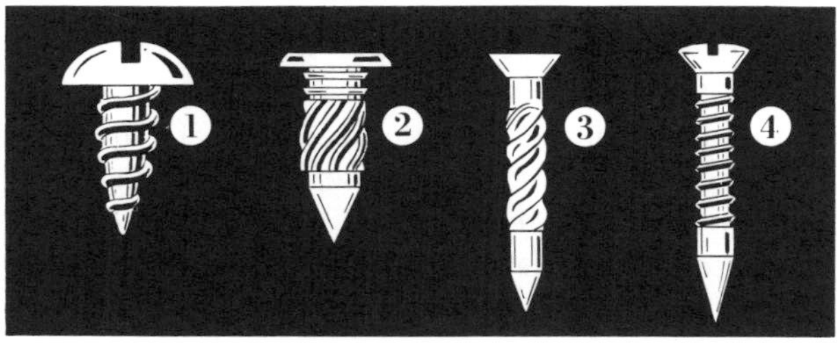

Fig. 374. Drive and Self-Tapping Screws

and practice. If the stock is rather thin, leaving very little of it around the screw, a thin screw should be used. Such a screw should have a gauge number representing one of the smallest diameters available for the particular length of screw to be used. See Fig. 371 for a list of gauge numbers usually available for each length of screw. If a heavy screw for gaining strength is needed, select one with a high gauge number for its length.

The larger the number representing the screw gauge, the larger the screw. Each length of screw may be secured in several gauges. Screw gauge and wire gauge are not the same. The length of the flat head screw is measured from the top to the point of the screw. The length of round head screws is measured from the bottom of the head to the point of the screw. Oval head screws are measured from the widest part of the head. See Fig. 372.

Buying Screws

Screws, except large ones, are packed in boxes containing one gross. A change to packing in units of 100 may be made for convenience in pricing. Large screws are packed in boxes containing one-half gross. It is possible to purchase screws in any quantity, small or large, but the smaller quantities of less than a full box will cost more in proportion than does the larger amount. Assorted sizes and kinds are available in small boxes.

Phillips Screws for Wood

There are many other types of screws used in wood construction. The Phillips screw, Fig. 373, is probably one of the most widely used in shop and industry. This screw has a cross-shaped recess in place of a slot. It is easier to start than the standard screw, because the driver point centers itself, and the screwdriver is less likely to slip. They are used in radio, television, and automobile construction.

Drive and Self-Tapping Screws

The drive screw combines the driving feature of a nail and the holding power of a screw. See Fig. 374.

1. The self-tapping screw, *1* in Fig. 374, has threads much like the standard

screw. Although it is self-tapping, it must be driven home with a screwdriver. This type of a screw is usually used to attach sheet metal, plastic, and composition material to wood.

2. The special drive screw, *2* in Fig. 374, is especially useful in attaching leather or cardboard to wood.
3. A typical common drive screw for use in wood is shown as *3* in Fig. 374.
4. A special drive screw for fastening light metal to wood is shown as *4* in Fig. 374. It is driven through the metal and part way through the wood with a hammer, and then seated with a screwdriver.

Questions

1. Do screws have greater holding power than nails?
2. Tell how the first screws were made.
3. Name the three general types of screws.
4. Most screws are made of what two metals?
5. For what kind of work are brass screws more desirable than iron screws and why?
6. What is meant by the gauge of a screw?
7. What is the proper way to write a 1¾ inch number nine flat head brass screw?
8. How many screws are packed in a box?

UNIT 54 Common Hardware Used in Woodworking

In addition to the nails and screws used in assembling, many other hardware items are necessary to complete a cabinet or to give a piece of furniture a final trim or touch. Among such items of hardware are various kinds of hinges, locks, pulls, knobs, and handles.

Hinges

The *butt hinge* is the most commonly used hinge, however it is usually the most difficult to apply. A butt hinge consists of three parts: the two leaves (including knuckles) and the connecting pin. The pin in a butt hinge may be riveted to the knuckle as in a box hinge or it may be loose as on a butt hinge for a common door, Figs. 375 and 376.

Surface hinges may be purchased in a greater variety of shapes than butt hinges. A typical surface hinge is shown in Fig. 377. They are attractive, easy to apply, and are used on many kinds of cabinet doors.

Chest hinges, Fig. 378, are made with one leaf of each hinge bent at a right angle so that when attached they are invisible from the outside of the chest. Only one gain is needed for both leaves of a chest hinge. The depth of the gain is equal to twice the thickness of one leaf.

In Fig. 379, is shown a screen or *double action* type of hinge. Hinges of this type make it possible for a screen or special door to swing two ways. They are attached to the edges like regular butt hinges.

The long or *continuous hinge* shown in Fig. 380 is often called a *piano hinge*. It is commonly used on desks and piano lids and on other fine cabinets such as radio and television cabinets. It is really a long butt hinge.

The hinge shown in Fig. 381 is a *kitchen-cabinet-visible type* for an offset or overlapping door. Hinges for kitchen cabinets or similar cabinets are made for rabbeted, lipped, offset, or flush doors. Some of these hinges are of the semi-concealed type in which one leaf is fastened to the stile of the cabinet and the other leaf to the edge or on the back face of the door. Kitchen cabinet hinges are usually fastened like regular surface hinges.

Invisible hinges of the Soss type are used in fine cabinets or furniture pieces such as desks, radio, and television cabinets, Fig. 382. When they are set or mortised in the edges of frames, lids, or doors, they become invisible. The mortises for Soss hinges are usually made with a brace and bit.

Hasps are combination locking devices commonly used on cabinets of many types, on boxes, and on swinging doors of garages and barns. There are two general kinds of hasps, the T-hinge hasp and the strap hinge hasp. They come in various sizes, from the small jewelry box size to the large, heavy, door size. The hasp shown in Fig. 383 is a strap hinge hasp.

Cabinet Locks and Catches

Many kinds and types of cabinet locks are used in woodworking. Locks are used on desks, cabinets, drawers, chests, boxes, and cabinets of various kinds. The *mortise lock* shown in Fig. 384 and the *rim lock* shown in Fig. 385 are the two most commonly used locks in cabinet making. A mortise must be cut in the edge of one side of the chest in order to receive the body of the lock. It is possible to install a mortise or a rim lock so only the keyhole shows from the outside. The rim-type

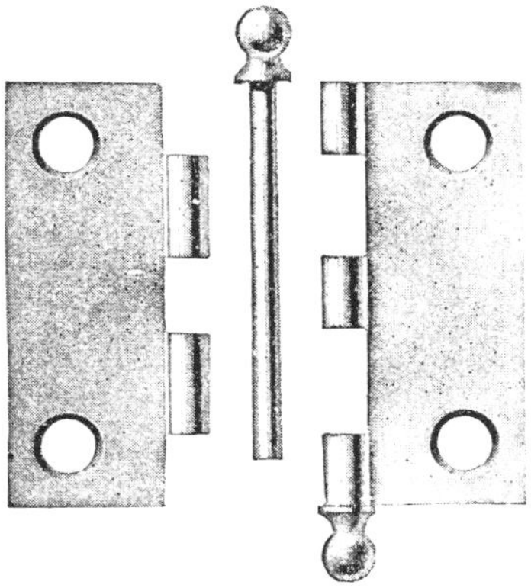

Fig. 375. Loose-Pin Butt Hinge

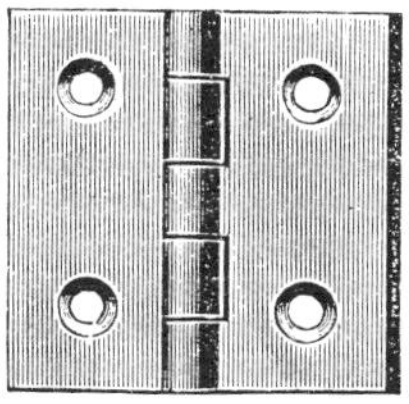

Fig. 376. Solid Butt Hinge

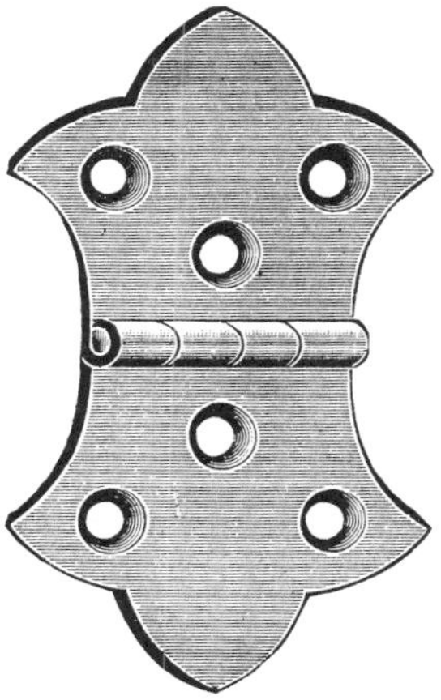

Fig. 377 Surface Hinge

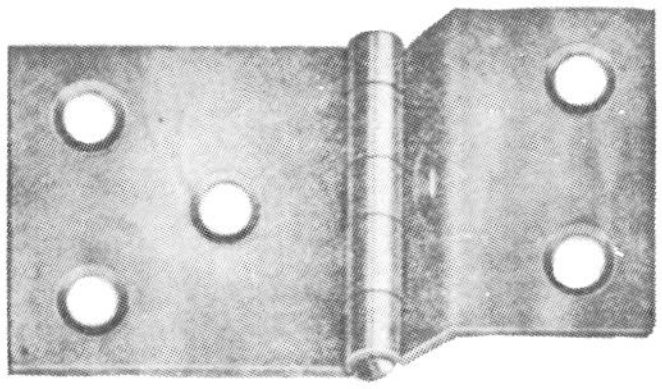

Fig. 378 Chest Hinge

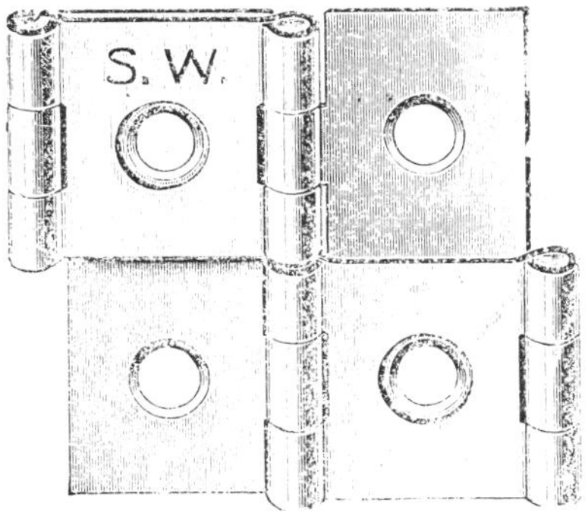

Fig. 379. Double Action Hinge

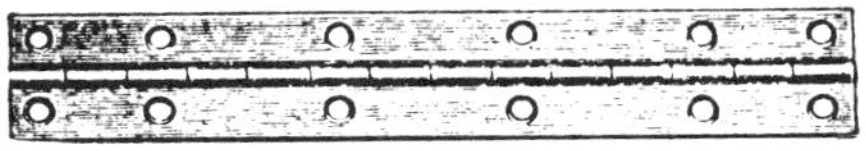

Fig. 380. Continuous or Piano Hinge

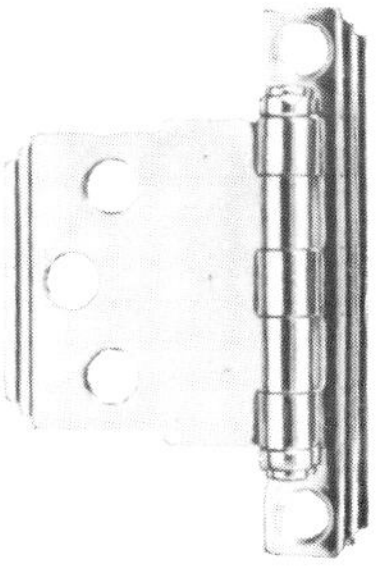

Fig. 381. Cabinet Hinge

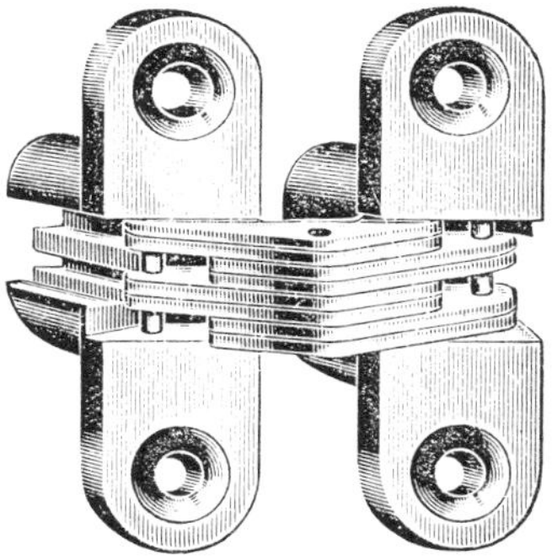

Fig. 382. Soss Hinge (Brodhead-Garrett)

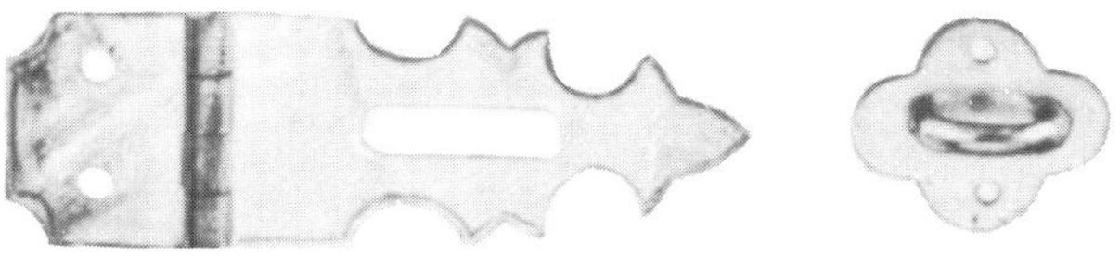

Fig. 383. Strap Hinge Hasp (Brodhead-Garrett)

cabinet locks are usually used on chests, Fig. 385.

Escutcheons are trim plates used to cover the rough edges of keyholes. They give a chest a finished tough. Escutcheons are often attached to chest fronts with fancy, round-head copper nails, Figs. 386 and 387.

It is frequently necessary to fit doors, wall cabinets, kitchen cabinets, and other types of cabinets with special devices to keep them closed. Some of these devices are the *catches, turns,* and *latches. Magnetic catches* are very commonly used. They are easy to install and do not require as much precision in their location as some other types. In Fig. 388 is shown a common *cabinet door latch* that has been available for many years. It is often necessary to use a catch of the *elbow* type, Fig. 389, to hold one of the doors closed when double doors are used in a cabinet. The latches shown in Figs. 390 and 391 are other common

Fig. 384. Mortise Lock

Fig. 385. Rim Lock

Fig. 386. Round Escutcheons

Fig. 387. Oval Escutcheons

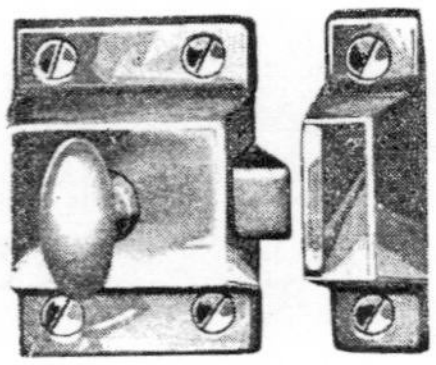

Fig. 388. Cabinet Latch

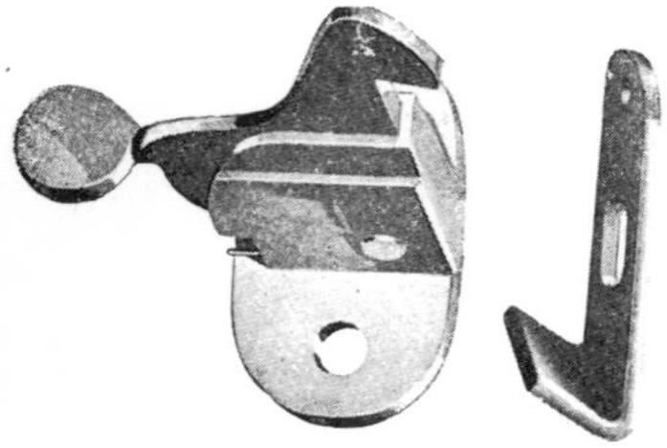

Fig. 389. Elbow Catch

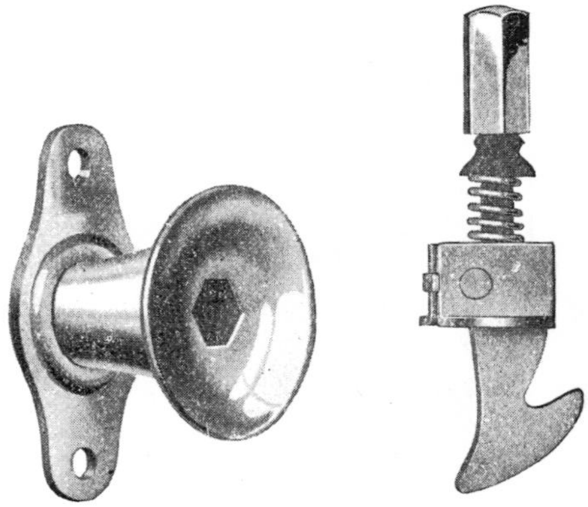

Fig. 390. Cabinet Catch

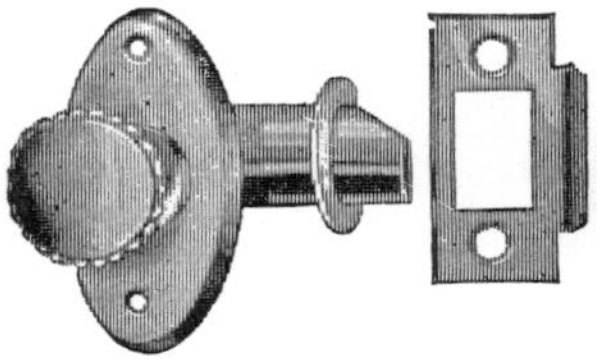

Fig. 391. Cabinet Catch

Fig. 392. Ball Catch

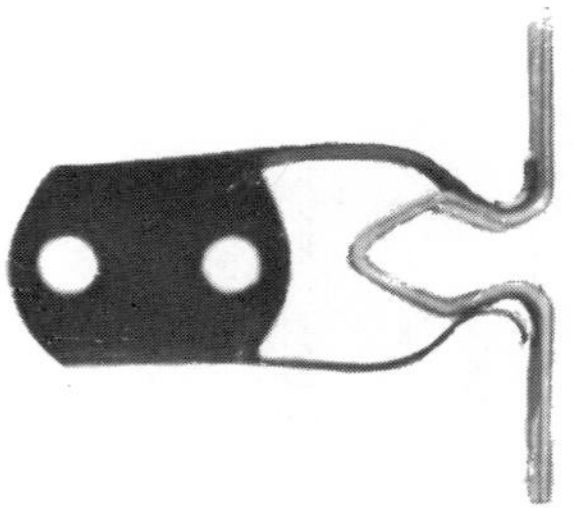

Fig. 393. Friction Catch (Brodhead-Garrett)

devices used on kitchen and medicine cabinets. Many other types of holding devices are available for use. When purchasing them, consideration should be given to the finish as well as to other hardware used on the cabinet or project.

The *ball catch* shown in Fig. 392 is especially useful on kitchen, radio, and television cabinets. The small brass cylinder contains a steel spring which operates a small steel ball. This ball fits into an opening in a piece of metal or catch which is attached to one edge of the cabinet.

The *friction catch* shown in Fig. 393 is easy to apply and is especially useful on shop supply and tool cabinets.

Knobs and Handles

Knobs are made in various designs and of many materials. Four types of knobs are shown: Figs. 394 and 395 are metal knobs, Fig. 396 is a wooden knob, and Fig. 397 is a glass knob. They are available in many other patterns at your hardware dealer. It is important to select carefully so the knob matches materials and other hardware.

Fig. 394. Round Metal Knob (Acme)

Fig. 395. Antiqued Knob (Acme)

Fig. 396. Wood Knob (Acme)

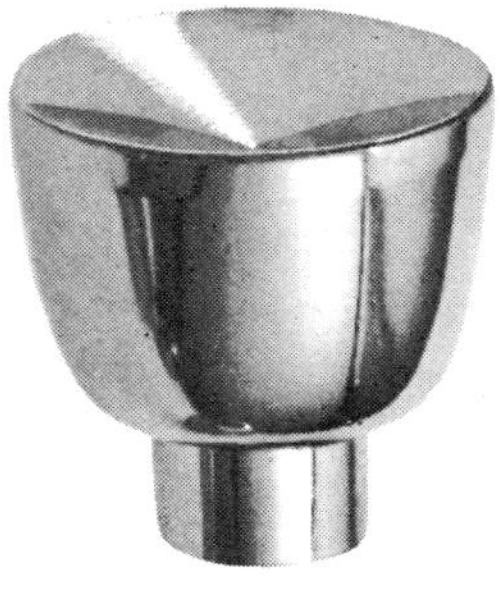

Fig. 397. Glass Knob (Acme)

Handles, like knobs, are made in various designs and materials. Four types of handles are shown: In Figs. 398, 399 and Fig. 400 are three common metal handles; and in Fig. 401 is a period metal handle. Handles should be selected to harmonize with the wood and other hardware used. The size of a drawer determines the number of handles or knobs needed. A small drawer will need but one handle or knob, and it should be located just above the center of the drawer front.

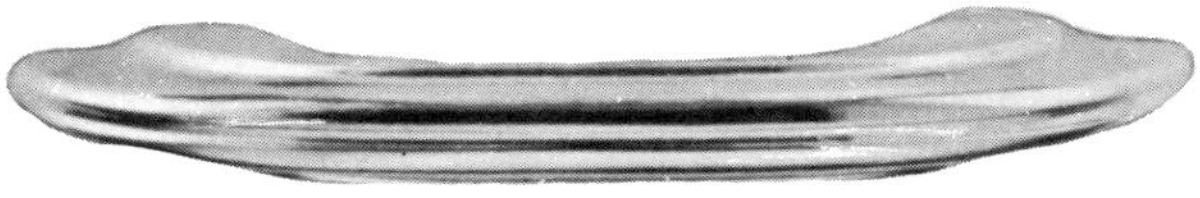

Fig. 398. Metal Handle

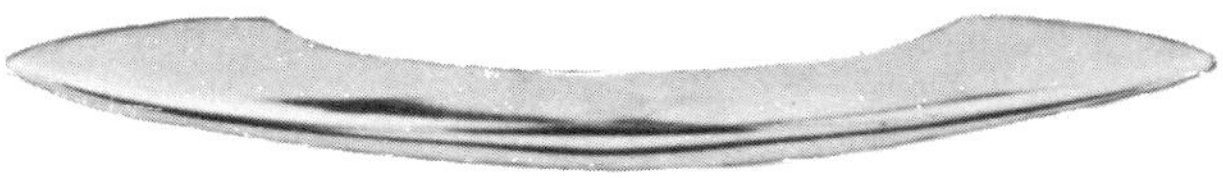

Fig. 399. Metal Handle

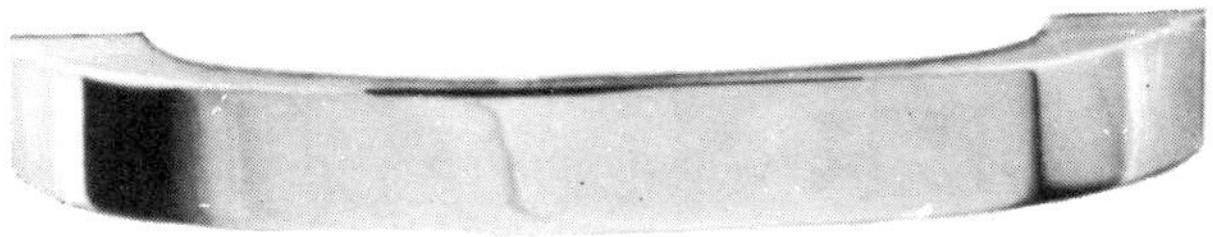

Fig. 400. Metal Handle

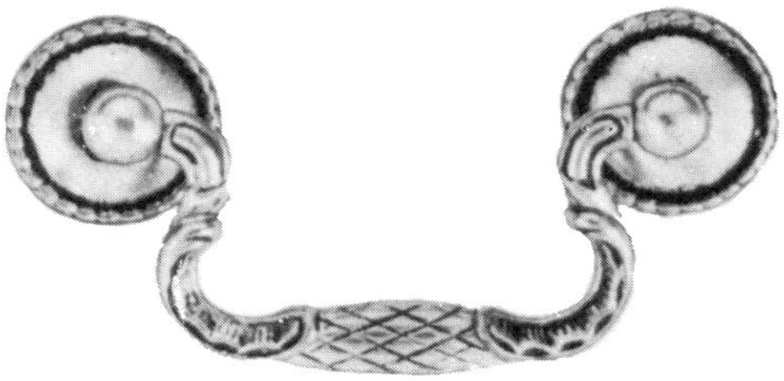

Fig. 401. Period Style Metal Handle

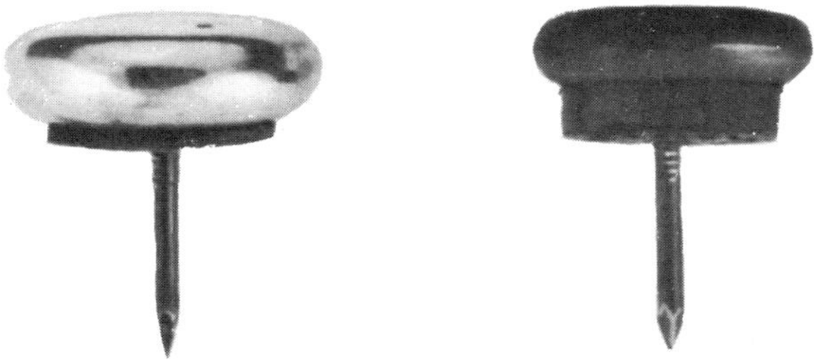

Fig. 402. Chair Glides

Only a small selection of the extensive amount of hardware available for use in woodworking can be shown in this book. A visit to your hardware dealer will indicate the many kinds of hardware available. You will find hardware for special purposes such as the chair glides shown in Fig. 402.

Questions

1. What are two common types of butt hinges?
2. What is meant by surface hinges?
3. What kind of hinges would you use on a cedar chest?
4. Where would you use an escutcheon?
5. What is a ball catch? A friction catch?
6. Name three kinds of furniture knobs.
7. Where would you make use of the Soss type of hinge?
8. What are hasps?
9. What is the difference between a handle and a pull?

UNIT 55

Fitting Butt Hinges

There are many kinds of hinges of various shapes and sizes. The kind that is most used is known as the butt hinge. The sizes of butt hinges are indicated in inches for length and as *broad, middle,* and *narrow* for width. The pin in a butt hinge may be either riveted to the knuckle as in box hinges, or removable from the knuckle as in butt hinges on a common door. Fig. 403 shows the parts for a butt hinge. Other types of hinges and hardware were described in Unit 54.

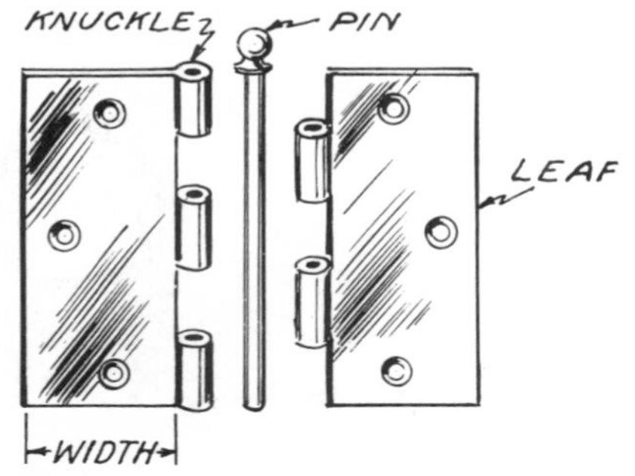

Fig. 403. Parts of Butt Hinge

Fig. 404. Mark Along Each End with Pencil

Marking the Gain for the Hinge

1. In attaching a butt hinge, it is essential to cut *gains,* Fig. 408, to sink the leaves of the hinge into the wood to a depth equal to the thickness of the knuckle. Should the knuckle be ⅛″ in diameter, each leaf should be set $\frac{1}{16}$″ into the wood.
2. The gains may be cut in one or in both of the pieces to be hinged together. In hanging a door the gains are usually cut in both the door and frame. In many types of cabinet work the gains are cut in one member only.
3. Determine the position of the hinge. Lay out the position of each gain by holding the hinge in place while marking along each end with a sharp pencil or a knife, Fig. 404.
4. Set the marking gauge so as to mark the width of one of the hinge leaves as shown in Fig. 405.

5. If the gains are to be cut in both members, mark the depth by setting the marking gauge to half the thickness of the knuckle. Make this mark on the side into which the gains open. This will be the side on which the knuckles of the hinge appear.
6. If the gains are to be cut in only one member as on a box, mark the depth of the gains equal to the thickness of the knuckle.

Cutting the Grain

1. Place a chisel in a vertical position on the line which locates the end of one hinge and with a mallet drive the chisel down to the gauge line which marks the depth of the hinge. Repeat this for the ends of all hinges.
2. Make a series of cuts with the chisel as shown in Fig. 406.
3. Pare the bottom of the gain to the gauge line, keeping the depth uniform, Fig. 407. Be careful not to go below the gauge line or to cut through the back of the gain.
4. Trim the walls of the gain and test by putting the hinge in place. Do not force the hinge into the gain, but carefully pare the walls until the hinge fits easily.

Attaching the Hinges

1. When attaching hinges to hard wood, drill a hole in the wood through one hole in each hinge leaf. The holes should be slightly smaller than the screws.

Fig. 405. Mark Width with Marking Gauge

2. Drive the screws with a screwdriver until the hinges are pulled into place.
3. Test to see if the door or cover fits properly. If it does not fit accurately, remove the screw in each leaf. It may be necessary to trim the gain deeper or to put paper shims under the leaves. Drill a new hole for each hinge, fasten the hinges and test again.
4. When the hinges are fitted properly, drive all the screws.
5. Be sure to bore the holes accurately or the screws will twist and break. Small brass screws are soft and twist off easily.

Fig. 406. Make a Series of Cuts with Chisel

Fig. 407. Pare Carefully to Gauge Line

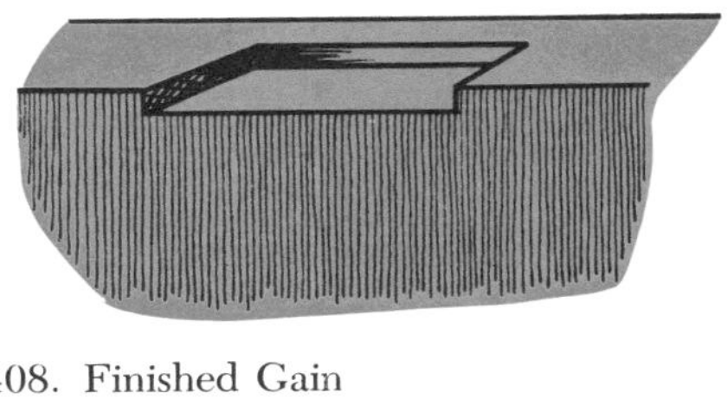

Fig. 408. Finished Gain

Apply wax or soap to them before driving.
6. It is not necessary to drill holes for screws in soft wood; mark the right spot with a nail or a brad awl.

Questions

1. What kind of hinge is in most common use?
2. How are the sizes of this hinge indicated?
3. What is a gain?
4. In hanging a door are the gains cut in both the door and the frame?
5. How deep are gains cut?
6. What tools are used in cutting gains?
7. Is it necessary to drill pilot holes for the screws?
8. When hinging a cover or door, how can you tell whether it fits properly before driving in all screws?

UNIT 56 Holding with Handscrews and Clamps

When gluing, handscrews and clamps serve as temporary devices for holding the stock together until the glue sets. There are many ingenious ways in which clamps can be used for holding stock while it is being worked. When an extra vise or a "third hand" is needed, handscrews and clamps supply this need very conveniently.

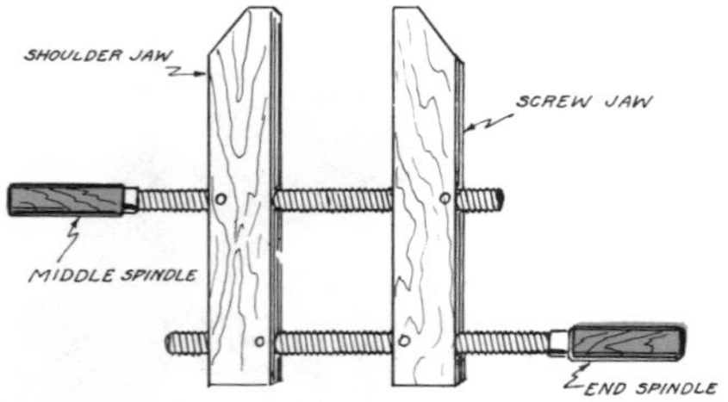

Fig. 409. Handscrew

Adjusting Handscrews

1. Handscrews vary in size from those with jaws four inches long to those with jaws twenty-two inches long.
2. The handscrew, Fig. 409, consists of four parts: the shoulder jaw and the screw jaw, both of which are made of maple; and the middle and end spindles made of steel. The jaws are already oiled when purchased. A few drops of machine oil should frequently be placed on the spindles.
3. To adjust the handscrew to fit as desired, hold the handle of the middle spindle in one hand and the handle of the end spindle in the other hand. Revolve the spindles together until the opening is about as desired.

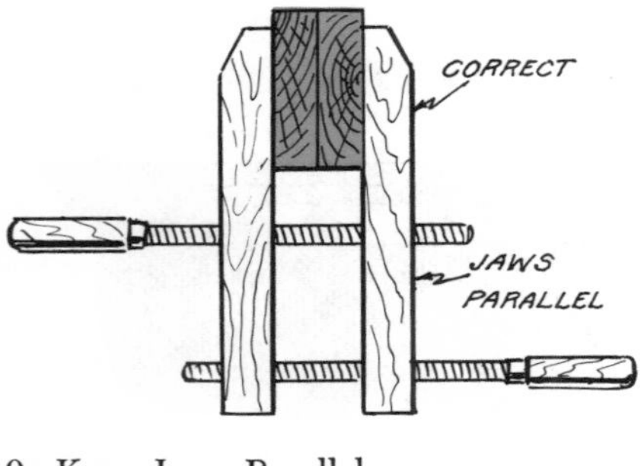

Fig. 410. Keep Jaws Parallel

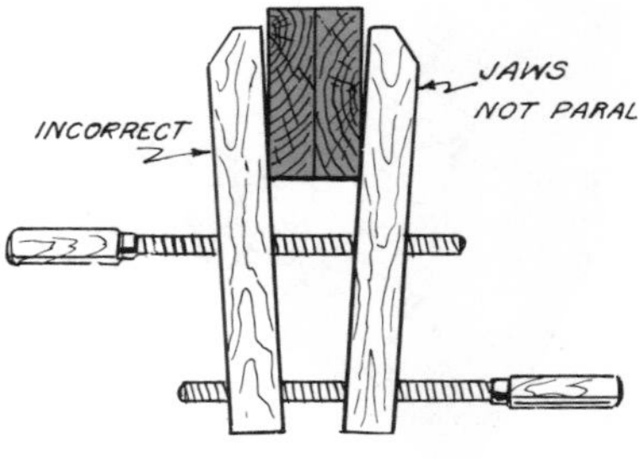

Fig. 411. Jaws Not Parallel – Pieces Will Slip

4. Adjust the jaws to the stock and screw the middle spindle tight. Adjust the end spindle next, being sure to keep the jaws parallel so as to press evenly on the stock, Fig. 410.
5. When you wish to take off the handscrew release the end spindle first and thus force the jaws apart.
6. In Fig. 411 is shown the incorrect way to use handscrews.

Adjusting Bar Clamps

The bar clamp, Fig. 413, is one of the most widely used of the various types of clamps. It is used chiefly when gluing edge-to-edge joints in wide pieces, for gluing up stock which is too wide to be spanned by other clamping devices, and in assembling furniture and frames. Bar clamps are made in sizes varying from one to eight feet in length, Fig. 412. They are made of steel with a screw at one end and an adjustable jaw at the other. This jaw can be adjusted so that any length, up to full length of the bar, can be obtained.

1. Before attempting to use the clamps, prepare blocks or strips of wood from waste stock. These pieces should be placed next to the wood and inside the jaws.
2. Determine the number of clamps to be used before starting to glue your work. Locate the position of the clamps on the boards, placing them about one foot apart.
3. Adjust all necessary clamps to the boards and tighten them to almost the required pressure. Test and inspect your work to see that it goes together properly and remove the clamps. Lay them aside, but have them at hand so they may be used quickly. Make sure that all clamps are drawn up uniformly when testing.
4. When making a table top or an edge-to-edge joint, use the clamps with handles all on one side as in Fig. 413. Use handscrews and wooden cleats as in Fig. 414 to keep the boards from buckling.
5. The clamps can also be used alternately on opposite sides. Place them at about one-foot intervals with one at each end of the assembled boards.

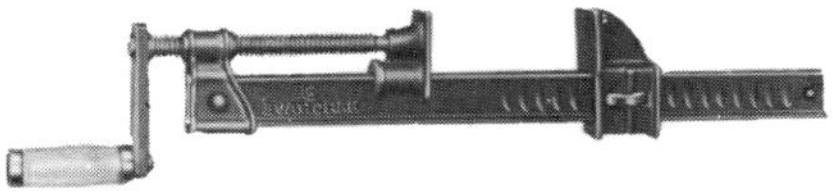

Fig. 412. "I" Bar Clamp (Cincinnati)

Fig. 413. Position of Clamps on Table Top

Fig. 414. Cleats Keep Top from Buckling

Clamping After Applying Glue

Apply the glue and place the clamps in position, beginning with the one at the center. See that the bars of the clamps are touching the stock at all points and draw them tightly. The clamps should be just tight enough to bring the matched edges of the pieces together. Do not force so tight that the edges of the wood are crushed.

Clamping Legs to Rails in Furniture Assembly

1. Place protecting pieces between the stock and iron jaws. Place the clamps in position, being sure that the pressure will be directly across the rails. Draw the clamps up snugly.
2. With the try square, or framing square, test the inside corners to see that the frame will draw up square. Correct any

error by tapping the ends of the legs with a mallet or by moving the clamp jaws from the center adjustment. If the frame will not draw up square, examine the joints to see that there are no obstructions or that they are cut properly.

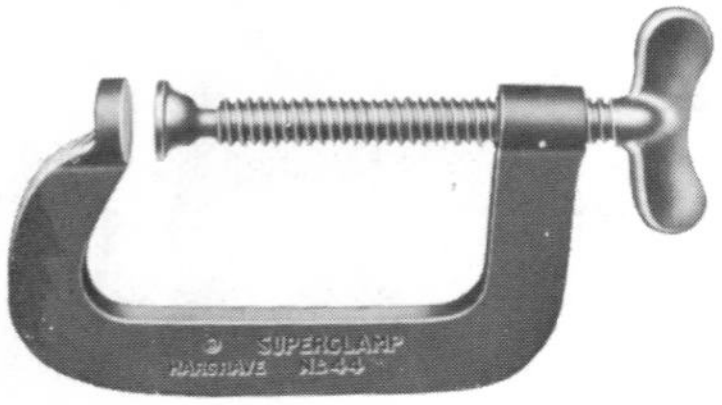

Fig. 415. C-Clamp (Cincinnati)

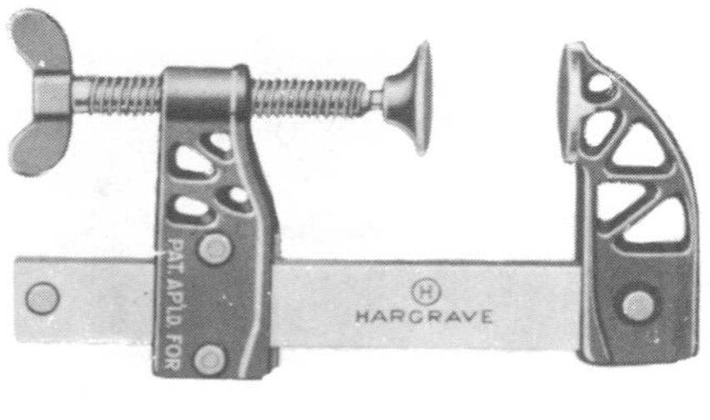

Fig. 416. Quick Clamp (Cincinnati)

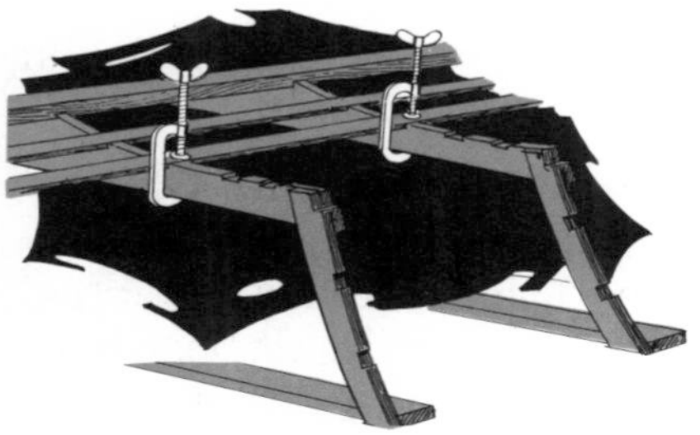

Fig. 416A. Typical Use of C-Clamp

3. Remove the clamps, being careful not to change their adjustment, and apply the glue. Replace the clamps and draw them up tightly. Do not force them.
4. Test again to make sure that the frame is square and set the work carefully aside in such a position that there will be no wind or twist while the glue is setting.

C Clamps

The C clamp, Fig. 415, is used in clamping small parts face-to-face or in holding pieces in place in large projects as in Fig. 416A. They are used in repair work and in clamping several pieces together when laying out work and when laying out duplicate parts. They are also used in holding temporary adjustments on a circular saw table or on a band saw table. An illustration of this would be the holding of a special fence for sawing balsa wood. The C clamp is made of steel or iron. It comes in several sizes, the smallest of which has a 1″ opening and the largest a 12″ opening. Essentially this clamp is used in the same manner as are bar clamps. Fig. 416 shows a convenient small adjustable steel clamp, similar to a C clamp, that is used on small work.

Questions

1. How are glued joints held in place until the glue sets?
2. What kind of clamps are used when gluing pieces edge to edge?
3. Before applying the glue, what besides the clamps should be made ready?
4. How tight should the clamps be made?
5. What is a C clamp?

UNIT 57 Kinds and Preparation of Glue

Glue is one of the oldest of the various materials used to fasten wood. Early Egyptian and Roman furniture assembled with glue hundreds of years ago is still in good condition in our museums.

Good glue will cement joints and parts together so that the glued parts will be stronger than the wood itself. Wood is more or less porous and when glue is applied, it spreads over the surface and seeps into the wood itself. There are several kinds of glue available and these have their special characteristics and properties which determine how and when to use them. Continued research will likely produce even better glues than the many good ones now available.

Glues may be divided into the following general classes:

- Animal glue
- Fish glue
- Casein glue
- Synthetic resin glue
- Resorcinal formaldehyde glue
- Polyvinyl resin glue
- Contact cements

Animal Glue

Animal glue has proved reliable through many years of use. Much of the furniture made hundreds of years ago was fastened with animal glue and the joints still hold. The better qualities of glue are made from hides, although most glue is made from both hides and bones. This glue may be purchased in flakes, sticks, or in powdered form. There are several grades, of which No. 2 is the poorest and No. AA-Ex is the best.

Good glue will absorb its own weight in water. The flakes should remain firm and keep their original shape when thoroughly soaked. Prepare the glue by soaking the dry flakes, or powder, in water until thoroughly softened, then add enough water to cover the resulting gelatinous mass. This should be heated to a temperature of 160° to 180° Fahrenheit while it is being used.

The exact consistency of glue is difficult to determine without special apparatus for testing. In shops with the ordinary glue pot equipment, the consistency is considered good when it is creamy and when long strings form as it runs from the brush.

The glue pot must be clean for each new batch of glue. *Do not add new glue to old glue.* In order to secure the best results, it is necessary that the hot glue be applied quickly and clamped quickly. It is also desirable to heat the stock to be glued so that the glue will not be chilled when it is applied. Large quantities of glue are of no advantage since the excess glue is squeezed out and wasted. When using animal glue, keep in mind that freshly prepared glue is best.

Fish Glue

Although hot animal glue is considered excellent for fastening joints, cold fish glue has become popular for general woodworking use. It is ready prepared and convenient to use on small work. Liquid fish glue is made from the tissues and scales of fish and occasionally from heads and bones. Acetic acid in the glue keeps it liquid if the container is kept tightly closed when not in use.

Casein Glue

Milk and certain chemicals are used in making casein glue. It is sold in a powdered form in either yellow or white color. This glue is strong and very water resistant. It can be quickly prepared and it is lasting and tough when used on such woods as spruce and pine, but it does not adhere well to oak. A ten percent solution of caustic soda should be applied to the joint surfaces of oak and allowed to dry before applying casein glue. This makes a strong joint.

The directions for use always appear on the casein glue containers and they should be followed closely so as to make sure of the greatest possible strength. Casein glue is used thicker than animal or liquid glues and must be applied with a stiff brush. It is used cold, and the brush and container must be washed after use. It cannot be kept in solution from day to day.

Synthetic Resin Glue

Synthetic resin glue is made from urea or phenol resin. It is usually purchased in powder form and mixed with water. There are several types, each developed with special characteristics. Some types set slowly, others quickly. Some are highly resistant to moisture, but others are only moderately so.

Follow the manufacturer's instructions carefully. Some synthetic resin glues are used to bond metal to wood, metal to plastic, glass to other materials, as well as wood to wood. They are often set rapidly by high temperatures or electronic equipment.

Resorcinol Formaldehyde Glue

Resorcinol formaldehyde glue is a very strong waterproof resin glue used in outdoor work. It is sold in two parts, liquid resin and a catalyst, packaged in a double container. Directions on the container must be followed closely. It is excellent for gluing projects that will be exposed to weather.

Polyvinyl Resin Glue

Polyvinyl resin glue is clean, white, and nonstaining. It is fast setting, strong, and easy to use. It is excellent for general furniture making. It is always ready to use at any temperature above 68°.

Fig. 416B. Apply Contact Cement to Edge of Stock

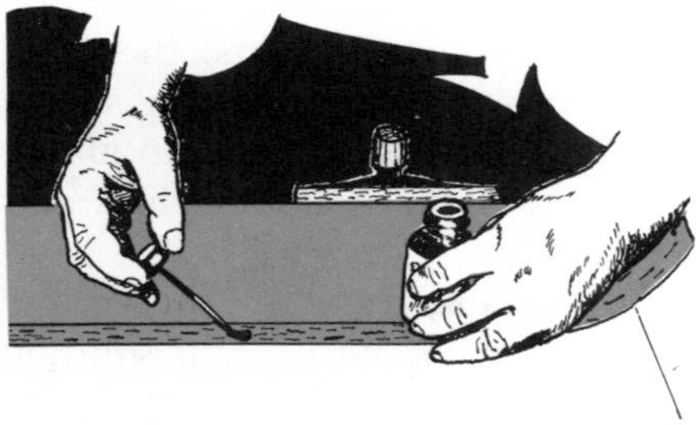

Fig. 416C. Apply Contact Cement to Surface of Wood Trim

Fig. 416D. Press Parts Together with Light Mallet Taps

Contact Cements

Contact cement has become popular as an adhesive in the woodworking shop. It is especially useful for bonding plywood and for fastening veneer trim to furniture edges. It is excellent for bonding formica and other decorative pieces to table tops and counters. Contact cement bonds quickly and permanently with very little pressure and without the use of clamps. It is odorless when dry, and transparent and nonstaining. It resists heat and is moisture resistant. Follow instructions on the container for your special use.

General Directions

1. Apply the cement to both clean surfaces.
2. Let the cement dry until it is glossy. This will require 15 minutes or more. See Figs. 416B and 416C.
3. Press the parts together, or tap very lightly with a mallet, Fig. 416D.
4. *Important*: Align the surfaces carefully before they touch together. Adjustment is very difficult once contact is made.

Questions

1. Name five kinds of glue.
2. Which glue is considered one of the best for general use?
3. Should animal glue be heated frequently?
4. From what is fish glue made?
5. What keeps fish glue in liquid form?
6. From what is synthetic resin glue made?
7. How is synthetic resin glue purchased?
8. Name two uses of synthetic resin glue.
9. Name a glue especially useful for outside work.
10. Name some characteristics of polyvinyl resin glue.
11. From what is casein glue made and for what kind of work is it used?
12. What is a common use for contact cement?

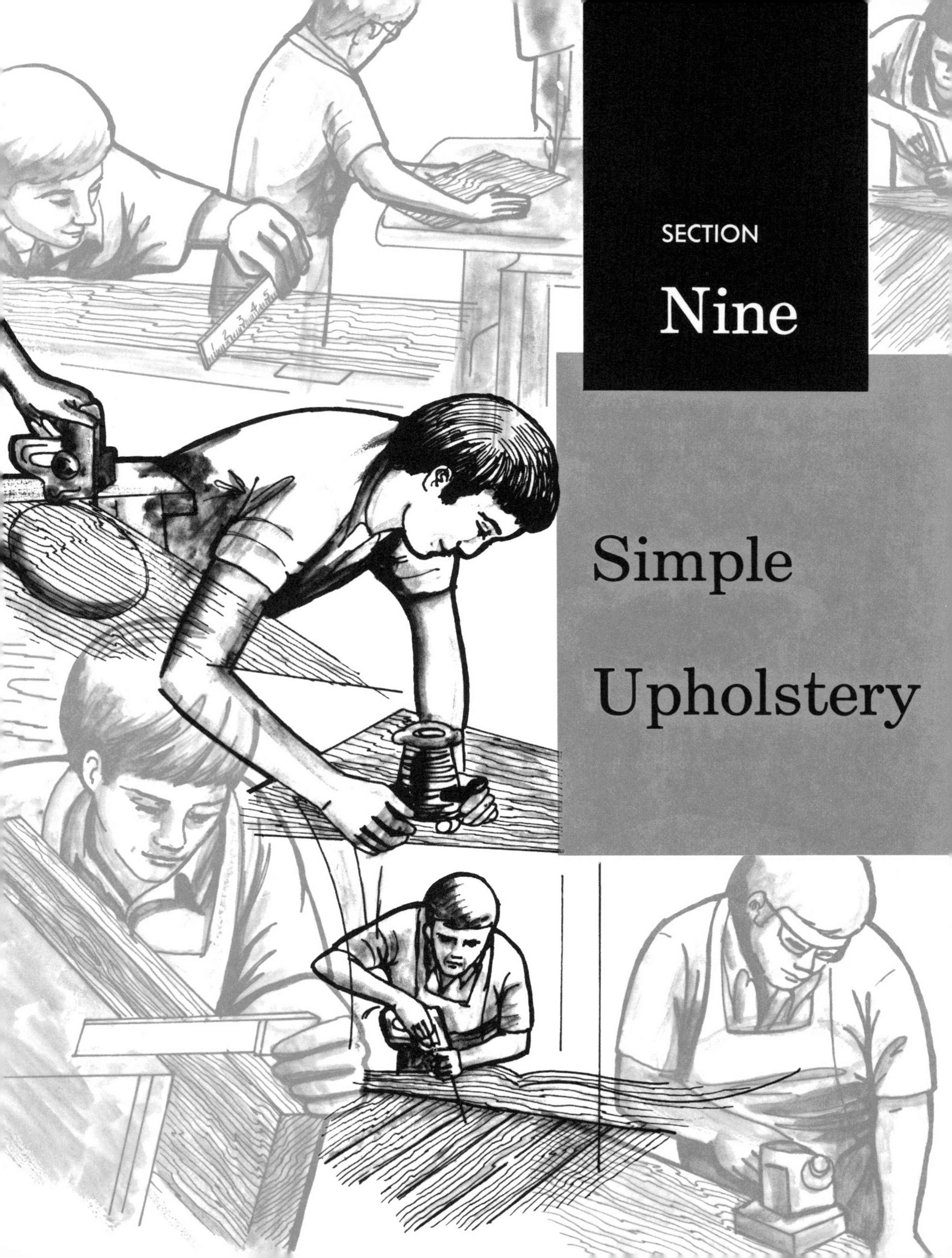

SECTION

Nine

Simple Upholstery

UNIT

58

Simple Upholstery

A good upholstered seat can be made by following the procedure outlined here. Two similar projects provide instruction in two methods that can be applied to a good many objects that do not require spring construction. If you wish to do more advanced upholstering, consult an upholstery text.

Fig. 417. Upholstered Seat in White Cover

Fig. 418. Upholstered Seat in Black Cover

The two seats illustrated are ten inches high and fourteen inches square. The cover can be brought to the lower edge of the rails as in Fig. 417 or short of half-way down the rails as in Fig. 418.

The stuffing can be rubberized fiber, foam rubber, or polyfoam. The base for the cushion may be webbing or ¾″ plywood. Webbing makes a softer seat than does plywood.

Materials and Tools

Webbing is made of jute, linen, or cotton and is sold in 3″, 3½″, and 4″ widths. The 3½″ width is most widely used. *Unbleached muslin* is used over the webbing and also under the cover to enclose the stuffing. Tacks are of three kinds – *webbing, upholstery,* and *gimp.* Each type is made in several sizes. Webbing tacks have flat heads and barbs on the shank which keeps the tacks secure. Upholstery tacks are quite like common tacks. Gimp tacks have small round heads and are used when they are likely to show.

Modern stuffing materials include *foam rubber, polyfoam, tufflex* (a cotton substitute), *rubberized fiber,* and *rubberized hair.* These are odorless and allergy proof.

Foam rubber *slab stock* is made in thicknesses from ½″ to 2″, Fig. 419A. *Cored stock* has large round openings in the underside,

Fig. 419A. Slab Foam Rubber

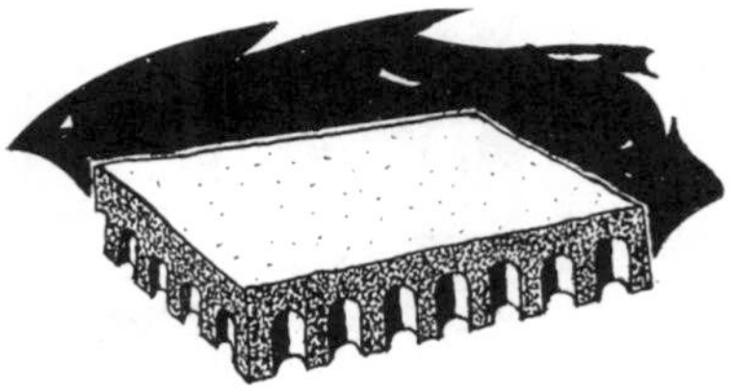

Fig. 419B. Cored Foam Rubber

Fig. 419C. Pincore Foam Rubber

Fig. 419B, but many dealers prefer to stock *pincore* slab, which has small holes about 3/16″ in diameter on both sides, Fig. 419C. Cored and pincore stock are made 3/4″ to 4 1/2″ thick. Foam rubber is made in densities of extra soft, soft, medium, firm, and extra firm.

For the seats shown, use 2″ stock of medium or firm density. The large core stock is used with or without spring construction. Cored foam rubber in special shapes may be obtained from many suppliers.

Foam rubber can be trimmed to size with scissors or with a 1/4″ band saw. Dip the scissors in water for easier cutting.

Rubberized fiber and *rubberized hair* are similar in appearance, Fig. 420. Vegetable fiber and animal hair are bonded with latex. These are made in 3/4″ to 2 1/2″ slabs. When used for stuffing, cover with 1/2″ foam rubber or cotton padding to prevent scratching. Shredded foam rubber is also used for stuffing.

Polyfoam contains no rubber but is especially light in weight and has a fine texture. It is made in soft, medium, and firm densities and in thicknesses from 1/2″ to 4″.

Rubber cement is used in joining foam rubber and also in fastening it to tacking tape. *Tacking tape* has a strip of adhesive which adheres to the rubber. The other edge, without adhesive, is tacked to the frame, Fig. 421. Muslin may be used by applying a one-inch strip of rubber cement along one side and allowing it to dry. Rubber cement must also be applied to the foam rubber and allowed to dry before applying the tape.

Cover fabrics are available in almost limitless materials and colors and should harmonize with the room. Plain or small patterned fabric is used on small projects. Vinyl plastic or artificial leather in black or off-white is attractive on either of these seats.

You will need three tools — an *upholstery hammer* for tacking, a *webbing stretcher* for tightening the webbing, and a sharp pair of six-inch scissors. You can make a webbing stretcher from the sketch in Fig. 422. Glue some fabric or a split section of garden hose on the end that is to touch the rail so as not to mar the wood. Other tools, such as the stuffing rod, regulator, pliers, upholsterer's pin, and ripping tools are used by the upholsterer.

Making the Base

1. Make the drawing and plan the procedure.
2. Make the base as shown in Fig. 423. If you plan to make a complete base, you will want to use furniture wood. The rails should be flush with the legs. The 1 3/8″ legs taper on the two inside surfaces. The rails are 3/4″ x 4″.

   If you plan to buy legs such as shown

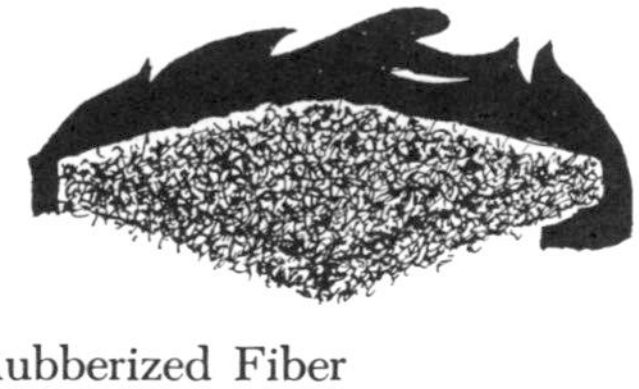

Fig. 420. Rubberized Fiber

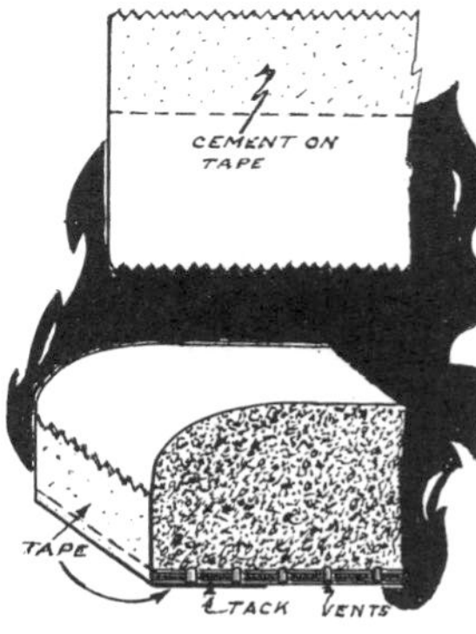

Fig. 421. Tacking Tape Applied on Corner

Fig. 422. Scissors, Stretcher, and Hammer

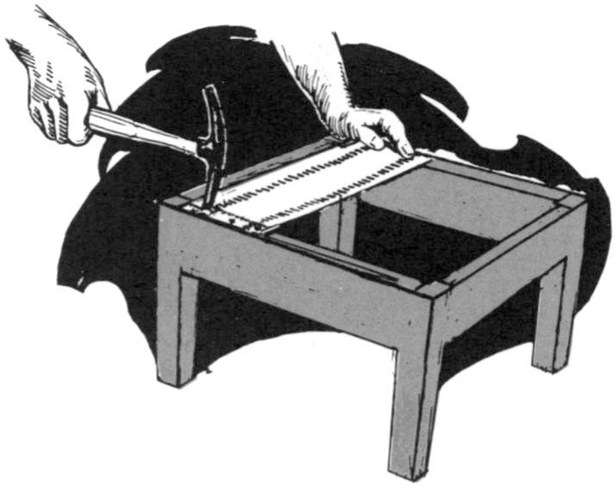

Fig. 423. Fasten the Webbing Near the Corner

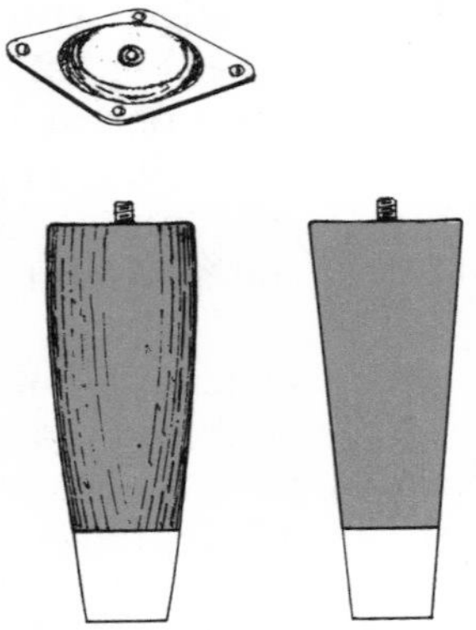

Fig. 424. Two Styles of Purchased Legs

Fig. 425. Using the Webbing Stretcher

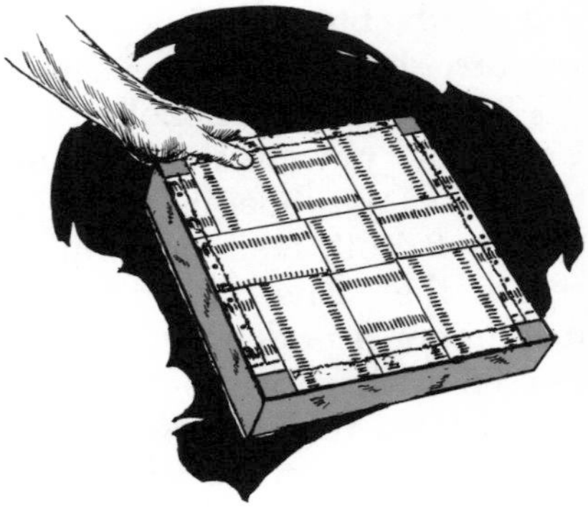

Fig. 426. Webbing in Place

in Fig. 424, make a square frame of soft wood, especially if the fabric is to cover the rails. The corners of the frame can be made with butt or rabbet joints and fastened with glue and nails. An angle brace 1½″ thick and 2½″ on each side should be screwed into each lower corner. It will strengthen the frame and provide a place for fastening the legs.

Construction with Webbing

1. Fasten the webbing to the top edges of the seat, starting near the corner, Fig. 423. Double one end and fasten it with five ten-ounce tacks. If the wood is hard, use six-ounce tacks.
2. Stretch the webbing tight with the stretcher, Fig. 425, and tack the end next to the stretcher to the top of the rail with three ten-ounce tacks, Fig. 423. Fold the webbing over and back again and fasten with two tacks. Space and fasten three strips of webbing.
3. Weave and tack three webbing strips across the first three strips, Fig. 426. Make sure the ends are doubled.
4. Cover the webbing with a piece of muslin, Fig. 427. Tack the muslin with 4-ounce tacks, about 2 inches apart, working from the center to the ends.
5. If you plan to use rubber slab, it should now be cut. Make it one inch larger than the seat in each dimension. If you use slab stock, omit Steps 6 and 7.
6. If you plan to use fiber, or shredded stuffing, attach another piece of muslin. Secure three sides only and leave it loose enough to hold the stuffing, Fig. 428. Be sure to double the edges of the muslin before nailing.

Fig. 427. Applying Muslin Cover Over Webbing

Fig. 428. Inserting Stuffing Between Muslin Covers

7. Insert the stuffing, working it well into the corners and the edges so they will be round and smooth, leaving a slight crown at the top of the cushion.
8. Tack the last side of the muslin cover.

Construction with Plywood Base

1. Fasten a piece of ⅜″ plywood to the top with 3d nails. The plywood should fit flush with the outside of the rails. Round the outside edges so there will be no sharp edges.
2. Bore about 25 ½″ holes in the plywood to allow movement of air.
3. There are several ways to form edges. One way is to cut the top outside edges at an angle with the scissors as in A, Fig. 429. Measure in and down ¾″ from the top edge and draw guide lines parallel with the edge. The amount of crown desired will determine how much more you may want to measure inward on the top. With the scissors, cutting a little at a time, make a chamfer around the pad. Smooth the ridges with sandpaper. In place of cutting, you can feather the edge as shown in B, Fig. 429.
4. Apply rubber cement to the lower edge of the pad and let it dry.
5. Fasten the cemented edge of the tape to the cemented area of the pad, and tack the lower part under the plywood base, Figs. 421 and 429.
6. You can also use a one-inch thick rubber slab and build it up by placing two smaller pieces under the top pad. Make one about ⅔ the size of the top and the bottom one ⅓ the size of the top pad. Cement them together.

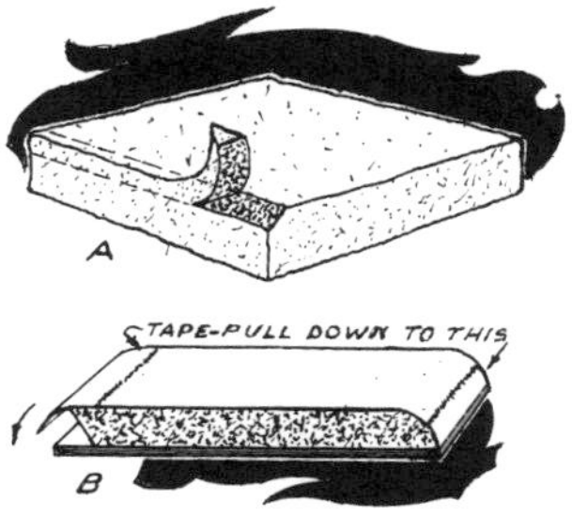

Fig. 429. Types of Rounded Edges

Fig. 430. Folding the Corner

Applying the Cover

1. Fit and place the cover fabric. Tack it, working from the center to within about two inches from the corner.
2. Fold the corners as shown in Fig. 430 and fasten with four-ounce tacks. Make sure the cover is snug and smooth.
3. If the edges of the cover are to be part way down the side as in Fig. 418, use gimp to finish the edge. Fasten it with metaline nails. If the fabric covers the rails as in Fig. 417, you need not use gimp, and the metaline nails can be placed head to head. Brass nails are suggested for leather. Fold the fabric under so as not to leave a raw edge at the same time strengthen it.
4. Nails can be spaced with a strip of cardboard. For example, if the nails must be ¾″ apart, cut a strip of cardboard ¾″ wide. Place the first nail at one corner, tapping it lightly. Set the spacer against the first nail, place another nail against the spacer, and tap it in place. Continue to the corner, then seat the nails.

Questions

1. Why is webbing more desirable than a board as a foundation for a seat?
2. What is the advantage in using foam rubber or polyfoam for stuffing?
3. Why use muslin over the webbing?
4. Why is genuine leather not frequently used for cover fabric?
5. Tell how to space metaline nails.
6. Name a few fabrics other than those listed that may be used for covers.

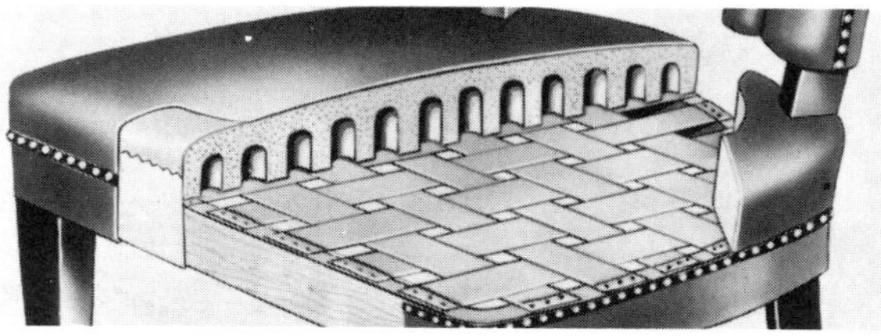

Fig. 430A. Section ofCommercial Chair (U.S. Rubber)

SECTION

Ten

Finishing Your Project

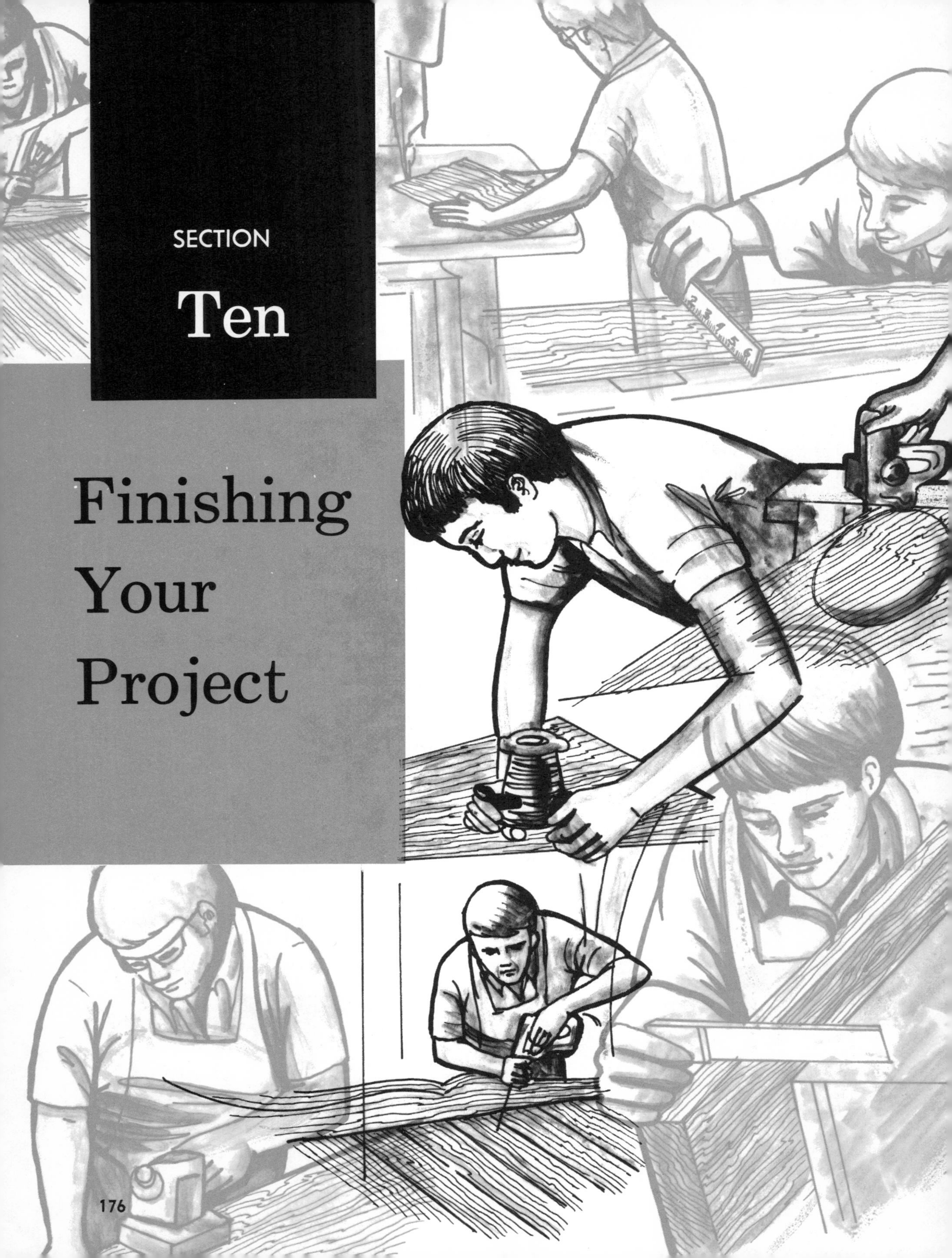

UNIT 59

Sanding Wood Surfaces

Sanding is the final step in the preparation of a surface for finishing. Sandpaper is not a substitute for the plane, chisel or other edge tools, but rather it is used only to produce a very smooth surface before applying the desired finish. Make sure that the surfaces to be sanded are properly worked with edge tools before using sandpaper. One should not use the plane or other edge tools on surfaces that have been sanded.

The commercial size of a sheet of sandpaper is 9″ x 11″, but smaller pieces can also be purchased. The 9″ x 11″ piece is torn into four or six parts. A piece thus torn is held on a block when in use which insures thorough and uniform sanding of a surface.

Tearing Sandpaper

There are several ways to tear sandpaper for use on a sanding block, but the following are well known and very effective procedures. Before tearing, work the smooth side over the edge of the bench to limber the paper and keep it from cracking when tearing.

Tear by Folding

1. Fold the sheet in the center with the sanded side inward. Crease at at the fold with your fingers and then fold it back with the sanded side out and crease again. Make sure that you have formed or "broken" a straight line down the center of the sheet.
2. Hold one half of the sheet in the left hand and the other half in the right hand and tear quickly with a sharp movement of the right hand. The paper will tear on the creased line.
3. To tear the sheet into four parts, fold the halves in two and tear as just described. The most economical way, however, is to fold the halves into three parts, thus making six small sheets from the large one.

Tear with a Straightedge

1. Another method of tearing sandpaper is to first fold the sheet as just described and then tear the sandpaper on the edge of the bench, Fig. 432.

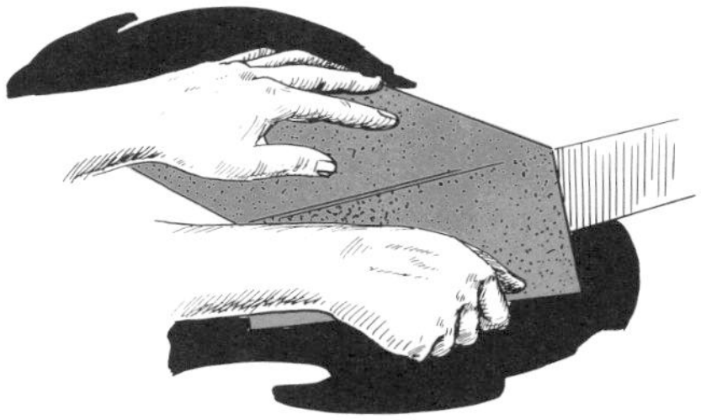

Fig. 432. Tearing Sandpaper on Edge of Bench

Fig. 433. Tearing Sandpaper with Straightedge

2. You can also use a straightedge as shown in Fig. 433 to hold the sheet of sandpaper while tearing on the line.

Making a Sandpaper Block

1. Make a block to fit your sandpaper pieces if you do not have one. The blocks shown in Fig. 434 work nicely for most types of work. Make the block ¾″ x 2½″ x 4″, of scrap stock.
2. Wrap the sandpaper tightly over the block to form a perfectly flat surface, Fig. 434.

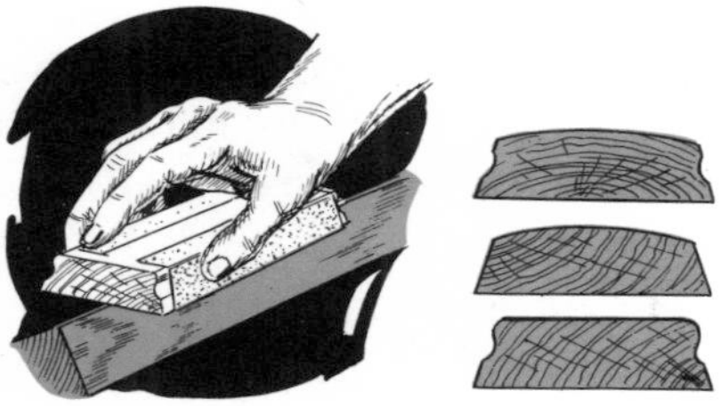

Fig. 434. Sandpaper Blocks

Fig. 435. Use Both Hands when Sanding

Fig. 436. Hold Stock in Vise to Sand Edge

Sanding Flat Surfaces

1. Select the sandpaper best suited for your work. For the first sanding No. ½ sandpaper is satisfactory and No. 2/0 for the final sanding.
2. Use both hands as shown in Fig. 435. Hold the sanding block flat on the surface and draw the block back and forth, working with the grain of the wood. Apply even pressure.
3. Make sure not to sand across the grain of the wood or in a circular motion. Leave the surface as it was planed except to make it smoother. Be careful that you do not sand down the surfaces near the edges of the stock.

Sanding Edges and Ends

1. When sanding edges, fasten the stock in the vise as in Fig. 436, and use both hands to hold the sanding block.
2. Remember that it is just as important to sand an edge true as it is to plane it true.

Fig. 437. Sand End Grain in One Direction Only

Fig. 438. Use Block when Sanding Curves

Fig. 439. Sand in One Direction when Rounding Corners

3. When sanding end grain, sand in *one direction only* as shown in Fig. 437. Sanding in one direction will result in a glass-smooth surface that will take a finish as readily as a surface with the grain.

Sanding Curves

1. When sanding rounded corners or other convex curves, use the sandpaper block to back up your sandpaper, as in Figs. 438 and 439. Hold the sanding block firmly in both hands and work it in one direction.
2. When sanding rounded or oval edges, hold the sandpaper in one hand as in Fig. 440 without using a sanding block. The palm of your hand forms a cushion that fits nicely around the stock.
3. When sanding a concave surface or an inside curve, place sandpaper around a rod or a round piece of wood and sand with the grain of the wood. Tool handles frequently work well for this, Fig. 441.
4. Make sure to sand until the work is perfectly smooth and entirely free of blemishes.
5. Remove sharp arrises by light sanding, with sandpaper on a block. One stroke is usually enough, Fig. 434.

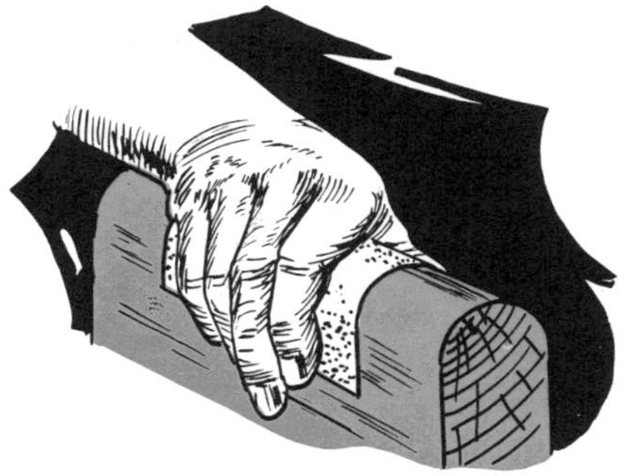

Fig. 440. Hold Sandpaper in Palm when Sanding Rounded Edges

Fig. 441. Wrap Sandpaper Around Rod when Sanding a Concave Surface and Inside Curves

Questions

1. Is sandpaper a substitute for a plane or chisel?
2. Should sanding be with the grain of the wood or across it?
3. What is used to back sandpaper to give it a broad even cutting surface?
4. How is sandpaper graded? How do you know what grade to use?
5. Why sand end grain only in one direction?
6. How should a rounded convex edge be sanded?
7. How should you sand a concave surface or an inside curve?

UNIT 60

Power Sanding Machines

There are several kinds of power machines available for the preparation of wood for final finishing. The disk sander, stationary belt sander, portable electric belt sander, and the orbital motion finishing sander are some of the common known power sanders.

There are several kinds of abrasives that can be used on these machines such as the natural abrasives which include flint, garnet and emery and the artificial abrasives which include silicon carbide and aluminum oxide. See Unit 57, Finishing and Polishing Abrasives.

Disk Sander

The disk sander is a disk covered with an abrasive paper or cloth which is driven by a motor. The diameter of the disk determines the size of the machine. Disks of 8½″ and 12″ diameter are two common sizes. The disk sander shown in Fig. 442 is a direct driven sander with a 12″ diameter disk.

Disk sanders are used for sanding the edges of small stock. There is an iron table on which the stock rests when sanding. The table can

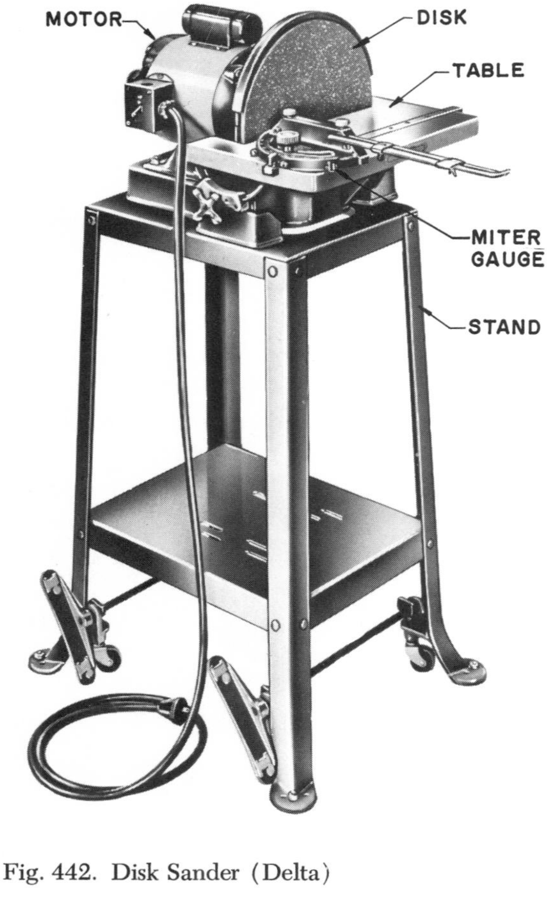

Fig. 442. Disk Sander (Delta)

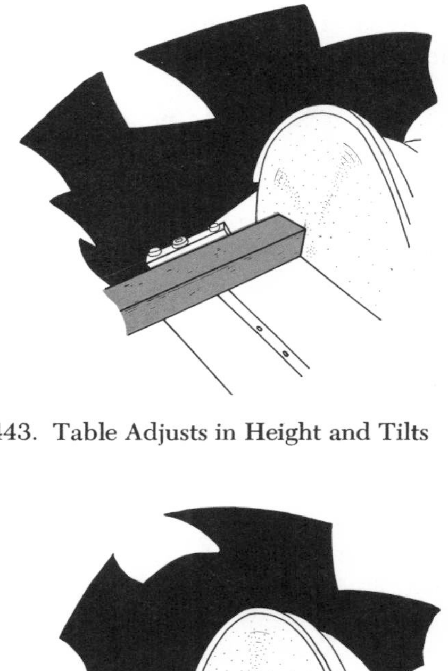

Fig. 443. Table Adjusts in Height and Tilts

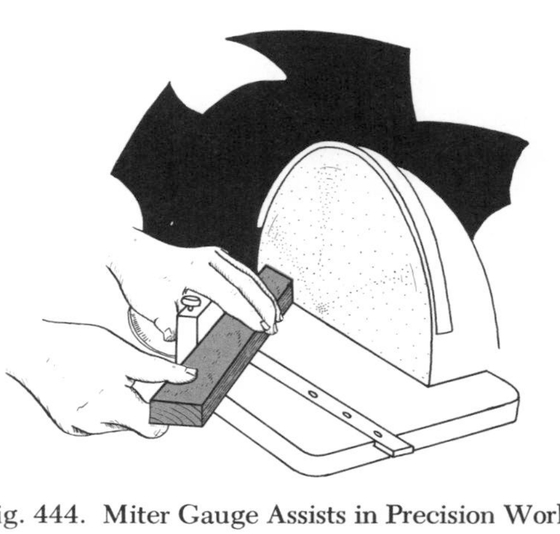

Fig. 444. Miter Gauge Assists in Precision Work

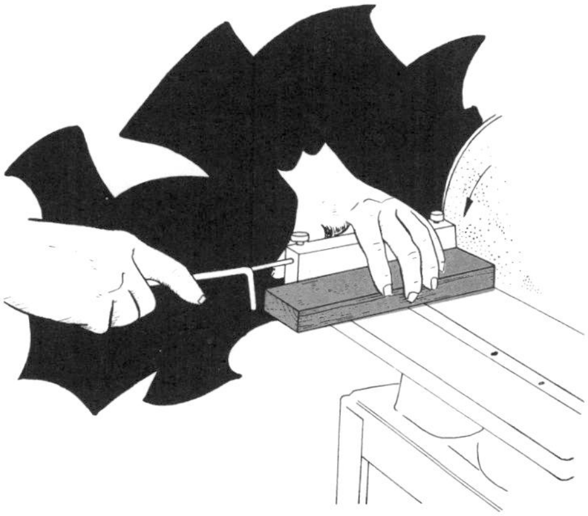

Fig. 445. Stop Rod on Miter Gauge Often Useful

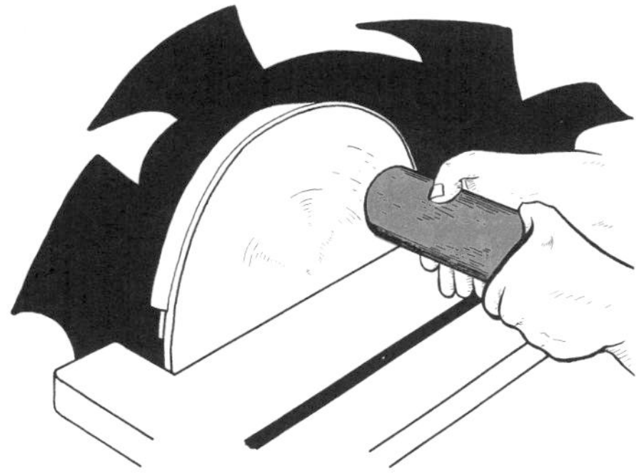

Fig. 446. Applying Stick Shellac

be raised, lowered, and tilted at any angle up to 45 degrees, Fig. 443. There is a mitered gauge that slides in a groove so bevels and chamfers can be sanded on end stock, Fig. 444. A stop rod is provided as shown in Fig. 445.

Safety Instructions

1. The disk sander is safe to use, but you can be injured if you get your hand on the disk. Keep your fingers away from the disk.
2. Get permission from your instructor before using the sander.
3. Check the setting of the table and inspect the paper on the disk to make sure it is cemented firmly.
4. See that there are no nails and screws in the stock.
5. Stop the machine if you must reset it.

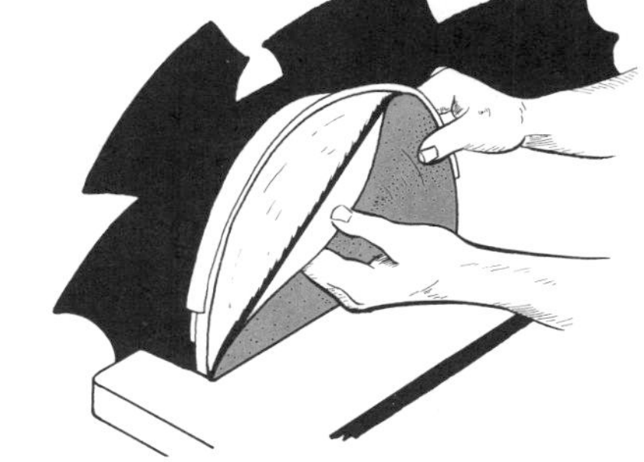

Fig. 447. Pressing Abrasive Disk in Place

Fig. 448. Use Light Pressure in Freehand Sanding

6. Avoid wearing loose clothing and a necktie when working at the sander.
7. Always sand from the inside to the outer edge of the disk. If you start at the edge, the paper may get caught and tear.
8. If you must talk, stop the machine.

Sanding with the Disk Sander

1. Attach the abrasive to the disk with glue, a special adhesive or stick shellac. See Figs. 446 and 447 for mounting the abrasive.
2. Do sanding freehand. Hold the stock flat on the table and push it lightly into the disk, Fig. 448.
3. The pivot jig shown in Fig. 449 is useful in obtaining uniform sanding on circular stock. A simple device can be made by driving a brad into a board. Clamp the board to the sander table with the brad at the proper distance from the sanding disk.

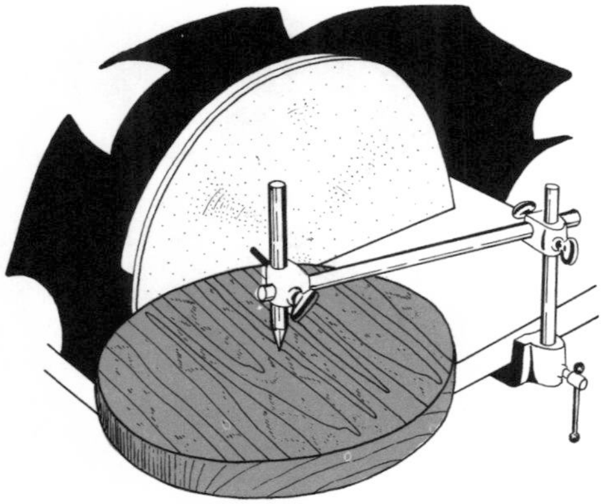

Fig. 449. Pivot Jig Helpful in Sanding Circular Pieces

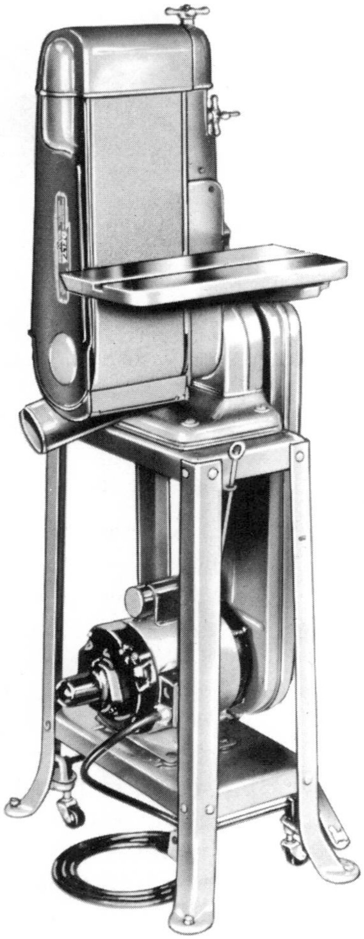

Fig. 450. Variety Table Belt Sander (Delta)

Variety Table Belt Sander

The table or stationary belt sander is probably the most versatile of mechanical sanders. There is an abrasive belt on it that operates on pulleys at either end of the table or unit, Fig. 450. The width of the belt determines the size of the sander. The table can be adjusted to do vertical, horizontal and angular sanding. This sander will give a surface speed between 2800 to 3200 feet per minute. Sanding belts can be purchased to fit any type of belt sander.

Safety Instructions

1. Get permission from your instructor before using the belt sander.
2. Check the sander carefully to make sure that all parts are in proper condition.
3. Lock the table in the position desired before turning on the power.
4. Do not attempt to sand small pieces on the machine.
5. See that there are no nails and screws in the stock.
6. Do not wear loose clothing or a necktie when sanding.
7. Keep fingers away from the belt.
8. If you must talk, stop the machine.

Sanding with the Variety Sander

1. To do surface sanding, adjust the sanding unit to the horizontal position, Fig. 451. Apply light but firm pressure on the

Fig. 451. Sanding a Surface

stock, being careful not to press at the edge of the belt.

2. Do end sanding with the belt sanding unit adjusted to the vertical position while resting the stock on the table, Fig. 452.
3. Curves can be sanded freehand on the outer drum.
4. Forms are useful in turning out quantity work. Forms of various shapes can be adjusted to your sander. See Figs. 452A and 452B. Make the form of wood and fasten it to the table.

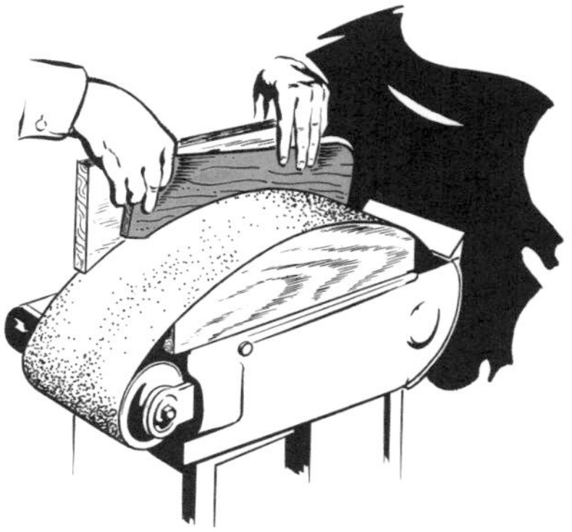

Fig. 452A. Special Form Fitted to Table

Portable Electric Orbital Sander

The portable electric orbital motion sander shown in Fig. 453 is the ready substitute for hand sanding. It works at least ten times faster and it is one of the most useful of the many mechanical sanding devices. The base or shoe is covered with sponge rubber on which the sandpaper is fastened. Short rapid strokes move back and forth in slight orbit (circle) from which it gets its name.

Safety Instructions

1. Keep your fingers away from the sanding surface when the sander is in use.
2. Get permission from your instructor before using the sander.
3. Hold the sander in your hands while you plug the cord.
4. Turn off the power and lay the sander on its side when not in use.

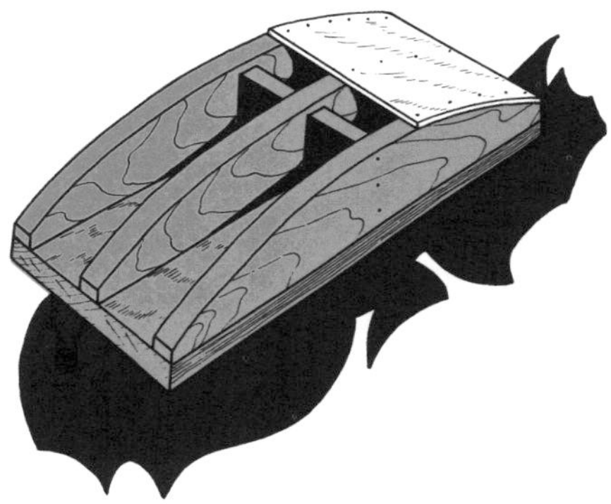

Fig. 452B. Typical Form Construction

Fig. 452. Sanding End Grain

Fig. 453. Portable Electric Orbital Sander (Porter-Cable)

Fig. 454. Dustless Portable Electric Sander (Porter-Cable)

5. Never turn on the power while the sander is resting on the belt.
6. Make the required ground connection before using the sander.

Sanding with the Orbital Sander

1. Fasten the stock firmly to a table or bench.
2. Select an abrasive of very fine grit.
3. Use both hands in sanding, but guide the sander with the right hand. The weight of the sander will provide the necessary pressure, so do not force it.
4. Although it is best to sand with the grain of the wood with an orbital sander, it can be used in any direction.
5. Work with the cord over the shoulder. This prevents running over the cord.

Dustless Portable Electric Sander

The dustless portable electric sander shown in Fig. 454 can be used for coarse, medium or fine sanding on many kinds of material such as wood, plaster, metal and plastics without the dust that accompanies machine sanding.

1. Follow the safety rules given for portable belt sander as well as the rules for other machines.
2. The dustless sander is used in the same manner as is the orbital sander.

Questions

1. Name three kinds of power sanders.
2. What is an abrasive?
3. What is a pivot jig? Miter gauge?
4. How is the size of a belt sander determined?
5. Name three safety rules for operating any type of sander.
6. Why should a portable sander be lifted when starting and stopping?
7. How does the portable electric orbital sander get its name?
8. Is the orbital sander always used with the grain of the wood?
9. Name the two most common types of portable sanders.
10. Does the weight of a portable sander provide enough pressure without using force?
11. What will happen if the sander is left running on one spot too long?
12. What do we mean by sanding freehand?
13. Which side of the disk or a disk sander should you use?
14. Should a sander be used for cutting down stock?
15. Should clean goggles be used when sanding with power machine?
16. Should a ragged or torn belt be used?

UNIT 61 Finishing and Polishing Abrasives

We usually think of finishing abrasives in terms of sandpaper and powder. Sandpaper has long been associated with wood finishing and will very likely continue to be a part of the wood finishing language regardless of the kind of finishing abrasive used.

Types of Abrasives

The abrasives used in wood finishing today can be divided into two main classifications. *Natural* and *Manufactured*. The natural abrasives are *flint, garnet,* and *emery*.

Natural Abrasives

Flint is a hard, grayish, sand-like quartz material used for the grit of flint abrasive or the regular sandpaper. Sea sand is too soft to be used in any type of finishing abrasive. Flint rock is found in New Hampshire and Maryland and has long been used for making sandpaper.

Garnet is a reddish-colored rock found in the Adirondack Mountains in New York State. Garnet is harder than flint and is one of the best finishing abrasives known.

Emery is a very hard and durable finishing abrasive. It is jet black, and it is usually imported from Turkey and the Grecian Islands. It is named after Cape Emeri. Although emery is sometimes used in wood finishing, it is more often used for polishing metal.

Manufactured Abrasives

There are two main manufactured or manmade, finishing abrasives; namely, silicon carbide and aluminum oxide.

Silicon carbide is a very hard abrasive produced by a chemical process from a mixture of coke, sand, and sawdust. It is used quite extensively in fine wood finishing, machine woodworking, and leather finishing. Silicon carbide finishing abrasives are sold under various trade names such as: "Durite," "Crystolon," and "Tri-M-Ite."

Aluminum oxide is also a hard abrasive. It is made principally from bauxite rock treated with special chemicals. It is used in fine wood finishing and metal polishing. Aluminum oxide finishing abrasives are sold under trade names such as "Alundum," "Adalox," "Aloxite," and "Three-M-Ite."

Size of Abrasive Grains

The size or the number of the grit of finishing abrasives is determined by the fineness or the coarseness of the sifting screen used. Abrasive rocks are first crushed and then sifted through screens of the desired numbered mesh. Finishing abrasives can now be obtained in both the number and grit size. Aluminum oxide, silicon carbide, and garnet are graded with screens of the same size. See the table below for abrasive grit sizes.

Abrasive Backing Materials

There are three common backing materials used in finishing abrasives: *paper, cloth,* and *combination*. Paper backing for abrasives must be very tough and strong. It comes in four weights, the "A," "C," "D," and "E" weights. The "A" paper is used for fine abrasives and weighs 40 pounds per 480 sheets of 24″ x 36″ size. The "C" paper weighs 75 pounds, and the "D" paper weighs 100 pounds. These grades are used for medium coarse abrasives.

FINISHING ABRASIVE, GRIT NUMBER AND MESH SIZE

Emery	Flint	Garnet		Aluminum Oxide		Silicon Carbide	
number	number	number	mesh	number	mesh	number	mesh
					600		600
					500		500
				10/0	400		400
	7/0			9/0	320		320
	6/0	8/0	280	8/0	280	8/0	280
	5/0	7/0	240	7/0	240	7/0	240
	4/0	6/0	220	6/0	220	6/0	220
3/0	3/0	5/0	180	5/0	180	5/0	180
2/0	2/0	4/0	150	4/0	150	4/0	150
1/0	1/0	3/0	120	3/0	120	3/0	120
1/2	1/2	2/0	100	2/0	100	2/0	100
1	1	1/0	80	1/0	80	1/0	80
1½	1½	½	60	½	60	½	60
2	2	1	50	1	50	1	50
2½	2½	1½	40	1½	40	1½	40
3	3	2	36	2	36	2	36
		2½	30	2½	30	2½	30
		3	24	3	24	3	24
		3½	20	3½	20	3½	20
				4	16	4	16

HARDNESS OF FINISHING ABRASIVES*

Emery	Flint	Garnet	Aluminum Oxide	Silicon Carbide
8.5 to 9.1	6.2 to 6.7	6.5 to 7.5	9.5 to 9.6	9.5 to 9.9

*The scale of hardness used for abrasives is Mohs' scale. The diamond is rated 10.0, the highest of all rating on this scale.

The "E" paper is used in abrasives where great strength is required and weighs 135 pounds per 480 sheets.

The *cloth* backings most commonly used are strong, lightweight cloth known as *jeans* (J) and a tough, flexible, medium cloth drill (X) especially used for belt and disc sanders.

The *combination* backing consists of a mixture of paper and cloth. It is strong, and it is used in abrasives that require flexibility and endurance.

There are two ways in which the abrasive grit is applied to the backing material. In the *gravity method,* rolls of paper or cloth are passed through printing press-like machines. The top side of the paper or cloth is covered with a good animal glue. Then a uniform layer of the desired abrasive grit is sprinkled in the glue or adhesive. The application of the grit is closely regulated to produce a smooth, even coating. In making "wetordry" or waterproof finishing abrasives, synthetic resin is used.

In the electrostatic method, the abrasive particles are attracted or pulled onto the glued backing while it passes through an electrically charged field. The abrasive particles travel on a belt conveyor which moves through the electrically charged field parallel with the coated paper or cloth.

How Finishing Abrasive is Packed and Sold

Sandpaper or finishing abrasive is usually sold in sheets 9 x 11 inches in size. The number and size of the grit is indicated on the back of each sheet and on the sleeves and units. Sandpaper or finishing abrasive is packaged in "sleeves" and "units." A sleeve may contain 25, 50, or 100 sheets. There are ten sleeves in a unit, Fig. 455.

Polishing Abrasives

Pumice stone is powdered lava from the volcanoes of Sicily and Italy. It is used for rubbing and polishing wood, ivory, marble, leather, and metal surfaces. There are many colors and varieties of pumice stone. The pumice most commonly used for wood finishing is white or grayish in color. The stone is ground into fine powder which is graded for fineness and coarseness. No. FF and FFF pumice are recommended for rubbing wood surfaces. The pumice powder is mixed with fine motor oil or paraffin oil to form a rubbing paste. The friction of the oil and the pumice causes the surface to become highly polished and smooth during the rubbing process.

Rottenstone is a very fine, dark brown powder ground from shale of limestone. It is similar to pumice stone but much softer and finer. It is used in finishing and polishing wood surfaces when a high polish and high luster is desired. It is mixed with fine motor oil or paraffin oil. A thorough rubbing with rottenstone will produce a very high, pleasing luster on finished wood surfaces.

Steel wool is a mild polishing abrasive consisting of fine strands of wire or metal shavings. It is commonly used to clean or polish metal objects. It is frequently used as a sandpaper substitute in polishing wood surfaces, especially concave places. Steel wool gives much the same results as pumice stone in rubbing down metallic articles to attain a fine finish. Buffing with fine steel wool is a common practice in treating lacquer finishes. Steel wool is available in one-pound, five-pound, and ten-pound packages in grades from number 4/0 (very fine), to number 3, (very coarse).

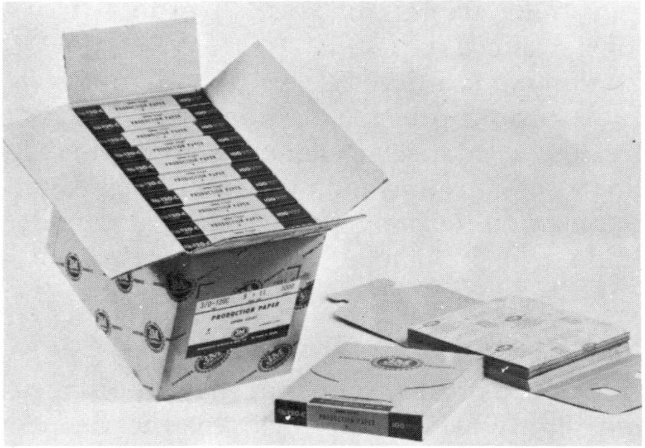

Fig. 455. Coated Abrasives (3-M)

Questions

1. Which finishing abrasive is known as sandpaper?
2. What are three kinds of finishing abrasive?
3. Name two kinds of artificial abrasives.
4. What kind of finishing abrasive is best suited for the school woodshop?
5. What kind of backings are used in finishing abrasives?
6. What is pumice stone? Rottenstone?
7. How are finishing abrasives or sandpaper packaged?
8. What are two methods used in coating finishing abrasives?
9. How are sandpaper and finishing abrasives graded?

UNIT 62

Modern Wipe-On Finishes

Wipe-on penetrating finishes are easy to apply and dustproof. Apply the finishing material evenly and smoothly with a soft cloth.

Producing a Sealacell Finish

Sealacell, Varnowax, and Royal Finish are used in the Sealacell process. Although good results can be obtained by using Sealacell and Varnowax, the best results are obtained by using all three preparations.

Applying Sealacell

Sealacell is applied first to form a protective base. It penetrates and protects the subsurface, sealing the walls and thus preventing absorption of moisture.

1. Sand the wood carefully. Preparing the wood is important in all finishing. Eliminate any scratches with 3/0 and finish with 6/0 and 8/0 garnet paper.
2. Wood surfaces must be clean, free of dust, and thoroughly dry. Use turpentine, benzine, or cleaner's naphtha.
3. Wood should be not less than 65 degrees Fahrenheit in temperature. A special finishing room is not required.
4. A soft cloth pad that is free of lint is used to apply Sealacell.
5. If a stain is desired, mix the ground-in-oil color with the Sealacell.
6. Apply Sealacell to the surface and spread it evenly and freely.
7. Allow to dry for 24 hours. When dry, sand with the grain lightly with 8/0 garnet paper or fine steel wool.
8. Wipe the surface with a dry cloth.
9. On open-grained wood, mix Sealacell with regular silex wood filler.

Applying Varnowax

Varnowax consists of a penetrating blend of gums and waxes.

1. With a soft cloth pad, apply a very thin coat of finish wiping with the grain.
2. Varnowax sets quickly so do not work a large surface at one time.
3. Allow to dry 24 hours. Sand lightly with 8/0 garnet paper or steel wool.
4. Wipe the surface with a soft dry cloth, then apply a second coat of Varnowax.
5. Allow 24 hours for this coat to dry. Sand again with 8/0 garnet paper, then wipe the surface with a dry cloth.

Applying Royal Finish

Royal Finish is applied as the final coat in the Sealacell process of finishing.

1. Apply the Royal Finish material. Either dip the soft pad in the liquid or pour it directly on the surface.

2. Spread the liquid to a thin film and let it dry for 24 hours.
3. If a second coat is desired, sand the surface lightly.
4. Clean the surface of dust and then apply the final coat of Royal Finish.
5. For a very high luster, the final coat may be rubbed with rotten stone and oil as described in Unit 68, page 195.

CAUTION: Soak all oily cloths in water and then throw them in the fireproof container when you are through for the day.

Deft Wipe-on Penetrating Finish

Deft is a clear semi-gloss finish for all interior woodwork, paneling, and furniture. It seals and finishes in one operation.

1. Make sure that the wood surfaces are clean, free of dust, and thoroughly dry.
2. Any room with good ventilation may be used for finishing with Deft.
3. Use a soft cloth pad about four to six inches square. Either dip the cloth in the liquid or pour it directly on the surface. Spread it evenly with the pad.
4. It will dry in thirty minutes, but it is better to let it dry for 12 to 24 hours before applying a second coat.
5. When dry, sand lightly with 8/0 garnet paper, or buff with very fine steel wool.
6. Wipe the surface with a dry cloth.
7. Wipe on a second coat, spreading it very evenly and then wipe off the surplus.
8. For a very high luster, the second coat may be rubbed and polished with rotten stone and oil. On most woods, two coats produce a beautiful semi-gloss finish.

Watco Danish Finish

Watco Danish Finish produces a soft natural finish. Preparation of the wood for finishing is the same as for other finishes and as described in Unit 59. It may be applied with a cloth pad, brush, spray, roller, or flowed onto the surface. Instructions are provided by the manufacturer.

For open-grained woods, paste wood fillers may be mixed with Watco before application.

Minwax

Minwax is a well known stain-wax finish. The surface must be properly prepared as for other finishes. Two coats are usually applied, with either a brush or cloth. The first coat is allowed to dry for two to four hours. The second coat is then applied, allowing it to dry for twelve hours, after which rubbing with a clean cloth brings out a hard finish. A finishing room is not necessary, but ventilation is desirable.

Questions

1. How should the surface of wood be prepared for wipe-on finishes?
2. What are the advantages of wipe-on finishes?
3. How should open-grained wood be treated?
4. Name three wipe-on finishes and tell the procedure for applying them.
5. Why soak oily rags in water and then put them in the metal container?

UNIT 63 Applying Water Stain

Water stains bring out the full beauty of the grain in nearly all woods. They resist fading and help produce transparent, clear finishes. Aniline dyes in powdered form are dissolved in hot water at the time the stain is to be used. They are usually mixed in proportion of one part powder by volume and eight parts water. They should always be mixed in a glass jar or earthenware container. An excellent water stain powder is obtained from the lignite coal of North Dakota. Water stains are inexpensive and may be obtained in many colors and shades.

Water stains have a tendency to raise the grain of the wood, and for that reason the wood should be sponged with water and sanded before the stain is applied. The sponging opens the fibers and raises the grain of the wood. When dry, the raised grain is sanded smooth to make an even surface for the stain. Water stains cannot be used over oil stains, shellac, wax, and varnish until every bit of the gum or oil has been removed.

Preparing the Surface

1. Examine the surface to see that tool marks, dirt, and grease spots have been removed.
2. Sponge the surface, including the ends, with warm water to raise the grain. Let it dry for twelve hours.
3. Sand very lightly with No. 5/0 (180 mesh) garnet paper. This sanding will reduce the raised grain to a smooth even surface.

Applying the Stain

1. It is better to apply a stain that is too light than a stain that is too dark.
2. Apply the stain by dipping the brush in the stain about one-fourth the length of the bristles and brushing with long strokes with the grain.
3. Be sure to brush out the laps and streaks quickly before the stain dries. Dip the brush in the stain often.
4. Complete one section of the project at a time such as a rail, the back, a side, or a panel. Do not daub around here and there. The most important surface or part should be stained last.
5. If one coat of stain is too light, apply a second coat. Be sure the first coat is thoroughly dry or has set at least twelve hours before applying a second coat.
6. It is more desirable to apply two or three coats of thin stain than to apply one coat of strong or thick stain.
7. When finished, clean the brush with hot water and wrap it in paper or clean cloth to dry.

Questions

1. How do water stains compare with other stains in price and ease of application?
2. Should water stain be applied across the grain or with the grain?
3. Why is it best to have the stain too light than too dark?
4. How should brushes used in water stain be cleaned?
5. What kind of a container should you use in mixing water stain?
6. What is the object of sponging the wood with water?

UNIT 64
Applying Oil Stains

Oil stains are more expensive than most other stains, but they are easily applied. They do not raise the grain of the wood, dry more slowly than other stains, and do not show brush marks. They can be used with excellent results on either soft or hardwood.

Types of Oil Stains

There are three general types of oil stains: the pigmented, the penetrating, and the preservative. All are available in a wide range of colors. The pigmented oil stains, also known as wiping stains, are made by dissolving oil

Fig. 457. Remove Surplus on Edge of Can

Fig. 458. Brush Toward Ends

soluble colors in light oil, such as linseed oil.

Penetrating oil stains are made from oil soluble dyes dissolved in such solvents as naphtha, benzol, benzine, or turpentine. Oil dyes may be purchased in powder form to be mixed with the proper solvent, or they may be obtained in liquid form ready for use.

Preservative stains, commonly known as creosote oil stains, are made from pigments and creosote mixed with linseed oil, turpentine, benzine, or japan dryer. Preservative stains are used out - of - doors, especially on shingles. Preservative stains can best be applied in warm weather.

Applying Oil Stain

1. Make sure you have sufficient stain of the desired color to complete the entire job. One pint of oil stain covers approximately twenty-five square feet of surface.
2. Mix the stain thoroughly by stirring it with a metal rod, breaking up any color pigment that may have settled to the bottom of the container. Wipe off the stirring rod when it is removed from the stain.
3. If the stain is too dark, reduce it to the desired shade with the solvent indicated in the directions on the can. A darker shade can be obtained by adding a darker shade of a similar stain.
4. Dip the brush into the stain about one-fourth the length of the bristles. Remove the surplus stain by pressing the brush lightly against the edge of the can, Fig. 457.
5. Apply the stain evenly and rapidly, brushing with the grain. Begin staining on the under surfaces or the back of a project.
6. Where inside corners are to be stained, begin in the corners and work away from them. On vertical surfaces, begin at the top and work down at the same time brushing outward toward the arrises, Fig. 458. When getting close to the arrises, brush carefully to prevent the bristles from throwing stain.
7. On a flat horizontal surface, brush with the grain the entire length of the surface.
8. Wipe the surface with a clean rag to produce an even shade. Don't cover too much area at one time because the wiping must be done before drying begins.
9. Allow the stain to dry at least twenty-four hours before beginning to apply the remaining coats of finishing materials.
10. Clean the brush carefully with whatever liquid is used as a solvent in the stain. Do not leave the brush in the stain.
11. Return all tools and materials to their proper places. Wipe empty cans or cups with rags moistened with kerosene. Clean up any stain that may have fallen on the floor or bench.
12. Place oily rags in a fireproof container.

Questions

1. About how many square feet of surface will a pint of oil stain cover?

2. What stains are flammable and should not be placed near a fire?
3. How should the brush be dipped to secure the proper amount of stain for best results?
4. Explain how to apply the oil stain with a brush.
5. On vertical surfaces, how should you apply the stain?
6. Why should the stained surface be wiped with a clean rag?
7. Why is it considered necessary to place all oily rags and waste in covered metal containers?

UNIT 65

Applying Spirit Stains

Spirit stains are made from aniline dyes and alcohol. They come in powdered or liquid form or ready to use and in nearly all the colors common to oil and water stains. Alcohol is the solvent used in most spirit stains.

Spirit stains are commonly used for patching in repair work. They are very seldom used on new work. They set fast and produce visible gaps and streaks unless applied very quickly, a characteristic that makes them difficult for beginners in finishing. Like all other kinds of stain, the more solvent used, the lighter will be the color. The better types of liquid spirit stains use a mixture of volatile oil and spirit stains. Benzol and thinners in addition to alcohol slow down the fast drying of spirit stains.

1. Prepare the surface. Make sure that tool marks, dirt, and grease spots have been removed.
2. Sponge the surface of the wood, including the ends, with warm water to raise the grain.
3. When the surface has dried for 24 hours, sand it lightly with the grain with 5/0 (180 mesh) garnet paper.
4. Apply the stain with a brush. Dip the brush in the stain about one-fourth the length of the bristles. Be sure the brush is well loaded with stain. Brush with long strokes with the grain, and work rapidly to even up the stain before it dries.
5. Apply the stain to the most difficult places first.
6. If one coat of stain is too light, apply a second coat. Be sure the first coat is thoroughly dry before applying a second coat.
7. When through staining, clean the brush in alcohol and wrap it in paper or a lintless cloth to dry.

Questions

1. Are spirit stains commonly used?
2. What is the solvent for spirit stain?
3. What kind of dyes are used in spirit stain?
4. What are the common uses of spirit stains?
5. Do spirit stains dry faster than other stains?
6. In what form can they be purchased?
7. Why is it difficult to get an even finish with spirit stains?
8. How should brushes used in spirit stain be cleaned?

UNIT 66

Bleaching or Blonding Wood

Bleaching is a process of lightening the color of wood with chemicals without injuring the wood fibers. Blond finishes require the use of bleaches to obtain the various blond effects.

Simple household laundry bleaches are quite effective on light-colored woods, and they will lighten dark wood to a considerable extent.

Commercial bleaches are available and are very satisfactory. It is possible to remove the original color partially or entirely from most woods, including mahogany and walnut. One type of bleach does the bleaching with one solution, while another type requires two solutions. Bleaching solutions are very strong chemicals and special care is necessary in applying them. When working with these chemicals, use rubber gloves and an apron.

Blonding with a Two-Solution Commercial Bleach

1. Pour enough of No. 1 solution in a glass bowl or jar for one complete application.
2. Apply the No. 1 solution with a sponge, swab or a brush. The brush is the quickest and most efficient method of applying a bleach solution on large surfaces. Cover the surface well, but make sure no runs are allowed to form. Runs will cause streaks.
3. Allow the first solution to dry for about 15 minutes, then apply the No. 2 solution.
4. Pour enough of No. 2 bleach solution in another clean glass jar or bowl and apply it in the same way you applied the first solution.
5. Let the second solution dry for about one hour or more, and then cover the surface with a neutralizing solution such as acetic acid, vinegar, or a household laundry bleach. Let this neutralizing solution dry for 24 hours.
6. Bleaching and neutralizing solutions tend to raise the grain of the wood so a light sanding with 8/0 (280 mesh) garnet paper is necessary when the wood is thoroughly dry.
7. The next step is the final blonding application. This is done with flat white paint or white lead the consistency of heavy cream.
8. Apply a coat of white paint mixture to the surface and let it set for about ten minutes.
9. Wipe the surface with a rag leaving only enough white paint in the pores to give the desired effect. You can vary the blonding by using gray paint with natural filler instead of the white paint, or you can use both.
10. Let this coat dry at least 24 hours before proceeding with the final finish. Sand lightly with 8/0 (280 mesh) garnet paper when thoroughly dry.
11. Seal the surface with a wash coat of white shellac and let it dry for 12 hours. Prepare the wash coat by mixing one part of four-pound-cut white shellac to eight parts of alcohol.
12. Sand lightly with 8/0 (280 mesh) garnet paper when dry, and wipe the dust off with a damp cloth.
13. You can now apply a final finish.

Questions

1. What does bleaching or blonding wood mean?
2. What are the advantages of the commercial bleaches?

3. Does bleaching require special equipment?
4. How can bleaches be applied?
5. What is the advantage of using glass containers?
6. Is it necessary to use white paint or lead in the bleaching process?
7. Is it necessary to seal the surface before applying the final finish?
8. What are some factors you should consider when deciding on the final finish for a project?

UNIT 67

Applying Wood Filler

Wood filler fills the pores of the wood and forms a smooth, hard, non-absorbent surface on which finishes are applied. Filler may be classified into four types: the *paste filler,* the *liquid filler,* the *sealer* and the *crack filler.*

Paste Fillers

Paste fillers are made of finely ground silicon or silex mixed with linseed oil, turpentine, Japan drier, and suitable coloring material. Silex paste filler does not shrink when it dries and is excellent for open grained wood. Paste fillers are packaged in containers of various sizes and mixed in various wood colors as well as transparent natural clear. A good practice in using paste filler is to buy natural filler and add oil color to match the stain.

Applying Paste Filler

1. If the surface has been stained, the stain must be perfectly dry before applying filler.
2. Although paste filler can be applied directly to a stained or a natural surface, better results are obtained if a sealer is used first.
3. Apply a wash coat of shellac as a sealer. Use one part of four-pound-cut shellac to 8 parts alcohol in this wash coat. Sand lightly with 8/0 (280 mesh) garnet paper when dry.
4. The filler should be the same color as the stain. You can color natural filler with stain, or you can buy a filler of the desired color.
5. Stir the filler in the container thoroughly and thin it with turpentine or benzine until it is a thin cream-like consistency. A filler the consistency of thick cream is not as satisfactory as a thin filler for most purposes. Walnut, mahogany, oak, butternut, and chestnut require paste filler.
6. One pound of filler covers approximately thirty square feet of oak or similar open-grained woods.
7. Apply the filler with a stiff bristle brush. Work it into the pores by brushing with the grain and across the grain.
8. Allow the filler to dry until the gloss has disappeared. This takes about twenty minutes.
9. Force the filler into the grain by stroking it in with the palm of the hand.
10. Wipe off the surplus filler with a coarse cloth or burlap. Work across the grain with even pressure in one direction until the surface is clean. With a soft cloth wipe lightly with the grain.
11. Allow the filler to dry for 24 hours and sand lightly with 5/0 (180 mesh) garnet paper to produce a smooth surface.
12. Apply a second coat of paste filler if necessary. One coat is usually enough, but on woods such as oak a second application is advisable.

Liquid Filler

Liquid paste filler can be used on medium close-grained woods such as beech, birch, cherry, gumwood, and redwood. Paste filler thinned with turpentine or benzine makes a good liquid filler. It contains a smaller portion of pigments than the original paste filler.

There are a number of ready-mixed liquid fillers that can be used as sizing material on rather soft, close-grained woods. These are often made from a low grade varnish mixed with a small amount of silex. These are applied much like a coat of varnish, but are not recommended for filling hardwood or bringing out the natural color of the wood.

Applying Liquid Filler

1. Liquid filler is a paste that has been thinned with turpentine or benzine to a liquid form. It contains a smaller portion of pigments than does the paste filler.
2. Liquid paste filler can be used on medium close-grained woods such as beech, birch, cherry, gumwood, and redwood.
3. Apply liquid paste filler in the same manner as you apply regular paste filler.

Sealers

A sealer is a thin filling solution that can be used as a first and second finishing coat directly on a natural close-grained wood such as poplar, basswood, pine, or cherry. It is also used over paste and liquid fillers to seal the filler and produce a smooth surface. A stained surface is usually given one or two coats of sealer before a regular paste filler is applied.

The most common sealers used in wood finishing are: the wash coat of shellac, the lacquer sanding sealer, and the ready-mixed penetrating sealer. Many good ready-to-use sealers are available commercially.

The shellac wash coat is an excellent sealer, and it is usually made by mixing one part of four-pound-cut white shellac with seven parts of alcohol.

Lacquer sanding sealer is used especially as an undercoat for lacquer. It is made from synthetic resins, nitrated cotton, and lacquer thinner and it seals stain and filler coats effectively.

The penetrating sealers are designed to build a sub-surface by penetrating the wood and sealing the wall of the wood cell to prevent absorption of moisture.

Applying Sealers

1. Wash coats of shellac must be applied rapidly. Apply the shellac with a brush, working one way with full length brush-wide strips from the center of the surface to the outside, applying only light pressure. Do not brush it back and forth.
2. Use a very light or "feathering" stroke to even up the coating before the shellac starts to set.
3. A lacquer sealer can be applied with a brush satisfactorily. It should be spread thin and quickly as in applying lacquer, flowing it on by working from the center of the surface to the sides. Do not brush it back and forth.
4. The wiping sealer is the easiest of all to apply. Wipe it on or rub it into the wood with a rag and then wipe it off smooth with a clean rag.

Crack or Crevice Filler

Nail holes, dents, checks, torn fibers, and other wood imperfections can be filled with one of several types of crack fillers such as plastic wood, stick shellac, water putty, sand dust and glue, and wood wedges, pegs, or plugs. Shallow dents and imperfections may be removed by steaming the wood and causing it to return to shape.

Plastic wood is a paste which is available in many colors and shades. It dries quickly and should be applied rapidly. Remove the required amount from the can and replace the cover immediately. When dry, the filled place is sanded even with the surface.

Stick shellac is another wood filler that can be obtained in various colors to match the wood. It is applied by melting a portion of a shellac stick in the wood cavity or crevice. It is then sanded even with the surface.

Water putty is especially useful in filling imperfections in soft wood before applying a paint or enamel finish. It is purchased in powder form and mixed with water to produce a thick paste filler. Water putty dries quickly and must be applied rapidly, usually with a knife.

Sand dust mixed with glue or varnish makes a good crevice or nail hole filler. The sand dust should be from the wood which is to be filled. Mix the sand dust and glue to a thick, paste-like consistency.

If dents or similar wood imperfections are not too deep, they may be removed by swelling with steam or hot water. This can be done satisfactorily by placing a wet cloth over the dented part and then passing a hot iron over the wet cloth.

Wood wedges, pegs, or plugs are used to repair large defects such as knot holes and torn pieces. This kind of repair requires accurate work but produces a very satisfactory and substantial job.

Applying Crack and Crevice Filler

1. Press the filler into the crevice or dent with a putty knife or a similar tool.
2. Let the filler dry thoroughly and sand with 3/0 (120 mesh) garnet paper until it is even with the surface.

Questions

1. Name two types of good wood fillers.
2. What is the purpose of wood filler?
3. How is a paste filler applied?
4. What are the materials in paste filler?
5. How long should a paste filler be left to set before rubbing it smooth?
6. Name three kinds of wood that require a paste filler.
7. Name three kinds of wood on which liquid filler may be used.
8. What is the difference between paste and liquid filler?
9. What is the difference between a liquid filler and a sealer?
10. Should fillers be applied before or after a stain?
11. Name two kinds of common sealers.
12. What is considered the best kind of liquid filler?
13. What is the difference between a paste filler and a crevice filler?
14. How can you fill wood imperfections, dents and nail holes?

UNIT 68

Applying Shellac

As early as the fifteenth century the Greeks used shellac as a dye for making various ornaments such as beads and earrings.

Production of Shellac

Shellac is a resinous substance produced in Southern Asia or East India by small insects known as the Tachardia Sacca or Coccus Lacca. The term "lac" is derived from the native word, lakh, meaning 100,000, which suggests the large number of insects necessary to produce the shellac gum on trees. These many small insects attack certain trees in Asia, sucking the sap and producing a resinous secretion or gum. The gum-covered branches and twigs are cut from the trees and broken into small pieces to dry. The gum is scraped from the larger branches while the smaller twigs are crushed and washed in hot water. Next the gum is melted, squeezed through cloth bags, and placed in shallow vats to cool where it becomes solid sheets. These sheets are broken into flakes and packed in bags for shipment.

Shellac is made by dissolving shellac flake or resin in high-proof denatured alcohol. The United States formula No. 1 provides for one hundred gallons of 190-proof ethyl (grain) alcohol and five gallons of methyl (wood) alcohol. To thin shellac further, denatured alcohol of 160-proof is sufficient.

Types of Shellac

Liquid shellac as purchased usually consists of four pounds of shellac gum dissolved or "cut" in each gallon of pure alcohol. This mixture is known as a four-pound-cut shellac but is too thick to be used for any type of finishing. It must be thinned or "cut" further to a one-pound, two-pound or wash-coat solution. A two-pound-cut shellac solution consists of one part of four-pound-cut shellac to one part of alcohol. A wash solution usually consists of one part of four-pound-cut shellac to seven parts of alcohol.

Shellac in the liquid form is available either in the white or in the original orange color. White shellac is produced by bleaching the orange shellac with caustic potash and chlorine. White shellac is the best form for general use.

Uses of Shellac

It is recommended that shellac be stored in tightly sealed glass containers to prevent evaporation of the alcohol. It should be shielded from strong light and kept in a fairly warm room during cold weather. Inasmuch as the alcohol in shellac evaporates quickly, the shellac naturally sets quickly. It is hard when dry, but it is likely to become soft and turn white when exposed to moisture. It cannot be applied over a varnish, lacquer, wax, or enameled surface since it will not adhere.

Shellac can be applied over a stained surface or over a natural wood. It can be used alone as a finish by building a smooth protective finish with several coats. Thin shellac makes an excellent sealer for almost any type of finish.

Shellac is used in finishing furniture, floors, toys, musical instruments, and wood patterns. It is used in making cement, phonograph records, telephone receivers, leather dressing, sealing wax, buttons, grinding wheels, and many other similar items. It is also used for many kinds of insulation in electrical work, as an undercoat on paper fiber goods, willow, rattan, and for sizing straw hats.

Producing a Shellac Finish

Shellac has been used as a finish for many years. It dries more rapidly than all durable wood finishes. White shellac is a favorite finishing material. The finest antique pieces are finished with many thin coats of shellac, each carefully rubbed by hand. Shellac can be applied directly on natural wood or on a stained surface.

Preparing the Surface

1. Remove tool marks, dirt, and grease spots from the project.
2. Sponge the surfaces with water, preferably warm water. Let dry for twelve hours. The water application raises the grain of the wood. Sponging is especially recommended on soft woods.
3. When dry, sand the surfaces and edges with 5/0 (180 mesh) garnet paper. Remove all dust with a lintless cloth slightly dampened with alcohol.
4. If the piece is to be stained, it should be done before the shellac is applied.

Applying White Shellac

1. Pour into a glass container enough wash shellac solution for the first coat. Place the project to be finished in position to insure good lighting.
2. Select a 1½″ varnish brush with long, good quality bristles.
3. Dip the brush into the shellac about one-third the length of the bristles. Gently press the bristles against the inside of the container as in Fig. 457. Apply the first coat of wash shellac as evenly as possible with long, fast, even strokes. Brush one way from the center of the

surface to the outside and apply only light pressure.

4. Use a very light or "feathering" stroke to even up the finish before it starts to set. Work fast and do not try to brush the surface once the shellac has started to set. Spots that seem to have been missed should be left to be covered with the next coat.
5. All strokes should be made from the center outward to the edge, Fig. 458.
6. Shellac any panels and sunken surfaces before covering the raised portions. Whenever possible place the project so the surface to be shellacked is horizontal.
7. Allow at least eight hours for the first coat to dry, then sand it very lightly with 8/0 (280 mesh) garnet paper. Use a small piece of sandpaper held with the finger tips. Work carefully on a small area at a time. Sand with the grain and feel for smoothness with finger tips.
8. If the wood has an open grain such as oak, walnut, or chestnut, apply a paste filler at this time.
9. Remove all dust with a damp cloth and apply a second coat of wash shellac.
10. Allow eight hours for the second coat to dry, then sand it lightly with 8/0 (280 mesh) garnet paper.
11. Remove the dust and dirt with a damp cloth and apply a third coat of wash shellac.
12. Allow eight hours for the third coat to dry and again sand lightly with 8/0 (280 mesh) garnet paper.
13. Prepare a two-pound-cut solution for the fourth and possibly a fifth coat of shellac. Mix one part of four-pound-cut shellac with one part or less of alcohol.
14. Apply the fourth, and a fifth coat if necessary, of the two-pound-cut shellac in the same manner that you applied the wash shellac.
15. When you are through with the shellacking, clean your brush thoroughly in alcohol. Wrap the brush in paper or a clean cloth before putting it away.
16. Give the final coat of shellac a rub down with No. FF pumice stone when it is dry.
17. Prepare a pad of soft cloth and saturate it with rubbing or paraffin oil.
18. Sprinkle some pumice powder on the pad and rub the surface, working with the grain of the wood. Be careful to put only a small amount of pumice on the pad.
19. Rub until a high polish is produced. Wipe off the oil and pumice mixture and polish the surface with a soft dry cloth.
20. For a higher polish use rottenstone and oil in the same manner as pumice and oil.
21. As a final touch to this finish, apply one or two coats of wax.
22. Apply the wax evenly with a cloth and let it dry for ten or fifteen minutes. Cover a small surface at one time.
23. After the wax is fairly dry, wipe it off and rub it to a high polish with a dry soft cloth.

Questions

1. How is shellac obtained?
2. Will turpentine or linseed oil readily mix with shellac?
3. What are Coccus Lacca?
4. What is the original color of shellac?
5. How is white shellac produced?
6. What is the solvent for shellac?
7. What is meant by a four-pound-cut shellac?
8. Name twelve uses for shellac.
9. What is the purpose of sponging the surface before applying the shellac finish?
10. Why is shellac more difficult to apply than varnish?
11. Is shellac being discarded for other finishes?
12. What is meant by a wash coat of shellac?
13. How is shellac applied?
14. How long should shellac dry before applying a second coat?
15. Why sand the shellacked surface when dry?
16. How can the final coat of shellac be treated after it is dry?

UNIT 69 Varnish

Varnish is a transparent finishing material that has been used to beautify and preserve materials, especially wood, throughout the ages. Varnish as a finish on wood is unsurpassed by any other type of finishing material. It is especially noted for its durability, hardness, transparency, and depth of film.

Varnish is made from natural copal gum resins or from man-made synthetic resin gums. Many fine varnishes are made from natural copal gums, but the general trend is toward the use of synthetic varnishes because of their fast-drying qualities.

Natural Varnish

Copal gums are the most important ingredients in the manufacturing of natural varnish. They are resinous substances found on decayed pine trees which grew several hundred years ago. These resinous substances are fossil gums. The term *copal* is a family name for all types of fossil gums. Although the supply of some of the best copal gums is exhausted, large quantities of excellent copal gum are found in many places. The copal gum, buried several feet under the ground, is found in certain sections of Africa, New Zealand, Brazil, Belgium, and the Phillippine Islands.

After the copals are dug out of the ground, they are cleaned, melted, and boiled with linseed oil for several days. After it has cooled, turpentine is added and stirred thoroughly thus producing varnish. The varnish is then placed in large tanks to age and ripen. Several months are required for this aging. The quality of natural varnish depends upon the grade of copal gum used, the proportions of turpentine and oil, and the care and time given to the boiling process. There are many kinds of natural varnishes, but cabinet rubbing varnish, spar varnish, and floor varnish are among the best.

Cabinet rubbing varnish contains more than the usual proportion of copal gum, usually Congo gum, together with China wood or tung oil. This high quality varnish can be rubbed to a hard, fine finish when dry. It is used in finishing fine furniture, cabinets, and other high grade woodwork.

Spar varnish is an excellent long-oil varnish that is tough, hard, elastic, and highly resistant to dampness. Natural varnishes are classified according to their oil content such as short-oil, long-oil, or medium-oil varnishes. Spar varnish contains forty to one hundred gallons of drying oil per one hundred pounds of resin and for that reason is called a long-oil varnish. It is called "spar" varnish because it was originally used to varnish the spars and other outside parts of ships. The high grade gum used in this varnish makes it very durable, and the large proportion of oil makes it tough and elastic. China wood oil is used in the manufacture of high grade spar varnish because it forms a more waterproof finish than does linseed oil. For general use, either inside or outside finishing, there is no other varnish that is as lasting as spar varnish. It is used generally on all outside work requiring varnish such as on boats, doors, and fishing rods.

Natural gum floor varnish consists of a carefully prepared mixture of oil and copal gum to produce a hard, long-wearing surface. The usual floor varnish is a medium-oil varnish containing from thirteen to forty gallons of oil to each one hundred pounds of resin. It is used especially on surfaces subject to constant wear such as school desks, countertops, stools and floors.

Many other natural gum varnishes are manufactured for special purposes such as architectural varnish, enamel, flat, marine, sizing, automobile, and piano varnishes.

Synthetic Varnish

In recent years, synthetic varnishes have become strong competitors of natural gum varnishes and in some instances have replaced them. Chemists analyzed the various natural copal gums and found that these natural resins could be duplicated by a chemical reaction of some simple material such as coal, moth balls, certain acids, linseed oil, soya oil, and other similar materials. A great many types of synthetic resins have been developed since the first discovery of artificial varnish gum. Synthetic resins or gums may be classified into three main divisions: ester gum, phenoformaldehyde resin, and alkyd resin.

Ester gum is a modified synthetic resin which is made by combining natural resins or copal gums with glycerin or some higher alcohol.

Phenolformaldehyde resins are used in the production of fast-drying varnishes. These gums are made from bakelite gums, formaldehyde, and carbolic acid. Much of the four-hour varnish is of this type.

Alkyd resin is made mostly from glycerine and phthalic coal tar products. Alkyd synthetic varnishes are used especially for finishes on automobiles, refrigerators, and numerous other articles of metal.

Using Varnish

Varnish is easy to apply, but unless certain precautions are taken, a rough, ugly surface rather than a nice smooth finish will result. The finishing room should be free of dust with a temperature between 70 and 80 degrees and a humidity of 35 to 45 per cent.

A number of excellent quick-drying varnishes of the rubbing type are available. It is recommended that varnish be purchased in small containers or in the amount that you are likely to use in one application. Once a container is opened, a scum forms on the surface which is hard to remove.

Preparing the Surface for the Varnish

1. Complete the final sanding, remove dust, and examine the surface for marks, dirt, and grease that may need attention before varnish is applied.
2. Sponge all surfaces with water, preferably warm water. Let it dry for twelve hours. The sponging raises the grain of the wood. Sponging is especially recommended on soft wood.
3. When dry, sand all surfaces with 5/0 (180 mesh) garnet paper. Remove all dust with a lintless cloth slightly dampened with alcohol.
4. If the piece is to be stained, it should be done at this time.
5. Apply a wash coat of white shellac to seal the stain, or if you are to have a natural wood finish, the shellac coat is the first coat.
6. Allow eight hours for this coat to dry and then sand it lightly with the grain with 8/0 (280 mesh) garnet paper.
7. If you are working with an open-grained wood such as walnut, oak, or chestnut, the next step is to apply a paste filler, allowing it to dry for twenty-four hours.
8. Sand the filler coat with 8/0 (280 mesh) garnet paper when dry.
9. Seal the filler with a coat of wash shellac. When dry sand again with 8/0 (280 mesh) garnet paper.
10. If close-grained wood is used, such as birch, pine, red gum, or cherry, proceed from step No. 6 with the varnish finish.

Applying Varnish

1. Select a quick-drying rubbing varnish of high grade.
2. Select a long-haired varnish brush of good quality. A width of 1½″ is satisfactory for projects of average size.
3. See that the varnish brush is perfectly clean. A new one cleaned in turpentine is preferred.
4. Have a glass jar or china cup container at hand. It must be clean so wipe out all dust with a clean cloth dampened with turpentine.
5. If a special finishing room is not available, it is better to use a room other than the shop. Even when the shop is clean, there is more dust in the air than

in an ordinary room. The advantage in using quick-drying varnish is that it sets before a great amount of dust can settle and stick to the surface.

6. Do not move around unnecessarily in the finishing room. Do not slam doors. Do not allow anyone to pass in and out while you work. Such activity will stir up the dust in the room. Observe the sun rays coming through a window, and you will see how much dust is always in the air.
7. Open the can of varnish. Pour into the glass jar or cup, enough of the varnish for the first coat. Quickly put the lid back on the can and press it down tightly.
8. Pour a small quantity of turpentine into the varnish to thin it down for the first coat.
9. Dip the brush into the varnish lightly to prevent the formation of bubbles. Remove the surplus on the edge of the container as in Fig. 457.

NOTE: Do not lay the brush down anywhere during the process of the application. It will pick up dust and transfer it to the surface being varnished.

10. Brush the varnish from the center toward the outer edges, Fig. 458. This will prevent the varnish from running at the edges.
11. When the first coat of varnish is applied, clean the brush carefully in turpentine and wrap it in a piece of clean paper for storage.
12. Allow twenty-four to forty-eight hours for the varnish to dry. A four-hour varnish may set in four hours, but it does not dry sufficiently in that time to proceed with the second coat.
13. When dry, sand carefully with 8/0 (280 mesh) garnet paper with the grain. Do your sanding in the shop and not in the finishing room. Sand with a small piece of sandpaper held with the finger tips. Work carefully on a small area at a time. Sand with the grain and feel for smoothness with your finger tips.
14. Brush off the particles resulting from the sanding.
15. Carry the project to the finishing room and wipe the surfaces carefully with a clean cloth dampened with turpentine.
16. If there is scum in the varnish, strain it through a silk or muslin cloth before using it. Apply the second coat, but use the varnish without diluting it.
17. Allow the second coat to dry for forty-eight hours or more.
18. Apply the third or last coat as you did the second coat.

NOTE: Open a new can for the last coat and use a new brush if possible.

19. Be sure to clean the brush with turpentine and wrap it with a clean piece of paper when you are through using it.
20. Allow the third or final coat to dry for three or four days; rub it down with No. FF pumice stone and rottenstone. Follow directions in Unit 68 starting with step No. 16 for polishing with pumice stone and rottenstone.
21. One or two coats of wax can be applied as a final touch for the rubbed varnish finish.

Questions

1. What are the ingredients of natural gum varnish?
2. Where and how are the best copal gums obtained?
3. Upon what does the quality of natural varnish depend?
4. What kind of varnish is used on boats and fishing rods?
5. How does rubbing varnish differ from the non-rubbing varnish?
6. What is synthetic varnish?
7. Name two general synthetic gum classifications.
8. What is one advantage of synthetic varnish over natural gum varnish?
9. What are some of the ingredients used in synthetic varnish?
10. Why is varnish used as a finish?
11. What should you do to a project before applying varnish?

12. What are some important factors to consider when applying varnish?
13. In what way can varnish be considered easy to apply?
14. Is it good practice to use a varnish directly from the original container?
15. Why not use varnish over new wood surfaces without sealers or fillers?
16. How can you remove scum from the surface of varnish in a container?
17. Does the room temperature and humidity affect the drying of varnish?
18. How should a varnish brush be cleaned? When? Why?
19. In what order would you use the following: wax, sealer, and finish.

UNIT 70

Producing a Lacquer Finish

Lacquer is a popular and an excellent finishing material. It is produced by dissolving nitrated cotton in a solvent consisting of banana oil (amyl acetate), alcohol, benzol, and solvent naphtha. Copal gums of the highest quality, such as filtered shellac or synthetic resins, are added to the lacquer solution to give a good body which is necessary in building a smooth surface quickly. Lacquer is made in a transparent varnish form and also in the form of colored enamel. The colored lacquer enamel is made by adding spirit-soluble color pigments to the solution.

Lacquer dries quickly and produces a hard, durable surface which is not affected by changes in temperature. It compares well with a good grade of spar varnish when exposed to moisture. It is usually used in the form in which it comes from the manufacturer. A special thinning fluid is made for each brand of lacquer. The different brands and thinners are usually *not* interchangeable. The thinning fluid is also used for cleaning the brushes.

Uses of Lacquer

Lacquer cannot be used over paste wood filler, oil stain, varnish, and paint if the finish is less than a few months old, unless a thin coat of shellac is first applied. Lacquer dissolves most newly applied paint finishes. The directions on the container usually cover this point. It is applied commercially with a sprayer, but excellent results can be obtained when applied with a brush. Some spraying lacquers dry too rapidly to be applied successfully with a brush. Manufacturers produce lacquers for both types of application. Care and speed are necessary in applying lacquer with a brush, but skill can be readily developed under proper guidance.

The use of certain materials in lacquer to slow the drying, such as castor oil and camphor, makes possible application with a brush.

Chinese Lacquer

Lacquer was used in its early form by the Chinese several hundred years ago. It was known as Chinese lacquer. The difference between Chinese lacquer and modern lacquer can be briefly stated as follows: Chinese lacquer was composed chiefly of thin varnish and materials called "japans." It was a modified varnish. When applied, it dried in a brief period through the combination of the thinning fluids with oxygen. This process is called *oxidizing*. This chemical action changes the lacquer film from a liquid to a solid. Modern lacquer dries entirely by *evaporation* of the solvent or thinning fluid. It is much like shellac in this respect.

Preparing the Project for the Lacquer

1. Thoroughly sand the project removing any marks, dirt, and grease.

2. Sponge the surfaces and edges with warm water and allow to dry for twelve hours. The sponging raises the grain of the wood. It is especially recommended on soft wood.
3. Sand all surfaces with 5/0 (180 mesh) garnet paper when dry. Remove all dust with a lintless cloth slightly dampened with alcohol.
4. If stain is to be used, apply a coat of water stain of your choice at this time. Let it dry for twenty-four hours. A water stain is recommended under lacquer. See Unit 63 on how to apply water stain.
5. Apply a wash coat of white shellac to seal the stain, or as the first application if you are applying a natural finish.
6. Allow eight hours for the wash coat to dry, then sand it lightly with the grain using 8/0 (380 mesh) garnet paper.
7. Open-grained wood such as walnut, oak, or chestnut, should be filled at this time. See Unit 67 on how to apply filler.
8. Sand the filler with 8/0 (280 mesh) garnet paper when dry and remove dust and dirt with a cloth dampened with alcohol.
9. Seal the paste filler application with a coat of wash shellac and sand it with 8/0 (280 mesh) garnet paper when dry.
10. A close-grained wood such as birch, pine, gum, or cherry, need not be filled before applying lacquer.

Applying a Special Lacquer Sealer

1. A lacquer sanding sealer may be applied on top of the wash shellac, preceding the lacquer. Lacquer sealer of the sanding type is like a thin, clear lacquer. Lacquer thinner is the solvent for both lacquer sealer and lacquer.
2. If a special finishing room is not available, use a room or space away from the shop if possible to avoid the dust of the shop.
3. Pour into a glass container enough of the lacquer sealer solution for one coat.
4. Apply the lacquer sanding sealer with a good brush, 1½″ to 2″ in width.
5. Apply or flow the lacquer sealer on quickly as you would lacquer. Lacquer sealer cannot be brushed back and forth like varnish or paint. Work from the center to the edges.
6. Clean the brush with lacquer thinner and wrap it in a piece of clean paper or a soft cloth.
7. Allow the sealer to dry for twenty-four hours and sand it lightly with 8/0 garnet paper.

Applying a Clear Brushing Lacquer

1. Pour into a glass container enough of the brushing lacquer for one coat. Thin it with lacquer thinner.
2. Apply the lacquer with a good quality brush, 1½″ to 2″ in width.
3. Dip the brush about one-third the length of the bristles into the lacquer. The brush should be well filled so do not remove the surplus lacquer on the side of the jar.
4. Flow the lacquer on quickly with your brush. Do not brush it back and forth. The lacquer will flow together into an even, clear surface.
5. Allow the lacquer to dry for twenty-four hours and then sand it lightly with the grain with 8/0 (280 mesh) garnet paper. Feel for smoothness with finger tips while sanding.
6. After each coat of lacquer, clean the brush carefully with lacquer thinner and wrap it in a clean piece of paper or a piece of soft cloth.
7. Wipe the surface carefully when dry with a cloth dampened with alcohol.
8. Apply a second coat of lacquer in the same manner you did the first coat.
9. Allow the second coat to dry twenty-four hours or more and then sand it lightly with 8/0 (280 mesh) garnet paper or buff with No. 2/0 steel wool.
10. Apply a third or final coat of lacquer. Allow it to dry forty-eight hours or more.
11. Rub and polish the final coat with rottenstone and oil. Follow the directions given in Unit 68.

Applying Colored Lacquer

1. Prepare the project for colored lacquer as if clear lacquer were to be used. Of course, a stain will not be used.
2. Pour enough colored lacquer in a glass container for one coat and stir it thoroughly. Thin it with lacquer thinner if necessary.
3. Spread the liquid to a thin, even film and let it dry for twenty-four hours or more.
4. If a second coat is desired, sand the surface lightly with 8/0 (280 mesh) garnet paper.
5. Clean the surface of dust and apply a final thin coat.
6. For a very high luster, the surface may be rubbed with rottenstone and oil.

Questions

1. What are the main ingredients of lacquer?
2. How does lacquer compare with other finishes for outside work?
3. How would you clean a lacquer brush?
4. What is used in lacquer to slow up the drying?
5. Is lacquer affected by temperature changes?
6. What causes lacquer to dry?
7. What will happen if lacquer is applied over a varnish finish?
8. What is the purpose of sponging the wood before applying the lacquer?
9. What is the best kind of stain to use under clear lacquer?
10. How do you seal a stain or filler before applying lacquer?
11. How is an open-grained wood treated before applying lacquer?
12. How do you apply a clear or a colored lacquer with a brush?
13. What is the solvent for lacquer?
14. How many coats of lacquer does it take to produce a good finish?
15. How is lacquer applied commercially?
16. Can lacquer be applied slowly with a brush like varnish or paint?

UNIT 71

Applying Inside Paint

Painting is not difficult. In order to obtain good results, however, it is necessary to use good quality paint and brushes. The surface must be properly prepared, and drying conditions must be good.

Preparing the Surface

1. There must be a smooth surface on which to work. Good results cannot be obtained on a rough surface. It is necessary, therefore, that every part of a project or surface to be finished be thoroughly sanded. First use No. ½ and then 2/0 sandpaper to make the surface smooth. Thorough sanding is also necessary when an old surface is to be refinished.
2. Cover pitchy places and knots with shellac. Yellow pine, fir and similar pitchy woods should be given a first coating of shellac. Shellac prevents the pitch from penetrating the paint and discoloring it. Shellac also tends to bind the knots in place.
3. Sand the surface again with 2/0 (100 mesh) sandpaper and dust it carefully.

Applying the Paint

1. Use a prepared flat paint of the desired color for the priming coat if the wood is not pitchy.
2. Before opening the can of paint shake it well. Remove the lid and pour off into

another container about two-thirds of the contents.

3. With a stirring rod or special stick, stir the part remaining which consists of pigment and oil. Loosen and dissolve every bit of pigment by stirring.
4. After the paint has been stirred to a smooth consistency, pour the oil back gradually while stirring. If the paint is too thick, add turpentine. In fact, it is good plan always to add a few teaspoonfuls of turpentine to a newly opened can of paint. It "cuts" the paint and makes it more workable.
5. Pour the paint back and forth from one container to another. This is called *boxing* by painters.
6. While painting, carry your paint in a tin pail or container of two-quart capacity and do not fill it more than one-half full.
7. Brush the first coat, or priming coat, thoroughly into the wood.
8. Fill all cracks, nail holes and crevices with putty, hard wax or plastic wood. These are all especially prepared and available for that purpose.
9. Allow the priming coat to dry for at least twenty-four hours and then sand it with 2/0 (100 mesh) sandpaper until the brush marks and rough places are removed.
10. Apply a second coat which should be of the kind of paint to be used for the final coat. For this coat the consistency of the paint should be reduced by adding ½ pint of turpentine to each gallon of paint. Allow 48 hours for this coat to dry.
11. Apply a third and final coat just as it comes from the can without thinning. Stir the contents of the can well before using. Brush out to a uniform smooth coat, being careful that brush laps do not show.
12. With turpentine or kerosene clean up any paint that may have fallen on the floor. Place all oily rags in a metal container provided for the purpose.
13. Clean the brush with turpentine or brush cleaner when you are through painting. Soap and hot water may also be used for cleaning brushes if used promptly. Never leave the brush in the paint.

Questions

1. What three important things are necessary for a good paint job?
2. Should cracks and nail holes be filled before or after the prime coat?
3. How can pitchy places and knots be sealed in to prevent the scaling of paint?
4. What is an effective way to stir paint?
5. What is meant by "box" the paint?
6. How long should the prime coat dry before the paint is applied?
7. How much and with what is the paint for the second coat reduced?
8. How should the paint for the third coat be prepared?

UNIT 72 Brushes, Finishing Materials and Their Care

Brushes of one kind or another have been in use for many centuries. The Egyptians used brushes of small bundles of reeds roughly fastened together. Later the Greeks made use of the rabbit's foot and tails of other small animals for brushes.

The word brush comes from the German word *brusta* meaning bristle. The quality of a brush depends on the material used for its bristles. One of the best all-purpose finishing brushes is the black, china bristle brush. It is made from the bristles of China hogs, and can be purchased in many sizes. The genuine bristles that make the best brushes are obtained chiefly from hogs of Russia, China, and Poland, but any contact material used in a brush is commonly regarded as the bristles of the brush. In the best finishing brushes, the ends of the bristles are split into a number of fine hairs known as flagged ends. The brushes with bristles of the flagged end variety hold more paint and produce a smoother finish than the straight bristle brushes.

Parts of a Brush

A brush consists of several parts: the handle, the ferrule, the plug or divider, and the bristles. The ferrule, which connects the handles with the bristle, is made from the light metal. The handle is usually of hard wood such as maple or birch although in larger brushes the handles are made of soft wood to reduce the weight of the brush. The ferrule is fastened to the handle with nails or rivets that do not rust. The plug or the divider piece is a filler of wood or hard rubber to spread the bottom of the bristles. In some of the finer brushes, the bristles are cemented or vulcanized in rubber.

Grades of Brushes

The XXX fitch hair brush is one of best soft brushes used in finishing. The XXX means that the bristles are fastened in three rows. The bristles of this fine brush are obtained from the American skunk.

The camel hair brush is a good quality brush especially suitable for applying varnish, lacquer, and tempera. The bristles of a camel hair brush are obtained from the tails of Siberian and Russian squirrels and not from camels.

The badger hair brush makes a good blending brush. The bristles used in a badger hair brush come from the badgers of Russia, Siberia, and Balkans.

The nylon brush is excellent for all types of finishing and is especially recommended for house painting. It was an invention of necessity during war time replacing much of the Russian and Chinese bristle brushes.

A full chisel brush consists of long and short bristles arranged to produce a chisel edge. It is widely used by painters and finishers.

Handling Finishing Materials

1. Most finishes are made from flammable materials and should be stored in a metal cabinet for fire prevention.
2. When using a finishing material, pour only enough of the finish in a glass container for one coat. Use a clean container for each finish and solvent you are using, Fig. 459.
3. Arrange the glass containers with finishing material on a tray or similar holder such as is shown in Fig. 459. A tray to hold finish and solvent containers provides for a handy and clean way of handling finishing materials.
4. When the finishing is completed, you can store the tray with sealed finishing jars in a metal cabinet.
5. Have many clean rags and pieces of cloth on hand when you are finishing, Fig. 459. These are needed to remove the dust from surfaces, to clean brushes, to rub and polish with pumice and oil.
6. Use a piece of metal to stir the finishing material. A screwdriver will do very nicely. When through stirring, promptly clean the metal piece with a rag. Place the soiled rag in a metal container like that shown in Fig. 460.

Fig. 459. Arrange Containers on Tray

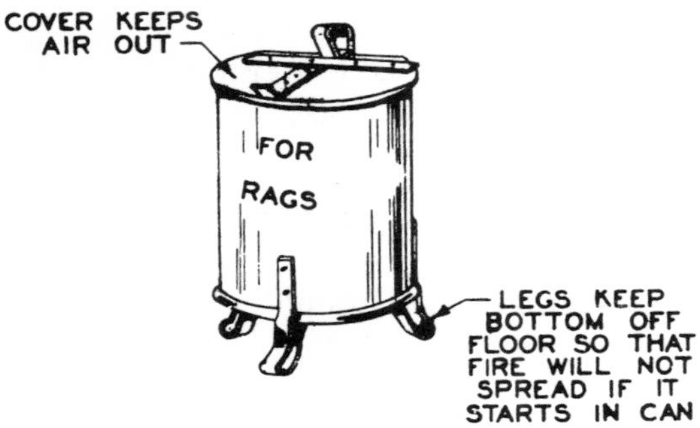

Fig. 460. Place Used Rags in Safety Container

Fig. 461. Wipe Finishing Material from Brush with Cloth

7. Never stir finishing materials such as shellac, lacquer, or paint with a stick. It is much easier to clean a metal rod with a rag than to find a place to dispose of the paint-covered stick. A messy stick usually lands on your clean bench or floor and leaves dirt in the finishing material.
8. Since most finishes are made from flammable materials, all rags, waste, or cloth used in cleaning brushes or in the rubbing operation must be placed in a metal container, Fig. 460.

Care of Brushes

1. Use a different brush for each finishing material. For example, use one brush just for white shellac, another brush for varnish, a third brush for lacquer, a fourth brush for oil stain, and so on. Label the brushes so they do not get mixed.
2. When you finish using a brush, clean it right away in the proper solvent. Do not set it aside carelessly and let it get gummy and hard.
3. Do not leave a brush standing on its bristles in a solvent or suspended in a solvent. There is always a certain amount of gum or material that will stick to a brush if it is left standing or suspended in a solvent. Clean it right away. It may be advisable to suspend a paint brush in a container of turpentine over night when doing outside painting.

SOME COMMON FINISHING MATERIALS AND THEIR SOLVENTS

Finishing Material	Solvent	Finishing Material	Solvent
Water Stain	Water	Paint	Turpentine
Tempera	"	Spirit Stain	Alcohol
Oil Stain	Turpentine	Shellac	"
Linseed Oil	"	Lacquer	Thinner
Varnish	"	Lacquer Sealer	"
Filler	"	Wipe-on-Finish	Turpentine

Cleaning a Brush

1. Remove surplus finishing material by squeezing the brush against the inside of the container.
2. Wash the brush in the proper solvent. If shellac, use alcohol for a solvent and not turpentine. See the table of solvents and finishing materials above.
3. Use clean pieces of cloth to pull finishing material from the brush as shown in Fig. 461. Wash the brush again in clean solvent and be sure to use another clean piece of cloth to draw out remaining material. Do not spare the clean cloth.
4. Wash the brush perfectly clean in soap and hot water.
5. Wrap the brush in a piece of paper or a soft, clean, lintless cloth and store it away to dry. If it is to be used the next day, place it on the tray next to the finish.

6. If brushes are to be stored for a considerable length of time, it is a good idea to give them a thorough soaking in a varnish remover. Varnish remover will soften the bristles and remove all dried finishing particles from the brush. Wash the brushes with soap and water and wrap in paper or cloth to dry.

Questions

1. What is the most important part of a brush?
2. What is the meaning of the word bristle?
3. What are the bristles of a fitch hair brush made from?
4. How are the ends of the bristles of good brushes treated?
5. What is the advantage of using glass containers?
6. Why not use a rough stick to stir a finish?
7. Why not use the same brush to apply lacquer and varnish?
8. What is the solvent for shellac? Varnish? Paint?
9. Why not leave the brush suspended in a solvent when not in use?
10. What will varnish remover do to a brush?

UNIT 73

Paint, Turpentine, and Linseed Oil

Paint is the most used and probably the oldest of finishing materials. It is used to preserve and to decorate surfaces, both inside and outside. Paint is opaque, available in any color, and has good resistance to moisture. Paint manufacturing is one of our leading industries.

Types of Paint

There are five main types of paints: lead base, zinc oxide, titanium, lithopone, and casein. Commonly, outside paint is made of white lead or white zinc, or both, mixed with linseed oil and thinned with turpentine. Titanium is frequently used to prevent chalking and preserve the color. White zinc and white lead are pigments or coloring materials, and the linseed oil and turpentine are the vehicles and binders of the paint. Raw, rather than boiled, linseed oil is preferred for outside use.

Lithopone is a synthetic pigment not frequently used in outside paints. It is used mostly in inside paints.

Casein paint is mixed with water, and this type is frequently classed as *emulsion paint*. The two general types are oil-resin and latex-emulsion. They dry quickly, do not have an objectionable odor, and have little fire hazard in use. Since water is the thinner or solvent, brushes and containers are easy to clean.

Inside paints are also made of white lead and white zinc, with linseed oil and turpentine for vehicles and binders.

Inside paint is applied to inside surfaces and to furniture when the beauty of the natural grain is lacking. There are several kinds of inside paints: flat paints for plastered walls and ceilings; enamels for woodwork and furniture; tough, wear-resisting paints for wood floors, concrete floors, and screens; and heat-resisting paints for radiators. Each is especially adapted and mixed for its particular use.

A larger portion of turpentine than oil is used in making paints for inside use.

Turpentine

Turpentine is considered the most appropriate and most perfect solvent for both varnish and oil paint. Over ninety percent of the turpentine manufactured in this country is distilled from crude gum taken from the long leaf pine trees of the South and is called gum turpentine. The gum is extracted from the trees by tapping the trees as is done with rubber trees. The gum runs or flows into containers fastened to the trees. The liquid-like gum is then gathered and distilled in large copper stills into turpentine.

Turpentine made from stumps and dead roots of trees is known as wood turpentine. The stumps and roots are dug out of the ground, shredded into small pieces by power machines, steam-heated in a boiler, and finally distilled into wood turpentine. Only about three or four percent of the turpentine manufactured in the United States is wood turpentine. Gum turpentine is far superior to wood turpentine.

Turpentine is used mainly as a thinner or solvent for paint and varnish. It is used too in making floor and furniture polish, waxes, inks, dyes, and medicine.

Linseed Oil

Linseed oil is the most important drying oil used in paint and varnish. Linseed oil has been used in the manufacture of paints and varnishes for centuries. It is usually pressed from flax seeds. The pressed seeds are known as linseed cakes, a byproduct which makes an excellent livestock food.

Either raw or boiled linseed oil can be purchased. Raw linseed oil is used mainly in ready-mixed paints. Boiled linseed oil has been heated to about 250 degrees Fahrenheit, and such driers as lead and manganese have been added. Because it dries quickly, boiled linseed oil is used quite extensively in fine varnishes and by itself as a natural finish on fine wood. Linseed oil is also used in making oil cloth, oil silks, linoleum, putty, and printing inks.

Questions

1. What are two purposes of painting?
2. Name the general classifications of paint.
3. What the ingredients of good outside paint?
4. What is called the body of the paint?
5. Name three kinds of inside paints.
6. What are some uses of turpentine?
7. How is turpentine manufactured?
8. How is linseed oil used?
9. How is linseed oil manufactured?
10. What is the difference between raw and boiled linseed oil?

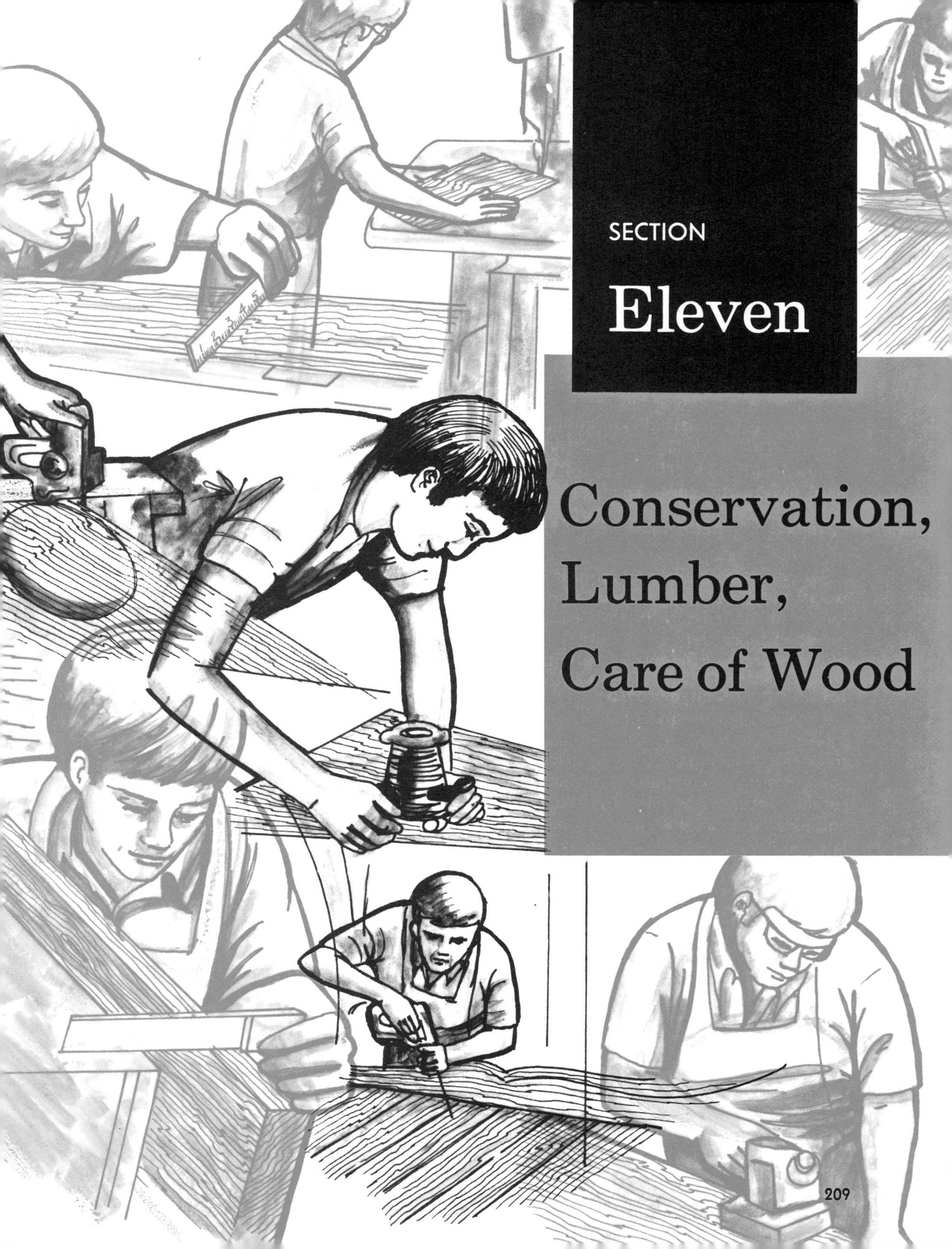

SECTION

Eleven

Conservation, Lumber, Care of Wood

UNIT

74 Conservation of Our Forests

A great variety of timber grows in American forests. There are more than 100 kinds of commercial woods. There are soft woods and hard woods, structural woods and decorative woods, and there are food-bearing trees such as the maples, the nut trees and the fruit trees of several kinds.

Wood is a crop just as is farm produce. The wood plants are larger, and require much longer to reach maturity than common farm plants. Timber trees must be cut when ripe; they mature and die just as do farm crops.

Meaning of Conservation

Conservation means not only the saving of forests, but also the systematic cutting of the trees and their preparation for market. In the deep forests, conservation begins with the careful cutting of only the trees that are ripe, and as soon as they are ripe, so there will be but a minimum of fallen, over-ripened trees. In the states where old growth is still plentiful, the harvest has not caught up with the ripening of the trees. There are so many fallen trees in the path of the harvest of these older forests that there frequently is serious delay and increase in the costs of cutting. These dead trees are fire hazards as well as a hindrance to logging operations.

Forest Lands

Forests are always growing. Besides the older forests there are new forests growing where former forests have been cut. A large part of all our lumber comes from "cut over" lands, that is, those lands from which timber has already been cut at least once. The Congress of the United States has established public forests from which timber crops will be cut again and again by future generations. There are more than a hundred million acres of such lands. If properly conserved, the timber supply of the future will be inexhaustible.

All minerals may some day be gone, but lumber will always be available. A tree can be cut and a new one will take its place. Minerals once taken from the earth are not replaced even when man would aid Mother Nature in this task if it were possible, as he is able to do in lumbering.

Persons who say that other materials will someday replace wood should know that in the future we shall have to find more uses for wood in order to conserve the minerals which cannot be replaced.

Trees in the forests must be cut systematically. The ripened trees must be removed while still maintaining the forest as a whole for future generations. There is much to be lost and nothing to be gained by leaving our forests to mature and fall before they can be harvested. It would be like delaying the wheat harvest. That which falls would be lost.

The Lumber Industry

It is good economics to put wood to every reasonable use. This not only prevents forest waste, but it creates a market for lumber that would otherwise be idle in piles. A ripened tree which is cut makes room for a new one. Lumber properly marketed keeps alive an industry that gives employment to 1,200,000 workers. The lumber industry can support one person in every twelve. It supplies the material for more than one hundred industrial activities not primarily concerned with the making of wood products. It supplies material for more than 5,000 wood products.

Forests Today

In the middle Western and Eastern States the anxiety of early settlers for acquisition of farm lands resulted in wholesale destruction of forests. It was quite natural and proper that forest lands should be cleared for cultivation. However, had there been planned lumber harvests, there could now be a continuous supply of lumber in these states, and there could be farm lands on which to grow all needed crops. Unfortunately, a large portion of these farm lands, which once supported an abundance of timber, are now waste lands having become too poor for farm crops. Where there could be large crops of timber there are now millions of acres of idle, tax delinquent, non-producing lands.

To the Middle West and East, where once thrived timber in plenty, there is shipped millions of feet of lumber from the West Coast and other places where the forests are still plentiful in timber. The annual bill for transporting this lumber runs into millions of dollars. That is indeed a high price for each generation to pay because of the lack of forethought on the part of their ancestors.

This does not mean that the forests in these sections are completely gone. There are still large areas that contain forests, but there are not enough for the future needs of the people in these sections. However, under careful rules of conservation, these forests will help in large measure to supply future lumber needs of these areas. Good management of these forests is now practiced, but one of the enemies of the forest tree, FIRE, is ever present.

Fire Prevention

Fire is a product of human hands. Man can preserve and he can destroy. In an earlier day he destroyed the forests through wilfullness. Today he destroys them through carelessness. There can be no forests; there can be no recreation grounds; there can be no game conservation unless man ceases to be careless and thoughtless. Every individual can be a good citizen without depriving himself of the good things of life. Those who travel our highways and visit our forests can do much to help Nature, who will always pay big dividends in return. If given a fair chance, Nature will not shirk; she is not careless, nor is she thoughtless even as man who has full control of his own actions. The good citizen of the forest stands ready to help in the great program of conservation.

Fig. 462. Forest Fires – Still Our Great Enemy
(U.S. Forest Service)

Preserving Our Forests

Every state in the Union has an interest in the preservation of forest lands. Wherever you live:

1. Heed the signs of the Forest Service in your state.
2. Enjoy the trees. Do not hack, cut, or otherwise mutilate living trees.
3. If you are an adult and if you smoke, do not throw the cigarette and match out the car window even if you believe they are not lighted. There is every reason to believe that cigarettes thrown from car windows, fanned into flames by the winds of passing cars, have been responsible for devastating fires. In some states there are laws against throwing cigarettes and matches out of moving vehicles. Make it *your law* in whatever state you travel.
4. Use only dead wood for your camp fires. Every dead stick burned in this way reduces the danger of a future fire, and a live tree is spared.
5. Build your camp fire in an open place away from flammable materials.
6. Do not leave your camp fire unattended. Someone must remain to watch it.
7. Extinguish your camp fire with water. If you cannot put your fingers in the coals, they are too hot to leave. Pour on more water.
8. Persons who smoke should grind pipe ashes, cigar stubs, and cigarettes into the ground with their feet.
9. Tell your friends to be careful with fire; and let them tell you.
10. Should you find fire in the woods, put it out. If you cannot put it out, go to the nearest telephone and call the local forest ranger. The telephone operator will help locate the proper authorities.
11. Be a clean camper and reduce fire hazard by burning all camp refuse.
12. Observe the game laws.
13. Keep the water clean and pure.
14. One careless and thoughtless act can undo all the good deeds of your many friends.

Be a Good Citizen

Questions

1. Who is the forest officer in your district? Where is his office located?
2. What are some of the duties of those engaged in forest conservation?
3. How long will our timber last if properly conserved?

UNIT 75 Lumbering

There is no more interesting topic for study in connection with woodworking than that of lumbering. Although lumbering is now highly mechanized, the general processes are practically the same as they were many years ago. The processes described here briefly concern the old and the new. The names given the workers are not necessarily used because all lumbermen use them, but rather they appear because they are used widely in a particular logging area.

Early Lumbering Practice

In former years, the first step in lumbering was to select a site. This was done by men whose duty it was to survey the forest from the point of view of economy in sawing and delivering of the logs to the market. Once the site was chosen for the camp, another force of men was hired to build roads from a railroad or highway to the camp site. There had to be trucks, power hoists, tractors, teams, wagons, saws and blacksmith tools, stoves, cooking utensils, and food supplies for those operations. A bunk house or two, an office, a mess house, blacksmith shop, and a stable had to be built.

Lumbering Today

Today the selection of sites and surveying the forest for cutting trees is much the same as it ever was. Camps are still set up in many places, but they are modern camps. Tractors, loading devices, and other new inventions have replaced the wagon, the horse, and many of the old methods.

The road into camp is substantially built for hauling heavy loads. Smaller roads are cut from the main roads into the cutting area. On these roads logs are toted to the main road. At some location convenient for quantity loading, there are cleared areas called skidways. Logs are here piled to be loaded at a later time on trucks and transported directly to the mill, if nearby, or to the railroad or water's edge.

Workers in the Forest

Having completed all necessary camp construction, the logging operations start in earnest. A large force of lumberjacks are hired, each for his special ability in performing one of the many phases of logging. A cruiser marks the trees for cutting. With an axe, he blazes each tree to be cut on the side of the tree that he believes will be the side toward which it should fall. Two men called fallers saw each marked tree with a large power driven saw, Fig. 463. This is an important operation. There must not be loss of life when the tree falls, and it must not fall against other trees on the way down. A deep notch is cut on the side toward which the tree is to fall. The fallers start sawing on the side opposite the notch. From time to time during the sawing, an iron wedge is driven into the opening or kerf made by the saw. This wedge keeps the saw from being pinched, thus making easier operation of the saw and, at the same time, it tends to force the tree to fall in the desired direction. Sawing and wedging continue until the tree falls. As each tree falls, there is a cry

Fig. 463. Chain Saw being Used to Cut a Large Fir Tree (Forest Products Industries)

Fig. 464. Large Ponderosa Pine Topples to the Ground (Forest Products Industries)

of "*timber*" which is a warning for all nearby to get out of the way, Fig. 464.

Workers called swampers trim the tree of branches and cut it into logs of standard length. All branches that are not usable must be carefully piled and burned. It is interesting to know that science plays its part in modern lumbering by taking advantage of every opportunity to increase the number of wood products obtainable other than lumber. For example, insulating wool for homes and refrigerators is made from the branches and bark of trees. There is little waste in modern lumbering.

Moving Logs to the Mill

The next step in logging is that of skidding the logs to the skidways where they are piled awaiting transfer to the mill. The logs are dragged or snaked with tractors or horses, Fig. 465. The piles of logs at the skidways are called decks. Decking is a rather difficult as well as dangerous procedure even when power hoists are used. Those who do the decking must know the tricks that are necessary in order to put the logs safely in high piles.

Fig. 465. Loading Logs on Truck (Forest Products Industries)

All logs in the skidways are scaled or measured for the number of feet of lumber that can be cut from each. The men who do this are called *scalers*.

From this point, there may be variations in the manner in which the logs are sent to the mill. The locality is a factor that determines the means of transportation. The logs may be floated, shipped by rail, or trucked to the mill.

The oldest method of transporting logs was that of floating. This method is seldom used now. This was done in the spring when the ice thawed and the freshets filled the river. This phase of lumbering has provided experiences that have made background for interesting stories of exploits of lumbermen of bygone days. The lumberjacks wore spiked shoes and carried a pike pole, a long pole with a straight point and a curved hook at one end. Some men had to ride the logs and some had to follow them along the shore to keep them in motion. It wasn't uncommon for logs to become caught and tangled so that a *jam* was formed which was practically impossible to untangle. In most instances, however, the logs were moved one by one and started on their way. Dynamite was sometimes used to break these jams. This movement was called the *spring drive*.

Handling Logs at the Mill

Logs arriving at the mill, whether by rail, truck, or river, are kept in the mill pond, which is a portion of the river or lake set apart with booms. The booms are logs chained to each other, end to end. They form an enclosure that makes possible the sorting and arranging of the logs for entry to the mill. The men who do this are frequently called *boom rats*.

The logs will crack or check if they are not kept in the mill pond until sawed. Rapid drying of logs in the warm weather is conducive to cracking and warping. A special drying process of the sawed lumber is necessary in order to prevent checking and cracking of the sawed pieces.

The logs are started upward one by one into the mill in a trough or conveyor contain-

Fig. 466. Conveying Logs from Mill Pond to Mill (U.S. Forest Service)

ing a conveyor chain, Fig. 466. They are hauled in this way and loaded on a platform called a deck. This is just inside the mill. The logs are placed in such a position that they can be conveniently loaded one at a time on a *carriage*. This carriage is a moving platform mounted on wheels and operated by steam or by electricity. It is equipped with various mechanical devices for holding a log in place and for shifting the log in order to obtain various cuts of lumber. As the log is held securely in place, the carriage moves it into the saw where one slice of lumber after another is taken the full length of the log. In the early days, circular or round saws were used in cutting the logs. It was found that this was wasteful and practically all large mills are now equipped with band saws. In some mills the band saws have teeth cut on both edges so the log is cut as it returns to its starting position; the log is cut "coming and going."

As the boards drop from the log, they fall on rollers that carry them on to other machines that rip and cut the boards to length. Bark is trimmed from the edges of each board by a saw called an edger, and the uneven ends cut off by another saw called a trimmer. All this is done while the boards are moving.

The next step is that of sorting the boards for quality while they are still in motion on a conveyor. This is done in an open shed called the *sorting shed*. Here the boards are sorted according to grades or quality determined by national rules.

Questions

1. How are logs skidded?
2. What are skidways?
3. What are the duties of the fallers, the cruiser, the swampers, the scalers, the lumberjacks?
4. Name one byproduct of lumbering that has come as a result of scientific study.
5. What is a common method of transporting logs over long distances?
6. What is a log jam?
7. What kind of saws are generally used in cutting logs into lumber?
8. How are the logs transported from the mill pond to the saw mill?
9. Is lumber sorted into grades as it comes from the mill or is the sorting done later?

UNIT 76

Our Common Woods

Where does the wood come from that you are using? How does it grow? How is it classified? How is it different from other woods? What is its best use according to the experiences of others that have used it? What is the best wood for your purpose?

The Growing Tree

A tree may be defined as a hardy, long-lived plant more than ten feet in height with a single main stem or trunk which is crowned by leafy boughs. Like human beings, trees require food, the sun's warmth, and light.

The roots absorb water and food from the ground and hold the *trunk* of the tree in place. The water and food is carried to all parts of the tree by a liquid substance called *sap.*

The *crown* of the tree, which consists of branches and leaves, is the place where the liquid taken from the roots and the gases absorbed from the air are digested and sent to all parts of the tree. This digestive function of the leaves requires plenty of sunlight and heat.

The *bark* covers the trunk, all the branches, and even the roots. It grows in two layers, the outer bark and inner bark. The outer bark is hard, generally rough, and serves to protect the tree from injury. See *C* in the cross-section, Fig. 467. The chief function of the inner bark, *B,* is to distribute the digested food to all live parts of the tree. The root tips, the buds, and the cambium layer are all growing parts of the tree.

The *cambium layer, A,* Fig. 467, is the first thin growth between the wood and the bark. As growth progresses, the inside part of the cambium layer develops new wood and the outside part new bark. This growth forms separate layers each year which are known as the *annual rings.* By counting the annual rings

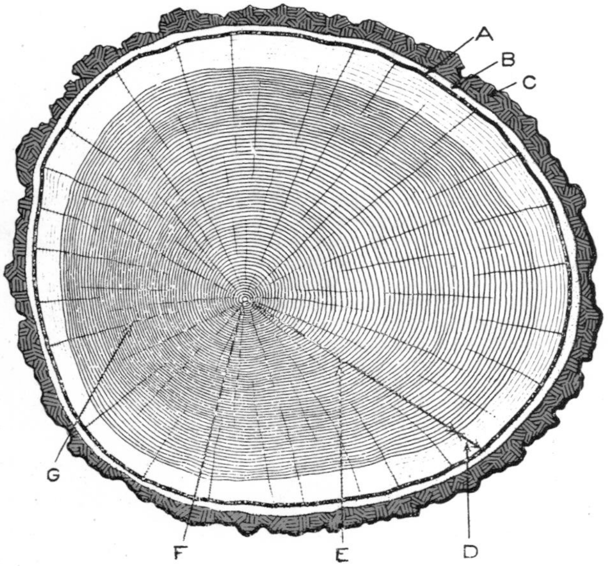

Fig. 467. The Tree Trunk (U.S. Forest Service)

after a tree is cut, the age of the tree can be determined.

Each annual ring consists of two parts, the springwood and the summerwood. The *springwood* of the ring is light in color and is developed in the early spring of the year. The *summerwood* is the darker part of the ring and is developed during the midsummer or the early fall.

The *sapwood, D,* Fig. 467, consists of the last several rings that are developed in the growth of a tree. This space of rings varies from 1 to 3 inches in width depending on the age of the tree.

The *heartwood* of a tree is the part which is made into finished lumber. It is developed by a constant change that takes place in the sapwood section. The greater part of a tree is this heartwood, or the matured wood, *E,* Fig. 467.

The center part of a tree is known as the *pith, F,* Fig. 467. It usually consists of a soft tissue but often becomes a hollow section.

Medullary rays are pitch rays or channels that radiate from the pith of the tree across the stem. These cell-like ducts, or rays, carry moisture and food across the trunk of the tree. When a tree is quarter-sawed, these rays produce beautiful, colored flakes and patches on both sides of a board. (See Unit 78.)

Hardwood and Softwood Trees

Our lumber supply comes from two main groups of trees, the softwood and the hardwood trees. Although there are several ways of classifying wood into soft and hard woods, one common way is according to the shape of the leaves and whether the leaves are shed. By this classification, hardwood trees have broad, flat leaves, and most of them are deciduous, meaning they lose their leaves every year. Oak, birch, maple, hickory, cherry, and walnut are good examples of this group.

The softwood trees are cone bearing trees and are usually known as "conifers." Most of the soft woods are evergreen trees and retain their needle-like leaves the year around. Fir, pine, cedar, cypress, spruce, balsam, and yew are common examples of the softwood trees.

The term "softwood" or "hardwood" does not mean that the woods are soft or hard. Many of the softwoods are harder than some of the hardwoods and vice versa.

Classification of Wood by Grain

The woodworker and the woodfinisher classify wood according to the coarseness or fineness of the grain. Wood is either open-grained, medium open-grained, or close-grained. Some examples are given below:

Open-grained — Oak, Ash, Walnut, Chestnut, Elm.

Medium open-grained — Butternut, Poplar, Cedar, Pine, Gum, Hickory.

Close-grained — Basswood, Cherry, Holly, Birch, Yew, Spruce.

Classification of Wood by Use

Perhaps the most practical way of classifying woods is according to their use. In this manner, woods are classified according to their real hardness and purpose. The following are examples in this classification:

Hard Wood — Oak, Birch, Maple, Ash, Southern Pine, Rosewood, Walnut, Yellow Pine, Hickory, Ebony, and Elm.

Medium Hard Wood — Red gum, Chestnut, Butternut, Mahogany, Cherry, Poplar.

Soft Wood — White Pine, Basswood, Fir, Cedar, Balsa, Spruce, Beech, Redwood, and Sycamore.

Balsa

Balsa is the lightest of all woods. The word balsa is the Spanish name for *raft*. This wood has long been used in making rafts upon which merchandise and heavier tropical timbers are carried down the river. It grows along the river banks in a few places in central America and the West Indies. It is found in abundance in the region around Lake Titicaca, the highest navigable body of water in the world, stretching from Peru into Bolivia. The logs of balsa are usually small and, therefore, wide long boards are hard to obtain. The tree grows rapidly and seldom attains a diameter of 12 inches. The young trees produce the lightest wood.

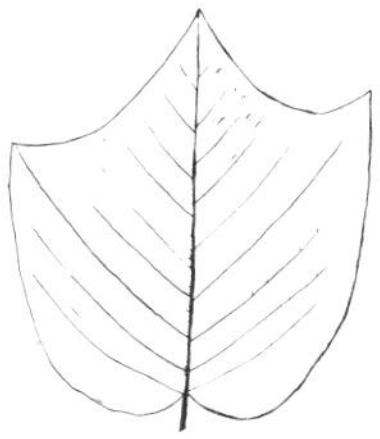

Fig. 468. Balsa Leaf

Fig. 469. Basswood Leaf

Balsa is lighter than cork and weighs 7.3 pounds per cubic foot. It is odorless, very soft, fine grained, and is strong for the weight of the wood. Because of its good heat insulating qualities, balsa is used for boxes in shipping food products, and linings of refrigerators. It is used for life preservers, life boats, loud speakers, soundproofing and air-conditioning devices and model airplane construction. Thousands of boys have used balsa in the construction of model airplanes.

Basswood

Basswood is one of the important commercial woods of America. It is similar in texture to white pine. It is a soft wood but classified as a hardwood. Basswood grows in the eastern and central parts of the United States, especially in Wisconsin, Michigan and West Virginia. It is also called the bee, lime, linden, whitewood and bass tree. The trees grow from 60 to 80 feet high, and have trunks 3 to 4 feet in diameter. The wood is soft, light, fine-grained, and not very durable. The heartwood and sapwood are the same in strength and in color. It is easy to work, takes screws and nails very well, and does not twist or warp readily. Basswood is used in the manufacture of furniture, drainboards, woodenware, novelties, boxes, excelsior and general millwork.

Butternut

Butternut is very much like walnut in color, but it is softer than walnut. It is as soft as white pine and basswood. It is also known as white walnut. Butternut grows in southern Canada, Minnesota, and throughout the eastern United States as far south as Alabama and Florida.

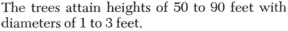

Fig. 470. Butternut Trees on Menominee Indian Reservation, Wisconsin (U.S. Forest Service)

Fig. 471. Yellow Birch Tree, Monongahela National Forest, West Virginia (U.S. Forest Service)

The trees attain heights of 50 to 90 feet with diameters of 1 to 3 feet.

The wood is soft, easy to work, coarse grained, a beautiful brown, and is fairly strong. Butternut is used in toy making, altars, woodenware, millwork, interior trim, furniture, boats, and scientific instruments. It is especially well suited for work in the school shops.

Birch

Yellow birch and sweet birch are the most common of the species of birch grown in the United States. Yellow birch grows in the areas from Newfoundland west to northern Minnesota, and South along the Appalachian Mountains to North Carolina. Sweet birch, which is also known as cherry birch and mahogany birch, grows in the east in the area from Newfoundland to northern Florida. Birch trees attain heights of 60 to 90 feet with diameters of 2 to 3 feet. Birch is of fine, even texture; it is hard, strong, and its heartwood is light to dark reddish brown in color. It takes a beautiful natural as well as a good stain finish. Birch forms an excellent base for a white enamel finish because of its hard, uniform, close-grained surface. It is also stained to imitate mahogany and walnut.

Birch lumber is used in the production of furniture, interior finish, doors, panels, flooring, veneers, novelties, handles, dowels, and musical instruments.

Cedar

Cedars are fragrantly scented softwoods. They include eastern red cedar, northern white cedar, western red cedar, southern white cedar, and yellow cedar.

The best red cedar to use for chest construction is the southern juniper. It is the well-known Tennessee red cedar. Southern juniper grows in central Tennessee, southern Virginia, northern Alabama, and Georgia. The wood is light, durable, aromatic, coarse grained, and generally knotty. The knots add to the beauty of the wood. Because the odor of the wood is repulsive to moths, Tennessee red cedar is especially adaptable for making clothes chests and for the lining of linen closets. Tennessee cedar is beautiful when finished in the natural color. It is the reddest of the cedars. This species of cedar grows to a height of 100 feet and a diameter of 4 feet.

Red Gum

Red gum is a beautiful wood that takes a very fine finish in the natural color of the wood. It is also known as sweet gum. It grows in the areas from New Jersey to the middle of Florida, and from Missouri to eastern Texas. It attains heights of from 100 to 150 feet, and diameters of from 4 to 6 feet. Red gum is a medium-textured wood, fairly soft and strong, which is beautiful either stained or in the natural finish. The heartwood is usually reddish brown, but irregular dark streaks and figured red gum can be found in many trees. The sapwood is pinkish white.

Although red gum has a tendency to warp, it is one of the leading furniture woods of the country. The better grade of furniture is made from the heartwood. Sapwood, however, is also used extensively for furniture. Red gum is a very good substitute for mahogany and walnut when properly stained and finished. It will closely imitate circassion walnut. Red gum is also used in the manufacture of store fixtures, musical instruments, picture frames, toys, and general millwork. The sap from the red gum tree is used in chewing gum and medicine.

Hickory

Hickory may be divided into two general classes: the true hickories, including the shag-

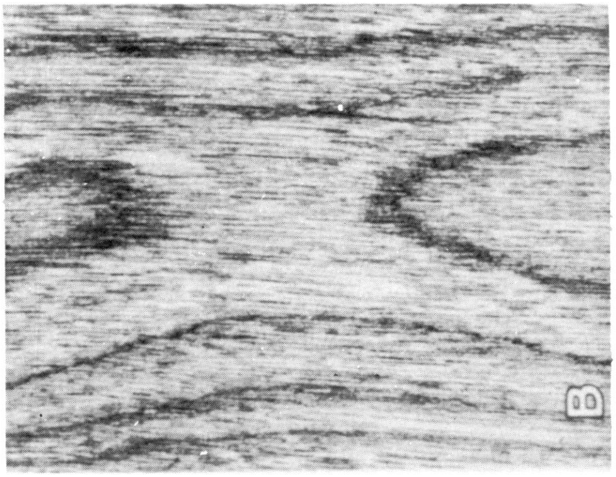

Fig. 472. Yellow Birch – Plain Sawed Surface (U.S. Forest Service)

Fig. 473. Western Red Cedar, Oregon (U.S. Forest Service)

bark, mockernut and pignut; and the pecan hickories, including pecan, water hickory, nutmeg hickory and bitternut. The hickories grow from 80 to 100 feet in height, and 3 to 4 feet in diameter. They are scattered in small groves among other broad-leaved trees rather than in forests. Hickory of the different species grows in the area from southern Ontario to Maine, and in Florida and Texas. Pecans grow in the states bordering on the Mississippi River from northern Illinois to central Louisiana. Water hickory is found in the lower Mississippi River valley and in the area from Virginia to Texas. Hickory is one of the toughest of woods and it is therefore used when great strength is necessary. The wood is heavy, strong, hard, rather coarse-textured and, us-

Fig. 475. Red Gum Trees, North Carolina (U.S. Forest Service)

Fig. 476. Pignut Hickory Tree (U.S. Forest Service)

Fig. 477. Mohogany Trees, British Honduras (U.S. Forest Service)

ually, straight grained. The heartwood of hickory is gray and reddish brown in color, while the sapwood is nearly white. It is used in the manufacture of vehicles, tool handles, agricultural implements, and bow staves.

Mahogany

There are many species of mahogany, but the true mahogany grows in the tropical parts of Florida, West Indies, central and northern South America. Some of the best kinds of mahogany come from Mexico and Cuba. The mahogany of Florida is the darkest and hardest of all mahoganies. Mahogany is a tropical tree that grows to a height of 50 to 190 feet, with a diameter ranging from 1 to 8 feet. Mahogany is usually divided into two classes, the figured and the plain. Figure in mahogany is called "broken stripe," "ribbon," and "crotch." The value of each tree depends upon the kind and amount of its figure.

The wood may be moderately open-grained, soft to strong, and from pinkish white to reddish brown in color, each color being typical of the locality where the wood is grown. Mahogany checks, swells, shrinks and warps only slightly. This quality of holding its shape and having a beautiful grain makes mahogany one of the most useful of cabinet woods. It takes a beautiful natural as well as stained finish. Mahogany is used in fine furniture construction, interior trim in expensive homes, office buildings, hotels, boats, musical instruments, and fixtures.

Sugar Maple

There are many kinds of maple trees, but they are usually divided into two main groups, hard maple trees and soft maple trees. The sugar maples are hard and the most important and abundant of all maples. They grow in the Great Lakes States, in southern Canada, along the Allegheny Mountains to Georgia and in western Florida. The trees grow from 50 to 100 feet in height with trunks from 2 to 4 feet in diameter. The sugar maple tree produces a sap which is made into sugar. Sugar maple wood is hard, stiff, heavy, and fine-grained. It has good wearing and bright finishing qualities, and is rather easy to work. Hard maple is frequently "figured." When figured, it is called bird's eye, blister, landscape, or curly maple. The heartwood is light brown, but the wider sapwood is nearly white. Besides being used in millwork products, such as flooring and fine interior trim, sugar maple wood is used extensively in veneering, in the manufacture of furniture, musical instruments,

Fig. 478. True Mahogany – Plain Sawed Surface (U.S. Forest Service)

Fig. 479. Sugar Maple Trees, Monongahela National Forest, West Virginia (U.S. Forest Service)

Fig. 480. Mature Kentucky Red Maple, Cumberland National Forest (U.S. Forest Service)

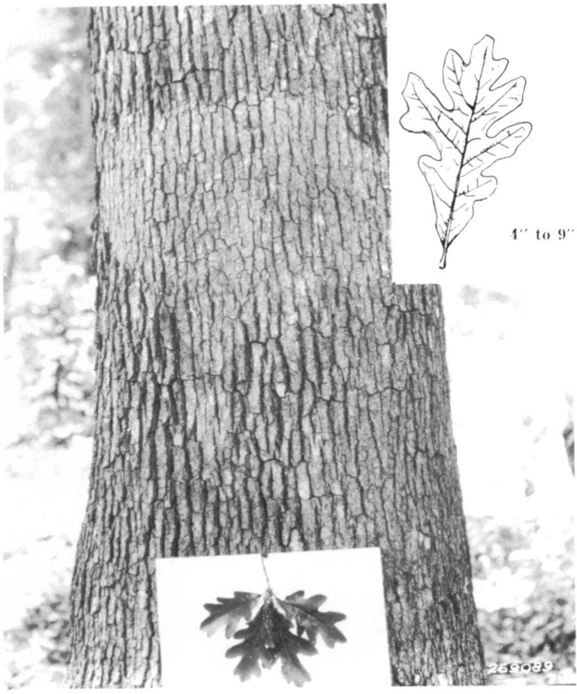

Fig. 481. White Oak, George Washington National Forest, Virginia (U.S. Forest Service)

woodenware, tool handles, ships, and school apparatus.

Red Maple

Red maple is one of the most beautiful of American trees. It is similar to sugar maple in properties and distribution, but is usually regarded as soft maple. It is also known as swamp maple, water maple, or white maple. It grows all over the eastern United States and Canada. Red maple attains a height of 50 to 100 feet and a trunk diameter of 2 to 4 feet. The wood is brown or reddish brown, close-grained, but somewhat lighter in weight and weaker than hard maple. Red maple has a good figure and is largely used for furniture, woodenware, musical instruments, handles, and novelties.

Fig. 482. Giant Red Oak Tree in White Sulphur Springs District, Monogahela National Forest, West Virginia. The Tree is Over Five Feet in Diameter (U.S. Forest Service)

White Oak

There are many species of white oak. Common among them are true white oak, live oak, and chestnut oak. White oak grows in the areas from Maine to Michigan, and south to Missouri, and from Florida to central Texas. The trees grow from 80 to 150 feet high and the trunks from 4 to 8 feet in diameter. White oak is strong, hard, tough, elastic, durable, beautiful and fine in grain, rather easy to work, and in color it is light grayish-brown with a reddish tinge. The medullary rays are large and outstanding, and present beautiful figures when quarter-sawed. The acorns of white oak ripen in one season.

White oak is used in the manufacture of furniture, cabinets, vehicles, boats, interior trim, paneling, tight barrels, wagons. It is strong and often used in heavy construction.

Red Oak

There are many species of red oak, but the common ones are the red oak, black oak, southern red oak, pin oak, willow oak, and Spanish oak. Red oak trees grow everywhere in the entire wooded area of the United States. Spanish oak grows along the coast from New York to Texas, and in Ohio and Missouri. Black oak grows in the areas from Minnesota to Texas, and from Maine to Florida. Pin oak grows from New York to Virginia, and west and south to Arkansas. The acorns of the red oak remain on the tree throughout the first winter and ripen the second summer.

The red oak tree grows from 80 to 100 feet in height and the trunk from 3 to 6 feet in diameter. Red oak is coarse, porous, strong, heavy, and has a beautiful figure when quarter-sawed. The heartwood is light red in color. Red oak is used in the manufacture of furniture, interior trim, and all types of cabinet and millwork.

Soft Pine

Western white pine is a soft white pine of the best quality. It is also known as Idaho white pine. It is grown in northern Idaho,

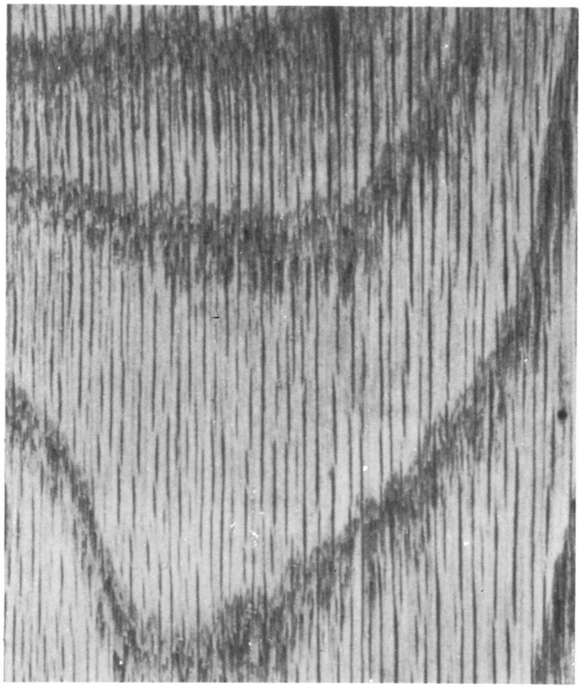

Fig. 483. Red Oak — Plain Sawed Surface (U.S. Forest Service)

Fig. 484. Group of Over-Mature White Pine, Kaniksu National Forest, Idaho (U.S. Forest Service)

Fig. 485. Northern White Pine, Butternut Lake, Wisconsin (U.S. Forest Service)

Fig. 486. Longleaf Pine, Vernon County, Louisiana (U.S. Forest Service)

Washington, western Montana, Oregon, and California. Heights of 80 to 100 feet and diameters of 3 to 10 feet are attained. It is light in color and weight, straight and medium grained, and very durable. The best grade of this pine is shipped to all parts of the United States. It is used in general millwork, cabinets, cornices, door frames, doors, interior finish, and pattern making.

Northern white pine is known as one of the best building woods. It is said that northern white pine was the first building wood to be used by the Pilgrims. Northern white pine is also called Canadian white pine, Minnesota white pine, white pine, soft white pine, and Wisconsin pine. It grows in the areas from Minnesota to Maine and from the Appalachian Mountains to Georgia. It attains heights from 80 to 175 feet with trunk diameters from 3 to 10 feet. This pine is soft, medium grained, and light. It is used in general millwork products such as doors, frames, interior finish, cabinets, and patterns for metal castings. The cheaper grades of this pine are used for general construction in carpentry.

Hard Pine

There are many species of hard, or yellow pine, but *Longleaf Pine* is one of the most valuable of the yellow pines. It is also known as Georgia pine and Southern pine. It grows throughout the southern Atlantic and gulf coasts of the United States from North Carolina to eastern Texas. From longleaf pines come most of the commercial resin and turpentine of the United States. The trees grow from 60 to 90 feet in height and from 2½ to 4 feet in diameter. The wood is hard, fine-grained, and the rings grow close together and dark in color. It is used for heavy structures, such as wharves, pilings, ship frames, and docks. It is also used for house sills, foundation timbers, and temporary construction, such as concrete form work.

Poplar

Yellow poplar is the tallest and one of the most beautiful hardwood trees in the United States and the largest in eastern United States. It is also known as the tulip tree and the whitewood tree. It is found in the Mississippi valley and in the Atlantic states south and west of Vermont. The finest grade of yellow poplar is found in the Appalachian Mountains. The trees attain heights of 125 to 250 feet and trunk diameters from 6 to 14 feet. The wood is soft, light, fine-textured, close and straight-grained, and rather easy to work. It does not readily warp, split, or shrink. The color of the heartwood is yellow or brown and often olive green. Poplar can be stained rather easily and is well adapted to paint or enamel finish. It is used in the manufacture of sash, doors, general interior trim, veneer backing, boxes, furniture, and general millwork.

Walnut

Black walnut is one of the finest and most beautiful of the hardwoods. It is valuable for its fine grain, rich color, and delicious nuts. It grows in scattered areas from Massachusetts to Florida, and from Minnesota to central Texas. The tree attains a height of 100 to 150 feet with a trunk diameter of 6 to 10 feet.

During colonial times, black walnut was used for fuel and fence building. Acres upon acres of black walnut trees were wasted when land was cleared for agricultural purposes. In spite of the fact that in the earlier days these trees were cut without regard for value or supply, we can be assured that in the American forests, under proper control, there is enough black walnut growing to meet the demands of our people for many years to come.

The heartwood of black walnut is rich chocolate brown in color, and it does not warp or check when properly seasoned. The wood is heavy, brittle, hard, strong, and coarse-grained. The sapwood is pale brown in color, and must be artificially darkened in order to match the heartwood. Walnut is used in high class furniture, cabinets, interior trim, gun

Fig. 487. Showing Bark of Yellow Poplar, Buncombe County, North Carolina (U.S. Forest Service)

Fig. 488. Black Walnut Tree, George Washington National Forest, Virginia (U.S. Forest Service)

stocks, musical instruments, fine boats, and many other articles of fine quality.

Western Yew

Western yew has been regarded as the best wood for the construction of bows for many years. It is the greatest bow timber in the world. It is found in the Sierra Nevada coast range of California, Oregon and Washington. Yew is an evergreen tree with leaves similar to fir and hemlock. It grows in the mountains, along streams, down narrow canyons. The wood is heavy, strong, elastic, dark red, and close-grained. Besides being used extensively for bows, it is used for canoe paddles, fishing rods, and novelties.

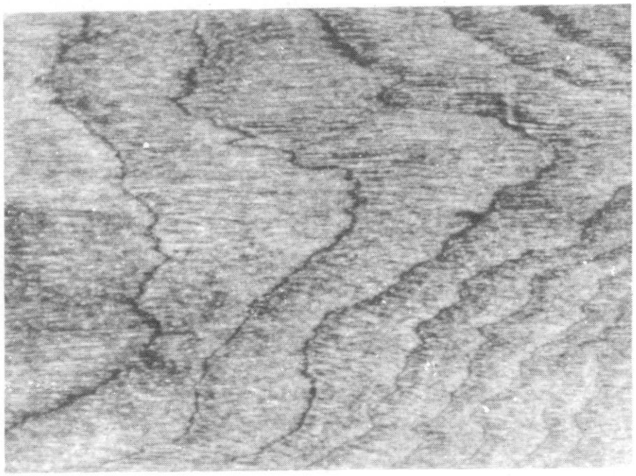

Fig. 489. Walnut – Plain Sawed Surface (U.S. Forest Service)

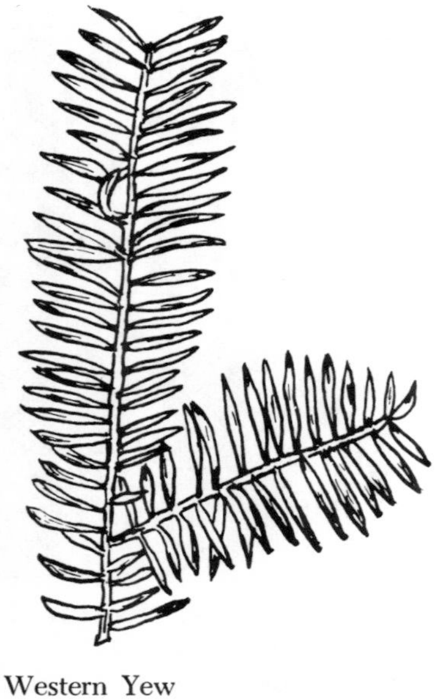

Fig. 490. Western Yew

Questions

1. What do we mean by annual rings?
2. What is considered the matured part of a tree?
3. What is the function of the sapwood?
4. What are medullary rays?
5. What are the two main groups of trees?
6. What is the most practical way of classifying woods?
7. What is the most common method of telling hardwood from softwood?
8. How does the woodworker or finisher like to classify woods?
9. In what part of the country would you find the following trees growing – butternut, red gum, poplar, oak, walnut, birch, balsa, red cedar?
10. Why is balsa wood so well suited to model making?
11. What are the characteristics of butternut wood that make it adaptable for use in the industrial arts shop?
12. Name five common uses of birch wood.
13. Why is fir not suitable for making bows?
14. What are some products made from the sap of gum trees?
15. What are the characteristics of hickory that make it suitable for tool handles?
16. Why is mahogany so popular for use in making fine furniture?
17. What are some of the common uses of maple wood?
18. Why is oak such a popular wood for use in making furniture?
19. What is the most common use made of pine lumber?
20. What is another valuable product obtained from pine trees?
21. What are some uses made of poplar lumber?
22. What are the characteristics of walnut lumber that make it so popular for shop projects and furniture?
23. What are the best lumbers for making bows? Why?

UNIT 77

Seasoning of Lumber

The thorough soaking of the logs in the mill pond is the first step in the drying or *seasoning* of lumber, Fig. 491. This soaking from the time of cutting until the drying begins helps to prevent checking and cracking. Large logs left to dry in the summer air do not produce the best lumber.

Drying Lumber

There are two methods of drying green lumber, namely, *air drying* (A.D.) and *kiln drying* (K.D.). In air drying, the lumber is piled in specially-constructed piles that protect it from the direct sun and rain, Figs. 492 and 493. The boards are kept from warping in the piles by their own weight. *Stickers,* or narrow boards, are placed crosswise like cleats between layers thus making it possible for air to circulate between the boards. Drying must be slow. Fast drying results in cracks and warping. The best air-dried lumber is usually

Fig. 492. Stacking Lumber (U.S. Forest Service)

Fig. 491. Logs Leaving Mill Pond in California (U.S. Forest Service)

Fig. 493. Lumber Being Air Dried – Pine, Right; Hardwood, Left (Forest Products Industries)

left in the piles for five years. Ordinarily one year's time is enough for air-dried lumber.

Even the best air-dried lumber is not dry enough for inside cabinet work and furniture. The *moisture content* is too high; there is still too much moisture to make possible the satisfactory construction of lasting joints.

Kiln Drying

Kiln drying is generally regarded as the most satisfactory method for the removal of moisture from lumber. Kiln-dried lumber is used in fine inside work because for such work the wood must be very dry to match the dry air in homes and offices.

Lumber is frequently kiln-dried after it has air-dried for about a year. The *kiln* may be either a large outdoor brick or concrete structure or it may consist of a special room within a building. This room is so constructed that circulation of hot air and ventilation is made possible. There is a problem of humidity involved, too. Temperature, ventilation, and humidity combine to form the necessary atmosphere for rapid drying in the kiln. Five years of air-drying without obtaining thorough seasoning is less satisfactory than two weeks of kiln-drying, which is more thorough.

Scientific Study

There are many opportunities available in the various phases of the scientific study and production of wood and wood products. So important is this science that the federal government has established a special laboratory for study. Any problem involving wood and wood products is here given careful study. Should you have problems related to wood, assistance can be obtained in your study by writing to the Forest Products Laboratory at Madison, Wisconsin.

Questions

1. Would the lumber be of better quality if the logs were not water soaked?
2. What are the two general methods of seasoning lumber?
3. What is considered the best method for seasoning inside cabinet lumber? Why is it the best?
4. How are lumber piles marked for identification?
5. How long does it take to air-dry lumber for cabinet work?
6. How does the time for kiln-drying compare with that for air-drying?

UNIT 78

How Lumber is Quarter-Sawed

A study of Fig. 494 will show how a log is cut to obtain *quarter-sawed* (Q.S.) and *plain-sawed* lumber. Plain lumber is sometimes said to be *slash-grained* (S.G.).

The *medullary rays* are seen as fine white radial lines on the end of a log. Some of these rays are as wide as two inches. Quarter-sawing shows these rays as broad light colored flakes and patches on both faces of a board. This is done by cutting the board as shown at *A* in Fig. 494. One edge of the board is at the center of the tree and the other edge is at the bark. The flakes which show are the "figure" of quarter-sawed oak used in furniture and interior house trim.

Oak and mahogany are the woods must commonly quarter-sawed because of the beauty of grain. There are other reasons, however, for quarter-sawing these and other woods. Flooring is frequently quarter-sawed. It is usually called vertical grained (V.G.) flooring. Quartered lumber and V.G. flooring wear evenly; they show less shrinkage and swelling; and they are less subject to warping than is plain-sawed lumber.

There are several possible "cuts" in quarter-sawing, but those shown in the drawing involve the least waste and the least time in sawing. The log is cut in halves and then into eighths. After each eighth section is cut, the log is turned and another eighth section is cut.

Questions

1. What part of the tree produces the flake in quarter-sawed lumber?
2. Tell how logs are sawed to produce quarter-sawed lumber?
3. What kinds of lumber are usually quarter-sawed?
4. Why is flooring quarter-sawed?
5. How does quarter-sawed lumber compare with others in cost?

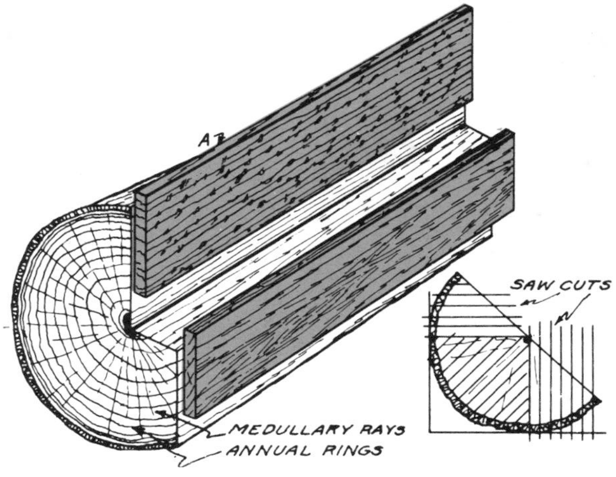

Fig. 494. Diagram of Quarter Sawing of Log

UNIT 79 The Moisture in Lumber

All wood products in which swelling, shrinking, warping, checking, and opening of glue joints may become troublesome should be manufactured at the moisture content and under atmospheric conditions corresponding to the average for the region in which they are to be used.

When the average temperature and humidity of any region is known, it is possible to determine what the moisture content of the wood should be for these conditions. Wood dried to this moisture content will undergo the least possible amount of shrinking, swelling, and warping in that particular region under normal conditions.

For example, a moisture content of 6% would be desirable where there is a 30% humidity at 70° F, but a moisture content of 13.5% would cause considerable shrinking and warping where there is a 30% humidity at 70° F. A humidity of 70% at 70° F would be a better atmospheric condition for lumber with a 13.5% moisture content.

The following table shows the moisture content in wood corresponding to various temperatures and humidities:[1]

Relative humidity of air	Moisture content of air dry wood		
Percent	At 70° F Percent	at 140° F Percent	at 212° F Percent
20	4.5	3.3	2.2
30	6.0	4.5	2.9
40	7.7	5.9	3.9
50	9.3	7.1	4.9
60	11.2	8.8	6.2
70	13.5	10.7	8.0
80	17.0	14.0	10.5
90	22.2	18.2	14.0
100	32.0	26.2	21.0

[1] Taken from Technical Note D-5, Forest Products Laboratory, Madison, Wisconsin.

UNIT 80 Determining the Amount of Moisture in Lumber

Lumber with a moisture content which is less than six percent may be considered thoroughly kiln dried. A moisture content of 10 to 15 percent indicates thoroughly air dried lumber. You may wish to learn how this is determined.

To test for moisture content, select several boards from different parts of the pile. Cut the boards at a point at least two feet from the end and then saw off a piece one inch long, the full width of the board, from one of these ends. Do not cut test pieces less than one foot from the ends of any board for testing moisture content because the ends may be affected by end drying.

Remove all splinters and loose particles from the outer surfaces of these sections and label each piece for future identification. Weigh the sections separately on an apothecary's balance, and record the weights of each.

Place the sections in an oven heated to 212° F., or lay them on a hot steam pipe. Weigh them at intervals of 10 to 15 minutes and record the weight. When they reach a constant weight subtract this constant weight from the first weight and you will have the weight of the water expelled from the wood.

To express the moisture content of the wood as a percentage, divide the weight of the water by the dry weight of the wood and multiply by 100. In order to establish reliability of the test, you should take at least four sections from as many boards at random from the pile.

Example

A piece of oak one inch long was cut from the center of the board. It weighed 27 grams. It was heated until it reached a constant weight of 25 grams. By subtracting 25 from 27, it is found that 2 grams of water were evaporated from the sample.

Divide 2 by 25 and multiply by 100 and you will have 8, or a moisture content of 8%. By cancellation it may be expressed as follows:

$$\text{M. C.} = \frac{2}{25} \times 100 = 8 \text{ percent}$$

Problem

Determine the moisture content of four samples of wood and record the data in your note book. Write out the plan of procedure and have it approved before starting.

UNIT 81 Influence of Temperature on Wood Products

All wood products are subject to the influence of temperature and humidity. It is because of this that it is necessary to dry all wood scientifically before it goes into wood products. Even when this has been carefully done, trouble may arise because of unusual air conditions at certain seasons of the year. During dry seasons and wet seasons difficulties frequently arise in connection with furniture, cabinet and room doors, dresser drawers and window frames. Even as thoroughly as wood is seasoned, it will take on moisture from the atmosphere if there is more moisture present in the air than in the wood.

During the rainy season, doors, windows and drawers swell so they can only be opened and closed with difficulty. In dry seasons, in hot rooms, or when furniture is placed too near radiators, the wood will dry too much and the joints will become loose. The finish may protect furniture to some extent, but the best of furniture protected with the best of finish cannot withstand the continuous exposure to high temperature when it is placed near radiators.

Swelling of doors and the opening of joints as a rule cannot be blamed on the builder or the furniture dealer. If a door or drawer is too tight, it can be made to fit better by one who is skillful in the use of a plane. Do not be too quick to make such an adjustment, however. If the season is unusually damp and if the door or drawer is not too tight, the condition may not exist again under normal conditions. Paint will protect most woodwork from moisture under ordinary conditions.

UNIT 82

Plywood and Manufactured Boards

Solid wood is subject to warping, twisting, cracking, and splitting. Also, it is difficult to obtain wide boards which are free of defects. Manufactured boards overcome many of these problems. In addition, scraps and pieces that otherwise would not have commercial value are used. Fine cabinet woods, as veneers applied to the outside surface of plywood, result in many more square feet of surface than if used as solid wood.

Plywood

The term plywood is used to designate built-up wood sheets made of thin layers of veneer glued together with the grain of each layer at right angles, 90°, with the adjacent layer, Fig. 495A.

A sheet of plywood is stronger than a sheet of metal of the same weight. Plywood is a very practical and sturdy building material which is made from almost any kind of wood that does not splinter easily.

For many years, solid wood was preferred to veneer because the early veneers were not sufficiently lasting. However, science through research has developed modern plywood which is superior to solid wood in strength and beauty.

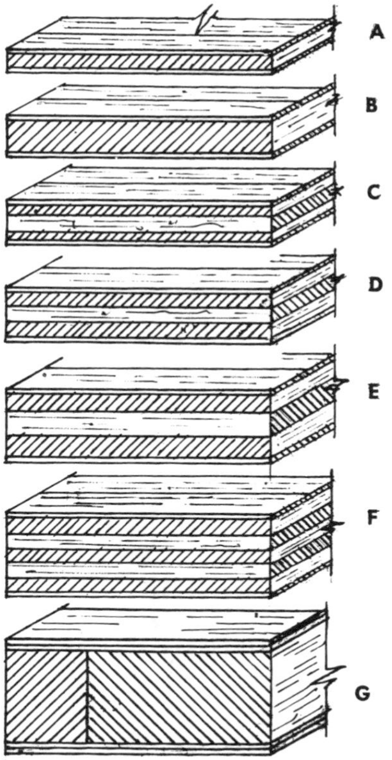

Fig. 495A. Plywood Generally Available in Lumber Yards. A = ¼″ 3 ply, B = ⅜″ 3 ply, C = ⅜″ 5 ply, D = ½″ 5 ply, E = ⅝″ 5 ply, F = ¾″ 7 ply, G = Lumber Core Plywood ½″ - 13/16″ and Thicker.

Plywood is now used extensively in making wood furniture, in building construction, aircraft, boats, cabinets of many kinds and wall panels, floors, doors, overseas packing cases, forms for concrete construction and more. In heavy building construction, built-up plywood timbers are preferable to solid wood timbers. There are two major classes of plywood. Examples are listed below although in softwood more than thirty species of wood are now used.

Softwood	Hardwood
Douglas Fir	Walnut
Western Hemlock	Oak
White Fir	Maple
Ponderosa Pine	Mahogany
Redwood	Birch

These are made for exterior and interior use. The exterior plywood is bonded with hot-press phenol resin glue and it is very sturdy when subjected to the elements. The interior type is bonded with soybean glue or phenol glue. It is not as sturdy under severe moisture conditions as is the exterior plywood.

There are special kinds available with exceptional wearing quality and beauty used in constructing overlays for table tops and counters. There are prefinished sheets in natural hardwood colors, and divided board patterns that give the appearance of solid boards.

Fig. 495. Cutting Continuous Sheets of Wood from Log (U.S. Forest Service)

Working Plywood

Operations for processing plywood are essentially the same as for solid wood. Instructions for these appear in the early chapters. Plywood can be processed into finished products with the simple joints such as the butt, dado, and the rabbet and fastened with finish nails and glue.

The Manufacture of Plywood

Large, thin sheets of wood, cut from straight logs, are used to make plywood. Before the sheets are cut, the logs are soaked in warm water for several hours. They are then placed in a large lathe and turned against a steel knife. As the log turns, continuous sheets of wood are shaved off in any desired thickness, Fig. 495. Some very fine-grained woods can be shaved in sheets only $\frac{1}{100}$ of an inch thick. In most mills the sheets used for plywood are between one-eighth and one-fourth of an inch thick. For decorative panels of fine cabinet woods, the log may be cut in straight sections rather than by turning. These sheets of veneer from a log are called a *flitch*. In making fine plywood, they are carefully selected and matched.

The long sheets are cut into sections, and the number of plies to be used is determined. The grain in each ply, or layer, is at a right angle to adjacent plies. Finished plywood is usually three plies, five plies, or seven plies thick, placed so the grain on both surfaces is the same direction. Glue is applied to the entire surfaces of the sheets to be glued. This wood sandwich is put into a press while the glue sets, Fig. 496. The finished plywood sheet is far stronger than solid wood. Because warping is caused by uneven pull on a board along the grain and across the grain, a plywood board resists warping.

Grades of Softwood Plywood

When ordering plywood, it is important to inform the vender what you plan to do with it. Tell him whether it is for inside or outside use and whether two finished sides are desired. If one side only is to be exposed, one side, the exposed side, need be finished. If you plan to use it for wall cover you would want natural finish hardwood veneer on one side. If it is to be used for sheathing under the finish floor or under the shingles on the roof, unfinished softwood plywood would be desired.

In hardwood natural finish plywood there are many kinds and patterns available. The core stock is of softwood. The following list includes about 90% of the vender's supply according to the demands for plywood in the softwood grades and there are more than twenty types listed by the American Plywood Association. Most venders have available for delivery 4′ x 8′ panels from ¼″ to ¾″ in thickness, but one inch or thicker is available on special order.

Plywood for exterior and interior use is classified by letters according to finish and sheathing grades.

Finish Grades

(available ¼″ – ¾″ in thickness)

Interior AD SO1S (sound one side, sanded both sides)

Interior AB SO2S (sound one side, solid one side, sanded both sides)

Exterior AC SO1S (sound one side, sanded both sides)

Exterior AB SO1S (sound one side, solid one side, sanded both sides)

Exterior AA SO2S Marine (sound two sides, sanded both sides)

Sheathing Grades

(available 5/16″ – ¾″ in thickness)

CD – Interior glue

CD – P&TS (plugged and touch sanded, interior glue)

CD – Exterior glue

CD – P&TS exterior glue

Hardboard or Pressed Board

Hardboard is frequently called "masonite," a trade name. It is made from wood chips

Fig. 496. Placing Plywood Sheets in Press (U.S. Forest Service)

which are exploded under high pressure into fibers. After the fibers are refined and felted, they are pressed into sheets. The lignin in the wood fibers holds the sheet together. If a harder surface is desired, as in tempered hardboard, a tempering compound is added and the sheet is baked after being pressed.

Masonite is available in at least 16 different hardwood finishes for interior use. It is factory finished and resists dents and is easily cleaned.

Hardboard is typically purchased in 4′ x 8′ sheets and in thicknesses of ⅛″ and ¼″, although other sizes and thicknesses may be obtained. It may be untempered, tempered one side, tempered two sides, or embossed and tempered. One of the most noticeable uses of hardboard is for display backgrounds, tool panels, and office dividers. Perforated hardboard, commonly called "Pegboard," permits very flexible arrangements of tools, merchandise, and shelving.

Hardboard is used for backs of cabinets, drawer bottoms, signs, toys, card table tops, and many other purposes. It resists moisture, mold, and fungus. It is very brittle though equally strong in all directions. It does not split, splinter, crack, shrink, or swell; and it resists dents, abrasion, and scuffing.

Hardboard can be worked with hand and power woodworking and metalworking tools. It can be painted, enameled, and varnished.

Flakeboard and Particle Board

Wood chips and flakes are also used to manufacture panels in which the chips are not disintegrated. These panels are more decorative than hardboard, and have many of the characteristics of plywood.

Particle board may be glued edge-to-edge. It has good screw and nail holding power. It is used as a veneer core, for desk and counter tops, panels, walls, and doors. Sheets of particle board are commonly 4′ x 8′, although larger sizes are produced. Many thicknesses, from ⅛″ to 1⅛″, are manufactured.

Index